CONTEMPORARY PAYMENT SYSTEMS

CASES, MATERIALS, AND PROBLEMS

■ ■ ■

Michael P. Malloy

Distinguished Professor and Scholar
University of the Pacific McGeorge School of Law
Director, Business and Law Research Division
Athens Institute for Education and Research

AMERICAN CASEBOOK SERIES®

WEST ACADEMIC PUBLISHING

American Casebook Series is a trademark registered in the U.S. Patent and Trademark Office.

© 2016 LEG, Inc. d/b/a West Academic
    444 Cedar Street, Suite 700
    St. Paul, MN 55101
    1-877-888-1330

West, West Academic Publishing, and West Academic are trademarks of West Publishing Corporation, used under license.

Printed in the United States of America

ISBN: 978-1-62810-227-7

This book is dedicated to
Claude D. Rohwer,
Friend, Colleague, and Guide

Preface

This book responds to the new demands of law and practice in the area of payment systems. While the mainstays remain drafts, notes and bank collections, contemporary practice embraces continuing developments in electronic funds transfers, new bodies of law and practice under the revised UCC Articles 4A (wire transfers) and 5 (letters of credit), and the explosive emergence of as yet untamed "cryptocurrencies" such as Bitcoin and the like. Contemporary conditions call for a more nimble pedagogy to bring the current law of payment systems to new generations of law students. My hope is that this book will offer a leaner, more systemic approach to the law of payment systems. It develops, within each chapter and across all chapters, a continuous narrative arc of problems and hypotheticals involving the continuing adventures of BayerCorp, SallerCo, and their executives, employees, banks, and other supporting characters.

With express intention, the casebook makes extensive use of graphics as an integral part of both the conceptual analysis and the narrative developing across the chapters. The inspiration and encouragement of my "technical advisors" in all of that – my children – was much appreciated. Likewise, the students in the various iterations of my *Commercial Law* class provided invaluable field research and behavioral data on the proper functioning and sequencing of a payment systems course.

I am grateful for the assistance of Ms. Janice Johnson and the staff of the Faculty Support Office in the preparation of various drafts of this book. A variety of student researchers assisted me as well from time to time, but I relied principally on my research assistant Ms. Riha Pathak, McGeorge Class of 2016, whose insights and determined efforts were invaluable.

This book also gained much from the advice – and patience – of my wife, Susie A. Malloy, who brought both clarity and practical perspective to bear on this project.

Michael P. Malloy
Oxford, England
Summer 2016

Acknowledgements

The author acknowledges and appreciates the permission to reprint excerpts from the following:

William B. Davenport, *Bank Credit Cards and the Code*, 85 Banking L.J. 941 (1968) (Publisher: LexisNexis A.S. Pratt).

David A. Frenkel (ed.), Selected Issues in Public Private Law 13 (Athens Institute for Education and Research, 2015).

Michael P. Malloy, *Payment Systems and Harmonization*, in Christian Cascante, Andreas Spahlinger & Stephan Wilske (eds.), Global Wisdon on Business Transactions, International Law and Dispute Resolution: Festschrift für Gerhard Wegen 273-285 (2015). © 2014 by Michael P.Malloy.

Michael P. Malloy, Principles of Bank Regulation (Concise Hornbook Series, West: 3d ed., 2011).

Stephen T. Middlebrook & Sarah Jane Hughes, *Virtual Uncertainty: Developments In The Law Of Electronic Payments And Financial Services*, 69 Bus. Law. 263 (2013) ©2013 by the American Bar Association. Reprinted with permission. All rights reserved. This information or any or portion thereof may not be copied or disseminated in any form or by any means or stored in an electronic database or retrieval system without the express written consent of the American Bar Association.

Arnold S. Rosenberg, *Better Than Cash? Global Proliferation of Payment Cards and Consumer Protection Policy*, 44 Colum. J. Transnat'l L. 520 (2006).

Summary of Contents

Table of Contents

Table of Cases

The principal cases are in bold type. Cases cited or discussed in the text are in roman type. References are to pages. Cases cited in principal cases and within other quoted materials are not included.

CONTEMPORARY PAYMENT SYSTEMS
CASES, MATERIALS, AND PROBLEMS

Chapter 1

HOW AND WHY WE USE PAYMENT SYSTEMS

A. INTRODUCTION

In this chapter we examine how payment systems operate and why we use them. Making a *payment* in exchange for some good or service is a commonplace occurrence. Indeed, it is the fundamental legal obligation of a buyer, just as delivery of the goods or services is the fundamental legal obligation of a seller.[1] So the real issues are how and why we make a payment within an established *system* for making payments.

A willing buyer and a willing seller could, of course, specifically negotiate what kind of return performance seller could expect from buyer – sheep for goats, servitude for room and board, guns for butter – and this is often implicit in contract terms denominating the currency in which the seller's goods or services are to be valued and paid for.[2] However, when the buyer's basic obligation is simply to pay for the seller's goods or services in a currency used by both of them (like US dollars), certain important practical questions remain. For example:

---

[1] See, e.g., UCC § 2-301 (concerning general obligations of parties to contract for sale of goods).

[2] *See generally* Gerhard Wegen, *2(b) or Not 2(b): Fifty Years of Questions– The Practical Implications of Article VIII Section 2(b)*, 62 FORDHAM L. REV. 1931 (1994) (discussing international law governing exchange contracts).

1

- Does buyer need to transfer dollars and cents to seller physically?
- If not, how is the amount of the payment to be "transferred" to seller?
- Aside from physically handing the payment to seller, what counts as a completed transfer from buyer to seller?

In typical exchanges, we assume that these questions can be (and are) successfully answered – so successfully that we may not even think about them. That we can comfortably ignore these questions in our daily lives is, in a sense, a triumph of our existing payment systems. Generally, they work well enough that we usually do not need to think about them.

A number of practical considerations lead societies to create conventional ways to make payments and systematic structures to facilitate them. (Some of these considerations underlie Alexander Hamilton's arguments in favor of establishing a national bank, excerpted below.) First, dealing with a metallic currency ("specie") is practically cumbersome, and for large payments in particular it can be a serious impediment to the performance of a transaction.

Large payments made with actual gold and silver can be burdensome.

Second, using physical currency – whether specie or a paper analog – involves obvious security risks. Addressing these risks then creates new transaction costs that inevitably increase as the payments grow in size. "Ideated" payments,[3] recorded in an established payment system, may help to contain some of these risks, or at least make the costs more manageable.

Using physical currency involves security risks and increased costs.

An efficient payments system generates more investments and payments.

---

[3] In this sense, an *ideated payment* is a virtual payment, a construction, that is represented by a record that can be replicated.

Finally, as Hamilton suggested in his *Treasury Report*, a system of ideated payments can be efficiently credited and turned over into new investments and loans, and this tends to generate more investments and payments. The result is that a greater quantity of credits is available to the economy, which in turn gives greater incentives to an efficient payments system.

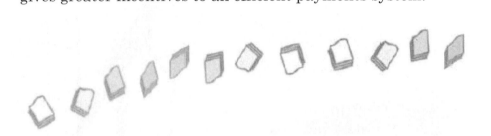

TREASURY REPORT ON A NATIONAL BANK
December 13, 1790
1 American State Papers 67

The following are among the principal advantages of a bank:

First. The augmentation of the active or productive capital of a country. Gold and silver, when they are employed merely as the instruments of exchange and alienation, have not been improperly denominated dead stock; but when deposited in banks, to become the basis of a paper circulation, which takes their character and place, as the signs or representatives of value, they then acquire life, or, in other words, an active and productive quality. This idea, which appears rather subtile and abstract in a general form, may be made obvious and palpable, by entering into a few particulars. It is evident, for instance, that the money which a merchant keeps in his chest, waiting for a favorable opportunity to employ it, produces nothing till that opportunity arrives. But if, instead of locking it up in this manner, he either deposits it in a bank, or invests it in the stock of a bank, it yields a profit during the interval, in which he partakes, or not, according to the choice he may have made of being a depositor or a proprietor; and when any advantageous speculation offers, in order to be able to embrace it, he has only to withdraw his money, if a depositor, or, if a proprietor, to obtain a loan from the bank, or to dispose of his stock—an alternative seldom or never attended with difficulty, when the affairs of the institution are in a prosperous train. His money, thus deposited or invested, is a fund upon which himself and others can borrow to a much larger amount. It is a well-established fact, that banks in good credit can circulate a far greater sum than the actual quantum of their capital in gold and silver. The extent of the possible excess seems indeterminate; though it has been conjecturally stated at the proportions of two and three to one. This faculty is produced in various ways. 1st. A great proportion of the notes which are issued, and pass current as cash, are indefinitely suspended in circulation, from the confidence which each holder has, that he can, at any moment, turn them into gold and silver. 2ndly. Every loan which a bank makes, is, in its first shape, a credit given to the borrower on its books, the amount of which it stands ready to pay, either in its own notes, or in gold or silver, at his option. But, in a great number of cases, no actual payment is made in either. The borrower, frequently, by a check or order, transfers his credit to some other person, to whom he has a payment to make; who, in his turn, is as often content with a similar credit, because he is satisfied that he can, whenever he pleases, either convert it into cash, or pass it to some other hand, as an equivalent for it. And in this manner the credit keeps circulating, performing in every stage the office of money, till it is extinguished by a discount with some person who has a payment to make to the bank, to an equal or greater amount. Thus large sums are lent and paid, frequently through a variety of hands, without the intervention of a single piece of coin. 3dly. There is always a large quantity of gold and silver in the repositories of the bank, besides its own stock, which is placed there, with a view partly to its safekeeping, and partly to the accommodation. These deposits are the immense consequence in the operations of a bank. Though liable to be redrawn at any moment, experience proves, that the money so much oftener changes proprietors than place, and that what is drawn out is generally so speedily replaced, as to authorize the counting upon the sums deposited, as an effective fund, which, concurring with the stock of the bank, enables it to extend its loans, and to answer all the demands for coin, whether in consequence of those loans, or arising from the occasional return of its notes.

These different circumstances explain the manner in which the ability of a bank to circulate a greater sum than its actual capital in coin is acquired. This, however, must be gradual, and must be preceded by a firm establishment of confidence—a confidence which may be bestowed on the most rational grounds, since the excess in question will always be bottomed on good security of one kind or another. This, every well-conducted bank carefully requires, before it will consent to advance either its money or its credit, and where there is an auxiliary capital . . . , which, together with the capital in coin, defines the boundary that shall not be exceeded by the engagements of the bank, the security may, consistently with all the maxims of a reasonable circumspection, be regarded as complete. ...

Secondly. Greater facility as to the government in obtaining pecuniary aids, especially in sudden emergencies. This is another and an undisputed advantage of public banks—one which, as already remarked, has been realized in signal instances among ourselves. The reason is obvious: the capitals of a great number of individuals are, by this operation collected to a point, and placed under one direction. The mass formed by this union, is, in a certain sense, magnified by the credit attached to it; and while this mass is already, and can at once be put in motion, in aid of the government, the interest of the bank to afford that aid, independent of regard to the public safety and welfare is a sure pledge for its disposition to go as far in its compliances as can in prudence be desired. There is, in the nature of things, as will be more particularly noticed in another place, an intimate connection of interest between the government and the bank of a nation.

Thirdly. The facilitating of the payment of taxes. This advantage is produced in two ways. Those who are in a situation to have access to the bank, can have the assistance of loans, to answer, with punctuality, the public calls upon them. . . . The other way in which the effect here contemplated is produced, and in which the benefit is general, is the increasing of the quantity of circulating medium, and the quickening of circulation. The manner in which the first happens has already been traced. The last may require some illustration. When payments are to be made between different places having an intercourse of business with each other, if there happen to be no private bills at market, and there are no bank-notes which have a currency in both, the consequence is, that coin must be remitted. This is attended with trouble, delay, expense, and risk. If, on the contrary, there are bank-notes current in both places, the transmission of these by the post, or any other speedy or convenient conveyance, answers the purpose; and these again, in the alternations of demand, are frequently returned, very soon after, to the place from which they were first sent: whence the transportation and re-transportation of the metals are obviated and a more convenient and more expeditious medium of payment is substituted. Nor is this all; the metals, instead of being suspended from their usual functions during this process of vibration from place to place, continue in activity, and administer still to the ordinary circulation, which, of course, is prevented from suffering either diminution or stagnation. . . .

The payment of the interest of the public debt at thirteen different places is a weighty reason, peculiar to our immediate situation, for desiring a bank circulation. Without a paper, in general currency, equivalent to gold and silver, a considerable proportion of the specie of the country must always be suspended from circulation, and left to accumulate, preparatory to each day of payment; and as often as one approaches, there must in several cases be an actual transportation of the metals, at both expense and risk, from their natural and proper reservoirs, to distant places. This necessity will be felt very injuriously to the trade of some of the States, and will embarrass not a little the operations of the treasury in those States. It will also obstruct those negotiations, between different parts of the Union, by the instrumentality of treasury bills, which have already afforded valuable accommodations to trade in general. . . .

Questions and Problems 1.1. Over the objections of Secretary of State Thomas Jefferson, who had a populist suspicion of banks and paper money, President Washington signed the bill based on Hamilton's proposal. It provided for a twenty-year charter for the Bank of the United States, with $10 million in capital. The charter was not renewed, however, because of the ascendancy of Jefferson's party in the interim. A *second* Bank of the United States was established in the aftermath of the War of 1812, and it was the constitutionality of this bank that was upheld in *McCulloch v. Maryland*, 17 U.S. (4 Wheat.) 316 (1819). It too was not renewed, because of the opposition of President Andrew Jackson, another adamant populist, in the 1830s.

1.2. Notice that, in addition to effects on payment systems and credit creation, Hamilton stressed the benefits to the government that flow from an effective central bank – creating a ready source of financing for government credit needs and facilitating payments *to* the government. Consider whether one or more of these benefits is present in the examples of other payment systems that are featured in the next section.

B. WALKING THROUGH HISTORICAL SYSTEMS

1. Barter and Specie

Barter – exchanging one type of goods or services in direct exchange for another – might seem to be an obvious alternative to the use of payments to obtain desired goods or services. However, this type of exchange is actually more complicated and less efficient for the immediate parties than a payment system might be. In effect, they are negotiating *two* contracts for the sale of goods or services simultaneously, and they need to worry about valuation of the consideration on both sides of the exchange, as well as the market price risks on each side. Nevertheless, barter (or "countertrade") still takes place in some specialized product markets.[1]

Trading goods or services in exchange for some well-recognized store of value, like specie – typically, gold or silver, often in the form of officially issued coinage – would seem to be the next logical step. But which precious metal should you accept? Which coins? And what should you do if the price of, say, silver begins to drop? Government can resolve some of this uncertainty by monopolizing coinage, standardizing its value, and

---

[1] *See, e.g.,* R. Michael Gadbaw, *The Implications of Countertrade under the General Agreement on Tariffs and Trade,* in B. FISHER & K. HARTE (eds.), BARTER IN THE WORLD ECONOMY (1985) (discussing the implications of countertrade under international trade rules).

enforcing rules that make coins "legal tender," *i.e.*, enforceable as payment for any public or private debt.

2. Currency

The U.S. Constitution follows this approach with respect to coinage. Congress has the authority to "coin Money, regulate the Value thereof, and of foreign Coin. . . ." U.S. Constit., art. I, § 8, cl. 5.[2] (Under the following clause 6, Congress has the authority to provide for the punishment of counterfeiting U.S. securities and coin.) "Currency," at least insofar as gold and silver coins are concerned, is under the exclusive control of the Congress. *Briscoe v. Bank of Commonwealth of Kentucky*, 36 U.S. (11 Pet.) 257 (1837).

Notice that this coinage authority says nothing about *paper currency*, although you might be able to tease out some authority for paper currency from the constitutional authority of Congress to borrow money "on the credit of the United States" (U.S. Constit., art I, § 8, cl. 2) and to regulate interstate and foreign commerce (*id.* § 8, cl. 3), particularly if coupled with the necessary and proper clause,

> The Congress shall have Power . . . [t]o make all Laws which shall be necessary and proper for carrying into Execution the foregoing Powers, and all other Powers vested by this Constitution in the Government of the United States, or in any Department or Officer thereof."

U.S. Const. art. I, § 8, cl. 18. At least until the Civil War, legal tender essentially meant specie, and paper "money" meant *bank notes*, debt instruments issued by state-chartered banks that would be redeemable in specie. Among so many other effects, the

---

[2] This authority includes the power to regulate the coins, and to require uniformity and parity in the coinage. *Laycock v. Kenney*, 270 F.2d 580 (9th Cir. 1959), *cert. denied*, 361 U.S. 933. The individual states in turn are prohibited from coinage and from issuing bills of credit under U.S. Constit., art. I, § 10, cl. 1. *Cf. Houston v. Moore*, 18 U.S. (5 Wheat.) 1, 49 (1820) (dicta, noting that exercise by states of power to coin money or emit bills of credit is prohibited by Constitution).

war was transformative for money and banking in the United States.[3]

LEGAL TENDER CASES
[Knox v. Lee; Parker v. Davis]
79 U.S. (12 Wall.) 457 (1871)

Mr. Justice STRONG delivered the opinion of the court.

The controlling questions in these cases are the following: Are the acts of Congress, known as the legal tender acts, constitutional when applied to contracts made before their passage; and, secondly, are they valid as applicable to debts contracted since their enactment? . . . If it be held by this court that Congress has no constitutional power, under any circumstances, or in any emergency, to make treasury notes a legal tender for the payment of all debts (a power confessedly possessed by every independent sovereignty other than the United States), the government is without those means of self-preservation which, all must admit, may, in certain contingencies, become indispensable, even if they were not when the acts of Congress now called in question were enacted. It is also clear that if we hold the acts invalid as applicable to debts incurred, or transactions which have taken place since their enactment, our decision must cause, throughout the country, great business derangement, widespread distress, and the rankest injustice. The debts which have been contracted since February 25th, 1862, constitute, doubtless, by far the greatest portion of the existing indebtedness of the country. They have been contracted in view of the acts of Congress declaring treasury notes a legal tender, and in reliance upon that declaration. Men have bought and sold, borrowed and lent, and assumed every variety of obligations contemplating that payment might be made with such notes. Indeed, legal tender treasury notes have become the universal measure of values. If now, by our decision, it be established that these debts and obligations can be discharged only by gold coin; if, contrary to the expectation of all parties to these contracts, legal tender

---

[3] On the transformation as it affected banking, see MICHAEL P. MALLOY, PRINCIPLES OF BANK REGULATION 9-12 (3d ed., 2011) (discussing origins of National Bank Act).

notes are rendered unavailable, the government has become an instrument of the grossest injustice; all debtors are loaded with an obligation it was never contemplated they should assume; a large percentage is added to every debt, and such must become the demand for gold to satisfy contracts, that ruinous sacrifices, general distress, and bankruptcy may be expected. These consequences are too obvious to admit of question. And there is no well-founded distinction to be made between the constitutional validity of an act of Congress declaring treasury notes a legal tender for the payment of debts contracted after its passage and that of an act making them a legal tender for the discharge of all debts, as well those incurred before as those made after its enactment. There may be a difference in the effects produced by the acts, and in the hardship of their operation, but in both cases the fundamental question, that which tests the validity of the legislation, is, can Congress constitutionally give to treasury notes the character and qualities of money? Can such notes be constituted a legitimate circulating medium, having a defined legal value? If they can, then such notes must be available to fulfill all contracts (not expressly excepted) solvable in money, without reference to the time when the contracts were made. Hence it is not strange that those who hold the legal tender acts unconstitutional when applied to contracts made before February, 1862, find themselves compelled also to hold that the acts are invalid as to debts created after that time, and to hold that both classes of debts alike can be discharged only by gold and silver coin. . . .

. . . It is impossible to know what those non-enumerated powers [in the necessary and proper clause] are, and what is their nature and extent, without considering the purposes they were intended to subserve. Those purposes, it must be noted, reach beyond the mere execution of all powers definitely intrusted to Congress and mentioned in detail. They embrace the execution of all other powers vested by the Constitution in the government of the United States, or in any department or officer thereof. It certainly was intended to confer upon the government the power of self-preservation. . . . That would appear, then, to be a most unreasonable construction of the Constitution which denies to the government created by it, the right to employ freely every means, not prohibited, necessary for its preservation, and for the fulfilment of its acknowledged duties. Such a right, we hold, was given by the [necessary and proper clause]. The means or instrumentalities referred to in that clause, and authorized, are not enumerated or defined. In the nature of things enumeration and specification were impossible. But they were left to the discretion of Congress, subject only to the restrictions that they be not prohibited, and be necessary and proper for carrying into execution the enumerated powers given to Congress, and all other powers vested in the government of the United States, or in any department or officer thereof. . . .

Indeed the whole history of the government and of congressional legislation has exhibited the use of a very wide discretion, even in times of peace and in the absence of any trying emergency, in the selection of the necessary and proper means to carry into effect the great objects for which the government was framed, and this discretion has generally been unquestioned, or, if questioned, sanctioned by this court. . . . Under the power to regulate commerce, . . . and other powers over the revenue and the currency of the country, for the convenience of the treasury and internal commerce, a corporation known as the [second Bank of the United States] was early created. To its capital the government subscribed one-fifth of its stock. But the corporation was a private one, doing business for its own profit. Its incorporation was a constitutional exercise of congressional power for no other reason than that it was deemed to be a convenient instrument or means for accomplishing one or more of the ends for which the government was established, or, in the language of the first article, already quoted, 'necessary and proper' for carrying into execution some or all the powers vested in the government. Clearly this necessity, if any existed, was not a direct and obvious one. Yet this court, in McCulloch v. Maryland . . . unanimously ruled that in authorizing the bank, Congress had not transcended its powers. So debts due to the United States have been declared by acts of Congress entitled to priority of payment over debts due to other creditors, and this court has held such acts warranted by the Constitution. . . .

. . . Even in *Hepburn v. Griswold*,[a] both the majority and minority of the court concurred in accepting the doctrines of *McCulloch v. Maryland* as sound expositions of the Constitution, though disagreeing in their application.

. . . Before we can hold the legal tender acts unconstitutional, we must be convinced they were not appropriate means, or means conducive to the execution of any or all of the powers of Congress, or of the government, not appropriate in any degree (for we are not judges of the degree of appropriateness), or we must hold that they were prohibited. This brings us to the inquiry whether they were, when enacted, appropriate instrumentalities for carrying into effect, or executing any of the known powers of Congress, or of any department of the government. Plainly to this inquiry, a consideration of the time when they were enacted, and of the circumstances in which the government then stood, is important. It is not to be denied that acts may be adapted to the exercise of lawful power, and appropriate to it, in seasons of exigency, which would be inappropriate at other times.

. . . Suffice it to say that a civil war was then raging which seriously threatened the overthrow of the government and the destruction of the Constitution itself. It demanded the equipment and support of large armies and navies, and the employment of money to an extent beyond the capacity of all ordinary sources of supply. Meanwhile the public treasury was nearly empty, and the credit of the government, if not stretched to its utmost tension, had become nearly exhausted. . . . The entire

---

[a] 75 U.S. (8 Wall.) 603 (1870). In *Hepburn*, decided by the Court in a reduced transitional size (eight when the case was considered in conference on November 27, 1869, and seven by the time the judgment was announced on February 7, 1870), the Legal Tender Acts were declared unconstitutional. Writing for the Court, Chief Justice Chase held that the acts were not "necessary," because their need "is far more than outweighed by the losses of property, the derangement of business, the fluctuations of currency and values, and the increase of prices to the people and the government, and the long train of evils which flow from the use of irredeemable paper money." *Hepburn*, 75 U.S. at 621. Likewise, he held that the acts were not "proper," because they unavoidably involved a taking of property without compensation or due process. Chase argued that it would be "difficult to conceive what act would take private property without process of law if [the Legal Tender Acts] would not." *Id.* at 625.

amount of coin in the country, including that in private hands, as well as that in banking institutions, was insufficient to supply the need of the government three months, had it all been poured into the treasury. . . .

. . . It is urged now, after the lapse of nine years, and when the emergency has passed, that treasury notes without the legal tender clause might have been issued, and that the necessities of the government might thus have been supplied. Hence it is inferred there was no necessity for giving to the notes issued the capability of paying private debts. At best this is mere conjecture. But admitting it to be true, what does it prove? Nothing more than that Congress had the choice of means for a legitimate end, each appropriate, and adapted to that end, though, perhaps, in different degrees. What then? Can this court say that it ought to have adopted one rather than the other? Is it our province to decide that the means selected were beyond the constitutional power of Congress, because we may think that other means to the same ends would have been more appropriate and equally efficient? That would be to assume legislative power, and to disregard the accepted rules for construing the Constitution. The degree of the necessity for any congressional enactment, or the relative degree of its appropriateness, if it have any appropriateness, is for consideration in Congress, not here. Said Chief Justice Marshall, in *McCulloch v. Maryland*, as already stated, 'When the law is not prohibited, and is really calculated to effect any of the objects intrusted to the government, to undertake here to inquire into the degree of its necessity, would be to pass the line which circumscribes the judicial department, and to tread on legislative ground.'

It is plain to our view, however, that none of those measures which it is now conjectured might have been substituted for the legal tender acts, could have met the exigencies of the case, at the time when those acts were passed. We have said that the credit of the government had been tried to its utmost endurance. Every new issue of notes which had nothing more to rest upon than government credit, must have paralyzed it more and more, and rendered it increasingly difficult to keep the army in the field, or the navy afloat. It is an historical fact that many persons and institutions refused to receive and pay those notes that had been issued, and even the head of the treasury represented to Congress the necessity of making the new issues legal tenders, or rather, declared it impossible to avoid the necessity. The vast body of men in the military service was composed of citizens who had left their farms, their workshops, and their business with families and debts to be provided for. The government could not pay them with ordinary treasury notes, nor could they discharge their debts with such a currency. Something more was needed, something that had all the uses of money. And as no one could be compelled to take common treasury notes in payment of debts, and as the prospect of ultimate redemption was remote and contingent, it is not too much to say that they must have depreciated in the market long before the war closed, as did the currency of the Confederate States. Making the notes legal tenders gave them a new use, and it needs no argument to show that the value of things is in proportion to the uses to which they may be applied. . . .

Concluding, then, that the provision which made treasury notes a legal tender for the payment of all debts other than those expressly excepted, was not an inappropriate means for carrying into execution the legitimate powers of the government, we proceed to inquire whether it was forbidden by the letter or spirit of the Constitution. It is not claimed that any express prohibition exists, but it is insisted that the spirit of the Constitution was violated by the enactment. Here those who assert the unconstitutionality of the acts mainly rest their argument. They claim that the clause which conferred upon Congress power 'to coin money, regulate the value thereof, and of foreign coin,' contains an implication that nothing but that which is the subject of coinage, nothing but the precious metals can ever be declared by law to be money, or to have the uses of money. If by this is meant that because certain powers over the currency are expressly given to Congress, all other powers relating to the same subject are impliedly forbidden, we need only remark that such is not the manner in which the Constitution has always been construed. ...

We come next to the argument much used, and, indeed, the main reliance of those who assert the unconstitutionality of the legal tender acts. It is that they are prohibited by the spirit of the Constitution because they indirectly impair the obligation of contracts. The argument, of course, relates only to those contracts which were made before February, 1862, when the first act was passed, and it has no bearing upon the question whether the acts are valid when applied to contracts made after their passage. The argument assumes two things, - first, that the acts do, in effect, impair the obligation of contracts, and second, that Congress is prohibited from taking any action which may indirectly have that effect. Neither of these assumptions can be accepted. It is true that under the acts, a debtor, who became such before they were passed, may discharge his debt with the notes authorized by them, and the creditor is compellable to receive such notes in discharge of his claim. But whether the obligation of the contract is thereby weakened can be determined only after considering what was the contract obligation. It was not a duty to pay gold or silver, or the kind of money recognized by law at the time when the contract was made, nor was it a duty to pay money of equal intrinsic value in the market. (We speak now of contracts to pay money generally, not contracts to pay some specifically defined species of money.) The expectation of the creditor and the anticipation of the debtor may have been that the contract would be discharged by the payment of coined metals, but neither the expectation of one party to the contract respecting its fruits, nor the anticipation of the other constitutes its obligation. There is a well-recognized distinction between the expectation of the parties to a contract and the duty imposed by it. Were it not so the expectation of results would be always equivalent to a binding engagement that they should follow. But the obligation of a contract to pay money is to pay that which the law shall recognize as money when the payment is to be made. If there is anything settled by decision it is this, and we do not understand it to be controverted. No one ever doubted that a debt of one thousand dollars, contracted before 1834, could be paid by one hundred eagles coined after that year, though they contained no more gold than ninety-four eagles such as were coined when the contract was made, and this, not because of the intrinsic value of the coin, but because of its legal value. The eagles coined after 1834, were not money until they were authorized by law, and had they been coined before, without a law fixing their legal value, they could no more have paid a debt than uncoined bullion, or cotton, or wheat. Every contract for the payment of money, simply, is necessarily subject to the constitutional power of the government over the currency, whatever that power may be, and the obligation of the parties is, therefore, assumed with reference to that power. Nor is this singular. A covenant for quiet enjoyment is not broken, nor is its obligation impaired by the government's taking the land granted in virtue of its right of eminent domain. The expectation of the covenantee may be disappointed. He may not enjoy all he anticipated, but the grant was made and the covenant undertaken in subordination to the paramount right of the government. We have been asked whether Congress can declare that a contract to deliver a quantity of grain may be satisfied by the tender of a less quantity. Undoubtedly not. But this is a false analogy. There is a wide distinction between a tender of quantities, or of specific articles, and a tender of legal values. Contracts for the delivery of specific articles belong exclusively to the domain of State legislation, while contracts for the payment of money are subject to the authority of Congress, at least so far as relates to the means of payment. They are engagements to pay with lawful money of the United States, and Congress is empowered to regulate that money. It cannot, therefore, be maintained that the legal tender acts impaired the obligation of contracts.

Nor can it be truly asserted that Congress may not, by its action, indirectly impair the obligation of contracts, if by the expression be meant rendering contracts fruitless, or partially fruitless. Directly it may, confessedly, by passing a bankrupt act, embracing past as well as future transactions. This is obliterating contracts entirely. So it may relieve parties from their apparent obligations indirectly in a multitude of ways. It may declare war, or, even in peace, pass non-intercourse acts, or direct an embargo. All such measures may, and must operate seriously upon existing contracts, and may not merely hinder, but relieve the parties to such contracts entirely from performance. It is, then, clear that the powers of Congress may be exerted, though the effect of such exertion may be in one case to annul, and in other cases to impair the obligation of contracts. And it is no sufficient answer to this to say it is true only when the powers exerted were expressly granted. There is no ground for any such distinction. It has no warrant in the Constitution, or in any of the decisions of this court. We are accustomed to speak for mere convenience of the express and implied powers conferred upon

Congress. But in fact the auxiliary powers, those necessary and appropriate to the execution of other powers singly described, are as expressly given as is the power to declare war, or to establish uniform laws on the subject of bankruptcy. They are not catalogued, no list of them is made, but they are grouped in the last clause of section eight of the first article, and granted in the same words in which all other powers are granted to Congress. And this court has recognized no such distinction as is now attempted. An embargo suspends many contracts and renders performance of others impossible, yet the power to enforce it has been declared constitutional. The power to enact a law directing an embargo is one of the auxiliary powers, existing only because appropriate in time of peace to regulate commerce, or appropriate to carrying on war. Though not conferred as a substantive power, it has not been thought to be in conflict with the Constitution, because it impairs indirectly the obligation of contracts. That discovery calls for a new reading of the Constitution.

If, then, the legal tender acts were justly chargeable with impairing contract obligations, they would not, for that reason, be forbidden, unless a different rule is to be applied to them from that which has hitherto prevailed in the construction of other powers granted by the fundamental law. But, as already intimated, the objection misapprehends the nature and extent of the contract obligation spoken of in the Constitution. As in a state of civil society property of a citizen or subject is ownership, subject to the lawful demands of the sovereign, so contracts must be understood as made in reference to the possible exercise of the rightful authority of the government, and no obligation of a contract can extend to the defeat of legitimate government authority. . . .

[W]e hold the acts of Congress constitutional as applied to contracts made either before or after their passage. In so holding, we overrule so much of what was decided in *Hepburn v. Griswold*, as ruled the acts unwarranted by the Constitution so far as they apply to contracts made before their enactment. That case was decided by a divided court, and by a court having a less number of judges than the law then in existence provided this court shall have. These cases have been heard before a full court, and they have received our most careful consideration.

The questions involved are constitutional questions of the most vital importance to the government and to the public at large. We have been in the habit of treating cases involving a consideration of constitutional power differently from those which concern merely private right. We are not accustomed to hear them in the absence of a full court, if it can be avoided. Even in cases involving only private rights, if convinced we had made a mistake, we would hear another argument and correct our error. And it is no unprecedented thing in courts of last resort, both in this country and in England, to overrule decisions previously made. We agree this should not be done inconsiderately, but in a case of such far-reaching consequences as the present, thoroughly convinced as we are that Congress has not transgressed its powers, we regard it as our duty so to decide and to affirm both these judgments. . . .

Mr. Justice BRADLEY, concurring:

. . . [A]t the time the Constitution was adopted, it was, and had for a long time been, the practice of most, if not all, civilized governments, to employ the public credit as a means of anticipating the national revenues for the purpose of enabling them to exercise their governmental functions, and to meet the various exigencies to which all nations are subject; and that the mode of employing the public credit was various in different countries, and at different periods-sometimes by the agency of a national bank, sometimes by the issue of exchequer bills or bills of credit, and sometimes by pledges of the public domain. In this country, the habit had prevailed from the commencement of the eighteenth century, of issuing bills of credit; and the revolution of independence had just been achieved, in great degree, by the means of similar bills issued by the Continental Congress. These bills were generally made a legal tender for the payment of all debts public and private, until, by the influence of English merchants at home, Parliament prohibited the issue of bills with that quality. This prohibition was first exercised in 1751, against the New England colonies; and subsequently, in 1763, against all the colonies. It was one of the causes of discontent which finally culminated in the Revolution. Dr. Franklin endeavored to obtain a repeal of the prohibitory acts, but only succeeded in obtaining from Parliament, in 1773, an act authorizing the colonies to make their bills receivable for taxes and debts due to the colony that issued them. At the breaking out of the war, the Continental Congress commenced the issue of bills of credit, and the war was carried on without other resources for three or four years. It may be said with truth, that we owe our national independence to the use of this fiscal agency. . . .

No one doubts at the present day nor has ever seriously doubted that the power of the government to emit bills exists. It has been exercised by the government without question for a large portion of its history. This being conceded, the incidental power of giving such bills the quality of legal tender follows almost as a matter of course.

I hold it to be the prerogative of every government not restrained by its Constitution to anticipate its resources by the issue of exchequer bills, bills of credit, bonds, stock, or a banking apparatus. Whether those issues shall or shall not be receivable in payment of private debts is an incidental matter in the discretion of such government unless restrained by constitutional prohibition.

This power is entirely distinct from that of coining money and regulating the value thereof. It is not only embraced in the power to make all necessary auxiliary laws, but it is incidental to the power of borrowing money. It is often a necessary means of anticipating and realizing promptly the national resources, when, perhaps, promptness is necessary to the national existence. It is not an attempt to coin money out of a valueless material, like the coinage of leather or ivory or kowrie shells. It is a pledge of the national credit. It is a promise by the government to pay dollars; it is not an attempt to make dollars. The standard of value is not changed. The government simply demands that its credit shall be accepted and received by public and private creditors during the pending exigency. . . .

No one supposes that these government certificates are never to be paid - that the day of specie payments is never to return. And it matters not in what form they are issued. The principle is still the same. Instead of certificates they may be treasury notes, or paper of any other form. And their payment may not be made directly in coin, but they may be first convertible into government bonds, or other government securities. Through whatever changes they pass, their ultimate destiny is to be paid. But it is the prerogative of the legislative department to determine when the fit time for payment has come. . . .

The CHIEF JUSTICE, dissenting:

We dissent from the argument and conclusion in the opinion just announced. . . .

A majority of the court, five [to] four, in the opinion which has just been read, reverses the judgment rendered by the former majority of five to three, in pursuance of an opinion formed after repeated arguments, at successive terms, and careful consideration; and declares the legal tender clause to be constitutional; that is to say, that an act of Congress making promises to pay dollars legal tender as coined dollars in payment of pre-existing debts is a means appropriate and plainly adapted to the exercise of powers expressly granted by the Constitution, and not prohibited itself by the Constitution but consistent with its letter and spirit. And this reversal, unprecedented in the history of the court, has been produced by no change in the opinions of those who concurred in the former judgment. One closed an honorable judicial career by resignation after the case had been decided, after the opinion had been read and agreed to in conference, and after the day when it would have been delivered in court, had not the delivery been postponed for a week to give time for the preparation of the dissenting opinion. The court was then full, but the vacancy caused by the resignation of Mr. Justice Grier having been subsequently filled[b] and an additional justice having been appointed under the act increasing the number of judges to nine, which took effect on the first Monday of December, 1869,[c] the then majority find themselves in a minority of the court, as now constituted, upon the question. . . .

We agree that much of what was said in the dissenting opinion in that case, which has become the opinion of a majority of the court as now constituted, was correctly said. . . . We assert

---

[b] Chief Justice Chase is referring to Justice Strong, appointed February 18, 1870, who eventually wrote the majority opinion in the *Legal Tender Cases*.

[c] This is a reference to Justice Bradley appointed March 21, 1870, who wrote a concurrence in the *Legal Tender Cases*.

only that the words of the Constitution are such as admonish Congress that implied powers are not to be rashly or lightly assumed, and that they are not to be exercised at all, unless, in the words of Judge Story, they are 'bonâ fide appropriate to the end,' or, in the words of Chief Justice Marshall, 'appropriate, plainly adapted' to a constitutional and legitimate end, and 'not prohibited, but consistent with the letter and spirit of the Constitution.'

There appears, therefore, to have been no real difference of opinion in the court as to the rule by which the existence of an implied power is to be tested, when *Hepburn v. Griswold* was decided, though the then minority seem to have supposed there was. The difference had reference to the application of the rule rather than to the rule itself. . . .

The reference made in the opinion just read, as well as in the argument at the bar, to the opinions of the Chief Justice, when Secretary of the Treasury,[d] seems to warrant, if it does not require, some observations before proceeding further in the discussion.

It was his[e] fortune at the time the legal tender clause was inserted in the bill to authorize the issue of United States notes and received the sanction of Congress, to be charged with the anxious and responsible duty of providing funds for the prosecution of the war. In no report made by him to Congress was the expedient of making the notes of the United States a legal tender suggested. He urged the issue of notes payable on demand in

---

[d] Salmon P. Chase was Lincoln's Secretary of the Treasury, and he was largely responsible for the currency acts – as well as the National Bank Act of 1864 – that were intended to assist significantly in the financing of the U.S. Government during the Civil War. With the decision in the *Legal Tender Cases*, they apparently succeeded beyond the objective contemplated by the then Secretary.

[e] For "his" and "he," the reader might accurately substitute "my" and "I," since Chase is speaking of himself and his direct involvement in these historical events. It reflects the sensibilities of the times that Chase did not recuse himself from *Hepburn* and the *Legal Tender Cases*, nor for that matter from the case of *Veazie Bank v. Fenno*, 75 U.S. 533 (1869), for which he wrote the majority opinion upholding other aspects of the legislation at issue in the *Legal Tender Cases*. On Chase's involvement in sponsoring the legislation and later upholding its constitutionality, see 1 MICHAEL P. MALLOY, BANKING LAW AND REGULATION 1B-11 – 1B-16 (2d ed. 2011).

coin or received as coin in payment of duties. When the State banks had suspended specie payments, he recommended the issue of United States notes receivable for all loans to the United States and all government dues except duties on imports. In his report of December, 1862, he said that 'United States notes receivable for bonds bearing a secure specie interest are next best to notes convertible into coin,' and after stating the financial measures which in his judgment were advisable, he added: 'The Secretary recommends, therefore, no mere paper money scheme, but on the contrary a series of measures looking to a safe and gradual return to gold and silver as the only permanent basis, standard, and measure of value recognized by the Constitution.' At the session of Congress before this report was made, the bill containing the legal tender clause had become a law. He was extremely and avowedly averse to this clause, but was very solicitous for the passage of the bill to authorize the issue of United States notes then pending. He thought it indispensably necessary that the authority to issue these notes, should be granted by Congress. The passage of the bill was delayed, if not jeoparded, by the difference of opinion which prevailed on the question of making them a legal tender. It was under these circumstances that he expressed the opinion, when called upon by the Committee of Ways and Means, that it was necessary; and he was not sorry to find it sustained by the decisions of respected courts, not unanimous indeed, nor without contrary decisions of State courts equally respectable. Examination and reflection under more propitious circumstances have satisfied him that this opinion was erroneous, and he does not hesitate to declare it. He would do so, just as unhesitatingly, if his favor to the legal tender clause had been at that time decided, and his opinion as to the constitutionality of the measure clear.

Was the making of the notes a legal tender necessary to the carrying on of the war? In other words, was it necessary to the execution of the power to borrow money? It is not the question whether the issue of notes was necessary, nor whether any of the financial measures of the government were necessary. The issuing of the circulation commonly known as greenbacks was necessary, and was constitutional. They were necessary to the payment of the army and the navy and to all the purposes for which the government uses money. The banks had suspended specie payment, and the government was reduced to the alternative of using their paper or issuing its own.

Now it is a common error, and in our judgment it was the error of the opinion of the minority in Hepburn v. Griswold, and is the error of the opinion just read, that considerations pertinent to the issue of United States notes have been urged in justification of making them a legal tender. The real question is, was the making them a legal tender a necessary means to the execution of the power to borrow money? If the notes would circulate as well without as with this quality it is idle to urge the plea of such necessity. But the circulation of the notes was amply provided for by making them receivable for all national taxes, all dues to the government, and all loans. This was the provision relied upon for the purpose by the secretary when the bill was first prepared, and his reflections since have convinced him that it was sufficient. Nobody could pay a tax, or any debt, or buy a bond without using these notes. As the notes, not being immediately redeemable, would undoubtedly be cheaper than coin, they would be preferred by debtors and purchasers. They would thus, by the universal law of trade, pass into general circulation. As long as they were maintained by the government at or near par value of specie they would be accepted in payment of all dues, private as well as public. Debtors as a general rule would pay in nothing else unless compelled by suit, and creditors would accept them as long as they would lose less by acceptance than by suit. In new transactions, sellers would demand and purchasers would pay the premium for specie in the prices of commodities. The difference to them, in the currency, whether of coin or of paper, would be in the fluctuations to which the latter is subject. So long as notes should not sink so low as to induce creditors to refuse to receive them because they could not be said to be in any just sense payments of debts due, a provision for making them a legal tender would be without effect except to discredit the currency to which it was applied. The real support of note circulation not convertible on demand into coin, is receivability for debts due the government, including specie loans, and limitation of amount. If the amount is smaller than is needed for the transactions of the country, and the law allows the use in these transactions of but one description of currency, the demand for that description will prevent its depreciation. But history shows no instance of paper issues so restricted. An approximation in limitation is all that is possible, and this was attempted when the issues of United States notes were restricted to one hundred and fifty millions. But this limit was soon extended to four hundred and fifty millions, and even this was soon practically removed by the provision for the issue of notes by the national banking associations without any provision for corresponding reduction in the circulation of United States notes; and still further by the laws authorizing the issue of interest-bearing securities, made a tender for their amount, excluding interest. . . .

Questions and Problems 1.3. The historical context – and the litigation history – surrounding the *Legal Tender Cases* are peculiar, to say the least.[4] The underlying disputes concerned whether or not the sale of confiscated sheep *after* the passage of the legal tender law (*Knox*) should be valued in Union "greenbacks," the federal notes at issue in the cases, and whether specific performance of a payment obligation that arose *before* the passage of the legal tender law (*Parker*) could be discharged in greenbacks. Tactically, discrediting the "legal tender" feature of the greenbacks would have defeated any claim or defense that depended directly or indirectly on valuation based on the greenback. The Court had said in *Hepburn* that it was unconstitutional to apply the legal tender clause retroactively, but the *Legal Tender Cases*, dancing past the precedential value of *Hepburn*, decided that the clause was constitutionally applicable to *both* preexisting and subsequently created obligations.

1.4. In another part of the opinion, Justice Strong touches on the issue of whether the Fifth Amendment might prohibit the constructive "taking" of the value of the contract that would result from requiring satisfaction of a debt in so many greenback dollars rather than in the same amount of gold or silver dollars. He argues that the Fifth Amendment

> has always been understood as referring only to a direct appropriation, and not to consequential injuries resulting from the

---

[4] For a useful examination of the historical context, see Randy E. Barnett, *From Antislavery Lawyer to Chief Justice: The Remarkable but Forgotten Career of Salmon P. Chase*, 63 Case W. Res. L. Rev. 653, 687-694 (2013).

exercise of lawful power. It has never been supposed to have any bearing upon, or to inhibit laws that indirectly work harm and loss to individuals. A new tariff, an embargo, a draft, or a war may inevitably bring upon individuals great losses; may, indeed, render valuable property almost valueless. They may destroy the worth of contracts. But whoever supposed that, because of this, a tariff could not be changed, or a non-intercourse act, or an embargo be enacted, or a war be declared? . . . [C]ertainly it would be an anomaly for us to hold an act of Congress invalid merely because we might think its provisions harsh and unjust. . . .

Do you agree with this characterization of the Fifth Amendment? Compensation for a "regulatory taking" – *i.e.*, excessive regulation of the use of property – was introduced in *Pennsylvania Coal Co. v. Mahon*,[5] holding that a prohibition on mining subsurface coal to protect surface structures was the equivalent to an eminent domain taking of coal. This doctrine gathered momentum in *Penn Central Transportation Co. v. City of New York*,[6] applying a three-factor test to determine whether a regulation constitutes a taking.[7] The doctrine has been subject to serious criticism.[8] but the viability of this non-categorical approach to regulatory takings was endorsed by the Supreme Court in *Tahoe-Sierra Preservation Council, Inc. v. Tahoe Regional Planning Agency*, 535 U.S. 302 (2002) (holding that question whether regional planning agency's temporary moratoria on development effected unconstitutional regulatory taking of property to be decided by applying *Penn Central* factors). In passing, *Tahoe-Sierra Preservation Council* acknowledged that *Pennsylvania Coal Co.* abrogated the narrow holding implicit in *The Legal Tender Cases* that a direct appropriation would be

---

[5] 260 U.S. 393 (1922).

[6] 438 U.S. 104 (1978).

[7] It should be noted, however, that, while endorsing the "regulatory taking" concept, the *Penn Central* Court finally rejected the takings challenge to New York City's historic preservation law, which had blocked the construction of a high-rise office building above Grand Central Terminal. *See Penn Central Transportation Co.*, 438 U.S. at 134.

[8] *See, e.g.*, Andrew W. Schwartz, *No Competing Theory of Constitutional Interpretation Justifies Regulatory Takings Ideology*, 34 STAN. ENVTL. L.J. 247 (2015) (presenting vigorous critique of regulatory taking doctrine).

necessary to trigger the Takings Clause. *Tahoe-Sierra Preservation Council, Inc.*, 535 U.S. at 326 n.21.

1.5. Chief Justice Chase's dissent offers a spirited – if bizarrely impersonal – defense of the holding in *Hepburn v. Griswold*, overruled by *The Legal Tender Cases*. To what extent does he actually differ from the majority opinion? Where do the two opinions agree, if at all? Can you explain why the issue of the constitutionality of the legal tender acts flip-flopped in the course of a single year?

1.6. Two other dissents, by Justice Clifford and Justice Field, focus in on the concept of what constitutes "money" in constitutional and legal terms. Here is Justice Clifford on the subject:

> Money, in the constitutional sense, means coins of gold and silver fabricated and stamped by authority of law as a measure of value, pursuant to the power vested in Congress by the Constitution. ...
>
> Even the authority of Congress upon the general subject does not extend beyond the power to coin money, regulate the value thereof and of foreign coin. . . .
>
> Intrinsic value exists in gold and silver, as well before as after it is fabricated and stamped as coin, which shows conclusively that the principal discretion vested in Congress under that clause of the Constitution consists in the power to determine the denomination, fineness, or value and description of the coins to be struck, and the relative proportion of gold or silver, whether standard or pure, and the proportion of alloy to be used in minting the coins, and to prescribe the mode in which the intended object of the grant shall be accomplished and carried into practical effect. . . .

What does this have to do with the dispute in the cases? And does gold and silver really have "intrinsic value," or is this just a traditional convention – or economic fetish – with no principled justification? Compare this with what Justice Field has to say on the subject:

> Now, money in the true sense of the term is not only a medium of exchange, but it is a standard of value by which all other values are measured. Blackstone says, and Story repeats his language, 'Money is a universal medium or common standard, by a comparison with which the value of all merchandise

may be ascertained, or it is a sign which represents the respective values of all commodities.' Money being such standard, its coins or pieces are necessarily a legal tender to the amount of their respective values for all contracts or judgments payable in money, without any legislative enactment to make them so. The provisions in the different coinage acts that the coins to be struck shall be such legal tender, are merely declaratory of their effect when offered in payment, and are not essential to give them that character.

Field's statement *assumes* that "money" and "gold and silver" are the same, but does his description of money and its functions necessarily and exclusively apply to specie?

1.7. Since 1870, claims and defenses based on theories discrediting paper currency have been repeatedly rejected by the courts as baseless and insufficient to withstand a motion to dismiss under Federal Rule of Civil Procedure 12(b)(6). *See, e.g., United States v. Condo*, 741 F.2d 238, 239 (9th Cir.1984) (theory that federal reserve notes are not valid currency was frivolous); *Foret v. Wilson*, 725 F.2d 254, 254-55 (5th Cir.1984) (argument that gold and silver is only legal tender in United States was hopeless and frivolous); *Tuttle v. Chase Home Finance, LLC*, --- F.Supp.2d ---, 2008 WL 4919263 at *3-4 (D.Utah 2008) (claim that only gold and silver coins were lawful currency seemed contradictory and absurd); *Sneed v. Chase Home Finance, LLC*, --- F.Supp.2d ---, 2007 WL 1851674 at *3-4 (S.D.Cal. 2007) (plaintiff's legal tender arguments were legally frivolous); *Carrington v. Federal Nat'l Mortgage Assoc.*, --- F.Supp.2d ---, 2005 WL 3216226 at *2-3 (E.D.Mich. 2005) (contention was "patently meritless and . . . universally rejected by numerous federal courts"); *Rene v. Citibank, N.A.*, 32 F.Supp.2d 539, 544-45 (E.D.N.Y.1999) (dismissing plaintiff's attempt to rescind home loan based on allegation that lender had provided "illegal tender"); *Nixon v. Indiv. Head of Saint Joseph Mortgage Co.*, 615 F.Supp. 898, 899-901 (N.D.Ind.1985) (rejecting plaintiff's argument that home loan was not backed by "legal" money; noting that "arguments and claims [were] absurd" and "smack[ed] of bad faith"). The following decision is representative of judicial attitudes expressed in such cases.

BEANER v. UNITED STATES
361 F.Supp.2d 1063 (D.S.D. 2005)

PIERSOL, Chief Judge.

Pending before the Court are Plaintiffs' motion to amend complaint, their renewed motion for temporary restraining order and preliminary injunction, and a motion for the Court to determine whether service has been perfected. Also pending are Defendants' Motion to Dismiss and Motion for Sanctions. For the reasons stated below, Plaintiffs' motions will be denied and Defendants' motions will be granted.

BACKGROUND

The Plaintiffs, Donald Beaner and Gloria Beaner ("Plaintiffs"), filed this civil rights action against the Defendants on June 24, 2003, seeking a temporary restraining order, declaratory and injunctive relief. Plaintiffs claim that the government is foreclosing on Plaintiffs' property unlawfully and based on a fraudulent mortgage. Plaintiffs state that "at no time after having pledged their real property as collateral for a loan guaranteed by the defendants, did Plaintiffs ever receive any legal tender or real money defined by Art. 10 Sec. 1 of the United States Constitution, in exchange for them putting up their property as collateral for the loan/mortgage the defendants are now claiming Plaintiffs' to be in default of." Plaintiffs apparently are claiming that since legal tender is gold or silver, and they received neither gold nor silver from the Defendants for their loan, the mortgage is void. Implicit in this claim is the idea that Plaintiffs received credit and money, but not gold or silver in return for their note and mortgage. . . .

The Court does not take lightly Plaintiffs' pattern of filing frivolous lawsuits, and it appears that the claims remaining in Plaintiffs' present lawsuit are frivolous and subject to dismissal. Plaintiffs assert that the mortgage they signed was fraudulent and that they did not receive legal tender as consideration for their mortgage. Plaintiffs apparently are claiming that legal tender is gold and silver and, because they received neither gold nor silver from the Defendants for their loan, the mortgage is void. Plaintiffs ask this Court to find unconstitutional the laws passed by Congress declaring United States currency to be legal tender. This Court has previously rejected a similar argument. *See United States v. Schiefen*, 926 F.Supp. 877, 881 (D.S.D.1995) (rejecting the plaintiff's argument that United States currency is unbacked paper), *aff'd* 81 F.3d 166, 1996 WL 148566 (8th Cir.1996) (table). The District of Columbia rejected this same claim made by Plaintiff Donald Beaner in *Beaner v. United States of America*, Civ. 02–1933. If Plaintiffs were to properly serve the Complaint on Defendants and if Defendants were to file a motion to dismiss the remaining allegations in Plaintiffs' Complaint, it appears that the motion would be granted. The Court will allow Plaintiffs an opportunity to dismiss their Complaint in this case in order to avoid the possibility of sanctions being imposed for filing the claims that remain in this case.

The Court's Order directed Plaintiffs to advise the Court whether or not they would voluntarily dismiss their Complaint. Plaintiffs' responded that they will not dismiss their Complaint. Indeed, Plaintiffs ask to amend the Complaint because Defendants have filed a foreclosure action against them. . . .

DISCUSSION . . .

Plaintiffs request permission to amend their Complaint because the government has filed a foreclosure action against them. . . .

. . . Plaintiffs' motion to amend their Complaint asserts frivolous claims and the motion will be denied. . . .

Defendants ask the Court to dismiss Plaintiffs' Complaint. The claims remaining in the Complaint challenge the legality of currency. As stated earlier, Plaintiffs ask this Court to find unconstitutional the laws passed by Congress declaring United States currency to be legal tender. They assert that the mortgage they signed was fraudulent because they did not receive legal tender as consideration for their mortgage.

The District of Columbia rejected this same claim made by Plaintiff Donald Beaner in *Beaner v. United States of America*, Civ. 02–1933.3 This Court rejected similar claims which were raised in defense to a foreclosure action in *United States v.*

Schiefen, 926 F.Supp. 877 (D.S.D.1995), *aff'd* 81 F.3d 166, 1996
WL 148566 (8th Cir.1996) (table). Schiefen argued that there
was insufficient consideration securing the promissory note he
signed because the FmHA loaned funds by "creating 'money' of
INtangible [*sic*] value by a bookkeeping entry[.]" . . . Schiefen alleged that United States currency is "irredeemable, unbacked
paper." . . . This Court dismissed Schiefen's claims, noting that
they had been rejected by numerous courts. . . . The similar
claims asserted by Plaintiffs in this case also necessitate dismissal for failure to state a claim. *See, e.g., Juilliard v. Greenman*,
110 U.S. 421, 448, 4 S.Ct. 122, 28 L.Ed. 204 (1884) ("Congress is
authorized to establish a national currency, either in coin or in
paper, and to make that currency lawful money for all purposes,
as regards the national government or private individuals"); *Ed-
gar v. Inland Steel Co.*, 744 F.2d 1276, 1278 n. 4 (7th Cir.1984)
(per curiam) (rejecting argument that "federal reserve notes are
not money"); *Foret v. Wilson*, 725 F.2d 254, 254–55 (5th
Cir.1984) (per curiam) (rejecting argument that "only gold and
silver coin may be constituted legal tender"). . . .

Defendants request that sanctions be imposed against Plaintiffs pursuant to Rule 11 of the Federal Rules of Civil Procedure.
. . .

"Rule 11 makes sanctions mandatory when a violation of the
Rule occurs, but whether a violation has occurred is a matter for
the court to determine, and this determination involves matters
of judgment and degree." *O'Connell v. Champion Int'l Corp.*, 812
F.2d 393, 395 (8th Cir.1987). The central issue is "whether the
person who signed the pleading conducted a reasonable inquiry
into the facts and law supporting the pleading." *Id.* The test for
whether Rule 11 is violated does not require a finding of subjective bad faith by the attorney or unrepresented party. *See
N.A.A.C.P. Special Contribution Fund v. Atkins*, 908 F.2d 336,
339 (8th Cir.1990) ("In determining whether a violation of Rule
11 has occurred, the district court must apply an 'objective reasonableness' standard.") A plaintiff's "subjective belief and pro
se status ... do not insulate him from the reach of Rule 11."
Carman v. Treat, 7 F.3d 1379, 1382 (8th Cir.1993). *See also
Business Guides, Inc. v. Chromatic Communications Enterprises,
Inc.*, 498 U.S. 533, 544–55, 111 S.Ct. 922, 112 L.Ed.2d 1140
(1991) (explaining that Rule 11 applies both to parties who are

represented by counsel and to pro se parties as well). As some courts have stated, one can no longer avoid "the sting of Rule 11 sanctions by operating under the guise of a pure heart and empty head." *Smith v. Ricks*, 31 F.3d 1478, 1488 (9th Cir.1994) (quoting *Zuniga v. United Can Co.*, 812 F.2d 443, 452 (9th Cir. 1987)).

The facts of this case justify Rule 11 sanctions. Plaintiffs have challenged the legality of United States currency in a number of lawsuits, and all of those challenges have been rejected. As stated earlier, in its Memorandum Opinion and Order of March 31, 2004, this Court informed Plaintiffs that their allegations regarding the payment of legal tender were frivolous, and Plaintiffs were given an opportunity to voluntarily dismiss their Complaint to avoid the possibility of sanctions. Plaintiffs informed the Court that they have no intention of dismissing their Complaint and, in fact, they want to amend it. In *Coleman v. Commissioner of Internal Revenue*, 791 F.2d 68 (7th Cir.1986), the Seventh Circuit imposed sanctions in the amount of $1,500 against tax protester plaintiffs who raised frivolous arguments. The Seventh Circuit stated, in part:

> Groundless litigation diverts the time and energies of judges from more serious claims; it imposes needless costs on other litigants. Once the legal system has resolved a claim, judges and lawyers must move on to other things. They cannot endlessly rehear stale arguments.... An obtuse belief-even if sincerely held-is no refuge, no warrant for imposing delay on the legal system and costs on one's adversaries. The more costly obtuseness becomes, the less there will be.

Id. at 72. This reasoning is applicable here. Plaintiffs may sincerely believe that United States currency is not legal tender, but they knew when they chose to continue pursuing this claim that it had been rejected previously by this and other Courts. Thus, Plaintiffs will pay sanctions for trying to litigate the same frivolous issue time and again.

Questions and Problems 1.8. While the *Legal Tender Cases* do not have the high-gloss reputation of *McCulloch v. Maryland*, scholarship has emerged that argues that the former cases are the key to understanding current interpretations of the necessary and proper clause. *See, e.g.,* Gerard N. Magliocca, *A New Approach to Congressional Power: Revisiting the Legal Tender Cases,* 95 GEO. L.J. 119, 123 (2006); Kenneth W. Dam, *The Legal Tender Cases,* 1981 SUP. CT. REV. 367 (focusing on financial details).

1.9. The final piece in this little puzzle is provided by the *Gold Clause Cases,*[9] decided in 1935, which considered federal actions that invalidated clauses in private contracts and public bonds and certificates mandating payment of obligation in gold coin. Collectively, in those cases the Supreme Court held that, even though the invalidation of contract and bond clauses requiring payment in gold was unconstitutional, no remedy was available, so long as payment was offered for the obligations in legal tender equal to the face amount owed. Is this consistent with the *Legal Tender Cases,* or does it make them more problematic? For a helpful discussion of the implications of the *Gold Clause Cases,* see Gerard N. Magliocca, *The Gold Clause Cases and Constitutional Necessity,* 64 FLA. L. REV. 1243 (2012).

3. Checks and Drafts

The payments system that most of us are familiar with is the one involving payment by check drawn on a banking account. In current practice, checks are governed by legal rules codified in *two* articles of the Uniform Commercial Code (UCC).

Article 3 governs the rights and obligations that are related to a *note,* a promise to pay, and a *draft,* an order to pay, of which a check is but one example. Checks and other drafts are a type of *negotiable instrument,* and they are the subject of Chapter 2.

---

[9] *Perry v. United States,* 294 U.S. 330 (1935) (concerning holders of U.S. gold bonds); *Nortz v. United States,* 294 U.S. 317 (1935) (concerning gold certificates deposited with the Treasury in exchange for legal tender); *Norman v. Baltimore & Ohio R.R. Co.,* 294 U.S. 240 (1935) (concerning bondholders of a private issuer in reorganization).

Checks are also governed by Article 4, which governs bank deposits and the rights and obligations of banks involved in payments. As we shall see in the next chapter, problems arising under these two articles are typically three-sided – for example, the maker or drawer of the instrument, the bank, and the payee. Other parties to whom the instrument is "negotiated" may also have rights and obligations not unlike the maker or drawer, or the payee. The case that follows offers a basic introduction to the transactional structure of checks and drafts, and the way in which the two articles interact.

TRAVELERS INDEM. CO. V. GOOD
737 A.2d 690 (N.J. App. Div. 1999)

CUFF, J.A.D.

Plaintiff, The Travelers Indemnity Company as subrogee of Stern, Lavinthal, Norgaard & Daly, appeals from a summary judgment entered in favor of defendant PNC Bank. We reverse and remand for additional discovery regarding PNC's actual conduct as measured by its policy for check verification.

Between October 1996 and December 1996, defendant Sobeyda Herrara Good was employed as a bookkeeper for Stern, Lavinthal, Norgaard & Daly, a law firm. During that time, Good forged the name of an authorized signatory on eight checks totaling $76,975 drawn on the firm's trust account at PNC Bank. The eight checks were made payable to either defendants Daniel Trainor or Glenn Davis and were negotiated by them. PNC paid seven of the checks and charged the attorney trust account. The firm discovered the fraud in December 1996 and notified PNC. Pursuant to the terms of a fidelity insurance policy, Travelers compensated the firm for the loss.

As the subrogee of the firm, Travelers filed a complaint against defendants Good, Trainer, Davis and PNC to recover the loss. The complaint alleged PNC breached its contract of deposit with the law firm and violated applicable provisions of Articles 3 and 4 of the Uniform Commercial Code (UCC), N.J.S.A. 12A:3-101 to -605, 4-101 to -504, by improperly charging the account with the forged checks. Finally, the complaint alleged PNC failed to exercise ordinary care and failed to act in accordance with the reasonable commercial standards of the banking industry in its handling of the checks.

In due course, summary judgment was entered against defendants Good, Trainor and Davis. Further, on May 4, 1998, partial summary judgment was entered in favor of PNC Bank, and Travelers' claim that the bank had improperly paid three checks presented at the local branch totaling $24,475 was dismissed. Travelers conceded that the branch bank procedures were reasonable concerning those checks. As to the remaining five checks issued between October 28 and November 20, 1996, all of which had been cleared through the bank's central processing unit, Travelers was given additional time to conduct discovery of PNC "related to the operations and procedures utilized by PNC to pay checks cleared at its central processing unit in 1996."

. . . The undisputed facts before the motion judge revealed that PNC's check clearing policy for checks which passed through its central processing unit required verification of the signature on any check in excess of $5000. PNC also provided training to the employees in this department and mentors were assigned to employees to supervise and assist the verification process. In response, Travelers conceded that $5000 was a reasonable threshold to trigger verification of signatures. However, it argued that it required additional discovery to determine whether PNC complied with its procedures.

In granting PNC's motion for summary judgment, the motion judge found that the law firm had not reviewed its October statement and had it done so would have detected the forgeries and could have taken appropriate action to prevent the issuance of the two December checks. He concluded that the inaction of the firm constituted negligence and precluded recovery against PNC for this loss. As to the remaining checks, the motion judge identified the controlling issue as whether the bank acted in a commercially reasonable manner. He found that there was nothing in the record to suggest that the bank's procedures were not commercially reasonable and further held that Travelers' request for additional discovery was too late.

On appeal, Travelers argues that PNC was not entitled to summary judgment because there was no evidence that it acted with ordinary care. It also contends that summary judgment was premature because discovery was incomplete. PNC responds that the law firm breached its duty to exercise reasonable care to prevent the forgeries and that further discovery would not enable Travelers to raise a genuine issue of material fact. ...

The UCC provides that an item is properly payable if it is authorized by the customer. N.J.S.A. 12A:4-401a. An item is not properly payable if it contains a forged drawer's signature or forged endorsement. N.J.S.A. 12A:4-401, UCC Comment 1. . . . The parties agree that the signature on the checks was unauthorized. See N.J.S.A. 12A:1-201(43). However, the parties disagree on where liability should attach.

Articles 3 and 4 of the UCC set forth the rights, duties and liabilities of banks and customers concerning commercial paper. . . . Effective June 1, 1995, the UCC established a comparative negligence test in which losses are allocated between the customer and the bank if each has failed to comply with its respective duties. [The court quotes the New Jersey version of UCC § 3-406.]

The phrase "substantially contributes" is read to be "a substantial contribution to the forgery rather than the negligence that must be substantial." . . . It "indicates causal relationship and is the equivalent of the 'substantial factor' test applied in the law of negligence generally." . . . What constitutes negligence depends on the circumstances of each case. . . .

"A lack of ordinary care on the part of the bank paying items under this provision of the UCC 'may be established by proof either that the bank's procedures were below standard or that the bank's employees failed to exercise care in processing the items.' " New Jersey Steel Corp. v. Warburton, 139 N.J. 536, 546, 655 A.2d 1382 (1995) (quoting First Nat'l Bank & Trust Co. v. Cutright, 189 Neb. 805, 205 N.W.2d 542, 545 (1973)). "For a payor bank to escape liability, it must establish that it acted in accordance with reasonable commercial standards and exercised ordinary care." A bank must use reasonable and proper methods to detect forgeries, but "the tellers and bookkeepers of the bank are not held to a degree of expertness which a handwriting expert possesses." Clarke v. Camden Trust Co., 84 N.J.Super. 304, 310, 201 A.2d 762 (Law Div.1964), aff'd o.b., 89 N.J.Super. 459, 215 A.2d 381 (App.Div.1965).

N.J.S.A. 12A:4-406 provides that if a bank makes available to its customer a statement of account, the customer has a duty to exercise "reasonable promptness" in examining the statement to discover any unauthorized signature or any alteration and to promptly notify the bank, if the customer should have reasonably discovered the unauthorized signature or the alteration. See Clarke, supra, 84 N.J.Super. at 308-12, 201 A.2d 762 (discussing the prior law dealing with a bank's liability to its depositor when forgery of the depositor's signature results in honoring the forged check). If a bank proves the customer failed to comply with this duty and the bank subsequently suffered a loss, the customer is precluded from asserting against the bank the customer's unauthorized signature or alteration on the item. N.J.S.A. 12A:4-406d(1). If the customer fails to report an unauthorized signature in breach of its duty and the bank subsequently pays other items in which the same wrongdoer is involved after the customer has had a reasonable time (not exceeding thirty days) to report the first item, the customer is precluded from asserting the alteration or unauthorized signature on subsequent items. N.J.S.A. 12A:4-406d(2).

If the customer is precluded but proves the bank failed to exercise ordinary care in paying the item and that failure substantially contributed to the loss, a comparative negligence test applies in which the loss is allocated between the customer and the bank. N.J.S.A. 12A:4-406e. If the customer proves the bank did not pay the item in good faith, the preclusion under 4-406d does not apply. Ibid. Without regard to care or lack of care the customer has one year within which to report the customer's unauthorized signature after receiving account statements. N.J.S.A. 12A:4-406f. See Villa Contracting Co. v. Summit Bancorp., 302 N.J.Super. 588, 595, 695 A.2d 762 (Law Div.1996) (holding the customer must be specific as to which items bear the forged signatures). . . .

The definition of "ordinary care" is the same for sections 3-406 and 4-406. Ordinary care in the case of a person engaged in business is defined as

> observance of reasonable commercial standards, prevailing in the area in which the person is located, with respect to the business in which the person is engaged. In the case of a bank

that takes an instrument for processing for collection or payment by automated means, reasonable commercial standards do not require the bank to examine the instrument if the failure to examine does not violate the bank's prescribed procedures and the bank's procedures do not vary unreasonably from general banking usage not disapproved by this chapter [Negotiable Instruments] or chapter 4 [Bank Deposits and Collections.]

[N.J.S.A. 12A:3-103a(7).] Good faith means "honesty in fact and the observance of reasonable commercial standards of fair dealing." N.J.S.A. 12A:3-103(4).

In *Globe Motor Car Co. v. First Fidelity Bank*, 273 N.J.Super. 388, 399, 641 A.2d 1136 (Law Div.1993), aff'd o.b., 291 N.J.Super. 428, 677 A.2d 794 (App.Div.), *certif. denied*, 147 N.J. 263, 686 A.2d 764 (1996), relied on by the motion judge in the present case, the court determined that an employer who has entrusted the examination of his account to a dishonest employee who is in a position to conceal the fraud is liable in the case of forgery by that employee. . . .

In *Putnam Rolling Ladder Co. v. Manufacturers Hanover Trust Co.*, 74 N.Y.2d 340, 547 N.Y.S.2d 611, 546 N.E.2d 904 (1989), relied on by Travelers, the court addressed which party should bear the loss for a series of checks forged by plaintiff's bookkeeper and cashed by the bank. During the bench trial in *Putnam*, plaintiff introduced as evidence of the bank's negligence five non-forged checks cashed by the bank during the same period the forged checks were cashed. Each bore only one signature in violation of the bank's resolution requiring two signatures to clear the check. *Id.* at 905. A bank manager testified each clerk had approximately four seconds to inspect each check that was processed through the bookkeeping center. . . . The court noted the bank introduced no evidence of general banking usage with respect to check-clearing procedures. . . . . After analyzing the shifting burdens of risk of loss in Articles 3 and 4 of the UCC, the court rejected application of comparative negligence principles and awarded plaintiff the full amount of its loss. *Id.* at 908.

As PNC correctly notes, *Putnam* is distinguishable from the present case because it applied a prior version of the UCC in which comparative negligence principles were absent. Furthermore, the prior version, unlike the current, did not define ordinary care. In that regard the New York Court of Appeals noted, "a customer could prove a bank lacked ordinary care by presenting any type of proof that the bank failed to act reasonably." *Id.* at 906. In *Putnam*, however, the evidence presented at trial delved into practice as well as procedure. The record established that clerks had only four seconds within which to examine checks. Here, the record contains no more than a statement of PNC's policy.

Viewing the record in the light most favorable to Travelers, the non-moving party, we conclude that summary judgment was entered prematurely. Further, the undisputed facts of record do not clearly establish that the law firm's negligence bars all recovery for the loss. . . .

Note. Revised Articles 3 and 4 (1990) were intended to modernize, reorganize and clarify the law at a time when payments were no longer as paper-based as the original version of the UCC assumed. For an excellent explanation and analysis by the former executive director of the Drafting Committee to Amend UCC Articles 3 and 4, see Fred H. Miller, *Benefits of New UCC Articles 3 and 4*, 24 UCC L.J. 99 (1991). As of 2014, 39 states plus the District of Columbia and the U.S. Virgin Islands have adopted revised Article 3 (1990). Ten other states have also adopted the limited amendments of the 2002 revisions. Curiously, New York is the one state that has retained its original 1962 adoption of the UCC articles, effective September 1964.[10]

The following case is a New Mexico decision dealing with a forged check situation, not unlike the one in *Travellers Indemnity*. However, the defrauded account holder in the next case is suing the bank where the forged checks were deposited (the *depository bank*), rather than the bank where its account is held (the *payor bank*), as was the situation in the previous case. Are the two cases consistent with one another?

---

[10] NY UCC §§ 3-101 – 3-805, 4-101 – 4-504 (McKinney).

WHITE SANDS FOREST PRODUCTS, INC. v.
FIRST NATIONAL BANK OF ALAMOGORDO
50 P.3d 202 (N.M. App. 2002)

ALARID, Judge.

INTRODUCTION

This case requires us to decide whether NMSA 1978, § 55–3–406 (1992) creates a statutory cause of action against a depositary bank for allegedly failing to exercise ordinary care in taking for collection numerous checks bearing a forged drawer's signature. We hold that Section 55–3–406 does not create a statutory negligence action against a depositary bank for alleged negligence in taking checks bearing a forged drawer's signature.

BACKGROUND

Plaintiff–Appellee, White Sands Forest Products, Inc. (White Sands), is a New Mexico corporation with its principal place of business in Alamogordo. Defendant–Appellant, First National Bank of Alamogordo (First National), is a national banking association, with its principal place of business in Alamogordo. In February 1999, White Sands brought suit against First National. White Sands' complaint asserted three counts: negligence, conversion, and recoupment. White Sands alleged that it maintained a checking account with Key Bank of Portland, Oregon (Key Bank), and that, beginning as early as January 1995, and continuing through February 1998, an employee (Forger) stole blank check forms for the Key Bank account and used those forms to make out checks naming herself as payee. According to the complaint, Forger, who did not have authority to sign checks on the Key Bank account, forged signatures of White Sands' employees having actual authority to sign checks for White Sands, indorsed the checks with her own signature, and cashed them at various branches of First National. White Sands alleged that during the period of January 1995 through February 1998, Forger forged 340 checks, totaling $433,375.95; and, that Forger presented the 340 checks to First National, which paid them.

The record contains evidence that Key Bank provided White Sands with monthly statements of its account; that the cancelled forged checks were returned with these statements; and, that White Sands did not have actual knowledge of the alleged forgeries until March, 1998. . . .

On remand [after a limited appeal on certain pleading issues], White Sands moved for summary judgment on the issue of First National's entitlement to assert the affirmative defenses available to payor banks under Section 55–4–406. In its response, First National argued that Section 55–3–406 did not create a cause of action in favor of White Sands against First National; but, that if it did, then First National should be entitled to assert statutory affirmative defenses available to payor banks. The district court granted summary judgment in favor of White Sands, ruling that White Sands was "entitled to judgment as a matter of law on defenses asserted by Defendant, First National Bank in Alamogordo."

In its order granting summary judgment, the district court found that "this decision involves a controlling question of law as to which there is [sic] substantial grounds for difference of opinion, and an immediate appeal from this decision may materially advance the ultimate termination of this litigation." . . .

DISCUSSION

Although considerable portions of the parties' briefs are devoted to the question of the affirmative defenses available to a depositary bank being sued by the purported drawer of forged checks for failure to exercise due care in taking the checks, we conclude that a more basic question is whether Section 55–3–406 even creates an affirmative cause of action in favor of drawers such as White Sands. As we explain below, Section 55–3–406 does not give rise to an affirmative cause of action in favor of a purported drawer against a depositary bank; consequently, the question of the scope of the defenses to such a claim does not even arise. [The court then quotes UCC § 3-406.]

As the district court observed in the course of the hearing on White Sands' motion for summary judgment, Section 55–3–406 appears to operate solely as a defense. . . .

We do not find support in Article 3 for a statutory negligence cause of action based upon Section 55–3–406 in favor of drawers against depositary banks. The official comments to the UCC are "persuasive authority." . . . As the district court recognized, the official comment to Section 55–3–406 expressly disclaims any intention to make a negligent party liable in tort. Further, as NMSA 1978, §§ 55–3–404(d) (1992) and 55–3–405(b) (1992) demonstrate, the drafters of Article 3 clearly understood how to create an affirmative cause of action based upon a party's failure to exercise ordinary care. The phrase "the person bearing the loss may recover from the person failing to exercise ordinary care" contained in Sections 55–3–404(d) and 55–3–405(b) is noticeably absent from Section 55–3–406. . . .

We recognize that some commentators have stated that UCC Section 3–406 does give rise to an affirmative cause of action. [2 JAMES J. WHITE & ROBERT S. SUMMERS, UNIFORM COMMERCIAL CODE § 19–1 at 239 (4th ed.1995).] However, these authors' discussion is noteworthy for its complete failure to address Official Comment 1 to Section 3–406. Other leading commentators are more cautious, observing merely that "[t]his provision seems to be purely defensive in nature, although conceivably it could constitute grounds for affirmative action by a party forced to reimburse a victim." 2A FREDERICK M. HART & WILLIAM F. WILLIER, NEGOTIABLE INSTRUMENTS UNDER THE UNIFORM COMMERCIAL CODE § 12.37 (2001).

We conclude that White Sands has not made out a persuasive case for superimposing a statutory negligence cause of action on the carefully crafted scheme of express statutory liabilities created by Article 3. "For the courts to interfere with the [UCC's] statutory scheme by superimposing tort rules, there must be sound policy reasons for finding the statutory scheme to be inadequate." *Spectron Dev. Lab. v. Am. Hollow Boring Co.*, 1997–NMCA–025, ¶ 24, 123 N.M. 170, 936 P.2d 852; *see also Bank Polska Kasa Opieki, S.A. v. Pamrapo Sav. Bank, S.L.A*, 909 F.Supp. 948, 956–57 (D.N.J.1995) (applying New Jersey law; declining to recognize common-law negligence cause of action in favor of drawer against depositary bank); *Lee Newman, M.D., Inc. v. Wells Fargo Bank*, 87 Cal.App.4th 73, 104 Cal.Rptr.2d 310 (.2001) (applying revised version of UCC; holding that Article 3's scheme of loss allocation has displaced common-law negligence action against depositary bank for failing to exercise ordinary care in taking checks with indorsements forged by dishonest employee of drawer; observing that plaintiff-drawer has express remedy under UCC Section 3–405(b)). . . .

Questions and Problems 1.10. As *White Sands* suggests, within the UCC there is a highly developed set of concepts categorizing different participants' negotiable instrument transactions and allocating specific rights and obligations to each. We shall address the practical implications of these concepts at length in the next chapter. What would have been the result if White Sands had sued Key Bank instead of First National?

4. Credit Cards and Debit Cards

INTRODUCTION

Over the past forty years, the traditional paper-based payments system of bank checks and deposits has been significantly overtaken by plastic – first credit cards, issued by a wide variety of credit providers, and increasingly debit cards, typically issued by banks and linked to accounts maintained by the issuer bank in the name of the card holder. How and to what extent credit and debit cards are governed by UCC rules, and what specifically tailored rules and regulations need to be in place with respect to these cards are perennial questions in an area of practice that continues to expand and morph over time.

THE CREDIT CARD PAYMENT SYSTEM

The following excerpt is from a seminal article on credit cards. It offers an initial exposure to the basic issues about what rules and procedures have developed with respect to credit cards.

WILLIAM B. DAVENPORT,
BANK CREDIT CARDS AND THE CODE
85 Banking L.J. 941 (1968)

Credit cards have existed as commercial instruments for approximately fifty years, although major developments with respect to them have occurred only within the past ten to seventeen years.

The first credit cards were issued about 1914 by oil companies to their customers for the purchase of gasoline, oil and accessories at the companies' stations. . . . Local department stores, like nationwide oil companies, began the practice of issuing single-purpose credit cards to their customers for purchases in the store or any of its branches. The advent of air travel brought with it the airline credit card. The rail travel credit card also came into existence.

In 1950, independent credit card companies began to emerge with an all-purpose card. In that year, the Diners' Club, Inc., which did not (and still does not) sell merchandise, began a credit and collection service for members of its plan. Members of the plan were of two kinds—cardholder members and establishment members. A directory of establishment members was issued to cardholder members to advise cardholders of establishments which would honor the card. Diners' Club executed one form of agreement with an establishment member and another form of agreement with a cardholder member. Each of the two agreements was independent of the other. Subsequent credit card plans have followed this pattern. In 1958 the American Express Company, an issuer of traveler's checks (whose function, like that of the credit card, was to avoid the necessity of carrying large sums of cash on the person), commenced operation of its system. In 1959 Hilton Credit Corporation initiated Carte Blanche. These three companies were the major independent issuers of credit cards until the entry of major banks into the credit card field in 1959. Users of credit cards issued by these three companies have been primarily businessmen for the purposes of travel and entertainment, and the practice of the issuer has been to transmit a monthly statement of credit card purchases for the preceding month payable on receipt.

In the late 1950's the nation's two largest banks, the Bank of America and the Chase Manhattan, entered the credit card field. Their credit card plans, like those of the three issuers mentioned, were tripartite arrangements. The bank card, however, served the needs of consumers and offered them an all-purpose credit card for consumer items under which statements for credit card purchases would be transmitted monthly, but would be payable, at the option of the cardholder, in full open receipt or upon an installment, revolving basis. . . .

This article will explain the mechanics of a bank credit card plan and discuss the body of law applicable to credit cards. It is the premise of this article that the credit card is a commercial instrument[20] . . .

Mechanics of a Bank Credit Card Plan and System

The basis of a single bank credit card plan is a tripartite arrangement involving: (1) an agreement between the issuing bank ("issuer") and cardholder; (2) an agreement between the issuer and the merchant seller of goods or services or both ("merchant"); and (3) a sales agreement between the cardholder and the merchant.

The Issuer-Cardholder Agreement

Bank credit cards are issued without charge to cardholders.[31] They may be issued either with or without application. In either case the bank has approved the credit of the cardholder to a maximum limit. . . . One difference between the situation in which a card is issued upon application and that in which it is transmitted on an unsolicited basis is in establishing the exist-

---

[20] The credit card itself is not a negotiable instrument. *Gulf Ref. Co. v. Plotnick*, 24 Pa. D. & C. 147, 150 (C.P. Lanc. 1935), commented upon at 2 U. Pitt.. L. REV. 117 (1936); *Lit Bros. v. Haines*, 98 N.J.L. 658, 660 121 Atl. 131, 132 (Sup. Ct. 1923) (credit coin). Neither is a letter of credit a negotiable instrument. *Orr & Barber v. Union Bank of Scotland*, 1 Macq. 513, 523 (H.L. 1854). The character of instruments drawn under or pursuant to these instruments is another question.

[31] This may be contrasted with the annual membership fee charged by some independent credit card companies.

ence of an issuer-cardholder agreement. If the cardholder executes a written application for the card, he, of course, agrees to
the terms set forth in the application, and they form the agreement. When an issuer transmits a credit card to a person,
whether or not he has signed a written application for the card,
the issuer also transmits with it a copy of its issuer-cardholder
agreement. If a person who has not requested the card receives
it along with a copy of the issuer-cardholder agreement, signs
his name on the signature pad on the reverse side of the card
and uses it, it seems clear that he has assented to the terms of
the enclosed issuer-cardholder agreement. . . .

The Issuer-Merchant Agreement

The second of the three agreements is that between the issuer or the participating bank and the merchant. Its provisions are
likewise fairly standard. The merchant agrees to sell goods or
services at his regular cash price to cardholders and reflect the
sale on a sales slip form furnished the merchant by a bank participating in the plan. This sales slip must show the total sales
price, be signed by the purchaser and imprinted with the basic
information on the credit card, together with the merchant's
name and number. Many issuer-merchant agreements obligate
the merchant to compare the signature on the reverse side of the
credit card with that on the sales slip.43 If the amount of the
proposed sale exceeds what is called a "floor limit"--e.g., fifty dol-
lars--the merchant must obtain authority for the sale from the
issuer's authorization center.44 The agreement contemplates
that the merchant will deliver the sales slip to the issuer within
three business days following the sale in a special envelope furnished by the issuer for that purpose. [Most of these steps are
now performed digitally, often with no paper copy at all, in the
absence of a customer request.]

A cardholder may also obtain a cash advance from a participating bank. Each cash advance must generally be cleared with
the issuer's authorization center by telephone. The cardholder
merely signs a cash advance slip, which has been inserted in the
bank's imprinter. [Again, this is now mostly digital, often via
bank ATMs.]

The Sales Agreement

The third agreement in the plan is the one between the card-holder member and the merchant member – *i.e.*, the sales agreement. The cardholder presents his card to the merchant and purchases goods or services. ...

Observations on Bank Credit Cards

As with everything else, credit cards have their advantages and their disadvantages. A cardholder may take advantage of special seasonal opportunities (for example, clearance sales) offering substantial savings without cash and make deferred payments at a more convenient time. A cardholder need not carry large amounts of cash or be concerned about the reluctance of merchants to accept personal checks. Credit card purchasing may simplify his personal bookkeeping and thereby save time, since payment is made for all charge purposes upon a single monthly statement with a single check. The merchant benefits by obtaining immediate cash for credit sales upon deposit of sales slips at his bank. To the extent of credit card sales he is liberated from bookkeeping, collection and bad debt problems and he has fewer receivables and more cash to invest in current inventory. The issuer or participating bank benefits to the extent that it establishes new sources of income from the discount percentages on merchant sales slips and from the monthly charges on cardholder purchases where the cardholder elects to pay on an installment basis spread over two or more months. The issuer also benefits from the merchant's bank account opened with it, and it may benefit from other business originating from the cardholder.

There are likewise disadvantages to all three parties. The two most frequently voiced complaints on the part of merchants have concerned the amount of the issuer's service charge and the lessening of customer contact. A possible disadvantage to the cardholder is that he may tend to overspend, since unlike an account kept in a check book, he may maintain no current record of his spending and his remaining balance. The issuer absorbs almost all risks of fraud and misuse of the card from all sources – the cardholder, a stranger into whose hands the card may come, and the merchant. Its share of fraudulent losses is probably greater than in instances involving checks and other negotiable instruments.[60] . . .

Conclusion

While bank credit cards are not a complete substitute for cash, they do represent a great commercial advance. Some believe that the bank credit card is one of the stations on our way to a checkless society. The economic impact of bank credit card plans seems clear. Banks will hold directly a considerably greater proportion of consumer debt than formerly, some of which they held indirectly in the form of loans to merchants secured by their accounts receivable. . . .

Questions and Problems 1.11. In your experience, does Davenport's description of the credit card system still seem accurate?[11] Since Davenport's article was published, it has long been the case that checks are governed by the UCC, while credit and debit cards have primarily been governed by a nest of private contracts. These include not just the one between card issuer and holder, but also between merchants who accept the card and their banks, and between those banks and credit card networks like MasterCard and Visa. The network agreements make the use of these cards efficient and almost universal. Typically, the bank-network contracts allocate liability among parties that handle a payment card transaction.[12]

1.12. As of 1 October 2015, network agreements experienced an "EMV Liability Shift,"[13] encouraging the adoption of EMV-

---

[60] In negotiable instrument cases some of the risk is allocated to other parties. *See* [UCC] §§ 3-406 and 4-406.

[11] For a very useful analysis of newer (post-Davenport) payment devices and the legal problems associated with them, see Gregory Maggs, *New Payment Devices and General Principles of Payment Law*, 72 Notre Dame L. Rev. 753 (1997).

[12] For a critique of these liability allocation rules, see Adam J. Levitin, *Private Disordering? Payment Card Fraud Liability Rules*, 5 Brook. J. Corp. Fin. & Com. L. 1 (2010).

[13] "EMV" is an acronym for "EuroPay, MasterCard, Visa," the three original adopters of the standard, but all major cards endorse EMV today. On the

chip cards that ultimately are supposed to replace the magnetic-strip cards prevalent in the United States. (To date, implementation of the shift is still in transition.) Under the EMV Liability Shift, risk of loss for certain types of unauthorized or fraudulent transactions shifts from the issuing bank and the credit card networks to the party that adopts the lowest level of EMV-compliant technology. So, for example, if a bank issues a cardholder an EMV-compliant card, and a merchant has not installed EMV-compliant card readers, liability for an unauthorized transaction at the merchant's location involving a counterfeit card is allocated to the merchant.

THE DEBIT CARD PAYMENT SYSTEM

There are many ways to transfer funds, both at the wholesale or commercial level and at the consumer level. The principal ones are explored in Chapter 5. However, today one prevalent way to transfer funds in payment of individual or consumer obligations is through the use of debit cards, the credit card look-alike that does not require credit approval and is routinely linked to ordinary retail checking accounts.

Questions and Problems 1.13. The following article takes a look at debit cards, as contrasted with credit cards. How do the characteristics of the former compare with the latter?

EMV Liability Shift, see *About EMV*, www.emvco.com/about_emv.aspx; Mark Scott, *Preparing for Chip-and-PIN Cards in the United States*, N.Y. Times Bits (Dec. 2, 2014), *available at* http://bits.blogs.nytimes.com/2014/12/02/preparing-for-chip-and-pin-cards-in-the-united-states/.

ARNOLD S. ROSENBERG, BETTER THAN CASH? GLOBAL PROLIFERATION OF PAYMENT CARDS AND CONSUMER PROTECTION POLICY
44 Colum. J. Transnat'l L. 520 (2006)

A global deluge of debit cards and prepaid cards--payment cards that do not require consumers to qualify for credit--is rapidly making electronic payment systems accessible to much of the world's population that previously paid in cash for goods and services. The global proliferation of payment cards is fraught with both risk and promise for consumers. . . .

[F]ees and charges imposed on consumers for payment card services are one of the most prolific sources of consumer complaints, yet they are not generally regulated by existing laws except through the imposition of disclosure requirements that are largely ineffective.[a] Bank fees are not even included in scholarship on "payment systems" and "payments Law." . . .

II. Payment Cards

A. Debit, Credit, and Charge Cards

Debit cards, sometimes issued as "ATM cards," "check cards," "cash cards," or "Smart Cards"[1] are proliferating worldwide at a staggering rate. Debit cards are distinguished from credit cards and charge cards in that the use of a debit card results in a direct debit to the user's bank account, while the use of a credit

---

[a] The situation has modestly changed pursuant to § 1075 of the Dodd-Frank Wall Street Reform and Consumer Protection Act, Pub. L. No. 111–203, 124 Stat. 1376, 2068 (2010) (codified at 15 U.S.C. § 1693o), which directed the Federal Reserve to regulate market abuses with respect to debit card fees. *See* 12 C.F.R. § 235.4 & App. A (Federal Reserve rules on debit card interchange fees and routing). *See also NACS v. Board of Governors*, 746 F.3d 474 (D.C.Cir. 2014), cert. denied, --- U.S. ---, 135 S.Ct. 1170 (2015) (generally upholding Federal Reserve rules imposing cap on debit card per-transaction fees and requiring at least two networks owned and operated by different companies be able to process transactions on each debit card).

[1] "Smart Cards," also called "chip cards," are multifunction cards that include a microchip. They can function as debit cards or credit cards, and perform other data functions. . . . "Check cards," too, can have both a debit and credit feature. ATM is the acronym for "automated teller machine."

card or charge card results in an extension of credit to the cardholder.

Credit cards, in turn, are distinguished from charge cards such as the American Express and Diners Club cards in that a credit card balance can be rolled over at the cardholder's option, while charge card balances must be paid in full each billing period. Charge cards, in other words, are intended entirely as convenience cards, while credit cards give the cardholder the right to an extension of credit by rolling over his or her outstanding balance. The distinction has blurred somewhat, however, as American Express has adopted rules permitting the cardholder to roll over certain types of charges, such as travel-related charges.

Although the volume of credit card transactions has grown, in 2003 debit cards overtook credit cards in aggregate dollar volume worldwide at Visa, by far the largest of the payment card networks, representing about half of the global payment card market. Debit cards are now the dominant card-based payment system in most countries other than the United States, Canada, and Japan, and the most widely used non-cash consumer payment system in the world. Even in the United States, debit card transactions have risen precipitously, and now represent a higher percentage of Visa point-of-sale (POS) transactions than credit cards.[5]

In China alone, according to the People's Bank of China, over 663 million debit cards were active in 2004, the overwhelming majority of them issued by domestic banks. As of 1995, the number stood at five million.

The key parties to a debit, credit, or charge card transaction are the cardholder (usually a consumer),[8] the merchant, the card issuer (a bank where the cardholder maintains an account or has deposited funds), the "merchant acquirer" (the merchant's bank), the processor that usually processes the transaction for

---

[5] Jonathan Zinman, Why Use Debit Instead of Credit? Consumer Choice in a Trillion-Dollar Market, Fed. Res. Bank of N.Y. Staff Report 91, July 15, 2004, at 2, available at http://www.newyorkfed.org/banking/debit_or_credit.pdf.

[8] . . . Many countries do not draw a distinction between consumer and non-consumer debit cardholders. The United States and certain European Union countries do.

the merchant acquirer, and the payment card association (e.g., Star and Cirrus in the United States) that provides facilities for clearing and settling the transaction between banks.

Debit card transactions resemble credit card transactions in most respects, apart from the debit posted directly to the cardholder's bank account and the fee structure. Debit card transactions in America may be processed through payment card networks such as Visa and MasterCard, or they may be processed through interbank networks such as the Star and Cirrus systems. Other countries like China have their own domestic interbank networks which in many cases are not linked to international networks.

Debit and credit card transactions are governed by a series of contracts.[9] The underlying contract between merchant and consumer gives rise to the payment obligation and authorizes the merchant to draw funds from the consumer's bank account to satisfy it. The consumer-card issuer contract governs the obligation of the bank to honor an authorized order to pay funds from the consumer's account. The merchant-acquirer contract governs the rights of the merchant to be credited with funds by the merchant acquirer once the merchant presents the transaction to the merchant acquirer, and the right of the merchant acquirer to deduct a fee, called a "discount." The merchant transfers its rights against the consumer to the merchant acquirer, who then transfers these rights to the card issuer in exchange for payment in accordance with payment card association rules that contractually bind both banks as association members. The card issuer then debits the consumer's account for the authorized amount in accordance with the payment order and its contract with the consumer.

The costs of processing payment card transactions generally are borne by merchants through discount fees paid per transaction to their merchant acquirers. The merchant acquirers are the merchant's banks, members of Visa, MasterCard, or another card association, which either own—as in the case of Chase—or

---

[9] Charge card transactions such as American Express are structured somewhat differently, in that American Express performs both the card issuer and merchant acquirer functions. This is beginning to change recently, as American Express has begun to allow banks to issue American Express cards.

are part of a bank association affiliated with, a processing entity, the largest of which in the United States is First Data Corporation. These banks are called "merchant acquirers" because by
contracting with the merchant to accept payment through Visa
or MasterCard they are said to have "acquired" the merchant for
the Visa or MasterCard association.[10]

Visa, the largest payment card network, is an association of
banks governed by a common set of bylaws and operating regulations. It is organized as the Visa International association,
comprised of six regional entities, the largest of which is Visa
U.S.A., Inc.[11] Each regional entity is owned by member banks in
the region. Worldwide, Visa has about 21,000 member banks.
Banks may join as card issuers, merchant acquirers, or both.
However, the merchant acquirer business, as a practical matter,
is concentrated in a few large banks while many smaller banks
join so they can issue payment cards with the Visa logo. The regional entities provide member banks with clearing and settlement facilities for payment card transactions within their region
and also with security technology and procedures. The Master-
Card association has a structure similar to Visa's.

So-called "private label" credit cards are cards that can only
be used at a particular retailer. These are common in the developing world at present, but have become a minor part of the
American card market. Private label credit cards were common
in the United States in the 1960s and 1970s, but today most
credit cards offered by American retailers to their customers
bear the Visa or MasterCard logo and therefore are usable anywhere that accepts Visa or MasterCard cards.

Debit cards are categorized as either personal identification
number (PIN) debit, also called "online" debit, or signature debit, also called "offline."[13] PIN debit card transactions require en-

---

[10] *Wal-Mart Stores, Inc. v. Visa U.S.A., Inc.*, 396 F.3d 96, 101-02 (2d Cir.
2005).

[11] Other regional organizations include Visa Latin America, Visa Asia Pacific, Visa Europe, and a region encompassing Africa and the Middle East.
See Visa Cards, http://corporate.visa.com/pd/merchant.jsp (last visited Jan.
20, 2006).

[13] "Offline" is really a misnomer. Stored value cards and cash are true "offline" payment devices. Signature debit transactions may be posted and
cleared electronically, but they are not posted and cleared in real time like
PIN debit transactions.

try of a PIN into a keypad and normally clear through interbank networks such as the Star and Cirrus systems. Signature debit cards are mainly issued in the United States by Visa and MasterCard member banks and bear the Visa or MasterCard logo. In most other countries, such as Canada, all debit cards are PIN-based. A signature is required, as with a credit card.

Although most consumers do not know it, there are significant differences between the two types of debit cards. PIN debit card transactions clear and are debited to the consumer's bank account almost instantaneously. They are real-time transactions. In the United States, the consumer often will be charged a fee by her bank for using another bank's or a merchant's facilities to consummate the PIN debit transaction. Such fees are uncommon in many other countries.

Signature debit transactions, like most checks, take two to three days to clear and to be posted to the consumer's bank account. They are riskier for the merchant, who could go unpaid if during those two to three days the consumer closes or depletes his bank account. However, signature debit is favored by American banks, which receive higher fees from merchants, paid in the form of discounts from what is credited to the merchant's account, than they do in PIN debit transactions. In contrast, merchants benefit from PIN debit in the form of lower discounts, but American consumers have resisted PIN debit due to the fees passed on to them by merchants and banks.

Many newer debit cards are actually "Smart Cards." Rather than a magnetic strip, Smart Cards contain a microchip. This makes them capable of storing a greater volume of data and performing multiple functions. Smart Cards can have both debit and credit functions, of which the consumer can choose either at the point of sale. They can collect, utilize, and send data about purchases, benefit entitlements, and other information.

For the card issuer, Smart Cards represent an additional source of information about the consumer and a possible source of additional revenue through the use or sale of that information. For the consumer, there is a risk of loss of privacy in the collection of this information. This risk is not new; the ability to collect information about the consumer proved to be a selling point when Visa and MasterCard were building their bank networks in the United States in the 1970s. The inability to share customer information with other banks was one reason that, in the late 1960s, Bank of America ceded control of its BankAmericard franchise network, the predecessor of Visa, to what became the Visa International association.[14]

B. Payroll, Stored Value, and Other Prepaid Cards

In a massive change that has accelerated during the past few years, instead of cash, millions of employees from Russia to Mexico—and increasingly in the United States[15]—are now paid through prepaid cards called "payroll cards," which they can swipe at a store to make a purchase and have the price debited from an account funded by wages deposited by their employer.

Prepaid cards are not limited to payroll cards, but include phone cards, gift cards, benefit cards, and travel cards, among others. Prepaid cards also are increasingly used to pay public benefits, especially in the many countries in which checks are rarely used as a method of payment.[17] Prepaid cards may be prepaid debit cards, the use of which results in a debit to a bank account opened for the benefit of the cardholder (*e.g.*, by an employer), or they may be "stored value cards" in which value is stored on the card itself.[18] While some prepaid cards—so-called

---

[14] See David S. Evans & Richard Schmalensee, Paying With Plastic: The Digital Revolution in Buying and Borrowing 72-73 (2d ed. 2005). . . .

[15] *See* Mark E. Budnitz, *Payment Systems Update 2005: Substitute Checks, Remotely-Created Items, Payroll Cards, and Other New-Fangled Products*, 59 Consumer Fin. L.Q. Rep. 3, 6-7 (2005); Christopher B. Woods, *Stored Value Cards*, 59 Consumer Fin. L.Q. Rep. 211 (2005); Christoslav E. Anguelov, Marianne A. Hilgert & Jeanne M. Hogarth, *U.S. Consumers and Electronic Banking, 1995-2003*, Fed. Res. Bull., Winter 2004, at 5, available at http:// www.federalreserve.gov/pubs/bulletin/2004/winter04_ca.pdf.

[17] In South Africa, for example, chip-based Smart Cards are now being used to pay government pension benefits. *World Wide Worx: Smart Card market explodes in South Africa* (Oct. 4, 2004), http://www.theworx.biz/smart card04.htm. . . .

[18] *See generally*, Budnitz, *supra* note 15, at 6-7; *Prepaid Cards in Europe and the US 2004*, DataMonitor, Mar. 5, 2004, available at http:// datamonitor.com/~ec641c4fc0a346018e7b491430411c27~/industries/research/? pid=BFFS 0243&type=Brief; Julia S. Cheney, *Prepaid Card Models: A Study in Diversity*, (Payment Cards Ctr., Fed. Res. Bank of Phila., Discussion Paper, Mar. 2005), available at http://www.paymentsnews.com/2005/03/philadel phia_fe.html; Mark Furletti & Stephen Smith, *The Laws, Regulations, and*

"closed loop" cards, including most gift and phone cards–are usable only for purchases from a particular retailer or service provider, prepaid cards are increasingly network-branded "open loop" cards, transactions with which are processed through Visa, MasterCard, and other payment card networks.[19]

Because prepaid cards do not require either creditworthiness or bank accounts, they are proliferating especially in areas such as Africa and parts of Latin America where relatively few people have bank accounts. Prepaid debit and stored value cards are a kind of "poor man's credit card," allowing access to electronic payments networks for those who cannot qualify for credit or lack bank accounts. Even in the United States, prepaid phone cards have become popular and payroll cards are catching on as a way to pay wages to the many, usually low-income employees who lack a bank account, sometimes referred to as "the unbanked."[21]

Questions and Problems 1.14. *What's in your wallet?* Take a moment to consider the plastic in your wallet or purse. Credit card? ATM card? Charge card? Payroll card? Phone card? Gift card? Other cards? What does each get you? How do you use

---

Industry Practices That Protect Consumers Who Use Electronic Payment Systems: ACH E-checks and Prepaid Cards, (Payment Cards Ctr., Fed. Res. Bank of Phila., Discussion Paper, Mar. 2005), available at http://www.paymentsnews.com/2005/03/philadelphia_ fe.html; Beth S. DeSimone & Carrie A. O'Brien, *Payroll Cards: Would You Like Your Pay With Those Fries?*, 9 N.C. Banking Inst. 35 (2005).

[19] Prepaid cards may also be divided into "online" and "offline" cards. The latter are stored value cards such as copy cards used in copy machines, which carry value stored internally on the card. The former are cards that electronically access value stored in an account maintained on a database at a bank, payroll processor, retailer, or other external location. In the United States, stored value cards are not currently covered by Federal Reserve Regulation E[, 12 C.F.R. pt. 205]. The Federal Reserve Board (FRB) has proposed to extend Regulation E coverage to payroll cards, and the Federal Deposit Insurance Corporation has proposed extending deposit insurance to cover funds accessed with certain payroll cards. *See* Budnitz, *supra* note 15, at 6.

[21] Budnitz, *supra* note 15, at 6-7; *see also* Debra Wolfe, *Card Usage Climbs: New Survey Shows Prepaid Card Usage Doubled in the Last Two Years*, Intele-Card News, Jan. 1 2002, available at http://www.intelecard.com/factsandfigures/03factsandfig.asp?A_ID=97.

each, and *how often*? Do you think that the diverse nature, terms, and uses of these cards make sense?

5. Letters of Credit

INTRODUCTION

Letters of credit (L/Cs) have a long historical pedigree. They come in several varieties, and at least some of these operate as a payment mechanism. This feature makes the L/C an appropriate  topic for this book. As you will see more clearly in Chapter 4, the L/C exhibits several characteristics in common with checks and deposits. There are typically three parties interacting with respect to the letter – the *issuer* (usually a bank), the *applicant* (*i.e.*, the bank customer who has requested that the bank issue the L/C), and the *beneficiary* (the party who has been promised payment by the applicant). There may be other intermediary parties facilitating the movement of the payment through the system – *depositaries* in the case of checks, confirmers and advisers in the case of L/Cs. Finally, the basic risks are similar in each case – *e.g.*, fraudulent demands for payment, unauthorized parties, wrongful dishonor of a payment demand. The following case offers a useful introduction to the risks and stresses in the L/C payment system.

VOEST-ALPINE INTERN. CORP. v.
CHASE MANHATTAN BANK
288 F.3d 262 (5th Cir. 2002)

CLEMENT, Circuit Judge:

The Bank of China appeals an adverse judgment in its dispute with Voest–Alpine Trading USA Corporation regarding the validity of a letter of credit. After conducting a bench trial, the district court concluded that the bank improperly refused payment on the letter and awarded Voest–Alpine damages and attorney's fees. We affirm the district court's judgment. . . .

In June 1995, Jiangyin Foreign Trade Corporation ("JFTC"), a Chinese company, agreed to purchase 1,000 metric tons of styrene monomer[a] from Voest–Alpine Trading USA Corporation ("Voest–Alpine"), an American company. At Voest–Alpine's insistence, JFTC obtained a letter of credit from the Bank of China for the purchase price of $1.2 million. The letter of credit provided for payment to Voest–Alpine after it delivered the monomer and presented several designated documents to the Bank of China in accordance with the Uniform Customs and Practice for Documentary Credits of the International Chamber of Commerce, Publication No. 500 ("UCP 500").[b]

By the time Voest–Alpine was ready to ship its product, the market price of styrene monomer had dropped significantly from the original contract price. JFTC asked for a price concession, but Voest–Alpine refused. After shipping the monomer to JFTC, Voest–Alpine presented the documents specified in the letter of credit to Texas Commerce Bank ("TCB"), which would forward the documents to the Bank of China. TCB noted several discrepancies between what Voest–Alpine presented and what the letter of credit required. Because it did not believe any of the discrepancies would warrant refusal to pay, Voest–Alpine instructed TCB to present the documents to the Bank of China "on approval," meaning that JFTC would be asked to waive the problems.

---

[a] Styrene monomer is a clear, oily liquid, ranging from colorless to yellow, with a sweet odor at low concentrations. It is used in the manufacture of plastics, paints, synthetic rubbers, protective coatings, and resins. N.J. Department of Health, *Hazardous Substance Fact Sheet*, *available at* http://nj.gov/health/eoh/ rtkweb/documents/fs/1748.pdf. It looks like this:

[b] The UCP, which has been updated since the decision in this case, is a set of recommended standard terms for L/Cs. In international transactions they are often designated by contract to substitute for otherwise applicable national law, like UCC Article 5. The UCP is discussed and compared with UCC Article 5 in Chapter 4.

The Bank of China received the documents on August 9, 1995. On August 11 the bank notified TCB that the documents contained seven discrepancies and that it would contact JFTC about acceptance. On August 15, 1995, TCB, acting on behalf of Voest–Alpine, responded that the alleged discrepancies were not adequate grounds for dishonoring the letter of credit and demanded payment. On August 19, the Bank of China reiterated its position that the documents were insufficient and stated, "Now the discrepant documents may have us refuse to take up the documents according to article 14(B) of UCP 500." JFTC refused to waive the discrepancies, and the Bank of China returned the documents to TCB on September 18, 1995.

In October 1995, Voest–Alpine filed the instant action for payment on the letter of credit. . . . After conducting a bench trial, the district court ruled in favor of Voest–Alpine, finding that the Bank of China's August 11, 1995 telex failed to provide notice of refusal and that the discrepancies noted in that telex were not sufficient to allow rejection of the letter of credit. . . .

The Bank of China's primary contention on appeal is that the district court erroneously concluded that the bank failed to provide proper notice of refusal to Voest–Alpine. In order to reject payment on a letter of credit, an issuing bank must give notice of refusal to the beneficiary "no later than the close of the seventh banking day following the day of receipt of the [presentation] documents." UCP 500 art. 14(d). If the Bank of China did not provide timely notice, it must honor the letter of credit despite any questions as to Voest–Alpine's compliance. *See Heritage Bank v. Redcom Lab., Inc.*, 250 F.3d 319, 327 (5th Cir.2001) (stating that an issuing bank waives its right to reject a letter of credit if it does not give notice of refusal within the time allotted by Article 14(d) of the UCP 500). . . .

The Bank of China received Voest–Alpine's documents on August 9, 1995. Since August 12 and 13 were Chinese banking holidays, the deadline for giving notice of dishonor was August 18, 1995. The Bank of China's only communication before the deadline was its telex of August 11, 1995. Accordingly, the issue is whether that telex provided notice of refusal.

The bank's August 11 telex stated:

UPON CHECKING A/M DOCUMENTS, WE NOTE THE FOLLOWING DISCREPANCY:

1. LATE PRESENTATION.[c]

2. BENEFICIARY'S NAME IS DIFFER (sic) FROM L/C.

3. B/L SHOULD BE PRESENTED IN THREE ORIINALS (sic) I/O DUPLICATE, TRIPLICATE.

4. INV. P/L. AND CERT. OF ORIGIN NOT SHOWING "ORIGINAL."

5. THE DATE OF SURVER (sic) REPORT LATER THAN B/L DATE.

6. WRONG L/C NO. IN FAX COPY.

7. WRONG DESTINATION IN CERT. OF ORIGIN AND BENEFICIARY'S CERT.

WE ARE CONTACTING THE APPLICANT FOR AC-CEPTANCE OF THE RELATIVE DISCREPANCY. HOLDING DOCUMENTS AT YOUR RISK AND DISPOSAL.

The district court found that the telex failed to provide notice of refusal because (1) the bank did not explicitly state that it was rejecting the documents; (2) the bank's statement that it would contact JFTC about accepting the documents despite the discrepancies "holds open the possibility of acceptance upon waiver" and "indicates that the Bank of China has not refused the documents"; and (3) the Bank of China did not even mention refusal until its August 19 telex in which it wrote: "Now the discrepant documents may have us refuse to take up the documents according to article 14(B) of UCP 500." In light of these circumstances, the district court concluded that the August 11 telex was merely a status report, that the bank would not reject the documents until after it consulted JFTC, and that the bank did not raise the possibility of refusing payment on the letter of credit until August 19. Accordingly, the district court held that the Bank of China forfeited its right to refuse the documents and was obligated to pay Voest–Alpine.

We find ample evidence supporting the district court's decision. The court's determination that the August 11 telex did not

---

[c] While the Bank of China originally cited late presentation as one of its reasons for refusing to honor the letter of credit, the district court noted that the bank later conceded that Voest–Alpine presented the documents in a timely fashion. *Voest-Alpine Trading Co. v. Bank of China*, 167 F.Supp.2d 940, 943 n.1 (S.D. Tex. 2000).

reject the letter of credit is based primarily on the Bank of China's offer to obtain waiver from JFTC. The offer to solicit waiver, the district court reasoned, suggests that the documents had not in fact been refused but might be accepted after consultation with JFTC. In reaching this conclusion, the district court relied heavily on the testimony of Professor James Byrne ("Byrne"), Voest–Alpine's expert witness on international standard banking practice and the UCP 500. Byrne testified that the bank's telex would have given adequate notice had it not contained the waiver clause. The waiver clause, he explained, deviated from the norm and introduced an ambiguity that converted what might otherwise have been a notice of refusal into nothing more than a status report. Faced with this evidence, the district court correctly decided that the Bank of China noted discrepancies in the documents, and, instead of rejecting the letter of credit outright, contacted JFTC for waiver.

Byrne further explained that the Bank of China's actions, viewed in light of standard banking practices, were ambiguous. The UCP 500 contemplates a three-step procedure for dishonoring letters of credit. First, the issuing bank reviews the documents presented for discrepancies. Second, if the bank finds problems, it contacts the purchaser for waiver. Finally, after conferring with the purchaser, the bank may issue its notice of refusal. This sequence ensures the issuing bank's independence in making its decision while also giving the purchaser an opportunity to waive discrepancies, thus promoting efficiency in a field "where as many as half of the demands for payment under letters of credit are discrepant, yet, in the vast majority of cases, the account party waives the discrepancies and authorizes payment." *Alaska Textile Co., Inc. v. Chase Manhattan Bank, N.A.*, 982 F.2d 813, 824 (2d Cir.1992). In light of the generally accepted procedure outlined by Byrne, we agree with the district court that the Bank of China's notice of refusal was ambiguous and inadequate.

The Bank of China also contends that the district court improperly accepted Byrne's expert opinion because TCB employees Sherry Mama ("Mama") and Deborah Desilets ("Desilets") both testified that they understood the bank's August 11 telex to be a notice of refusal. However, in contrast to Byrne's reasoned explanation of why the waiver clause deviates from standard banking practice, Mama and Desilets, who were both fact witnesses, offer nothing more than their subjective beliefs. Moreover, the determinative question is not whether the Bank of China provided adequate notice of refusal to TCB, but whether it gave notice to Voest–Alpine; and the bank presented no evidence of Voest–Alpine's interpretation of the telex.

Viewed in the context of standard international banking practices, the Bank of China's notice of refusal was clearly deficient. The bank failed to use the standard language for refusal, failed to comply with generally accepted trade usages, and created ambiguity by offering to contact JFTC about waiver, thus leaving open the possibility that the allegedly discrepant documents might have been accepted at a future date. Accordingly, the district court properly found that the August 11 telex was not an adequate notice of refusal. Since we agree with the district court that the bank failed to provide timely notice, we need not reach the question of whether the alleged discrepancies warranted refusal. . . .

Questions and Problems 1.15. Why does Voest-Alpine entertain *two* lawsuits – one against the issuer bank and one against JFTC? And once Bank of China pays the judgment due to Voest-Alpine, is it forced to eat that loss, or does it have any remedy against the applicant JFTC? In answering these questions, consider the following case.

BANCO NACIONAL DE MEXICO, S.A. v. SOCIETE GENERALE
820 N.Y.S.2d 588 (N.Y. App. Div. 2006)

CATTERSON, J.

Plaintiff Banco Nacional De México, S.A. Integrante Del Grupo Financiero Banamex (hereinafter referred to as "Banco Nacional") commenced this action seeking reimbursement for payments made to the beneficiary of a letter of credit. The letter of credit (hereinafter referred to as "the Letter") was issued on December 10, 2002, in connection with the construction of a power plant in Mexico. It was issued at the request of nonparties Alstom Power and Rosarito Power (hereinafter referred to as "Alstom" and "Rosarito") in favor of the Comision Federal de Electricidad (hereinafter referred to as "CFE") up to an amount of $36,812,687.68. The issuing bank was Societe Generale (hereinafter referred to as "SG"), a French bank doing business in New York, which subsequently requested Banco Nacional to be the confirming bank.[a]

The parties to the Letter agreed that it was to be governed by the UCP.[19] Further, despite the fact that the agreement was executed in Mexico and involved Mexican parties, they agreed that where there was no contradiction with the UCP, the Letter was to be governed and interpreted under New York law. The Letter additionally provided that "any dispute arising herefrom shall be resolved exclusively before the courts of the United States of America with seat in Manhattan, New York City, State of New York".[20]

The Letter also provided that CFE had the right to demand from the issuing bank, SG, partial payments or full payment "upon presentation of a signed written request [...] specifying the amount of the request for payment and that at that time the commission [CFE] has a right to receive such payment from the companies [Alstom and Rosarito] pursuant to the provisions of the agreement." The Letter further provided that if a request for payment did not comply with its terms and conditions, SG must immediately notify CFE in writing.

On September 1, 2004, CFE hand-delivered a signed written request for payment to plaintiff Banco Nacional pursuant to the terms of the Letter. The request demanded the full amount obligated under the Letter. The payment demand strictly conformed to the terms of the Letter.

---

[a] A *confirming bank* – or *confirmer*, under current UCC terminology – is used to "confirm" the L/C, which means that it takes on the obligation to make payment to the beneficiary under the L/C, with a subsequent presentation of demand to the issuer for reimbursement.

[19] The Uniform Customs and Practice for Documentary Credits ("UCP") is a compilation of internationally accepted commercial practices issued by the International Chamber of Commerce. "Although it is not law, the UCP applies to most letters of credit because issuers generally incorporate it into their credits". *See Alaska Textile Co. Inc., v. Chase Manhattan Bank N.A.*, 982 F.2d 813, 816 (2d Cir.1992).

[20] This wording is from the English language translation of the Letter.

Subsequently, Banco Nacional informed defendant SG of CFE's conforming Payment Demand and provided supporting documentation and a reimbursement request indicating the complete amount to be paid to Banco Nacional.

On September 3, 2004, SG informed Banco Nacional that Alstom and Rosarito had questioned CFE's right to payment on the grounds that no final arbitration award had been rendered against them. Within days, Alstom and Rosarito commenced an action against CFE in two Mexican courts and obtained ex parte Mexican orders purporting to stay payment on the Letter pursuant to the application of Mexican law. The first order was a provisional order to stay, which specifically stated that the stay was not based on the merits. The second order was also a provisional order to stay, which subsequently was revoked on appeal. Based on the two Mexican court orders, Alstom and Rosarito maintained that CFE was not entitled to payment under the agreement.

Banco Nacional responded that pursuant to the law governing the Letter, the UCP and the laws of the State of New York, disputes between parties to the agreement are irrelevant to the bank payment obligations under the Letter.

On September 8, 2004, Banco Nacional paid CFE the full amount obligated under the Letter, and immediately requested reimbursement from defendant. SG refused to reimburse plaintiff on the grounds that the Mexican orders excused it from payment.

Banco Nacional commenced this action seeking reimbursement plus interest. SG asserted that the Mexican injunctions prevented it from paying any party under the Letter. Subsequently, plaintiff moved for summary judgment on the grounds that payment was required under the terms of the Letter and that the orders of the Mexican court did not constitute a proper basis for refusal of payment. SG opposed, arguing that plaintiff was aware that CFE had no right to demand payment and therefore the payment was fraudulent.

The motion court rejected SG's claim of fraud, and held that SG would have had to comply with the Letter and would have been required to reimburse Banco Nacional if not for the doctrine of comity which required the court to honor the injunctions of the Mexican courts since the place of performance of the Letter was Mexico. The court thus denied plaintiff's motion for summary judgment. For the reasons set forth below, we reverse, and grant summary judgment to plaintiff, and order defendant to reimburse plaintiff with interest.

The motion court erred in invoking the doctrine of comity. It is true that under certain circumstances, the doctrine of comity requires New York courts to honor foreign judgments. *See Lasry v. Lasry*, 180 A.D.2d 488, 579 N.Y.S.2d 393 (1st Dept.1992). However, there is no such requirement in the instant case.

At the heart of this action lies a commercial letter of credit transaction. The transaction in the instant case involves, as do all letter of credit transactions, three separate contractual relationships. *See Blonder & Co. Inc., v. Citibank, N.A.*, 28 A.D.3d 180, 181, 808 N.Y.S.2d 214, 216 (2006). In *Blonder*, this Court itemized the three relationships as: the underlying contract for the purchase and sale of goods or services; the agreement between the issuer, usually a bank, and its customer, the applicant for the letter of credit; and the letter of credit itself in which the issuer/bank undertakes to honor drafts presented by the beneficiary upon compliance with the terms and conditions specified in the letter of credit. *Id.*, 808 N.Y.S.2d at 216.

The fundamental principle governing letters of credit, as reflected in the UCP, and long-recognized by New York courts, is the doctrine of independent contracts. The Court of Appeals has explained the doctrine thus: "[T]he issuing bank's obligation to honor drafts drawn on a letter of credit by the beneficiary is separate and independent from any obligation of its customer to the beneficiary under the sale of goods contract and separate as well from any obligation of the issuer to its customer under their agreement." *First Commercial Bank v. Gotham Originals, Inc.*, 64 N.Y.2d 287, 294, 486 N.Y.S.2d 715, 719, 475 N.E.2d 1255, 1259 (1985); *see also Gillman v. Chase Manhattan Bank, N.A.*, 73 N.Y.2d 1, 12–13, 537 N.Y.S.2d 787, 792, 534 N.E.2d 824, 829 (1988); *Nissho Iwai Europe, PLC v. Korea First Bank*, 99 N.Y.2d 115, 120, 752 N.Y.S.2d 259, 263, 782 N.E.2d 55, 59 (2002); *3Com Corp. v. Banco do Brasil, S.A.*, 171 F.3d 739, 741–744 (2d Cir.1999).

In November 2000, this independence principle was codified in a general revision of Article 5 (Letters of Credit) of the Uniform Commercial Code. [The court quotes UCC § 5–103(d).]

In other words, the "letter of credit" prong of any commercial transaction concerns the documents themselves and is not dependent on the resolution of disputes or questions of fact concerning the underlying transaction. *Blonder v. Citibank*, 28 A.D.3d at 181, 808 N.Y.S.2d at 216, citing, *First Commercial Bank v. Gotham Originals Inc.*, 64 N.Y.2d at 294–295, 486 N.Y.S.2d at 715, 475 N.E.2d 1255.

In the instant case, the contractual relationships are comprised as follows: the underlying contract was made between Alstom/Rosarito and CFE; the issuer of the Letter was SG, whose customers are Alstom/Rosarito; and the letter of credit is an undertaking by SG to honor any drafts presented by CFE according to the terms of the Letter. Further, the dispute here is between banks. SG is the bank which issued the Letter, and Banco Nacional confirmed it, which created a relationship separate and independent of the underlying transaction in Mexico between CFE, the beneficiary, and Alstom and Rosarito, the applicants for SG's Letter of Credit.

Consequently, based on the doctrine of independent contract, SG's obligation to honor Banco Nacional's presentation to SG is dependent only on the validity of the presentation which the Letter subjects exclusively to New York law and the New York forum.

Indeed, the motion court properly observed that pursuant to the UCP and under New York law, SG "must honor a demand for payment which complies with the terms of the [Letter] regardless of whether there is a contract dispute." The court further properly found that payment on the Letter was not conditioned on any "arbitral award" and that the written request for payment under the Letter delivered to plaintiff strictly conformed to the terms of the Letter. Further, the court observed that there is no evidence in the record to suggest that defendant ever notified plaintiff or CFE in writing of any discrepancy between the Payment Demand and the Letter. Nor did it return the presented documents, or claim non-conformities. Defendant simply questioned CFE's underlying right to the funds, which was not a statement by defendant that the Payment Demand failed to conform to the documentary conditions of the Letter. The court consequently found that all conditions to payment on the Letter were satisfied under New York law.

However, even while acknowledging that the Letter contained the exclusive choice of New York law and forum clauses, the court conducted a "place of performance" analysis and erroneously determined that, in this case, the doctrine of comity supersedes that of independent contract. The court reasoned that because the performance of the Letter, that is, "presenting the demand and then Request, the issuance of the Confirmation, [and] the notice by SG", all took place in Mexico City, the doctrine of comity applied and therefore the injunctions of the Mexican courts staying payment on the Letter "must" be recognized. This was error.

The motion court ignored the provision of revised UCC § 5–116(a) that states that "the jurisdiction whose law is chosen [to govern the letter of credit] need not bear any relation to the transaction." This provision requires application of New York substantive letter of credit law when the parties choose it, regardless of any relationship or lack thereof with New York State. *Blonder & Co., Inc. v. Citibank, N.A.*, 28 A.D.3d at 182, 808 N.Y.S.2d at 217.

Section 5–116 became effective when Article 5 was revised in 2000, so that it conformed to international trade practice. The section replaced former § 1–105(1) which required a "reasonable relation" between New York and the letter of credit for New York law to apply. A "contacts" and "place of performance" analysis, therefore, is neither necessary nor permissible under UCC § 5–116. Thus, even though the Mexican courts may have jurisdiction of the underlying transaction under the "contact" and the "place of performance" analysis, their injunctions have no bearing on the letter of credit.

On appeal, SG argues, nevertheless, that the change in the law resulting from the enactment of UCC § 5–116(a) did not alter the principles of comity or preclude New York courts from recognizing foreign orders in the letter of credit context. SG relies on *Fleet Natl. Bank, N.A. v. Liag Argentina, S.A.*, 4 Misc.3d 1025(A), 798 N.Y.S.2d 344 (Sup.Ct.N.Y.Co.2004), to support its position that New York courts have continued to apply the doctrine of comity to determine whether to recognize foreign orders relating to letters of credit. However, such reliance is misplaced because the promissory note in Fleet permitted the holder to choose either the law and courts of New York or the law and courts of Argentina. There was no explicit choice of law clause in *Fleet.* Here, by contrast, there was an explicit choice of law clause that established New York law as the exclusive governing law and forum. Moreover, as plaintiff correctly asserts, public policy considerations favor enforcing explicit choice of New York law clauses in letter of credit agreements. As a primary financial center and a clearinghouse of international transactions, the State of New York has a strong interest in maintaining its preeminent financial position and in protecting the justifiable expectation of the parties who choose New York law as the governing law of a letter of credit. *J. Zeevi & Sons, Ltd. v. Grindlays Bank, Ltd.*, 37 N.Y.2d 220, 227, 371 N.Y.S.2d 892, 898, 333 N.E.2d 168, 172–173 (1975), cert. denied, 423 U.S. 866, 96 S.Ct. 126, 46 L.Ed.2d 95 (1975). The doctrine of independent contract, as codified in UCC article 5, allows the letter of credit to provide " 'a quick, economic and trustworthy means of financing transactions for parties not willing to deal on open accounts.' " *Mennen v. J.P. Morgan & Co. Inc.*, 91 N.Y.2d 13, 21, 666 N.Y.S.2d 975, 980, 689 N.E.2d 869, 874 (1997), quoting *All Serv. Exportacao, Importacao Comercio, S.A., v. Banco Bamerindus Do Brazil, S.A.*, 921 F.2d 32, 36 (2nd Cir.1990). Indeed, the utility of the letter of credit rests heavily on strict adherence to the agreed terms and the doctrine of independent contract. *First Commercial Bank v. Gotham Originals, Inc.*, 64 N.Y.2d at 298, 486 N.Y.S.2d at 721, 475 N.E.2d 1255.

In any event, even under the traditional comity analysis, there is no basis for the motion court to recognize the Mexican injunctions because they are non-final, ex parte orders of Mexican courts. . . .

Questions and Problems 1.16. How can the construction contract and the L/C be "independent contracts" when the L/C is the payment mechanism specified by the construction contract? And why is it so important for the court to identify and outline the "contractual relationships" involved in the case?

6. Cryptocurrencies

"Cryptocurrencies" like Bitcoin are virtual currencies supported by a peer-to-peer network and no central issuing authority like a central bank.[14] Arguably, they represent an emerging payment system that as yet is not clearly subject to any one body of payment law.

Questions and Problems 1.17. The following article explores some of the problems raised by the virtual currency phenomenon. How should we characterize virtual currencies for purposes of legal analysis and regulation?

MICHAEL P. MALLOY, THERE ARE NO BITCOINS, ONLY BIT PAYERS
SELECTED ISSUES IN PUBLIC PRIVATE LAW 13 (2015)

[T]here has been an explosion of interest – and a frenzied up-swing in trading – in Bitcoins.[1] From a socio-economic perspective, this offers an unusual opportunity to observe the emergence and development of an entirely new, and so far unregulated, kind of market. Scholars interested in the law and policy of financial services regulation are also presented with an important opportunity to test assumptions that we blithely make about the ways in which regulation interacts with business and commercial activity.[2] Policymakers may confront a moment of truth – to regulate or not to regulate, and when, and how. . . .

. . . The Financial Crimes Enforcement Network (FinCEN) of the U.S. Treasury Department has in fact been addressing these issues since 2011, when it amended definitions and other regu-

---

[14] *See generally* European Central Bank, *Virtual Currency Schemes* 21-26 (Oct. 2012), available at http://www.ecb.europa.eu/pub/pdf/other/virtualcur rencyschemes201210en.pdf.

[1] More than a hundred virtual currencies exist as of this writing, with the largest capitalized virtual currency, and the one that historically has received the lion's share of attention from investors and users, being Bitcoin. [Kessler, M. (2014). 'States Seek Approach to Protect Consumers While Allowing Innovation in Virtual Currency' BNA Banking Daily (April 25, 2014), available at http://www.bna.com (last visited June 20, 2014).] [Footnotes have been renumbered consecutively for the sake of clarity.]

[2] *Cf., e.g.*, [W.C. Turbeville, W.C. A New Perspective on the Costs and Benefits of Financial Regulation: Inefficiency of Capital Intermediation in a Deregulated System, 72 Maryland L. Rev. 1173 (2013)] (offering masterful critique and reconception of predominant approach to measuring efficiency in relation to evaluation of costs and benefits of regulation).

lations relating to money services businesses, among other things, to refine the definitions of dealers in foreign exchange and money transmitters,[3] and to amend regulations relating to prepaid access to currency.[4] In March 2013, it issued its own interpretive guidance to clarify that certain activities involving "convertible" cryptocurrencies as media of money transmission may be subject to the Bank Secrecy Act[5] and the FinCEN regulations.[6] Firms that create, obtain, distribute, exchange, accept, or transmit virtual currencies may be subject to FinCEN's registration, reporting, and recordkeeping requirements. In November 2013, FinCEN announced that it was working collaboratively with government and industry partners to close gaps in U.S. regulations that might be exploited by criminals using virtual currencies for illegal activities like money laundering.[7] In addition to FinCEN, other agencies looking at the regulatory implications of cryptocurrencies include the Securities and Exchange Commission, the Internal Revenue Service, the Federal Election Commission, and the Federal Reserve.

ORIGIN AND OPERATION

The Bitcoin enterprise started in 2009 based on a computer science research paper by the pseudonymous "Satoshi Nakamoto," an individual or group of individuals that developed complex algorithms the solution of which earns players digital tokens

---

[3] *Bank Secrecy Act Regulations - Definitions and Other Regulations Relating to Money Services Businesses*, 76 Fed. Reg. 43,585 (July 21, 2011).

[4] *Definitions and Other Regulations Relating to Prepaid Access*, 76 Fed. Reg. 45,403 (July 29, 2011).

[5] 31 U.S.C. §§ 5311 *et seq.*

[6] Financial Crimes Enforcement Network, *Application of FinCEN's Regulations to Persons Administering, Exchanging, or Using Virtual Currencies*, http://fincen.gov/statutes_regs/guidance/html/FIN-2013-G001.html (last visited June 20, 2014). . . . [For a useful discussion of the application of FinCEN's regulations to persons administering, exchanging, or using virtual currencies, see Stephen T. Middlebrook & Sarah Jane Hughes, *Virtual Uncertainty: Developments in the Law of Electronic Payments and Financial Services*, 69 BUS. LAW. 263 (2013).]

[7] [A. Alexis & M. Ferullo, 'Virtual-Currency Oversight Is High Priority, Officials Say' BNA Banking Daily (Nov. 19, 2013), available at http://bna/com (last visited June 20, 2014).]

called Bitcoins.[8] As early users entered the network, they became a part of a decentralized infrastructure that hosts Bitcoin's open-source program. The computers joining the network immediately began capturing virtual coins. The network's protocol was designed to release a new block of Bitcoins every 10 minutes until all 21 million were released, with the blocks getting smaller as time goes on. If the user takes more than 10 minutes to guess the correct code, the Bitcoin program adapts to make the puzzle easier. If the user solves the problems in less than 10 minutes, the code becomes harder.

Within this peer-to-peer network, earned Bitcoins can be passed among players and other participants digitally by computer or phone.[9] Apparently from the very beginning, this decentralized network used Bitcoins as a form of currency in exchange for real-world goods and services from willing providers.[10] A participant with the necessary free, open-source software can send or receive Bitcoins from other participants, all of whom remain anonymous,[11] while the Bitcoin itself acts as a digital marker recording the series of trades.[12]

Until the second half of 2013, most Bitcoin origination was done on the individual computers of digital-money fanatics.[13] However, as the value of a single Bitcoin skyrocketed, the competition for new coins quickly turned into "mining" as an industrial enterprise. Efficiencies were achieved through the use of "miners," specialists that vie to solve algorithms at competitive rates to generate large quantities of Bitcoins. One such mining

---

[8] This description is based on European Central Bank, *Virtual Currency Schemes* (2012), *available at* http://www.ecb.europa.eu/pub/pdf/other/ virtualcurrencyschemes201210en.pdf ("*Virtual Currency Schemes*"), and [N. Popper, Into the Bitcoin Mines, N.Y. Times, Dec. 22, 2013, at BU 1].

[9] *Virtual Currency Schemes* at 21.

[10] *Id.* at 21, 24. It is widely believed that the first commercial transaction in which Bitcoins were used as a means of payment occurred in Jacksonville, Florida, in 2010, when a software programmer named Laszlo Hanyecz exchanged 10,000 Bitcoins in payment for two Papa John's pizzas worth approximately $30.00. [N. Bilton, N. (2013). 'Betting on a Coin With No Realm,' N.Y. Times, Dec. 23, 2013, at B8.] Mr. Hanyecz had "mined" the Bitcoins by solving a series of algorithms set by a Bitcoin mine in Iceland.

[11] *Virtual Currency Schemes* at 21-23.

[12] *Id.* at 21.

[13] Popper (2013) at 1.

operation, Cloud Hashing, was profiled in the *New York Times* in December 2013, "[o]n the flat lava plain of Reykjanesbaer, Iceland, near the Arctic Circle."[14] "Reykjanesbaer" seems an appropriately mythic-sounding location for the mining of virtual gold. At Reykjanesbaer, high-capacity computers run an open-source Bitcoin program, performing complex algorithms 24 hours a day. If they identify the correct answers before competitors around the world, they win a block of 25 new Bitcoins from the virtual currency's decentralized network. While the network is programmed to release 21 million coins eventually, as of year-end 2013, slightly more than half of the anticipated maximum number of bitcoins was already out in the world. However, since the system is designed to release Bitcoins at a progressively slower rate, the complete mining of all bitcoins could take more than 100 years.

A further important feature has been the emergence of digital exchanges, like Mt. Gox, the largest until its recent collapse. The exchanges operate as secondary markets where persons could buy or sell Bitcoins using conventional currencies, with a fee paid to the respective exchange.[15]

LEGAL CHARACTERIZATIONS

The emergence of these "conversion" trades – cryptocurrency for conventional currency – has created a critical problem. There is "a growing trend of real monetary trading . . . , the exchange of virtual objects with real currencies,"[16] without a clear understanding of the legal nature of cryptocurrencies. Despite the generic way in which cryptocurrencies are often referred to, there are at least three distinct types of arrangements to be addressed. A 2012 study by the European Central Bank (ECB) divides virtual currencies into three categories: (1) closed; (2) unidirectional; and (3) bidirectional.[17]

A closed virtual currency is used exclusively in the *internal* trade of *virtual* goods in a virtual world, like the game *Monopoly*

---

[14] Popper (2013).

[15] Mt. Gox was sold to a Japanese Bitcoin firm in 2011. Bilton (2013).

[16] [Yang, R. (2013). 'When Is Bitcoin a Security Under U.S. Securities Law?' Journal of Technology Law & Policy 18:99-129], at 100.

[17] *Virtual Currency Schemes* at 5.

or its online equivalents.[18] Contextually, the cryptocurrency mimics real-world currency, but without practical or legal consequences.

A unidirectional virtual currency involves a purchase-only framework, in which real-world currency is used to buy a virtual currency or scrip, essentially allowing a prepayment or credit against online purchases of real-world goods or services.[19] This is very common as a customer-loyalty or advance-revenue device,[20] as in the case of marketers such as Amazon and Facebook.

A bidirectional virtual currency involves free-flowing interactions between real and virtual contexts.[21] The interplay between these two contexts raises the possibility of significant fraud or manipulation as transactions flow back and forth across the permeable boundary between the two.

While it is clear that Bitcoin trading is bidirectional, how to characterize, as a legal matter, what is involved in Bitcoin origination and trading remains a critical issue. The outcome of this issue could determine the appropriate regulatory approach, if any, to be taken with respect to cryptocurrencies like Bitcoin. For example, if Bitcoins really are a "virtual currency" – a meaningless phrase, a glib metaphor – then fiscal supervision by the Federal Reserve might be the most appropriate approach to regulating Bitcoin activity.[22]

Further, if they are in any significant sense "currency," then treatment under the U.S. securities regulation framework is categorically ruled out, since "currency" is excluded from the statutory definition of "security."[23] In contrast, under that char-

---

[18] *Id.* at 13.

[19] *Id.* at 5.

[20] *Virtual Currency Schemes* at 18.

[21] *Id.* at 16-17.

[22] *See* [M.P. Malloy, Principles of Bank Regulation 31-32 (3d ed., West 2011) (discussing purposes and functions of Federal Reserve).

[23] *See, e.g.,* 15 U.S.C. § 78c(a)(10):

    The term "security" . . . shall not include currency or any note, draft, bill of exchange, or banker's acceptance which has a maturity at the time of issuance of not exceeding nine months, exclusive of days of grace, or any renewal thereof the maturity of which is likewise limited.

acterization, Bitcoins, at least if involved in a contract for future delivery, would be "commodities" subject to supervision by the Commodity Futures Trading Commission (CFTC).[24] On the other hand, if we consider the term "currency" – undefined in the federal securities and commodities laws – as referring only to conventional, government-sponsored currency, then we may need to consider whether the financial obligation represented by a Bitcoin may actually be a form of "note." As a "note," a Bitcoin would be a "security" for certain purposes under the securities laws.[25]

Furthermore, recent news reports have indicated that Bitcoins are beginning to be accepted by more and more vendors as a form of payment.[26] If in fact it becomes a commonplace that Bitcoins operate as a payment mechanism, then we must deal with the possibility that they should be subject to transactional rules of article 3 of the UCC, and possibly other selected provisions of the Code. It is at this point that we begin to think about the contractual aspects of Bitcoins.

Bitcoins as Property

At a very elementary level, we could simply characterize Bitcoins as intangible property, worth whatever willing buyers and sellers consider them to be worth. This approach is implicit in the FBI seizure in October 2013 of the assets of Silk Road and its founder, Ross "Dread Pirate Roberts" Ulbricht, on hacking,

---

[24] Commodity Exchange Act (CEA), 7 U.S.C. § 1a(4). *See Commodity Futures Trading Com'n v. International Foreign Currency, Inc.*, 334 F.Supp.2d 305, 312 (E.D.N.Y. 2004) (holding that "currency is a commodity as defined under the CEA" and that currency transactions "for future delivery" fall within the CEA).

[25] *Reves v. Ernst & Young*, 494 U.S. 56 (1990) (holding that notes that are subject of common trading and bear a "family resemblance" to securities fall within definition of "security" for purposes of federal securities laws).

[26] In December 2013, Overstock.com, a major online discount retailer, announced that it would begin accepting Bitcoin within the next six months. [Wingfield, N. (2013). 'Overstock.com, Signaling Mainstream Support, Plans to Accept Bitcoin,' N.Y. Times, Dec. 27, 2013, at B3.]

money laundering and narcotics trafficking charges.[27] Silk Road was an Internet site that hosted anonymous, Bitcoin-based drug and gun sales. The seized assets included one of the world's largest accumulations of Bitcoins, a portion of which were publicly auctioned on 27 June 2014 as property of a criminal enterprise.[28] The obvious difficulty that results from this characterization is that there will be no clear and consistent institutional setting within which to determine valuation, outside of specific transactions.

Within specific transactions, however, one would have a very concrete measure of the value of the Bitcoin. For example, in March 2014 the U.S. Internal Revenue Service released guidance indicating that it would treat Bitcoin and other cryptocurrencies as property for tax purposes, not as currency.[29] As a result, determinations of income and valuation would apply rules that govern stocks and barter transactions. If this logic is followed consistently, Bitcoins held for more than a year and then sold or traded would pay significantly lower capital gains tax rates, as opposed to rates applicable to ordinary income. Likewise, in a falling Bitcoin market, losses from sales of or trades involving Bitcoins held for more than a year could be deducted from capital gains, but only up to $3,000.00 in such losses could be deducted from ordinary income.

Bitcoins as Securities

One obvious alternative is to characterize Bitcoins as securities, subject to the federal securities laws.[30] In 2013 article, Ruoke Yang argued that unorthodox settings like Bitcoins should be treated as "investment contracts," one identified type of "se-

---

[27] [J. Fingas, FBI seizes black market website Silk Road, arrests its founder, available at http://www.engadget.com/2013/10/02/fbi-seizes-black-market-site-silk-road/ (last visited June 1, 2014).]

[28] [D. Cooper, 'US to begin selling off its Silk Road Bitcoin hoard' available at http://www.engadget.com/2014/06/13/us-silk-road-Bitcoin-auction/?ncid=rss_truncated&cps=gravity (last visited June 20, 2014).]

[29] Notice 2014-21, 'IRS Virtual Currency Guidance,' *Internal Revenue Bulletin* 2014-16 (April 14, 2014), *available at* http://www.irs.gov/irb/2014-16_IRB/ar12.html (last visited June 23, 2014). . . .

[30] *See generally* Yang (2013) (considering arguments that Bitcoins are securities).

curity" in the definition of the term within the federal securities laws.[31] This is subject to a three-factor test adopted by the U.S. Supreme Court in the classic case *SEC v. W.J. Howey Co.*[32] The Court interpreted the term "investment contract," undefined by the statute, to mean "a contract, transaction or scheme whereby a person invests his money in a common enterprise and is led to expect profits solely from the efforts of the promoter or a third party"[33] The first factor – an investment of money – seems easily met in the case of the Bitcoin, since it is a bidirectional crypto-currency.[34]

Second, the investment must be in a common enterprise, and this is where Yang's analysis becomes problematic. The anonymous peer-to-peer nature of the network, and the fact that there is no enterprise to which Bitcoin value relates may make any notion of a common enterprise a difficult one to sustain. As Yang notes, the cases themselves are not particularly consistent in their approaches to interpreting "common enterprise."[35] Cases often take off in quite disparate directions, looking for "horizontal" relationships among investors or "vertical" relationships be-

---

[31] 15 U.S.C. § 77b(a)(1) ("The term 'security' means any . . . investment contract. . .").

[32] 328 U.S. 293 (1946).

[33] *W.J. Howey Co.*, 328 U.S. at 298.

[34] I am skeptical, however, of Yang's alternative argument that "investment" of electricity would constitute an "investment of money" for these purposes. (*See* Yang (2013) at 109-110.) At best, this would probably represent a commodity trade, but in any event the argument is unnecessary, given the bidirectional nature of the Bitcoin itself. Yang recognizes this later, in observing:

> Note that this result would apply to other virtual currencies in the bidirectional and unidirectional categories that normally would only require real currencies in exchange for virtual currencies. Here, the case with Bitcoin is even stronger than most virtual worlds that allow bidirectional RMT [*i.e.*, "real money trading"] because whereas some users in Second Life may argue that their interests do not require them to participate in the RMT exchange, all users in Bitcoin engage in bidirectional RMT – the alternative currency purpose of Bitcoin.

Yang (2013) at 110-111 (footnotes omitted).

[35] *See, e.g., W.J. Howey Co.*, 328 U.S. at 301.

tween investors and promoter.[36] The problem with cryptocurrencies like the Bitcoin would seem to be that the relationships, horizontally or vertically, are too disparate and individualized to support commonality.

This observation leads to a critical problem for the third factor underlying the "investment contract" concept, the requirement that there be an expectation on the "investor's" part that profits will be derived solely from the efforts of the promoter or third parties. Again, the disparate, peer-to-peer nature of the Bitcoin network would seem to presuppose the active participation of those involved, not a passive reliance on the efforts of third parties.[37]

While we may have doubts about the legal argument that cryptocurrencies are "securities," there is little doubt that swaps and derivatives contracts based on these currencies – arrangements that are a near reality already[38] - would themselves be classifiable as securities or commodities subject to regulation and disclosure requirements.[39]

Bitcoins as "Currency"

The Securities Exchange Act of 1934 expressly excludes from the definition of the term "security" for purposes of the act "currency or any note, draft, bill of exchange, or banker's acceptance which has a maturity at the time of issuance of not exceeding nine months, exclusive of days of grace, or any renewal thereof the maturity of which is likewise limited."[40] The term "currency"

---

[36] *See, e.g., SEC v. ETS Payphones, Inc.*, 300 F.3d 1281 (11th Cir. 2002) (concerning horizontal commonality); *SEC v. Eurobond Exch., Ltd.*, 13 F.3d 1334 (9th Cir. 1994) (concerning vertical commonality).

[37] *Cf., e.g., ETS Payphones, Inc.*, 408 F.3d 727 (11th Cir. 2002) (emphasizing essential managerial efforts of placement, collection and maintenance of products).

[38] *See* [M. Leising. & S. Brush, 'Bitcoin Swaps Near Reality As Tera Creates Legal Framework,' BNA Elec. Comm. & L. Rep. (Mar. 26, 2014), available at http://www.bna.com (last visited June 20, 2014)] (describing the development of Bitcoin swaps).

[39] It is reported that the Commodities Futures Trading Commission is already considering appropriate regulatory measures to govern such instruments as commodities. Leising & Brush (2014).

[40] 15 U.S.C. § 78c(a)(10).

is not defined by the securities laws. Cryptocurrency or "virtual currency" has commonly been characterized as "a medium of exchange without government backing that can be circulated over the Internet,"[41] but one might reasonably argue that the term "currency" ought to be read as referring only to conventional, government-sponsored currency.

Consider, for example, a December 2013 notice issued jointly by the People's Bank of China (PBOC) – China's central bank – and the Ministry of Industry and Information Technology, the China Banking Regulatory Commission, the China Securities Regulatory Commission, and the China Insurance Regulatory Commission that has banned financial and payment institutions from using Bitcoin.[42] This is a very significant development, for two reasons. First, the notice is an official response to the cryptocurrency phenomenon by the country with arguably the largest Bitcoin trading volume in the world, with multiple trading platforms, including BTA China, China's largest Bitcoin trading platform.[43]

Second, it represents a decisive choice to regulate Bitcoin trading as private transactional activity and to reject the characterization of Bitcoin as a currency, "virtual" or otherwise. The notice requires Bitcoin trading platforms to register with Chinese telecommunications regulators.[44] At the same time, the notice takes the explicit position that "Bitcoin is not issued by monetary authorities, is not the same as legal tender, and is not in any real sense an actual currency. . . . Since Bitcoin does not have a legal status or monetary equivalent, it cannot and should not be used as a currency in the market."[45]

In contrast, in an interesting development, in May 2014 Spanish tax authorities indicated that they are monitoring the

---

[41] Alexis & Ferullo (2013).

[42] PBOC, Yin Fa [2013] No. 289, *Notice on Guarding Against Bitcoin Risks, available at* http://www.pbc.gov.cn/publish/goutongjiaoliu/524/2013/ 20131205153156832222251/20131205153156832222251_.html (in Chinese). *See* [L.A. Pappas, 'China Bans Bitcoin Bank Transactions, Internet Use Allowed' BNA Int'l Bus. & Fin. Daily (Dec. 6, 2013), available at http://www.bna.com (last visited June 20, 2014)] (discussing PBOC notice on Bitcoin use).

[43] Pappas (2013).

[44] *Id.*

[45] Pappas (2013).

evolution of cryptocurrencies, given their potential use for money laundering.[46] Without clearly identifying Bitcoin as either currency or property, the Government stated in response to a parliamentary query, that the €2,500 limit placed on *cash* transactions could apply to *Bitcoin* transactions.[47]

3.4. Bitcoins as consumer transactions

One approach that seems to be favored by some U.S. jurisdictions is to treat cryptocurrencies as consumer transactions.[48] Indeed, the only concrete step taken so far at the state level in the United States has been the issuance of consumer-oriented "guidance" by the North American Securities Administrators Association and the Conference of State Bank Supervisors in April 2014.[49] While not mandatory in any sense, the *Model State Consumer and Investor Guidance on Virtual Currency* offers suggestions to state regulators in informing consumers about virtual currency. Consumers should be advised to consider, when trading or investing in virtual currencies, that virtual currencies may be unregulated; that they can be stolen or otherwise subject to cybercrime;[50] that they are volatile in value; that they have been connected to criminal activities; and, that virtual currency transactions may be taxable.

4. CONCLUSION

Until its own collapse amid fraud charges, Mt. Gox was a trading website for Bitcoins ("btc"). It provided public and readily accessible trading data that reflected Bitcoin market perfor-

---

[46] [B.A. King, 'Spain Eyes Bitcoin-Based Fraud; Stops Short of Cash Treatment for Now,' BNA Elec. Comm. & L. Rep., (2014), available at http://www.bna.com (last visited May 28, 2014).]

[47] *Id.*

[48] Kessler (2014).

[49] *Model State Consumer and Investor Guidance on Virtual Currency*, http://www.csbs.org/legislative/testimony/Documents/ModelConsumerGuidance--Virtual%20Currencies.pdf.

[50] A key risk is that Bitcoins are essentially computer files that can be stolen by hackers. [A. Alexis, 'Bitcoin Seen Facing Big Hurdles As Supporters Seek Wide Adoption' BNA Banking Daily (Dec. 2, 2013), available at http://bna/com (last visited June 20, 2014).]

mance.

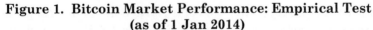

Figure 1. Bitcoin Market Performance: Empirical Test (as of 1 Jan 2014)

How have Bitcoins been performing? . . . (*See* Figure 1, [*supra*]. . . .) At least until the collapse of Mt. Gox, the values had been steadily cumulating from day to day.

The gains reached as high as 15.15 percent,[51] prior to the market adjustment that resulted from the collapse of Mt. Gox. The performance tends to flatten out when you look at a longer trading period, for example six months to the past year. . . . However, from the time that Bitcoin trading began attracting news coverage – roughly, from the Fall 2013 forward – the appreciation in value markedly increased. What is as yet unclear is the extent to which, if at all, these dramatic gains reflect market manipulation in Bitcoin trading.[52] Indeed, it is conceptually challenging to consider what manipulation would mean in this context.

We may never have a complete answer to that question. Mt. Gox, the Tokyo-based Bitcoin exchange, filed for bankruptcy in Japan in February 2014 after disclosing that it could not account for approximately 850,000 Bitcoin units, including more

---

[51] [In a market test, on] the downside, these gains may have been greater, but for the fact that my technical adviser periodically liquidated incremental gains from the account. On the upside, this practice protected us from greater account losses as the market decreased dramatically after the collapse of Mt. Gox.

[52] *Cf., e.g.,* 15 U.S.C. § 78i (prohibiting manipulation of securities markets).

than 700,000 units belonging to its customers.[53] (While Mt. Gox has since announced that approximately 200,000 Bitcoins had been located, customer losses still exceed $218 million.) Parallel suits were brought in the United States by U.S. customers against the company's U.S. affiliate, Mt. Gox principal Mark Karpeles, another company controlled by him, and other Mt. Gox insiders, as well as Mizuho Bank Ltd., the Japanese bank that processed transactions for the exchange. Whether the "losses" were the result of gross negligence or fraud,[54] these recent events underscore the need for clear transactional and regulatory frameworks appropriate to the Bitcoin context.

Questions and Problems 1.18. Bitcoin-denominated financial instruments do not rely on traditional intermediaries such as banks or public exchange markets. The "block chain" technology[15] that Bitcoin introduced for decentralized and transparent recordkeeping makes it even harder to imagine how cryptocurrency transactions would be effectively regulated.[16] The article excerpted next describes several approaches to regulating cryptocurrencies. Which ones, if any, seem likely to be effective and efficient?

---

[53] [A. Harris, 'Mt. Gox's U.S. Customers Ask Judge To Approve Deal to Revive Bitcoin Exchange,' BNA Elec. Comm. & L. Rep. (May 7, 2014), available at http://www.bna.com (last visited June 20, 2014).]

[54] *See generally* [D. McAuley, 'Mt. Gox Bitcoin Exchange Accused of Fraud, Negligence in Putative Class Action Lawsuit,' BNA Elec. Comm. & L. Rep. (Feb. 28, 2014), available at http://www.bna.com (last visited June 4, 2014)] (reporting on claims resulting from failure of Bitcoin exchange).

[15] For discussion of block chain technology underlying virtual currencies, see Judith Alison Lee, et al., *Blockchain Technology and Legal Implications of 'Crypto 2.0,'* 20 Electronic Commerce & Law Report 527 (2015).

[16] For a useful survey of the type of virtual financial instruments and transactions that might be susceptible to regulation, see Jerry Brito, Houman Shadab, & Andrea Castillo, Bitcoin Financial Regulation: Securities, Derivatives, Prediction Markets, and Gambling, 16 Colum. Sci. & Tech. L. Rev. 144 (2014).

STEPHEN T. MIDDLEBROOK & SARAH JANE HUGHES, VIRTUAL UNCERTAINTY: DEVELOPMENTS IN THE LAW OF ELECTRONIC PAYMENTS AND FINANCIAL SERVICES
69 Bus. Law. 263 (2013)

The legal landscape for virtual currencies remained undisturbed . . . until early 2013, when both regulators and law enforcement turned their attention to these alternative payment systems. Their actions were likely influenced by growing usage of virtual currencies, especially Bitcoin. The Financial Crimes Enforcement Network ("FinCEN") issued guidance clarifying the application of anti-money laundering rules to virtual currencies ("FinCEN Guidance").[8] That guidance was followed by two significant law enforcement actions. First, the Department of Homeland Security ("DHS") seized funds belonging to Mt. Gox, a major Bitcoin exchange. Shortly thereafter, the Department of Justice ("DOJ") indicted Liberty Reserve, a major international digital currency company, and its principals, on charges of money laundering. . . .

A. FinCEN Issues New Guidance on Virtual Currencies
On March 18, 2013, FinCEN issued interpretive guidance clarifying the application of the Bank Secrecy Act to virtual currencies. FinCEN had previously promulgated regulations governing money services businesses ("MSBs"), including currency exchanges and money transmitters, which are obligated to comply with registration, record-keeping, and other requirements ("MSB Rule").[12] This new guidance attempts to clarify if and when participants in virtual currency transactions might be engaging in "money transmission" and thus subject to the MSB Rule.

---

[8] Fin. Crimes Enforcement Network, U.S. Dep't of the Treasury, Application of FinCEN's Regulations to Persons Administering, Exchanging, or Using Virtual Currencies, FIN-2013-G001 (Mar. 18, 2013) [hereinafter FinCEN Guidance], available at http://www.fincen.gov/statutes_regs/guidance/pdf/FIN-2013-G001.pdf.

[12] Bank Secrecy Act Regulations; Definitions and Other Regulations Relating to Money Services Businesses, 76 Fed. Reg. 43585 (July 21, 2011) (to be codified at 31 C.F.R. pts. 1010, 1021 & 1022).

FinCEN begins its guidance by distinguishing "real" currency from ""virtual" currency. Real currency is the coin and paper money of the United States, or another country, that has the status of legal tender in the country of issue. Virtual currency does not have legal tender status and thus is not real currency. Some virtual currency, however, has an equivalent value in real currency or may be used as a "substitute" for real currency, and FinCEN deems this "convertible virtual currency." FinCEN is not explicit on this point, but presumably a virtual currency such as Bitcoin that can be exchanged for real currency would constitute a convertible virtual currency.

Because convertible forms of virtual currency may "substitute" for real currency, a transaction in these virtual currencies may qualify as a "money transmission." FinCEN defines "money transmission" as "the acceptance of currency, funds, or other value that substitutes for currency from one person and the transmission of currency, funds, or other value that substitutes for currency to another location or person by any means."[15] Whether a particular entity is or is not a "money transmitter" is "a matter of facts and circumstances," but the rules set forth a number of specific exemptions.[16] A person who takes a convertible virtual currency from one person and then transmits that convertible virtual currency to another person or location would be a "money transmitter," according to the FinCEN Guidance.

The FinCEN Guidance next divides participants in virtual currency arrangements into three categories: users, exchangers, and administrators. "Users" obtain virtual currency in order to purchase real or virtual goods and services. "Exchangers" engage in the exchange of virtual currency for real or virtual currency as a business. "Administrators" engage in the business of issuing and redeeming virtual currency. Users are not MSBs because they do not transmit the value of funds to another person or location. An exchanger or administrator will be a "money transmitter" if it (1) accepts and transmits a convertible virtual currency between persons or from one location to another, or (2) buys or sells convertible virtual currency, unless, in either case,

---

[15] 31 C.F.R. § 1010.100(ff)(5)(i)(A) (2013) (defining "money transmission services").

[16] Id. § 1010.100(ff)(5)(i)(B)(ii).

an exemption applies. An intermediary that accepts and transmits funds solely for the purpose of completing a bona fide purchase or sale of currency–real or virtual–is exempt and will not be treated as a "money transmitter." However, FinCEN views an exchange that takes funds from a user and then transmits those funds to the user's account at the administrator to be engaged in "money transmission."

In a virtual currency system such as Bitcoin, which operates without a central administrator, a person who creates units of the virtual currency (a ""miner" in Bitcoin parlance) and uses it to purchase real or virtual goods is merely a user and would not be a "money transmitter."[27] In contrast, FinCEN clarifies that "a person that creates units of convertible virtual currency and sells those units to another person for real currency or its equivalent is engaged in transmission to another location and is a money transmitter." Thus, a Bitcoin "miner" who creates and sells Bitcoins for real currency is apparently a "money transmitter." However, FinCEN's definitions of both an "exchanger" and an "administrator" contain the phrase "engaged as a business," which is not defined. It is unclear at what point an entity participating in the virtual currency market would be deemed to be "engaged as a business," and thus it is difficult to advise when the MSB Rule begins to apply.

While the FinCEN Guidance does not specifically reference Bitcoin, the applicable rules have drawn criticism from Bitcoin proponents. For example, Patrick Murck, legal counsel for the Bitcoin Foundation that promotes use of the virtual currency, said that the FinCEN Guidance "would be infeasible for many, if not most, members of the Bitcoin community to comply with."[30] At least three "exchanges" that traded Bitcoins shut down shortly after the new guidance was issued.[31] Treasury Undersecre-

---

[27] . . . How one obtains virtual currency may be described using various terms--such as "mining"--depending on the specific virtual currency model. See [FinCEN Guidance, supra note 8,] at 2 n.7.

[30] Jeffrey Sparshott, Web Money Gets Laundering Rule, Wall St. J. (Mar. 21, 2013), http://online.wsj.com/article/SB10001424127887324373204578374611-351125.

[31] Jon Matonis, FinCEN's New Regulations Are Choking Bitcoin Entrepreneurs, Am. Banker (Apr. 25, 2013, 10:00 AM), http://www.americanbanker.com/bankthink/fincen-regulations-choking-Bitcoin-entre-preneurs-1058606-1.html.

tary David Cohen stated that virtual currency exchanges that comply with the law "have nothing to fear from Treasury."[32] Given compliance challenges, however, those exchanges are unlikely to find much comfort in Cohen's statement.

B. Homeland Security Seizes Funds Held by
    Bitcoin Exchange Mt. Gox

On May 14, 2013, DHS obtained a seizure warrant directed to Dwolla, an Iowa-based [I]nternet payments company, ordering the seizure and forfeiture of an account belonging to Mutum Sigillum, LLC. According to the affidavit of a federal agent filed with the warrant application, Mutum Sigillum is the U.S.-based subsidiary of Mt. Gox, which is the world's largest Bitcoin exchange and which is based in Japan. The affidavit stated that a confidential informant residing in Maryland established an account at Dwolla that he used to fund an account at Mt. Gox and to purchase Bitcoins. In addition, the informant also exchanged Bitcoins for U.S. dollars that were transmitted back to him through Mutum Sigillum and Dwolla accounts. Apparently relying upon, but not citing to, the FinCEN Guidance, DHS asserted that those transactions demonstrated that Mutum Sigillum was engaged in "money transmission." The affidavit noted that Mutum Sigillum was not registered with FinCEN as required by 31 U.S.C. § 5330, and asserted that Mt. Gox consequently was in violation of 18 U.S.C. § 1960 and subject to legal penalties. One such penalty is the forfeiture of property as authorized by 18 U.S.C. § 981(a)(1)(A). The affidavit noted that Mutum Sigillum funds were also transmitted through an account at Wells Fargo and that a separate warrant was issued to seize funds in that account.[40] While law enforcement executed warrants to seize the funds of Mt. Gox located in the United States, as of June 12,

---

[32] Liberty Reserve Case No Comment on e-Currency Exchangers, United Press Int'l (May 29, 2013, 3:30 AM), http://www.upi.com/Business_ News/2013/05/29/US-Liberty-Reserve-case-no-comment-on-e-currency-exchangers/UPI-50571369812600/.

[40] . . . [S]ee also Brian Browdie, Bitcoin Exchange in U.S. Crosshairs Banked at Wells Fargo, Am. Banker (May 16, 2013, 8:43 AM), http://www.americanbanker.com/issues/178_95/Bitcoin-exchange-in-u-s-crosshairs-banked-at-wells-fargo-1059158-1.html.

2013, no indictments of Mt. Gox or its subsidiary Mutum Sigillum have been handed down. Mt. Gox subsequently implemented a new policy requiring identity verification before it would perform currency deposits or withdrawals.

C. Department of Justice Indicts Liberty Reserve
   for Money Laundering

On May 28, 2013, the U.S. Attorney for the Southern District of New York unsealed a criminal indictment charging Liberty Reserve and seven of its principals and employees with operating as an unlicensed money transmitter and engaging in money laundering. The indictment charges the defendants under 18 U.S.C. § 1960 with operating an unlicensed money transmitting business in violation of 31 U.S.C. § 5330 and its accompanying regulations. Defendants were also charged with conspiracy to commit money laundering in violation of 18 U.S.C. §§ 1956(a)(1)(B)(i) and 1956(a)(2)(B)(i). Liberty Reserve is alleged to have been a "financial hub of the cyber-crime world, facilitating ... credit card fraud, identity theft, investment fraud, computer hacking, child pornography, and narcotics trafficking." The government estimated that Liberty Reserve had 200,000 users in the United States and processed over twelve million transactions a year with a value of more than $1.4 billion.

Allegedly, Liberty Reserve did not require users to validate their identity, and criminals created accounts under false names such as "Russian Hackers." The government alleges that Liberty Reserve, in an effort to add an additional layer of anonymity, did not permit users to transmit funds directly to Liberty Reserve, but instead required them to make deposits and withdrawals through third-party exchanges. Liberty Reserve allegedly recommended third-party exchanges that tended to be unlicensed money transmitters operating without government oversight and that were concentrated in Malaysia, Russia, Nigeria, and Vietnam. Pursuant to 18 U.S.C. § 982(a)(1), the government seeks forfeiture of "at least $6 billion" held in accounts in Costa Rica, Cyprus, Russia, Hong Kong, China, Morocco, Spain, Latvia, and Australia, as well as one account at SunTrust Bank in the United States.

Of special interest to followers of cyberspace law, in a declaration filed in support of a post-indictment restraining order, seizure warrant, and injunction against Liberty Reserve, a Secret Service agent stated that the investigation included execution of "one of the first-ever 'cloud'-based search warrants, directed to a service provider used to process Liberty Reserve's Internet traffic." The government also sought an injunction preventing Amazon Web Services from providing services to support Liberty Reserve's website.

On the same day that indictment was unsealed, FinCEN issued a notice of proposed rulemaking to declare Liberty Reserve an institution of primary money laundering concern under section 311 of the [Uniting and Strengthening America by Providing Appropriate Tools Required to Intercept and Obstruct Terrorism Act of 2001, or "USA Patriot Act," 31 U.S.C. § 5318A].[53] The rule would prohibit all U.S. financial institutions from maintaining correspondent relationships with foreign banks that do business with Liberty Reserve. The measure would effectively cut off Liberty Reserve from the U.S. financial system.

While the Mt. Gox forfeiture order and the Liberty Reserve criminal indictment are quite different on a number of levels, both use 18 U.S.C. § 1960 to enforce the registration requirement for MSBs with severe penalties, including asset forfeiture and additional criminal sanctions. . . . These actions, following so soon after the publication of the FinCEN Guidance, signal the government's intent to police the virtual currency market robustly. These methods may be a convenient and effective way for law enforcement to deal with money launderers, but they have potentially significant collateral effects on small companies and start-ups that wish to operate within the confines of the law, but lack the resources or the expertise to navigate such tricky regulatory waters. Establishing appropriate compliance obligations without stifling innovation in emerging payments technology is always a concern. With regard to virtual currencies, it remains to be seen whether the government has found the proper balance. . . .

---

[53] Imposition of Special Measure Against Liberty Reserve S.A. as a Financial Institution of Primary Money Laundering Concern, 78 Fed. Reg. 34008 (proposed June 6, 2013) (to be codified at 31 C.F.R. pt. 1010).

VI. Conclusion

Despite attempts at clarification, many ambiguities remain following the FinCEN Guidance on virtual currencies and the application of the MSB Rule. . . . In addition to the FinCEN Guidance, virtual currency providers are also facing potential regulation from the Commodity Futures Trading Commission and from the states. These new regulations will add to compliance burdens and present new challenges to these emerging businesses. . . .

Chapter 2

Negotiable Instruments

One efficient way to move payments and credits through the financial system is by using a "negotiable instrument," one that will be recognized as a means of payment by almost anyone, and for which relatively clear and detailed rules exists. In the United States, those rules are found in articles 3 and 4 of the Uniform Commercial Code (UCC).[1] "Negotiability" for these purposes is the legal characteristic of a writing that can, with least interference, move through the payment system.[2] This chapter explores that legal characteristic in depth.

---

[1] Article 3, the subject of this chapter, covers negotiable instruments – drafts and notes – and Article 4 covers bank deposits and collections. Since checks are a type of draft, both articles will apply to many transactions involving negotiable instruments. If there is any conflict or inconsistency in the coverage of these two articles in relation to a particular transaction, Article 4 prevails. UCC § 3-102(b). Furthermore, since the banking system is to a significant degree federally regulated, applicable regulations of the Board of Governors of the Federal Reserve System (the "Fed" or "Federal Reseerve") and operating circulars of the Federal Reserve Banks supersede any inconsistent provision of Article 3, to the extent of the inconsistency. *Id*. § 3-102(c). (Unless otherwise specifically noted, in this chapter all references to the UCC, and especially UCC Article 3, are to the current revised official version.)

[2] Note that, in this context, "negotiation" does not refer to the process whereby contract terms are agreed to, but rather to the "transfer of possession, whether voluntary or involuntary, of an instrument by a person other than the issuer to a person who thereby becomes its holder." UCC § 3-201(a).

A. NEGOTIABILITY AND NEGOTIATION

Article 3 of the UCC covers *negotiable insruments*.[3] A "negotiable instrument" is a signed writing that evidences an unconditional *promise* or *order* to pay a fixed sum of money on demand or at a definite time to order or to bearer.[4] If the negotiable instrument is an order to pay, it is a "draft." *See* UCC § 3-104(e). If the draft is payable on demand and orders a bank to pay (*i.e.*, "is drawn on a bank"), it is a "check." *See* UCC § 3-104(f)(1).

Article 3 does *not* apply to money, to payment orders governed by Article 4A (covering funds transfers, discussed in Chapter 5), or to securities governed by Article 8. UCC § 3-102(a). It also does not include "documentary drafts," which we shall talk about in Chapter 4, where we consider letters of credit.

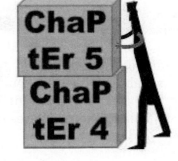

1. Concept and Process

To be negotiable – and hence covered by Article 3 – an instrument must exhibit the following characteristics:

- It must be payable to bearer or to order at the time it is issued or at the time it first comes into the possession of a holder.[5]
- It must be payable on demand or at a definite time.[6]
- Most significantly, it must *not* include any other undertaking or instruction by the person promising or ordering payment to do any act in addition to the payment of money.[7] However, the promise (if it is a note) or order (if it is a draft) may contain (a) an under-

---

[3] UCC § 3-101.

[4] *See generally* UCC §§ 3-103(1)(i), 3-104(1), 3-104 comment. 1.

[5] UCC § 3-104(a)(1). "Order" for these purposes means that the instrument has a written instruction to pay money signed by the person giving the instruction. UCC § 3-103(a)(8). For definitions of "payable to bearer" and "payable to order," see UCC § 3-109.

[6] UCC § 3-104(a)(2). For definitions of "payable on demand" and "payable at a definite time," see UCC § 3-108.

[7] UCC § 3-104(a)(3). This is why, among other reasons, letters of credit and the documentary drafts associated with them are not negotiable instruments. As we shall see in Chapter 4, there are all sorts of explicit conditions that will be imposed on the obligation of the issuer of the letter of credit to pay.

taking or power to give, maintain, or protect collateral to secure payment, (b) an authorization or power to the holder to confess judgment or realize on or dispose of collateral, or (c) a waiver of the benefit of any law intended for the advantage or protection of an obligor.[8]

Hence, we speak of a negotiable instrument as representing an *unconditional* promise or order. The promise or order is unconditional "unless it states (i) an express condition to payment, (ii) that the promise or order is subject to or governed by another record, or (iii) that rights or obligations with respect to the promise or order are stated in another record."[9]

Questions and Problems 2.1. Assume that Speedy wants to buy Sylvester's classic car. They discuss terms over dinner at the Arriba Lounge, and agree on a price and delivery terms. Sylvester knows about things like the Statute of Frauds, so he tells Speedy that he "want[s] the deal in writing." Speedy picks up a cocktail napkin, writes on it and hands it to Sylvester. Is this a check? (*See* UCC § 3-104(f).) If Sylvester signs the back of the napkin (*i.e.*, "indorses" it),[10] and presents it to the teller at the local branch of Banco Merca, can he

[handwritten note: No, it's a draft because it's order to pay but not payable.]

---

[8] UCC § 3-104(a)(3)(i)-(iii). So for example, a check might explicitly constitute the operative part of an accord and satisfaction of a debt (*cf. Webb Business Promotions, Inc., infra*), or a waiver of some right or obligation (*cf. American Nat. Bank & Trust Co., infra*).

[9] UCC § 3-106(a)(i)-(iii). However, a mere reference in the instrument to another record does not in itself make the promise or order conditional. *Id.* § 3-106(a), (b). (For purposes of Article 3, the term "record" is defined to mean "information that is inscribed on a tangible medium or that is stored in an electronic or other medium and is retrievable in perceivable form." UCC § 3-103(a)(14).)

[10] The indorsement of the instrument – and the legal consequences of indorsement – are governed by UCC § 3-204. Note that, although as a matter of ordinary practice, we expect to find indorsements on the back of the instrument, the UCC does not require that indorsing take place there. UCC § 3-204 defines indorsement as "a signature, other than that of a signer as maker, drawer, or acceptor . . . *made on an instrument* . . . unless the . . . *place of the signature, or other circumstances unambiguously indicate that the signature was made for a purpose other than indorsement.*" UCC § 3-204(a). The signature could be "made on an instrument" even if the signature appears on "a paper affixed to the instrument [as] a part of the instrument." *Id.* On the rules as to what counts as a signature and the consequences of signing, see UCC §§ § 3-308, 3-401 - 3-403, 3-419.

expect to receive payment from the bank in the stated amount? In answering these questions, consider the case that follows.   *Yes*

Here is what the napkin says:

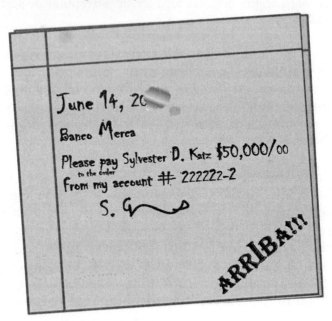

June 14, 20

Banco Merca

Please pay Sylvester D. Katz $50,000/00
to the order
from my account #: 222222-2

S. G

ARRIBA!!!

TELERECOVERY OF LOUISIANA V. GAULON
738 So.2d 662 (La. App. 1999)

CHEHARDY, Judge.

The primary issue before us is whether a casino patron's markers for gambling debts are enforceable negotiable instruments subject to the penalties imposed by the Nonsufficient Funds Checks statute.

TeleRecovery of Louisiana, Inc. filed suit on December 29, 1995 alleging that Lance D. Gaulon issued two checks to the Belle of Baton Rouge casino, totaling $10,000 and drawn on the First National Bank of Commerce; that payment of the checks had been refused by the drawee[a] as NSF [*i.e.*, Non Sufficient Funds]; and that the original creditor had assigned the account to plaintiff. . . .

. . . Defendant argued that the [Nonsufficient Funds Checks] statute was not intended to cover gambling markers and the markers did not constitute checks within the meaning of the statute. . . . Specifically, defendant argued that plaintiff failed to attach the credit payment

---

[a] The "drawee" is defined as the "person ordered in a draft to make payment," in the case of check, typically the bank where the checking account is established. UCC § 3-103(a)(4).

agreement on which the markers were predicated and failed to prove that the signature was authentic and that the casino's rights had been assigned to plaintiff.

. . . The district court ruled in favor of plaintiff, finding that the markers are checks under negotiable instruments law, that the plaintiff had complied with the other requirements of the NSF check statute, and that the plaintiff is entitled to penalties as set forth in La. R.S. 9:2782. On May 21, 1998 the trial court signed a judgment awarding plaintiff $10,000.00 in penalties, together with legal interest from date of judicial demand until paid, attorney's fees of 9.25% of the award and the interest, and all costs. The judgment specified the award was in addition to the amounts awarded in the judgment of April 16, 1996. Defendant appeals. . . .

ARE THE MARKERS NEGOTIABLE INSTRUMENTS?

. . . [D]efendant contends the bad check law cannot be applied here because the markers are not negotiable instruments. He contends the markers are *sui generis* and do not fall within the narrow precepts of the bad check law, which must be strictly construed. [The court quoted the Louisiana version of § 3-104(a)-(c), (e)-(f), defining "negotiable instrument."]

Defendant argues the casino markers are conditional because they refer to another document outside the face of the markers and, thus, do not satisfy the requirement of "unconditional promise to pay."

The following emulation approximates the markers in this case:

Each marker bears on its face the statement, "I agree to payment according to the terms of the Credit Payment Agreement previously executed by the undersigned." Defendant contends this requires a holder to examine another document to determine rights with respect to payment, making the marker conditional and non-negotiable.

Plaintiff rebuts by arguing that in order to be conditional the instrument must state that it is conditioned by, subject to or governed by another writing, and mere reference to another writing on the face of the instrument does not make it conditional. La. R.S. 10:3–106(a).

Δ's argument

La. R.S. 10:3–106(a) provides,

> Except as provided in this Section, for the purposes of R.S. 10:3–104(a), a promise or order is unconditional unless it states (i) an express condition to payment, (ii) that the promise or order is subject to or governed by another writing, or (iii) that rights or obligations with respect to the promise or order are stated in another writing. A reference to another writing does not of itself make the promise or order conditional.

Although Louisiana's adoption of the Uniform Commercial Code is recent, the underlying principle in question here has long been part of the law governing negotiable instruments in Louisiana. The issue-the type of reference to another document that makes a promise to pay conditional and an instrument non-negotiable-has seen little litigation in this state, however.

In *Newman v. Schwarz*, 180 La. 153, 156 So. 206, 207 (1934), the court held that the statement "Rent Note Subject to Terms of Lease Dated May 2, 1927," written in red ink across the face of the note, bore no relation to the unconditional promise of the maker[b] to pay the notes, amounted to "nothing more than a statement of the transaction which gives rise to the notes and which serves to identify them with the transaction," and did not render the note non-negotiable.

In *Tyler v. Whitney–Central Trust & Sav. Bank*, 157 La. 249, 102 So. 325, 329 (1924), the court concluded that because the expression "as per lease this date" was found in a separate sentence from the promise to pay it bore no relation whatever to the promise. "In fact, the entire sentence in which the reference appears amounts to nothing more than a statement of the transaction which gives rise to the notes and which serves to identify them with the transaction. Such a statement and means of identification do not render the notes nonnegotiable."

We find the following general statement useful:

---

[b] The "maker" is defined as the "person who signs or is identified in a note as a person undertaking to pay." UCC § 3-103(a)(7).

(4) Reference to other instruments or agreements. If the note or draft states that it is given "as per" a transaction, "in accordance with" a transaction, or that it "arises out of" a transaction, this does not destroy negotiability, but, if the instrument states that it is "subject to" or "governed by" any other agreement, then negotiability is destroyed. [Emphasis in original; footnotes omitted.]

2 FREDERICK M. HART & WILLIAM F. WILLIER, BENDER'S U.C.C. SERVICE, COMMERCIAL PAPER § 1B.04[3] (1995).

Examining the language at issue in this case, we conclude it does not destroy negotiability of the marker. Its location on the last line of the instrument as well as its use of "according to" simply references another document but does not make payment conditional.

APPLICABILITY OF NSF CHECK STATUTE

Having determined that the marker was a negotiable instrument, we must decide whether the trial court properly held the NSF check law applicable. La. R.S. 9:2782 provides for award of damages and attorney's fees against the drawer[c] of a dishonored check when certain conditions are fulfilled. It states, in pertinent part:

A. Whenever any drawer of a check dishonored for nonsufficient funds fails to pay the obligation created by the check within thirty days after receipt of written demand for payment thereof delivered by certified or registered mail, the drawer shall be liable to the payee or a person subrogated to the rights of the payee for damages of twice the amount so owing, but in no case less than one hundred dollars plus attorney fees and court costs.

B. The payee may charge the drawer of the check a service charge not to exceed fifteen dollars or five percent of the face amount of the check, whichever is greater, when making written demand for payment.

C. (1) Before any recovery under Subsection A of this Section may be claimed, a written demand in substantially the form which follows shall be sent by certified or registered mail to the drawer of the check at the address shown on the instrument:
[Form omitted.]

(2) Notice mailed by certified or registered mail evidenced by return receipt to the address printed on the check or given at the time

---

[c] The "drawer" is defined as the "person who signs or is identified in a draft as a person ordering payment," in the case of a check, typically the account holder or other person authorized to sign checks on the account. UCC § 3-103(a)(5).

of issuance shall be deemed sufficient and equivalent to notice having been received by the person making the check.

(3) It shall be prima facie evidence that the drawer knew that the instrument would not be honored if notice mailed by certified or registered mail is returned to the sender when such notice is mailed within a reasonable time of dishonor to the address printed on the instrument or given by the drawer at the time of issuance of the check.

Defendant does not contest that plaintiff followed the formalities of the statute, but argues that the NSF check law cannot apply because "gambling markers do not operate like checks, but more like a promise to pay." Defendant asserts that when the state legislature enacted the law in 1977 "it never envisioned that the law would be used by casinos as leverage against their patrons." Instead, defendant insists, the law was enacted "to discourage consumers from floating bad paper in the stream of commerce." Defendant concludes, "It would be unconscionable to allow casinos to wield the penalizing nature of the Bad Check Law against delinquent gamblers."

This argument has no merit. Legalization of riverboat gaming activities has placed casino operations in the stream of commerce. The marker fits within the definition of a check in La. R.S. 10:3–104(f); therefore, the trial judge did not err in applying the NSF check statute in these circumstances. . . .

Questions and Problems 2.2. How does the process of making a payment by check or other draft happen under UCC Article 3? Keeping the Arriba Lounge incident in mind, follow the road map below, and answer these questions in order to trace the path of a negotiable instrument:

> **a.** How is a negotiable instruments obligation created? *UCC § 3-104 (a)*
> **b.** To whom is the instrument payable? *the bearer*
> **c.** Is there a particular place that it is payable?
> **d.** Can *B*, the person to whom the instrument is payable, give it or transfer it to someone else? Would that require the permission of *A*, the person who "issued" the instrument? Does *B* have to sign the instrument to transfer it?
> **e.** If *B* transfers it to *C*, who has a right to enforce the instrument?
> **f.** What is the procedure for obtaining payment as specified in the instrument? Assume, for example, that it states that it is drawn on an account at Banco Merca.
> **g.** If *C* demands payment from Banco Merca, what are the bank's legal options? What are the legal consequences for Banco if it pays *C*? For *A*? For *B*?

h. What are the consequences for Banco if it refuses to pay *C*? For *A*? For *B*?

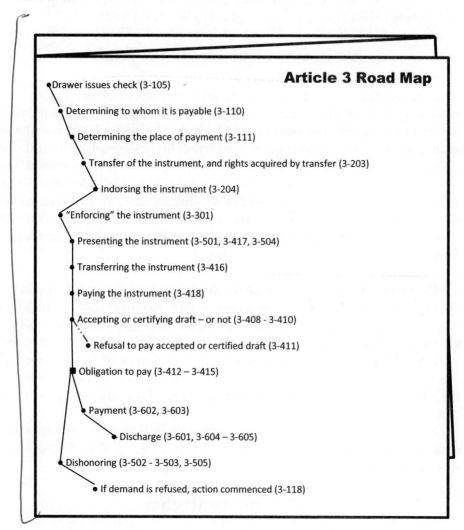

Questions and Problems 2.3. Would it make a difference to the negotiability of the napkin if, instead of "$50,000.00," it said "37,900 Euros"? *See* UCC § 3-107 (concerning instrument payable in foreign money).

2.4. What if the napkin says "Fifty Thousand Dollars ($5000.0)"? *See* UCC § 3-114 (providing rules to resolve contradictory terms in instrument).

2.5. What if Sylvester writes on the back of the napkin "Pay to the order of Tweety Byrd," and signs beneath those words? *See* UCC §§ 3-205 (concerning "special indorsement"), 3-206 (concerning restrictive indorsement).

2.6. What if the napkin says "Sylvester D" instead of "Sylvester D. Katz"? *Cf.* UCC § 3-115 (providing rules to deal with instrument that is incomplete but that signer intended to be completed).

2. Assignment of Contract Rights

A note represents a promise to pay an indicated amount, and a draft may at least imply a promise to pay, although not in any particular language of the instrument itself. Could the instrument be viewed as a contract, and governed by contract law principles? Could the rights represented by the instrument be assigned to a third party? The short answer of course is that statutory law – *i.e.*, UCC Article 3 – intervenes and supersedes any contrary contract law. To gain the rights of a person entitled to enforce the instrument, one needs a transfer that operates as a negotiation of the instrument, not just an assignment of the transferor's contract rights.[11]

Questions and Problems 2.7. Reconsider problem 2.1, involving Speedy's purchase of Sylvester's classic car. Assume that, in order to settle certain obligations of his car dealership, Sylvester assigns his current receivables to Max Factor. Max demands payment of $50,000 from Speedy. Can Speedy effectively raise defenses of Sylvester's failure to deliver the car on time, or breach of warranty with respect to the car in response to Max's demand? (*See* UCC §§ 3-301(i)-(ii), 3-302(a), 3-305(a)(2), (b).)
2.8. Would the result be any different if Sylvester indorses the back of the napkin as follows: "Pay to the order of Max Factor" and signs his name?

3. Property Rights

A negotiable instrument is someone's property, often more than one person's, but we tend to be focused on the Article 3 rights and obligations that arise *in relation to* the negotiation of the instrument, rather than on the classic "bundle of rights" that property represents in itself. Nevertheless, the UCC does recognize the rights to the instrument as property. Thus, a person taking an instrument, other than a person having rights of an HDC, would be subject to "a claim of

---

[11] *See* UCC § 3-201(a) (defining "negotiation" to mean "a transfer of possession ... of an instrument by a person other than the issuer to a person who thereby becomes its holder").

a property or possessory right in the instrument or its proceeds."[12] This would include a claim to rescind a negotiation and to recover the instrument or its proceeds.[13] However, an HDC would take the instrument free of any such property claim.[14]

      Questions and Problems 2.9. Henri Forgeré opens a checking account at a local branch of Issuer Bank in the name of the Grab Foundation, an international charity, and provides the bank with documents indicating that Henri is the U.S. executive representative of the Foundation authorized by it to open the account and to sign checks on the account. In fact, Henri is an accounts clerk at the national headquarters of the Foundation, and has been embezzling checks from the Foundation, which he deposits in the Issuer Bank checking account. The Foundation has now demanded that Issuer Bank return the checks to it or pay it the value of the checks. Can Issuer Bank successfully resist this demand? *See American Parkinson Disease Ass'n, Inc. v. First Nat. Bank of Northfield*, 584 N.W.2d 437 (Minn. App. 1998) (upholding judgment in favor of HDC bank). *Cf. Dixon, Laukitis, and Downing, P.C., infra* (discussing similar cases).

      2.10. Would it make a difference to the outcome of the dispute if Henri was known by Issuer Bank to be a trustee of the Grab Foundation? *See* UCC § 3-307(b) (indicating that notice of breach of fiduciary duty by fiduciary is notice of claim of represented person).

B. CONTRACT LIABILITY

      It is tempting to think of the rights and obligation of parties involved in the negotiation of an instrument as contract-like, and there are certain contract implications to negotiable instruments. However, it is important to keep in mind that many traditional contract defenses do not affect the validity of negotiation itself. Thus, negotiation will be effective even if obtained from a minor or someone who is incapacitated, or a corporation acting *ultra vires*.[15] Likewise, negotiation is still effective if effected by fraud, duress, or mistake,[16] or in breach of duty or as part of an illegal transaction.[17] Other legal principles might

---

    [12] UCC § 3-306. *See also* UCC § 3-309 (concerning right to enforce stolen instrument). *Cf.* UCC § 3-312 (governing claim against bank obligated under a lost, destroyed, or stolen cashier's check, teller's check, or certified check).

    [13] UCC § 3-306.

    [14] *Id.*

    [15] UCC § 3-202(a)(i).

    [16] UCC § 3-202(a)(ii).

    [17] UCC § 3-202(a)(iii).

allow for rescission or other remedies, but not against a subsequent "holder in due course" (HDC) or a person paying the instrument in good faith and without knowledge of facts that are a basis for rescission or other remedy.[18]

There will be defenses available to someone confronted by a demand for payment, but those will be significantly restricted if the person holding the instrument is considered an HDC. To be considered an HDC, one must meet the following criteria:

- The instrument when issued or negotiated to the holder must not bear "such apparent evidence of forgery or alteration or is not otherwise so irregular or incomplete as to call into question its authenticity."[19]
- The holder must take the instrument for value.[20]
- The holder must take the instrument "in good faith."[21]
- The holder must be "without notice that the instrument is overdue or has been dishonored,"[22] or – in the case of instruments that have been issued in a series (*e.g.*, bonds or other notes) – "that there is an uncured default with respect to payment of another instrument issued as part of the same series."[23]
- The holder is "without notice that the instrument contains an unauthorized signature or has been altered."[24]
- The holder is without notice of a claim to the instrument (described in Section 3-306).[25]
- The holder is without notice that a party that might otherwise be liable on the instrument has a defense or claim in recoupment (described in Section 3-305(a)).[26]

The following case illustrates some of the restrictions on the ability of an apparent maker or drawer to raise affirmative contract-based defenses in response to a claim under a negotiable instrument. Consider whether the court offers a satisfactory explanation of such restrictions.

---

[18] UCC § 3-202(b).

[19] UCC § 3-302(a)(1).

[20] UCC § 3-302(a)(2)(i). *See* UCC § 3-303(a) (indicating when instrument is taken "for value").

[21] UCC § 3-302(a)(2)(ii).

[22] On determining when an instrument is "overdue" for these purposes, see UCC § 3-304.

[23] UCC § 3-302(a)(2)(iii).

[24] UCC § 3-302(a)(2)(iv).

[25] UCC § 3-302(a)(2)(v).

[26] UCC § 3-302(a)(2)(vi). On defenses and claims in recoupment, see UCC § 3-305.

QAD INVESTORS, INC. V. KELLY
776 A.2d 1244 (Me. 2001)

DANA, J.

Laurence Kelly appeals from a judgment of the Superior Court . . . in favor of QAD Investors, Inc. on its claim against Kelly for failure to fulfill his obligations pursuant to a promissory note. Kelly contends that the court erred in finding him liable on a note that he did not sign, and was not signed or ratified on behalf of himself or the partnership he formed with Stephen MacKenzie; in awarding attorney fees to QAD pursuant to the note; and in awarding attorney fees in excess of QAD's costs of collection. We disagree and affirm.

BACKGROUND

The court found the following facts. In 1993, Kelly entered into a joint venture with MacKenzie to purchase a parking lot. Kelly and MacKenzie were two of the three members of a partnership that owned the Brian Boru Public House in Portland.[a] Kelly and MacKenzie obtained an option to purchase the lot for $280,000, paying $5000 per month to maintain the option while they raised the money to purchase the lot. While Kelly and MacKenzie were searching for investors, MacKenzie approached Russell Glidden, the principal of QAD, and provided him with a copy of Kelly's personal financial statement. Kelly, MacKenzie, and Glidden met together repeatedly thereafter. At the meetings, Kelly did not object to MacKenzie's characterization of him as a joint venturer in the project. By the end of the second meeting, Glidden had committed QAD to providing $20,000 to the venture.

Glidden delivered the check, after which MacKenzie gave Glidden a written receipt stating that the money procured a one-third interest in the parking lot. The receipt also provided that the $20,000 would be paid back pursuant to a note that Glidden would hold. The money was deposited into a bank account under Kelly's exclusive control.

The promissory note was prepared soon thereafter, providing, in relevant part:

---

[a] The pub was apparently named for BrianBorú, High King of Ireland from 1002 to 1014 A.D., who was killed during the Battle of Clontarf on 23 April 1014. He was preceded and succeeded by Máel Sechnaill mac Domnaill. The pub is still in operation – with live music. *See* brianboruportland.com/ for the schedule of pub performances.

FOR VALUE RECEIVED, the undersigned, STEPHEN H. MAC-
KENZIE and LAURENCE KELLY, promise to pay to QAD INVES-
TORS the principal sum of $20,000.00 at 14% per annum, payable as
follows:

I. Payments of principal and interest in the amount of $960.26
shall be paid monthly, commencing on January 15, 1994, until the
principal and accrued interest are fully paid;

....

III. The unpaid balance of principal and accrued interest shall be
paid in full upon the sale or transfer of all or any part of the real estate securing this note, or an interest therein, without the Holder's
prior consent....

....

The undersigned and all other parties liable hereon, whether
principals, endorser or otherwise, hereby jointly and severally waive
presentment for payment, demand of nonpayment, and notice of pro-
test of this note.

This note is secured by a pledge of any and all interests held by
Laurence Kelly and Stephen MacKenzie in the parking lot located at
57/59 Center Street, Portland, Maine, and is to be considered joint
and several as to the makers.

The note has lines for the signatures of Kelly and MacKenzie, but
only MacKenzie's line contains a witnessed signature; Kelly's line is
blank.

MacKenzie made the first two or three payments, but thereafter
Kelly made all payments out of the account over which Kelly exercised
exclusive control. Kelly communicated to QAD in the summer of 1994
that payments would not be kept current because the summer months
were slow. QAD received no payments from May 1994 to September
1994. Kelly, without MacKenzie, met with Glidden, Fergus O'Reilly
(the third owner of Brian Boru), and Justin O'Reilly (Fergus's broth-
er), to discuss the payment of the note. Kelly delivered one month's
payment after the meeting. Glidden wrote a letter to Kelly indicating
that he felt more comfortable about the payment schedule after the
meeting and made clear that he was looking to Kelly for future payments.

Kelly made another payment in October 1994, which prompted
Glidden to write Kelly a letter reminding him that he was four months
in arrears and again making it clear that he was looking to Kelly for
payment. Kelly delivered another payment in November, followed by
another letter from Glidden discussing the arrearage. At no time during the correspondence did Kelly suggest to QAD that he was not obligated by the note.

In November 1994, MacKenzie agreed to transfer his interest in the lot to Fergus and Justin O'Reilly. Nobody informed QAD of MacKenzie's agreement with the O'Reillys at that time. MacKenzie had been "eased out of" his partnership in Brian Boru and the joint venture in the parking lot. Kelly continued to make payments.

In February 1995, Kelly requested a copy of the note, which Glidden sent to him with another letter concerning the arrearage. Glidden indicated in his letter that he understood that an interest in the parking lot was being sold, and asked if arrangements had been made to pay off the note. Although aware of the note, Kelly had not seen the note before February 1995; when he did see it, he consulted with an attorney. Kelly did not inform Glidden that he believed he was not responsible for the note, but instead made one more payment that month, requesting that Glidden not cash the check immediately. Kelly was concerned that Glidden would disrupt a transaction that would transfer the ownership of the parking lot. The transaction closed and no further payments were made.

In May of 1995, Glidden met with Kelly and the O'Reillys to discuss restructuring the debt. Again, Kelly did not indicate that he believed he was not obligated on the note.

QAD filed a complaint against MacKenzie and Kelly on January 9, 1997, seeking payment due pursuant to the note, in addition to interest, costs, and attorney fees. Kelly filed his answer alleging, by way of affirmative defense, that (1) he never represented verbally or in writing that he agreed to be liable on the note MacKenzie signed, (2) he had never seen or signed the note, and (3) he never authorized MacKenzie to sign on his behalf. MacKenzie was discharged in bankruptcy. After a bench trial on April 27, 2000, the court concluded that Kelly was jointly liable on the note as a member of the joint venture, which is a partnership for a limited purpose. The court reasoned that Kelly authorized the execution of the note on behalf of the partnership, and that even if the partnership had not authorized the note, it ratified the loan based on Kelly's and MacKenzie's subsequent acts. ...

DISCUSSION

A. Kelly's Liability

Kelly contends that he cannot be personally liable on the note because he did not sign it in compliance with the Uniform Commercial Code, 11 M.R.S.A. § 3-1401 to -1402 (1995), and did not authorize MacKenzie to sign the note on his behalf. According to Kelly, the note was not binding on the partnership because it was not signed in the partnership name, nor was it executed in the ordinary course of business as required by the Uniform Partnership Act, 31 M.R.S.A. §§ 288 and 289 (1996). According to Kelly, he did not ratify the note either, because the note was not executed on his account, he conferred with an attorney to confirm that he was not liable on the note when he discovered there was a signature line for him on it, and his actions did not constitute an affirmance of MacKenzie's execution of the note on his behalf.

According to QAD, the plain language of the note indicates that the parties understood that Kelly was to be bound as a partner because a signature line is present on the note and the note pledges as collateral an interest in the property for which the partnership was formed. QAD contends, in the alternative, that MacKenzie had apparent authority to act for Kelly both personally and as a partner. Finally, it contends that Kelly ratified the note by making payments on it and failing to communicate that he did not believe he was liable. . . .

We disagree with QAD that the language of the note unambiguously establishes Kelly's personal liability on the note. The blank signature line and the security of the note against partnership interests are inadequate to establish Kelly's personal liability; instead, they create an ambiguity. We therefore review the court's resolution of that ambiguity for clear error. *Forrest Assocs.* [*v. Passamaquoddy Tribe*, 2000 ME 195, ¶ 9, 760 A.2d 1041, 1044].

Kelly does not contest the existence of a partnership between himself and MacKenzie. [The court quoted the Maine version of the Uniform Partnership Act § 9, including paragraph (2), which provides "An act of a partner which is not apparently for the carrying on of the business of the partnership in the usual way does not bind the partnership unless authorized by the other partners."]

. . . "As is made clear by the use of the adverb apparently, the partner need not be engaged in the actual business of the partnership; his acts need only be apparently within the scope of the partnership business." *Dayton Sec. Assocs. v. Morgan Guar. Trust Co. of New York (In re Securities Group)*, 926 F.2d 1051, 1054 (11th Cir.1991) (internal quotation marks omitted). The party seeking to enforce the agreement may "rely on any apparent authority only to the extent that it was being exercised in pursuance of partnership business 'in the usual way.' " *Luddington v. Bodenvest Ltd.*, 855 P.2d 204, 210 (Utah 1993).

"A contract does not need to be signed by all partners or even mention the name of the partnership in order to bind the partners." *Barnes v. McLendon*, 128 Wash.2d 563, 910 P.2d 469, 474 (1996). Moreover, the note need not be in the partnership name if the partnership has no name. *See First State Bank of Riesel v. Dyer*, 248 S.W.2d 785, 788 (Tex.Civ.App.1952).

Kelly also cites the UCC, which provides instruction on the requirement of a signature on a negotiable instrument. [The court quotes UCC §§ 3-401, 3-402.]

The law of partnership and the law of negotiable instruments direct us to determine whether MacKenzie had authority to sign the note for the partnership or for Kelly personally. . . .

The court did not commit clear error in finding that MacKenzie's and Kelly's conduct would lead a reasonable third party to believe that MacKenzie was acting as the agent of the partnership and with the requisite authority. Kelly attended meetings with Glidden and MacKenzie during which they discussed the possibility of obtaining money from Glidden for the joint venture. MacKenzie gave Kelly's personal financial statement to Glidden before negotiating with him. The facts found by the court adequately support its legal conclusion that MacKenzie was authorized to bind the partnership.[2]

Even if MacKenzie's apparent authority to bind the partnership was in doubt, Kelly's subsequent conduct ratified that authority. . . .

The court did not commit clear error in finding that, even if MacKenzie's execution of the note was unauthorized, Kelly's behavior following the execution of the note ratified MacKenzie's authority to sign the note. Kelly made payments in the precise amount specified by the note, he met with Glidden repeatedly to renegotiate the payment schedule, he failed to indicate at any time before the commencement of this suit that he did not believe the partnership was bound by the note, and he made a payment even after he knew that his signature did not appear on the note. We affirm the judgment. . . .

Kelly is liable for the note. [handwritten note]

Questions and Problems 2.11. In *QAD Investors*, Mr. Kelly tried to argue that he was not one of the parties to whom the rights and obligations of negotiable instruments law attaches. If you are a maker or a drawer, the impact of negotiable instruments law seems self-evident. What about other players? If you are a *non-customer* of a drawee bank who is a holder of a draft, can you compel the bank to recognize your right to be paid? If not, what remedies do you have? In answering these questions, consider the following case.

---

[2] We need not, therefore, address whether Kelly authorized MacKenzie to bind him personally.

MESSING V. BANK OF AMERICA, N.A.
821 A.2d 22 (Md. 2003)

HARRELL, Judge.

I.

The case sub judice involves a bank check. A check is defined as a draft payable on demand and drawn on a bank. Maryland Code (1974, 2002 Repl.Vol.), Commercial Law Article, § 3–204(f)(i). The circumstances which gave rise to the case before us are, in terms of its genesis, reminiscent of those described in the case of *Board of Inland Revenue v. Haddock*.[2] In that case, the protagonist, Mr. Haddock, after some dispute involving uncollected income-taxes owed, elected to test the limits of the law of checks as it existed at British common law at the time. Operating on the proposition that a check was only an order to a bank to pay money to the person in possession of the check or a person named on the check, and observing that there was nothing in statute or custom at the time specifying that a check must be written on paper of certain dimensions, or even paper at all, Haddock elected to tender payment to the tax collector by a check written on the back of a cow. The Collector of Taxes at first attempted to endorse the check, but, we are informed, the check "appeared to resent endorsement and adopted a menacing posture" at which point the Collector abandoned the attempt and refused to accept the check. Mr. Haddock then led the check away and was subsequently arrested in Trafalgar Square for causing an obstruction, upon which he was said to have observed that "it was a nice thing if in the heart of the commercial capital of the world a man could not convey a negotiable instrument down the street without being arrested." He subsequently was summoned by the Board of Inland Revenue for non-payment of income-tax.

The case sub judice arises from Petitioner's irritation with the Bank of America's Thumbprint Signature Program. Under the Thumbprint Signature Program, a bank requests non-customer presenters of checks over the counter to place an "inkless" thumbprint or fingerprint on the face of the check as part of the identification process. The program was developed . . . by the American Bankers Association, working with the Federal Deposit Insurance Corporation (FDIC), the Federal Reserve Banks, the Office of the Comptroller of the Currency, the Federal Bureau of Investigation, and other law en-

---

[2] *Board of Inland Revenue v. Haddock*, known commonly as "The Negotiable Cow" case, is, in fact, a fictitious case which originally appeared in the pages of the british humor magazine *Punch*, and since has been re-printed in A.P. Herbert, Uncommon Law: Being sixty-six misleading cases revised and collected in one volume (Dorset Press, 1991) (1935).

forcement officials and banking trade associations across the county in response to rising instances of check fraud. . . . It is undisputed that the Bank of America's Thumbprint Signature Program uses an inkless fingerprinting device that leaves no ink stains or residue

II.

At some point in time prior to 3 August 2000, Petitioner, as a holder, came into possession of a check in the amount of Nine Hundred Seventy–Six Dollars ($976.00) (the check) from Toyson J. Burruss, the drawer, doing business as Prestige Auto Detail Center. Instead of depositing the check into his account at his own bank, Petitioner elected to present the check for payment at a branch of Mr. Burruss' bank, Bank of America, the drawee.[3] On 3 August 2000, Petitioner approached a teller at Bank of America's 10 Light Street Banking Center in Baltimore City and asked to cash the check. The teller, by use of a computer, confirmed the availability of funds on deposit, and placed the check into the computer's printer slot. The computer stamped certain data on the back of the check, including the time, date, amount of the check, account number, and teller number. The computer also effected a hold on the amount of $976.00 in the customer's account. The teller gave the check back to the Petitioner, who endorsed it. The teller then asked for Petitioner's identification. Petitioner presented his driver's license and a major credit card. The teller took the endorsed check from Petitioner and manually inscribed the driver's license information and certain credit card information on the back of the check.

At some point during the transaction, the teller counted out $976.00 in cash from her drawer in anticipation of completing the transaction. She asked if the Petitioner was a customer of Bank of America. The Petitioner stated that he was not. The teller returned the check to Petitioner and requested, consistent with bank policy when cashing checks for non-customers, that Petitioner place his

---

[3] Petitioner's choice could be viewed as an attempt at risk shifting. Petitioner, an attorney, may have known that he could have suffered a fee charged by his own bank if he deposited a check into his own account and the bank on which it was drawn returned it for insufficient funds, forged endorsement, alteration, or the like. Petitioner's action, viewed against that backdrop, would operate as a risk shifting strategy, electing to avoid the risk of a returned-check fee by presenting in person the check for acceptance at the drawee bank.

thumbprint on the check.[4] Petitioner refused and the teller informed him that she would be unable to complete the transaction without his thumbprint.

Petitioner requested, and was referred to, the branch manager. Petitioner presented the check to the branch manager and demanded that the check be cashed notwithstanding Petitioner's refusal to place his thumbprint on the check. The branch manager examined the check and returned it to the Petitioner, informing him that, because Petitioner was a non-customer, Bank of America would not cash the check without Petitioner's thumbprint on the instrument. After some additional exchanges, Petitioner left the bank with the check in his possession. The branch manager advised the teller that Petitioner had left the bank with his check. In response, the teller released the hold on the customer's funds, voided the transaction in the computer, and placed the cash back in her teller drawer.

Rather than take the check to his own bank and deposit it there, or returning it to Burruss, the drawer, as dishonored and demanding payment, Petitioner, two months later, on 10 October 2000, filed a declaratory judgment action against Bank of America (the Bank) in the Circuit Court for Baltimore City. Petitioner claimed that the Bank had violated the Maryland Uniform Commercial Code (UCC) and had violated his personal privacy when the teller asked Petitioner to place an "inkless" thumbprint on the face of the check at issue. Petitioner asked the trial court to declare that: 1) Petitioner had provided "reasonable identification" without his thumbprint; 2) under § 3–501(b)(2), a thumbprint is not reasonable identification; 3) requiring a thumbprint of non-customers to cash a check is illegal, inappropriate, and unnecessary; 4) requiring non-customers to provide a thumbprint is a violation of the personal privacy of non-customers; 5) the Bank be required to cease requiring thumbprints in Maryland; 6) the Bank had "accepted" the check when presented by Petitioner; 7) the Bank "wrongfully dishonored" the check; and 8) the Bank wrongfully converted the check. Petitioner also sought injunctive relief directing Bank of America to cease participation in the Thumbprint Signature Program.

On 15 November 2000, the Bank filed a Motion to Dismiss or, in the alternative, for Summary Judgment. Petitioner opposed the Bank's Motion and filed a "cross" Motion for Summary Judgment. Af-

---

[4] The writing surface at each teller station at the branch was posted with a sign relating to the FDIC. Clearly visible in the lower right quadrant of each sign were the following words: "Thumbprint Signature Participating Member. For the protection of our customers, Thumbprint Signatures will be obtained from all non-account holders seeking to cash checks."

ter the Circuit Court heard oral arguments on the pending motions, it denied Petitioner's request for injunctive relief and entered summary judgment in favor of the Bank, dismissing the Complaint with prejudice.

[After the Court of Special Appeals concluded that the Circuit Court's decision was legally correct,] Petitioner petitioned this Court for a writ of certiorari. On 10 June 2002, we granted the petition. . . .

III.

Six questions are presented for our consideration. They are:

"1. Did the Court of Special Appeals err in construing the requirement of giving "reasonable identification" under . . . Section 3–501(b)(2), to require a thumbprint if demanded by a drawee to whom presentment of a check is made, notwithstanding the proffer of reasonable and customary documentary forms of identification?

"2. Did the Court of Special Appeals err in finding the [Respondent] did not accept the particular check at issue, as "acceptance" is defined in . . . Section 3–409(a)?

"3. Did the Court of Special Appeals err in finding that the [Respondent] did not dishonor the particular check at issue, as "dishonor" is defined in . . . Section 3–502(d)(1)?

"4. Did the Court of Special Appeals err in finding the [Respondent] did not convert the cash proceeds of the particular check at issue, as "conversion" is set out in . . . Section 3–420?

"5. Did the Court of Special Appeals err in not giving full effect to the plain language of . . . Section 3–111, that states that when no address is stated in an instrument, "The place of payment is the place of business of the drawee or maker. If the Drawee or maker has more than one place of business, the place of business is any place of business of the drawee or maker chosen by the person entitled to enforce the instrument"?

[The sixth question – not relevant for our purposes – was whether it was error to vacate the judgment and remand for entry of a *written* declaration of the rights of the parties. (The Maryland Supreme Court did conclude, as a procedural matter, that vacating and remand for this narrow purpose was appropriate.)]

IV.

. . . Where, as here, the material facts are undisputed, the reasonableness of the Bank's actions are for the court to decide. *Gillen v. Maryland Nat'l Bank*, 274 Md. 96, 102–03, 333 A.2d 329, 334 (1975) (question of bank's duty of care is one of law when the facts are undisputed). . . .

V.

A. Petitioner's Arguments:

Petitioner argues initially that he properly presented the check to the drawee bank and that the bank accepted the check. In Petitioner's view, the Bank's request for thumbprint identification was unreasonable as it would not aid the Bank in identifying the Petitioner as the proper person to pay at the time payment was made, but would be useful only at some later date, if at all. Petitioner's argument is fairly straight forward, adopting a "follow the bouncing ball" approach to the application of . . . Title 3 . . . to the facts of this case. Petitioner's argument is that § 3–111 instructs that the correct location for him to present the check at issue for payment was at the offices of the bank named on the check as the drawee.[7] [The court quotes UCC § 3–111, on place of payment.]

In short, Petitioner's position is that, assuming all else is in order, § 3–111 requires Bank of America to pay a check drawn on one of its customer's accounts if presentment is made over the counter at the Bank.[8] Petitioner then argues why his presentment was in order, according to the relevant code provisions, thus, in his view, requiring the Bank to pay the check.

Petitioner cites § 3–501, [concerning "presentment," and the court quotes the provision].

Petitioner argues that he correctly made "presentment" of the check to the Bank pursuant to § 3–111 and § 3–501(a), and demands that, as the person named on the instrument and thus entitled to enforce the check, the drawee Bank pay him. Petitioner further argues that his presentment was in the proper form set forth in § 3–501(b)(2). Petitioner points out that he exhibited the instrument when he arrived at the counter and that, upon request, he provided reasonable identification in the form of his driver's license and a major credit card, and that he surrendered the check to the teller, who stamped it in her computer. The subsequent request for Petitioner to place his

---

[7] *See also* Federal Reserve Board Regulation CC, 12 C.F.R. 229.36(b).

[8] Petitioner is incorrect. Section 3–111 merely requires the Bank to receive the presentment of a check for payment, return, or dishonor. Put another way, § 3–111 identifies the location where the check ultimately is to be sent so that the drawee Bank may have notice of the order to pay and make a decision with regards to that order. As is discussed infra, § 3–111 does not require the Bank to accept the check (§ 3–409), or to pay the check (§ 3–413 and § 4–215). Thus, the answer to Petitioners fifth question presented is "no."

thumbprint on the check was, in Petitioner's view, not "reasonable" and therefore improper under § 3–501(b)(2)(ii). Petitioner argues that the rightness of his view is because the purpose of providing reasonable identification at the time of presentment is so that a bank can assure itself that it is making payment to the proper person at the time payment is made. Petitioner argues that a thumbprint will not provide that information at the time payment is made over the counter, but only at some later date. While we shall address the reasonableness of the thumbprint identification, *infra*, the issue is not dispositive as to Petitioner's claims against the Bank, and is, in fact, largely collateral.

. . . Petitioner contends that the teller, by placing the check in the slot of her computer, and the computer then printing certain information on the back of the check, accepted the check as defined by § 3–409(a). . . .

Relying on § 3–401(b), Petitioner argues that the act of the Bank's computer printing information on the back of the check constitutes the Bank's signature, and thus effectuates acceptance of the check on the part of the Bank. . . .

In support, Petitioner points to part of the Official Comment 2 attached to § 3–409, as follows:

> Subsection (a) states the generally recognized rule that the mere signature of the drawee on the instrument is a sufficient acceptance. Customarily the signature is written vertically across the face of the instrument, but since the drawee has no reason to sign for any other purpose a signature in any other place, even on the back of the instrument, is sufficient. It need not be accompanied by such words as "Accepted," "Certified," or "Good."[9]

Thus, according to Petitioner, because the Bank's computer printed information on the back of the check, under § 3–401(b) the Bank "signed" the check, said "signature" being sufficient to constitute acceptance under § 3–409(a).

Petitioner's remaining arguments line up like so many dominos. According to Petitioner, having established that under his reading of § 3–409(a) the Bank accepted the check, Petitioner advances that the Bank is obliged to pay him, pursuant to § 3–413(a). . . .

Petitioner continues that because Bank of America accepted the check, but then failed to make payment, by the terms of § 3–502(d)(1)

---

[9] Among other things, Petitioner omits the last sentence of Comment 2, which reads: "The last sentence of subsection (a) states the generally recognized rule that an acceptance written on the draft takes effect when the drawee notifies the holder or gives notice according to instructions."

the Bank dishonored the check and became solely liable to Petitioner for payment. Section 3–502(d)(1). . . .

Petitioner claims that the drawee Bank of America solely would be liable as the acceptor because, under § 3–414(c), the drawer of the check is discharged upon acceptance by the Bank. Section 3–414(c). . . .[10]

Petitioner extends his line of reasoning by arguing that the actions of the Bank amounted to a conversion under § 3–420. . . .

Based on this, Petitioner argues that because the Bank accepted the check, an act which, according to Petitioner, discharged the drawer, he no longer had enforceable rights in the check and only had a right to the proceeds. Petitioner's position is that the Bank exercised unauthorized dominion and control over the proceeds of the check to the complete exclusion of the Petitioner after the Bank accepted the check and refused to distribute the proceeds, counted out by the teller, to him.

B. Acceptance under § 3–409(a).

Predictably, Bank of America argues that Petitioner's interpretation of Maryland's U.C.C. is incorrect. . . . Bank of America argues, correctly, that it had no duty to the Petitioner, a non-customer and a stranger to the Bank, and that nothing in the Code allows Petitioner to force Bank of America to act as a depository bank [§ 4–105] and cash a check for a non-customer. As the Supreme Court pointed out in *Barnhill v. Johnson*, 503 U.S. 393, 398–99, 112 S.Ct. 1386, 118 L.Ed.2d 39 (1992):

> Under the U.C.C., a check is simply an order to the drawee bank to pay the sum stated, signed by the makers and payable on demand. Receipt of a check does not, however, give the recipient a right against the bank. The recipient may present the check, but if the drawee bank refuses to honor it, the recipient has no recourse against the drawee. . . .
>
> This is because ... receipt of a check gives the recipient no right in the funds held by the bank on the drawer's account.

Absent a special relationship, a non-customer has no claim against a bank for refusing to honor a presented check. *City Check Cashing, Inc. v. Manufacturers Hanover Trust Co.*, 166 N.J. 49, 764 A.2d 411, 417 (2001). A "transient, non-contractual relationship" is not enough

---

[10] Petitioner, however, overlooks § 4–601. . . . No one was discharged on the instrument at the time Petitioner acquired rights in it. § 4–102(a). . . .

to establish a duty. *Id.* (quoting *FMC Corp v. Fleet Bank*, 226 A.D.2d 225, 641 N.Y.S.2d 25, 26 (1996)). It is also well settled that a check does not operate as an assignment of funds on deposit, *Ward v. Federal Kemper Ins. Co.*, 62 Md.App. 351, 357–58, 489 A.2d 91, 94 (1985), and the bank only becomes obligated upon acceptance of the instrument. This is made clear by § 3–408. . . .

Once a bank accepts a check, under § 3–409, it is obliged to pay on the check under § 3–413.[12] Thus, the relevant question in terms of any rights Petitioner had against the Bank turns not on the reasonableness of the thumbprint identification, but rather upon whether the Bank accepted the check when presented as defined by § 3–409. . . . [T]he question of the thumbprint identification is relevant only to the issue of whether the Bank's refusal to pay the instrument constituted dishonor under § 3–502, a determination which has no impact in terms of any duty allegedly owed by the Bank to the Petitioner.

. . . The mere fact that the teller's computer printed information on the back of the check does not, as Petitioner contends, amount by itself to an acceptance. Section 3–409(a). . . .

Petitioner relies on the first two sentences of the statute, while ignoring the balance. The statute clearly states that acceptance becomes effective when the presenter is notified of that fact. The facts demon-

---

[12] These rules of commercial practice are of considerable long standing. In *Moses v. President & Directors of Franklin Bank*, 34 Md. 574, 580–81 (1871), the Court stated:

A check does not, as contended by the appellant, operate as an assignment pro tanto of the fund upon which it is drawn, until it is accepted, or certified to be good, by the bank holding the funds. It is true, a bank, if in funds of the drawer, is ordinarily bound to take up his checks; but it can only be held liable to the holder for its refusal to do so, upon the ground of fraud, whereby he loses the money or some part of it, for which the check is drawn. It is certainly a general rule, that a drawee who refuses to accept a bill of exchange cannot be held liable on the bill itself; nor to the holder for the refusal to accept, except it be upon the ground of fraud and loss to the latter. A bank upon which a check is drawn occupies in this respect a similar position to that of the drawee of a bill of exchange. It is but the agent of the depositor, holding his funds upon an implied contract to honor and take up his checks to the extent of the funds deposited. The obligation to accept and pay is not to the holder of the check, but to the drawer. If, therefore, the depositor should direct that a check should not be paid, the bank would be bound to observe the direction, unless it had previously accepted the check by certifying it to be good, in which case it would be bound to pay; at any rate to a subsequent holder. The bank, therefore, ordinarily, owes no duty to the holder of a check drawn upon it, nor is it bound, except to the depositor, to accept or pay the check, though it may have sufficient funds of the drawer with which to do it.

strate that at no time did the teller notify Petitioner that the Bank would pay on the check. . . .

. . . [T]he negotiation of the check is in the nature of a contract, and there can be no agreement until notice of acceptance is received.[13] As a result, there was never acceptance as defined by § 3–409(a), and thus the Bank, pursuant to § 3–408 never was obligated to pay the check under § 3–413(a). Thus, the answer to Petitioner's second question presented is "no."

C. "Conversion" under § 3–420.

Because it never accepted the check, Bank of America argues that the intermediate appellate court also correctly concluded that the Bank did not convert the check or its proceeds under § 3–420. Again, we must agree. . . .

Nor was there a conversion of the cash proceeds. . . . [U]nder § 3–409(a), Bank of America never accepted the check, and thus never became obligated under § 3–413(a) to pay on the check. Pursuant to § 3–408, Petitioner never had a right to the funds on deposit, and Bank of America cannot convert funds to which Petitioner has no right in the first instance.

Similarly, as Bank of America never accepted the check, Petitioner's argument that he no longer has rights in the instrument is incorrect. Because Bank of America did not accept the check pursuant to § 3–409, the drawer was not, as Petitioner alleges, discharged under § 3–414(c). At the time Petitioner left the Bank, he retained all of his rights in the instrument, and was free to either present the check again and provide a thumbprint as requested, negotiate the check to some other third party, or to deposit the check in his own bank. . . . [W]ere the Bank's refusal to accept the check to amount to dishonor, Petitioner even may proceed against the drawer under § 3–414(b). *See Ward*, 62 Md.App. at 357–58, 489 A.2d at 94. The answer to Petitioner's fourth question presented is "no."

D. "Reasonable Identification" under § 3–501(b)(2)(ii) and "Dishonor" under § 3–502

We now turn to the issue of whether the Bank's refusal to accept the check as presented constituted dishonor under § 3–501 and § 3–

---

[13] Where a check is presented for payment over the counter, it is hard, given general business practices, to imagine where acceptance would be effective before the funds paying the check were handed over to the presenter, except where a certified or cashier's check was involved. *Rezapolvi v. First Nat. Bank of Maryland*, 296 Md. 1, 6, 459 A.2d 183, 186 (1983).

502 as Petitioner contends. Petitioner's argument that Bank of America dishonored the check under § 3–502(d) fails because that section applies to dishonor of an accepted draft. We have determined . . . that Bank of America never accepted the draft. Nevertheless, the question remains as to whether Bank of America dishonored the draft under § 3–502(b). . . .

The reason that § 3–502(b)(2) potentially is relevant to the case sub judice is because of § 3–501(b)(2) and (3). . . .

The question is whether requiring a thumbprint constitutes a request for "reasonable identification" under § 3–501(b)(2)(ii). If it is "reasonable," then under § 3–501(b)(3)(ii) the refusal of the Bank to accept the check from Petitioner did not constitute dishonor. If, however, requiring a thumbprint is not "reasonable" under § 3–501(b)(2)(ii), then the refusal to accept the check may constitute dishonor under § 3–502(b)(2). The issue of dishonor is arguably relevant because Petitioner has no cause of action against any party, including the drawer, until the check is dishonored.[16] *Ward*, 62 Md.App. at 358, 489 A.2d at 95; *Stewart v. Citizens and Southern Natl. Bank*, 138 Ga.App. 209, 225 S.E.2d 761 (1976).

Respondent Bank of America argues that its relationship with its customer is contractual, *University Nat'l Bank v. Wolfe*, 279 Md. 512, 514, 369 A.2d 570, 571 (1977); *Kiley v. First Nat'l Bank of Maryland*, 102 Md.App. 317, 326–27, 649 A.2d 1145, 1149 (1994), and that in this case, its contract with its customer, the drawer, authorizes the Bank's use of the Thumbprint Signature Program as a reasonable form of identification. The pertinent part of that Deposit Agreement states:

> You [customer] agree that we [Bank of America] may impose additional requirements we deem necessary or desirable on a payee or other holder who presents for cashing an item drawn on your account which is otherwise properly payable and if that person fails or refuses to satisfy such requirements, our refusal to cash the item will not be considered wrongful. You [customer] agree that, subject to applicable law, such requirements may include (but are not necessarily limited to) physical ... identification requirements....

According to Respondent, this contractual agreement allowed it to refuse to accept the check, without dishonoring it pursuant to § 3–501(b)(3)(ii), because the Bank's refusal was based upon the present-

---

[16] A cause of action for wrongful dishonor sounds in tort, not contract. See § 4–402; *Wright v. Commercial & Sav. Bank*, 297 Md. 148, 159, 464 A.2d 1080, 1086 (1983); *Siegman v. Equitable Trust Co.*, 267 Md. 309, 313, 297 A.2d 758 (1972); *Boggs v. Citizens Bank & Tr. Co.*, 32 Md.App. 500, 501, 363 A.2d 247 (1976).

ment failing to comply with "an agreement of the parties." . . . We, however, do not [agree with this argument].

The reason why the Bank's contract with its customer is not controlling on the issue of the reasonableness of requiring a thumbprint as identification is because the terms of § 3–501 are not modified by the terms of that contract. The terms of § 3–501(b) require an "agreement of the parties." The term "parties" does not refer to the parties of the Deposit Agreement, but rather, according to § 3–103(a)(8), refers to the parties to an instrument. While Petitioner is a party to the instrument, he is not a party to the Deposit Agreement, nor may he be deemed properly a third party beneficiary thereof. To be effective against the Petitioner, Messing, as the party entitled to enforce the instrument, would have to have been a party to the agreement. § 3–117. Thus, while the Deposit Agreement protects the Bank from a suit for wrongful dishonor brought by its customer, the drawer, as a result of the Bank's potential dishonor of the check because the Bank's demand for a thumbprint was not met, [§ 4–402], the contract has no impact on the determination of the "reasonableness" of the requirement for purposes of § 3–501(b), and subsequently whether the instrument was dishonored for purposes of § 3–502(b)(2). In other words, the Bank and its customer cannot through their contract define the meaning of the term "reasonable" and impose it upon parties who are not in privity with that contract. Whether requiring a thumbprint constitutes "reasonable identification" within the meaning of § 3–501(b)(2)(ii) is therefore a broader policy consideration, and not, as argued in this case, simply a matter of contract. . . . This also means that the Bank cannot rely on the contract as a defense against the Petitioner, on the facts presented here, to say that it did not dishonor the check.

Petitioner, as noted, argues that requiring a thumbprint violates his privacy,[17] and further argues that a thumbprint is not a reasona-

---

[17] *Homo Sapiens* possesses a truly opposable thumb. An opposable thumb is a necessary adaptation for a creature whose survival depends on having a firm grasp on the tools and instruments encountered in daily life. In the case sub judice, the instrument being grasped was a check. Because when grasping and transferring or receiving a paper, such as a check, one does so normally by holding the paper against the side of the index finger with the assistance of a firmly down pressed thumb, we deduce that on multiple occasions during the passing back and forth of the check while Petitioner attempted to cash it, he inevitably and repeatedly placed his thumbprint upon it. At best, therefore, Petitioner's objection appears not to be to placing his thumbprint on the check, but rather to placing a thumbprint on the check which would be longer lasting and more clearly identifiable over time than would otherwise be the case given normal handling conditions.

ble form of identification because it does not prove contemporaneously the identity of an over the counter presenter at the time presentment is made. According to Petitioner, the purpose of requiring "reasonable identification" is to allow the drawee bank to determine that the presenter is the proper person to be paid on the instrument. Because a thumbprint does not provide that information at the time presentment and payment are made, Petitioner argues that a thumbprint cannot be read to fall within the meaning of "reasonable identification" for the purposes of § 3–501(b)(2)(ii).

Bank of America argues that the requirement of a thumbprint has been upheld, in other non-criminal circumstances, not to be an invasion of privacy, and is a reasonable and necessary industry response to the growing problem of check fraud. The intermediate appellate court agreed, pointing out that the form of identification was not defined by the statute, but that the Code itself recognized a thumbprint as a form of signature, § 1–201(39), and observing that requiring thumbprint or fingerprint identification has been found to be reasonable and not to violate privacy rights in a number of non-criminal contexts. . . .

More compelling . . . is the reasoning of the intermediate appellate court in rejecting Petitioner's argument that § 3–501(b)(2)(ii) implicitly contains a present tense temporal element. . . .

The reason has to do with warranties. The transfer of a check for consideration creates both transfer warranties (§ 3–416(a) and (c)) and presentment warranties (§ 3–417(a) and (e)) which cannot be disclaimed. The warranties include, for example, that the payee is entitled to enforce the instrument and that there are no alterations on the check. The risk to banks is that these contractual warranties may be breached, exposing the accepting bank to a loss because the bank paid over the counter on an item which was not properly payable. See § 4–401; *C.S. Bowen Co., Inc. v. Maryland Nat. Bank*, 36 Md.App. 26, 36–38, 373 A.2d 30, 36–37 (1977). In such an event, the bank would then incur the expense to find the presenter, to demand repayment, and legal expenses to pursue the presenter for breach of his warranties.

In short, when a bank cashes a check over the counter, it assumes the risk that it may suffer losses for counterfeit documents, forged endorsements, or forged or altered checks. Nothing in the Commercial Law Article forces a bank to assume such risks. *See Barnhill*, 503 U.S. 393, 398–99, 112 S.Ct. 1386, 118 L.Ed.2d 39 (1992); § 3–408. To the extent that banks are willing to cash checks over the counter, with reasonable identification, such willingness expands and facilitates the commercial activities within the State. . . .

Because the reduction of risk promotes the expansion of commercial practices, we believe that the direction of § 1–102(2)(b) requires that we conclude that a bank's requirement of a thumbprint placed upon a check presented over the counter by a non-customer is reasonable. *Barclays Bank D.C.O. v. Mercantile National Bank*, 481 F.2d 1224, 1230–31(5th Cir.1973); *DaSilva v. Sanders*, 600 F.Supp. 1008, 1013 (D.D.C.1984). . . . [T]he Thumbprint Program is part of an industry wide response to the growing threat of check fraud. . . . Prohibiting banks from taking reasonable steps to protect themselves from losses could result in banks refusing to cash checks of non-customers presented over the counter at all, a result which would be counter to the direction of § 1–102(2)(b).

As a result of this conclusion, Bank of America in the present case did not dishonor the check when it refused to accept it over the counter. Under § 3–501(b)(3)(ii), Bank of America "refused payment or acceptance for failure of the presentment to comply with ... other applicable law or rule." The rule not complied with by the Petitioner-presenter was § 3–502(b)(2)(ii), in that he refused to give what we have determined to be reasonable identification. Therefore, there was no dishonor of the check by Bank of America's refusal to accept it. The answer to Petitioner's third question is therefore "no," as is the answer to Petitioner's first question. . . .

ELDRIDGE, Judge, concurring in part and dissenting in part.

. . . I cannot agree with the majority's holding that, after the petitioner presented his driver's license and a major credit card, it was "reasonable" to require the petitioner's thumbprint as identification.

Today, honest citizens attempting to cope in this world are constantly being required to show or give drivers' licenses, photo identification cards, social security numbers, the last four digits of social security numbers, mothers' "maiden names," 16 digit account numbers, etc. Now, the majority takes the position that it is "reasonable" for banks and other establishments to require, in addition, thumbprints and fingerprints. Enough is enough. The most reasonable thing in this case was petitioner's "irritation with the Bank of America's Thumbprint Signature Program." . . . .

Chief Judge Bell has authorized me to state that he joins this concurring and dissenting opinion.

Questions and Problems 2.12. In *Messing*, the court says that in the absence of a special relationship, a non-customer has no claim against a bank for refusing to honor a presented check. Does that mean that you need a contractual relationship to establish a duty? That issue, among others, is considered in the next case. Unlike the non-customer in *Messing*, the non-customer drawer of the check and the depositary bank have something more than a "transient, non-contractual relationship," sufficient to establish a duty. Consider whether this means a general negligence theory applies, or something relational.

CHICAGO TITLE INS. CO. V. ALLFIRST BANK
394 Md. 270, 905 A.2d 366 (2006)

GREENE, J.

In this case we must decide an issue of first impression, whether a depositary bank is liable in negligence to a non-customer drawer of a check. . . . [T]he instant case originated with the refinancing of Mark A. Shannahan's home in 1997. Petitioner, First Equity, an agent for petitioner, Chicago Title Insurance Company, [collectively "First Equity"] conducted Shannahan's settlement. Shannahan granted an indemnity deed of trust ("IDOT") to Farmers Bank of Maryland, where he also maintained several business and personal accounts.

While several checks exchanged hands in order to complete Shannahan's refinancing, the two checks at issue here were Check No. 1 and Check No. 2. Check No. 1 was delivered and made payable to Shannahan by First Equity to represent his "cash out" from the refinancing. Check No. 2 was made payable to Farmers Bank, and drawn on First Equity's checking account at Allfirst Bank, representing payment for an outstanding line of credit. Both checks were delivered to Shannahan, along with a letter instructing Farmers Bank to pay off and close out the line of credit. The letter was never delivered to Farmers Bank, and both checks were indorsed and deposited by Shannahan into his personal account. Eventually, Farmers Bank initiated foreclosure proceedings in connection with the IDOT because the line of credit balance was in default. Apparently, this occurred when First Equity became aware that Farmers Bank still had a lien on Shannahan's property, and that Shannahan did not pay off the line of credit. When First Equity notified Allfirst about Check No. 2, it requested that Allfirst re-credit its account, which Allfirst refused.

First Equity filed a declaratory judgment action against Farmers Bank and Allfirst in the Circuit Court for Anne Arundel County, to which both Farmers and Allfirst banks filed a Counter-Complaint for Interpleader against First Equity. The Circuit Court subsequently ordered Farmers Bank to release the IDOT lien on the property. It was also determined that Allfirst was not liable for debiting funds from First Equity's checking account through the processing of Check No. 2. First Equity filed a cross-appeal on that issue. The Court of Special

Appeals affirmed the judgment of the Circuit Court. . . . Chicago Title and First Equity filed a Petition for Writ of Certiorari, and Farmers Bank filed a Cross-Petition for Writ of Certiorari, both of which we granted. . . .

First Equity presents two questions for our review, which we have rephrased:

> 1. Did the Court of Special Appeals err in its holding that Check No. 2 was properly payable?
>
> 2. Did the intermediate appellate court err in concluding that an action in negligence against Farmers Bank was permitted under Maryland law?

We answer both questions in the negative and affirm the judgment of the Court of Special Appeals. Farmers Bank and Allfirst also presented three issues for our review,[3] which are addressed *infra*.

FACTS

. . . The intermediate appellate court ultimately held:

> We shall sustain the trial court's ruling that Farmers [Bank] was negligent in its handling of Check [No.] 2. We hold that the court erred, however, in failing to consider the contributory negligence of First Equity, and in resting its decision on Md.Code (1974, 2003 Repl.Vol.), section 7-106 of the Real Property Article ("RP") (authorizing [a] cause of action against [a] lienholder for its failure to release [a] lien whenever full payment is made and a release is requested in writing). Finally, we affirm the trial court in its holding that First Equity could not recover against Allfirst because the latter did not violate UCC section 4-401 when it charged Check [No.] 2 against First

---

[3] Farmers Bank and Allfirst ("respondents") are both represented by the same counsel and presented three issues that addressed both parties' positions:

> 1. Whether, as a matter of Maryland law, Farmers, as the [depositary] bank, owed a tort duty of care to Chicago Title and First Equity, neither of which were customers of the bank nor had an intimate nexus with the bank?
>
> 2. Whether a cause of action for common law negligence had been displaced by the statutory scheme of the Maryland Uniform Commercial Code as to actions by a drawer of a check against a [depositary] bank alleging improper negotiation of a check?
>
> 3. Whether the lower courts correctly found that the Check bore the indorsement of the payee, was effectively negotiated to Allfirst, and was therefore properly paid by Allfirst?

Respondents' questions will be addressed in our analysis below.

Equity's account. This is so because no signature on Check [No.] 2 was forged, and no indorsement was missing.

. . .

DISCUSSION

I.

Did the Court of Special Appeals err in its holding that Check No. 2 was properly payable?[a]

First Equity argues that Check No. 2 was not properly payable when presented to Allfirst because Check No. 2 lacked the requisite payee indorsement from Farmers Bank, and that a missing indorsement is equivalent to a forged indorsement for purposes of determining whether a check is properly payable. Specifically, First Equity contends that the Court of Special Appeals erred in its determination that Farmers Bank indorsed Check No. 2 as a payee. Instead, First Equity asserts that Check No. 2 was not properly payable under the Maryland UCC because it did not bear the necessary payee indorsement.

. . . Check No. 2 is both a negotiable instrument and a draft. Commercial Law § 3-104(a)-(f). First Equity signed, or was identified in, the draft as a "person" ordering payment; thus it is the drawer of the check. § 3-103(a)(3). Allfirst is the drawee, or person ordered in a draft to make payment, Section 3-103(a)(2), and is also the payor bank. § 4-105(3). Farmers Bank is a depositary bank pursuant to Commercial Law § 4-105(2), as it was "the first bank to take an item even though it is also the payor bank unless the item is presented for immediate payment over the counter."[7]

Indorsement of Check No. 2

First Equity argues that Farmers Bank did not indorse Check No. 2 as its payee. Farmers Bank was the designated payee on Check No. 2, issued by First Equity and made payable "to the order of" Farmers Bank. It is undisputed by First Equity that Farmers Bank deposited Check No. 2 directly into Shannahan's private account. First Equity contends, however, that Farmers Bank's indorsement on Check No. 2

---

[a] In the meantime, Allfirst Bank had withdrawn its argument that it was a holder in due course as to Check No. 2.

[7] . . . Official Comment 1 to § 4-105:

> The definitions in general exclude a bank to which an item is issued, as this bank does not take by transfer except in the particular case covered in which the item is issued to a payee for collection, as in the case in which a corporation is transferring balances from one account to another. Thus, the definition of "depositary bank" does not include the bank to which a check is made payable if a check is given in payment of a mortgage. This bank has the status of a payee[.]

is a depositary bank indorsement, placed on Check No. 2 after Shannahan deposited it into his private account with Farmers Bank, and after it had been sent by the bank to a "processing department" outside the Annapolis Branch of Farmers Bank.

First Equity argues that Farmers Bank's indorsement of Check No. 2 was intended to be that of a depositary bank, and urges us to evaluate the location of the physical characteristics of the Farmers Bank indorsement in relation to the deposit of that instrument into Shannahan's personal account, and its temporal and physical relationship with Shannahan's signature on Check No. 2. First Equity discounts the intermediate appellate court's notation that petitioners had not provided any expert testimony or otherwise that Farmers Bank's indorsement on Check No. 2 "could not serve the dual purpose of a [depositary] bank indorsement and a payee indorsement."

First Equity contends that Farmers Bank's signature on Check No. 2, by its placement on the instrument in "full compliance with C.F.R. 12 guidelines,"[b] and its temporal and spatial relationship to Shannahan's signature in the location "long established" by custom and usage as that of the payee, clearly indicates that Farmers Bank did not intend to provide a payee's indorsement on Check No. 2.

Farmers Bank and Allfirst note that Check No. 2 clearly bears four indorsements, one by Shannahan, two by Farmers Bank and one by Allfirst. The intermediate appellate court noted that the pattern of the indorsements placed by Farmers Bank on Check No. 2 is the same as that placed on the other check that was payable to Farmers Bank. . . . [The court quoted § 3-204(a).]

. . . The Official Comment to § 3-204(a) provides some guidance to its application:

> In some cases an indorsement may serve more than one purpose. For example, if the holder of a check deposits it to the holder's account in a depositary bank for collection and indorses the check by signing holder's name with the accompanying words "for deposit only" the purpose of the indorsement is both to negotiate the check to the depositary bank and to restrict payment of the check.
>
> The but clause of the first sentence of subsection (a) elaborates on former Section 3-402. In some cases it may not be clear whether a signature was meant to be that of the indorser, a party to the instrument in some other capacity such as drawer, maker or acceptor, or a person who was not signing as a party. *The general rule is that a signature is an indorsement if the instrument does not indicate an un-*

---

[b] The reference here, presumably, is to Title 12 of the Code of Federal Regulations, and specifically to the Federal Reserve's regulations concerning collection and payment of checks, 12 C.F.R. §§ 210.1-210.15, 229.1-229.60.

*ambiguous intent of the signer not to sign as an indorser. Intent may
be determined by words accompanying the signature, the place of the
signature, or other circumstances.*

(Emphasis added).

Although the "general rule" is worded in a manner that is somewhat unnecessarily obtuse, we attempt to simplify the rule. A signature on the back of an instrument is an indorsement unless it says
that it is not. If the instrument does not indicate any clear intent on
the part of the signer to sign as anything other than an indorser, the
signature is an indorsement. In the instant case, the intermediate appellate court was correct in finding that Shannahan's signature represented an anomalous indorsement.[9] Shannahan was not a "holder"[10] of
the instrument; therefore his signature on the back of the instrument
did not affect the manner in which it could be negotiated.

The only indorsement (other than Allfirst's subsequent indorsement as the payor bank) was that of Farmers Bank. We find no support for Farmers Bank's contention that it indorsed the back of Check
No. 2 as a depository bank and not as the payee of the instrument.
Farmers Bank states in its brief, "[t]here is no doubt that Farmers'
indorsement of Check No. 2 *was intended to be*, and was, that of a [de-
pository] bank." . . . (emphasis added). Whether Farmers Bank intended its indorsement to be that of a depository bank is irrelevant
under the facts of the instant case and under the definition of indorsement set forth in § 3-204(a). . . .

An examination of Check No. 2 indicates that there were no accompanying words with the stamp of Farmers Bank to indicate that
the indorsement was that of a depository bank only, or that the stamp
was not intended to be an indorsement. Farmers Bank directs us to

---

[9] *See* Md.Code (1975, 2002 Repl.Vol.) § 3-205(d) of the Commercial Law
Article ("'Anomalous indorsement' means an indorsement made by a person
who is not the holder of the instrument ... and does not affect the manner in
which the instrument may be negotiated.").

[10] Section 1-201(20)(a) of the Commercial Law Article defines a "holder"
in regards to a negotiable instrument as follows:

> (20) "Holder" means:
> (a) The person in possession of a negotiable instrument that is paya-
> ble either to bearer or to an identified person that is the person in posses-
> sion[. . . .]

Check No. 2 is a negotiable instrument but was not payable to either
"bearer" or Shannahan, who was the person in possession of the check. Therefore, Shannahan was not a "holder" of the check.

Official Comment 1 to § 3-204, which suggests that custom and usage may be used as a factor to determine intent, and contends that Farmers Bank's indorsement, "and its temporal and physical relationship with Shannahan's signature," demonstrate that it was solely that of a depository bank. We acknowledge that specifications are provided by the Code of Federal Regulations for the location of the stamp of a depositary bank. The fact that Farmers Bank's indorsement falls within those enumerated specifications does not negate the facts that Farmers Bank is the payee of the instrument; that the only other indorsement on the instrument is an anomalous indorsement; and that there is no accompanying information with its stamp to indicate that it is a depository bank indorsement only. Maryland law provides that an indorsement can be written anywhere on an instrument. *Leahy v. McManus*, 237 Md. 450, 454, 206 A.2d 688, 690 (1965). The fact that Farmers Bank's stamp on Check No. 2 was identical to that of its stamp on Check No. 1, where it was the payee, flies in the face of its contention that its stamp on Check No. 2 was unambiguously that of a depository bank.

Farmers Bank has not presented any expert testimony to support its contentions. Further, there was testimony from an experienced bank officer that stamped bank indorsements could appear anywhere on back of check. The words, or lack thereof, accompanying Farmers Bank's indorsement, the place of the stamp, and other circumstances surrounding Check No. 2 do not indicate a clear intent on the part of Farmers Bank not to sign as an indorser.

II.

Did the intermediate appellate court err in concluding that an action in negligence against Farmers Bank was permitted under Maryland law?

Farmers Bank and Allfirst argue that the Court of Special Appeals erred in recognizing the existence of a common law tort duty owed by a depositary bank to a non-customer. Farmers Bank notes that no contractual duty existed between First Equity and Farmers Bank, as First Equity was not a customer of Farmers Bank. In addition, First Equity did not maintain an account with Farmers Bank and had no contractual or direct relationship with Farmers Bank. In regard to a common law duty of care, [Farmers Bank claims] that the facts of the instant case are legally inadequate to impose a duty of care owed by Farmers Bank to First Equity. We must first discuss, however, the argument that . . . § 3-420 . . . expressly rejects the position that a depositary bank such as Farmers owes a duty to exercise reasonable care to non-customer drawers of checks that are presented for deposit.

Section 3-420 of the Commercial Law Article

Both the respondents and The American Banker Association, as amici, argue that § 3-420 of the UCC displaces the common law causes of action against a depositary bank by the drawer of a check. . . .

We disagree with amici and the respondents that our decision in the instant case implicates *Hartford Fire Ins. Co. v. Maryland Nat'l Bank, N.A.*, 341 Md. 408, 671 A.2d 22 (1996), and the subsequent amendment of § 3-420 of the UCC abolishing a drawer's common law action for conversion. The facts of the instant case are distinguishable in that the drawer in the instant case does not have an adequate remedy under the UCC because payment of the check was authorized pursuant to the guidelines of the UCC.[12]

Section 1-103 of the UCC provides that, unless displaced by Titles 1 through 10 of the Commercial Law Article, "the principles of law and equity, including the law merchant and the law relative to capacity to contract, principal and agent, estoppel, fraud, misrepresentation, duress, coercion, mistake, bankruptcy, or other validating or invalidating cause shall supplement its provisions."[13] The plain language of the statute states that actions in conversion are prohibited in specific situations. We disagree with the reading of the statute by amici. In our view, to conclude that the prohibition of one tort action by the UCC means the prohibition of all tort actions is unsupported by Maryland

---

[12] The Official Comment 1 to § 3-420 provides:

> Under former Title 3, the cases were divided on the issue of whether the drawer of a check with a forged indorsement can assert rights against a depositary bank that took the check. The last sentence of Section 3-420(a) resolves the conflict by following the rule stated in [*Stone & Webster Engineering Corp. v. First National Bank & Trust Co.*,] 345 Mass. 1, 184 N.E.2d 358 (1962). There is no reason why a drawer should have an action in conversion. The check represents an obligation of the drawer rather than property of the drawer. *The drawer has an adequate remedy against the payor bank for recredit of the drawer's account for unauthorized payment of the check.*

(Emphasis added). Our treatment of *Stone* in *Hartford Fire Ins. Co.*, *supra*, is inapplicable to the instant case as we have found that Check No. 2 was not unauthorized and was, in fact, properly payable.

[13] The exceptions to this statement are: "(a) the age of majority as it pertains to the capacity to contract is eighteen years of age; and (b) no person who has attained the age of eighteen years shall be considered to be without capacity by reason of age." Md.Code (1975, 2002 Repl.Vol. & 2005 Supp.) § 1-103(a)-(b) of the Commercial Law Article.

law. To allow a negligence action to proceed in the instant case, where Check No. 2 was properly payable, is not error.

Section 4-401(a) of the Commercial Law Article provides that "[a] bank may charge against the account of a customer an item that is properly payable from that account.... [A]ny item is properly payable if it is authorized by the customer and is in accordance with any agreement between the customer and bank." As we have discussed *supra*, there were no missing or unauthorized indorsements on Check No. 2. Farmers Bank's stamp constituted a proper indorsement of the check. The check was payable to Farmers Bank only, and there is no evidence on the record that Shannahan's signature constituted a forgery.[14] The loss in the instant case was indeed caused by events that occurred outside of the check itself, and therefore the UCC loss allocation rules do not apply to First Equity's claim. We look instead to the rules of common law negligence.

Negligence

We turn now to determine whether Farmers Bank may be held liable to First Equity in negligence for its handling of Check No. 2, notwithstanding the fact that First Equity was not a customer of Farmers Bank, and there was no formal contract between the parties. As we shall discuss, Maryland law provides that a contractual relationship, or its equivalent, may establish the necessary "intimate nexus" between the parties in a tort action where only economic loss results. *See Jacques v. First Nat'l Bank*, 307 Md. 527, 534-35, 515 A.2d 756, 759-60 (1986). The elements of negligence are well-established and require a plaintiff to assert in the complaint the following: "(1) that the defendant was under a duty to protect the plaintiff from injury, (2) that the defendant breached that duty, (3) that the plaintiff suffered actual

---

[14] The UCC does not define "forgery," but "forgery is equated with the concept of 'unauthorized' signatures or indorsements, as defined in § 1-201(43). A forged indorsements, in other words, under the law of Maryland and elsewhere, is one that is 'unauthorized' within the meaning of § 1-201(43)." *Northwestern Nat'l Life Ins. Co. v. Laurel Fed. Sav. Bank*, 979 F.Supp. 354, 356 (D.Md.1996) (citing *Citizens Bank of Maryland v. Maryland Indus. Finishing Co., Inc.*, 338 Md. 448, 458, 659 A.2d 313, 318 (1995)). Section 1-201(43) of the Commercial Law Article defines an unauthorized signature as "one made without actual, implied, or apparent authority and includes a forgery." Shannahan did not attempt to indorse the instrument as "Farmers Bank," nor is there any evidence as to what type of authority he purported to have while signing the check. As we have already discussed, Shannahan's signature was more fittingly an anomalous signature per § 3-205(d) of the Commercial Law Article.

injury or loss, and (4) that the loss or injury proximately resulted from the defendant's breach of the duty." *Valentine v. On Target, Inc.*, 353 Md. 544, 549, 727 A.2d 947, 949 (1999) (quoting *B G & E v. Lane*, 338 Md. 34, 43, 656 A.2d 307, 311 (1995) (citation omitted)). One of our primary concerns in the instant case is the element of duty:

> The duty to take precautions against the negligence of others thus becomes merely a matter of the customary process of multiplying the probability that such negligence will occur by the magnitude of the harm likely to result if it does, and weighing the result against the burden upon the defendant of exercising such care.

Hogge v. SS Yorkmar, 434 F.Supp. 715, 729 (D.Md.1977) (citation omitted). We must consider two elements when resolving whether a tort duty should be recognized based upon a particular set of facts:

> the nature of the harm likely to result from a failure to exercise due care, and the relationship that exists between the parties. Where the failure to exercise due care creates a risk of economic loss only, courts have generally required an intimate nexus between the parties as a condition to the imposition of tort liability. This intimate nexus is satisfied by contractual privity or its equivalent. By contrast, where the risk created is one of personal injury, no such direct relationship need be shown, and the principal determinant of duty becomes foreseeability.

Noble v. Bruce, 349 Md. 730, 739-40, 709 A.2d 1264, 1269 (1998) (quoting *Jacques*, 307 Md. at 534-35, 515 A.2d at 759-60). Absent a breach of duty, there is no liability in negligence. *Wells v. General Elec. Co.*, 807 F.Supp. 1202, 1204 (D.Md.1992).

We begin by acknowledging Chief Judge Bell's comprehensive analysis of the elements of duty and privity in *Walpert, Smullian & Blumenthal, P.A. v. Katz*, 361 Md. 645, 762 A.2d 582 (2000), and our decision in *Jacques v. First Nat'l Bank of Maryland*, 307 Md. 527, 515 A.2d 756 (1986).[17] Both cases discuss the concepts of duty and privity at great length. We have no desire to reinvent the wheel. Therefore, we discuss the analyses of those cases relevant to the facts of the instant case.

---

[17] In *Jacques*, individuals who were buying a home brought suit against the bank at which they applied for a home mortgage loan. *Id.* at 528, 515 A.2d at 756. We were called upon to determine whether a bank that has agreed to process an application for a loan owes a duty of reasonable care to its customer in the processing and determination of that application. *Id.*

Walpert involved the liability of an accountant for economic losses of a party who relied on a financial report which an accountant prepared. George and Shirley Katz (the "Katzses") sued Walpert, Smullian & Blumenthal, P.A. ("WS & B") in damages for negligence, gross negligence, negligent misrepresentation and breach of contract as a consequence of loans they made to Magnetics, Inc., George Katz's former company and WS & B's client. *Walpert*, 361 Md. at 648, 762 A.2d at 583. We affirmed the holding of the Court of Special Appeals in *Walpert* that an accountant's knowledge of a third-party's reliance on the accountant's work product was the legal equivalent of privity necessary to establish an accounting malpractice claim. *Id.* at 653, 762 A.2d at 586. In discussing the element of duty, we noted our analysis in *Jacques v. First Nat'l Bank of Maryland*:

> This Court extensively considered the duty element of negligence in *Jacques*. *See id.* at 532-37, 515 A.2d at 759-61. In that case, the issue was whether a bank that had agreed to process a loan application owed its customer a duty of care in the processing of that application. Duty, 'an obligation to which the law will give effect and recognition to conform to a particular standard of conduct toward another,' *id.* at 532, 515 A.2d at 758, citing J. Dooley, Modern Tort Law, § 3.03 at 18-19 (1982, 1985 Cum.Supp.), we said, 'has been defined as the expression of the sum total of those considerations of policy which lead the law to say that the plaintiff is entitled to protection.' *Id.* at 533, 515 A.2d at 759, quoting Prosser and Keeton on The Law of Torts, § 53 at 357 (1984). The Court also acknowledged two major considerations affecting duty: the nature of the harm likely to result from a failure to exercise due care, and the relationship that exists between the parties. *See id.* at 534, 515 A.2d at 759. With regard to the connection between the harm and the relationship between the parties, we observed:
> 'Where the failure to exercise due care creates a risk of economic loss only, courts have generally required an intimate nexus between the parties as a condition to the imposition of tort liability. This intimate nexus is satisfied by contractual privity or its equivalent. By contrast, where the risk created is one of personal injury, no such direct relationship need be shown, and the principal determinant of duty becomes foreseeability.' 307 Md. at 534-35, 515 A.2d at 759-60.

Id. at 657-58, 762 A.2d 582, 762 A.2d at 588-89 (quoting *Jacques*, 307 Md. at 532-33, 515 A.2d at 758-59). To illustrate the concept of the intimate nexus, it was necessary to note our reliance in *Jacques* upon two decisions from New York: *Ultramares Corporation v. Touche*, 255 N.Y. 170, 174 N.E. 441 (1931)[18] and *Glanzer v. Shepard*, 233 N.Y. 236,

---

[18] In *Ultramares,* the plaintiff sued for damages sustained as a result of

135 N.E. 275 (1922).[19] Our review of Maryland and New York case law led us to state in *Walpert* that "the rationale underlying the requirement of privity or its equivalent as a condition of liability for negligent conduct, including negligent misrepresentations, resulting in economic damages ... [is] to avoid 'liability in an indeterminate amount for an indeterminate time to an indeterminate class.'" *Walpert*, 361 Md. at 671, 762 A.2d at 596 (quoting *Ultramares*, 174 N.E. at 444). We explained that the reason for the privity requirement is to "limit the defendant's risk exposure to an actually foreseeable extent," allowing a defendant to control the risk to which he or she is exposed. *Id.* In support of this statement, we cited the facts of Jacques, where the Jacqueses were not strangers to the loan transaction as the bank in that case promised the Jacqueses to process their loan application as a specific locked-in interest rate for a specific period of time. *Id.* (citing *Jacques*, 307 Md. at 537, 515 A.2d at 761). Then, citing *Glanzer*, Chief Judge Bell, writing for the Court, stated that "a defendant's knowledge of a third party's reliance on the defendant's action may be important in the determination of whether that defendant owes that party a duty of care." *Id.* at 684, 762 A.2d at 603. The identity of the plaintiffs in Glanzer, and the class in which those plaintiffs belonged, was known by the defendant, as was the fact that the prospective plaintiffs would be relying on the information provided by the defendant. *Id.* at 687, 762 A.2d at 605.

---

misrepresentations of a firm of public accountants. *Id.* at 442. The accountants were employed by Fred Stern & Co. to prepare and certify a balance sheet exhibiting the condition of its business. *Id.* The business required extensive credit and borrowed large sums of money from banks and other lenders in order to operate. *Id.* The defendants were aware of this fact, and provided numerous certified copies of the balance sheet to the company, although it was not aware that a copy would be given to the plaintiffs. *Id.* at 442. The status of the company, contrary to what was stated in the balance sheet, was insolvent, due to the falsification of the books by those in charge of the business. *Id.* The plaintiffs loaned money to the company on the basis of the balance sheet and brought suit against the accountants to recover the loss suffered by the plaintiff in reliance upon the audit. *Id.* at 443.

   [19] The plaintiffs in *Glanzer* bought beans from a merchant, the price of which was determined by the weight of the beans. *Glanzer*, 135 N.E. at 275. The buyers were given a certificate noting the certified weight of the beans that was prepared by "public weighers" who, at the seller's request, weighed the bags. *Id.* at 275-76. When the purchasers learned that the actual weight was less than that amount specified in the certified weight sheet, the purchasers sued the public weighers. *Id.* Despite the fact that the plaintiffs had no contract with the weigher of beans, the court held that the purchasers were the "known and intended beneficiaries" of the contract between the seller and the weigher, and the purchasers were beneficiaries of the duty owed by the weigher. *Id.*

Credit Alliance Corp. v. Arthur Andersen & Co., 65 N.Y.2d 536, 493 N.Y.S.2d 435, 483 N.E.2d 110, 118 (1985),[20] subsequently clarified *Ultramares, supra,* in regard to the privity equivalent, or near privity requirement. ...

An Intimate Nexus

As the instant case presents a situation in which the failure to exercise due care creates a risk of economic loss only, we examine the relationship between Farmers Bank and Allfirst to determine if a sufficient intimate nexus between the parties existed, thus allowing the imposition of tort liability. Both Farmers Bank and Allfirst contend that Farmers Bank and First Equity were not in privity with one another, and that the only nexus between First Equity and Farmers Bank is that First Equity was the drawer of a check presented to Farmers Bank for deposit and collection. Allfirst further contends that such a connection is too attenuated to give rise to a duty of care owed by Farmers Bank to First Equity.

Because Bill Grippo, the Farmers Bank representative who handled Check No. 2, could not be found, the only evidence of what occurred from his perspective is contained in a memo he wrote:

> Mr. Shannahan went to the teller to deposit the check, the teller brought the check to me since it was over her limit. At that time I had Mr. Shannahan come into my office and I saw that the check was payable to Farmers Bank. At that time I retrived [*sic*] his accounts and saw that the bank had a trust on his property. At that time I called Matt Pipkin and told him what I had. Matt stated it was okay for Mr. Shannahan to deposit the check[.] I questioned the outstanding trusts and again Matt stated it was okay to deposit the check.
> It was my practice to review Mr. Shannahan's large deposit, as I did with any other customer. If I or Brenda Higdon had any questions, we usually contacted Matt as he was the primary officer on the account.

---

[20] In the two appeals involved in *Credit Alliance,* the plaintiff loaned money to an accountant's client in reliance on audited financial statements prepared by the accountants. The Court of Appeals of New York held that the plaintiffs failed to allege sufficient facts to demonstrate the existence of a relationship between the parties that amounted to privity. *Credit Alliance,* 493 N.Y.S.2d 435, 483 N.E.2d at 119. Specifically, the court found that there was no sufficient allegation of "either a particular purpose for the reports' preparation or the prerequisite conduct on the part of the accountants ... [and] there is simply no allegation of any ... action on the part of [the accountants] directed to plaintiffs ... which provided the necessary link between them." *Id.* at 119.

At deposition, Matt Pipkin denied ever having this conversation with Grippo.

We noted in *Walpert* that Glanzer "clearly recognizes that a defendant's knowledge of a third party's reliance on the defendant's action may be important in the determination of whether that defendant owes that party a duty of care." *Walpert*, 361 Md. at 684, 762 A.2d at 603. In the instant case, Farmers Bank was aware that the check presented by Shannahan was drawn on Allfirst Bank and, although endorsed by him, the check was not made payable to Shannahan. When asked at trial what a branch manager was supposed to do when receiving a check like Check No. 2, "payable to itself with no other restrictions or instructions," John Yaremchuk, president of Farmers Bank, responded that a bank officer or branch manager should make inquiries to the presenter on "how they wanted to use the funds" and should determine if the customer's request was reasonable. Despite Yaremchuk's testimony that "inquiries" should be made when a check like Check No. 2 is presented, the court ascertained that the only statement of the individual who handled the transaction with Shannahan, Bill Grippo, did not indicate that Shannahan was asked any questions.

As noted by the intermediate appellate court, Farmers Bank received a sizable check payable to itself from First Equity, an institution that was not indebted to it, and with no direction as to its purpose. Yaremchuk even testified that, in his experience, it would have been advisable to contact First Equity when a check like Check No. 2 was received. But Yaremchuk did not testify, and indeed there is no proof in the record that Farmers ever contacted First Equity to inquire about the check.

Here, Farmers Bank was aware that the funds drawn on Check No. 2 were not payable to Shannahan, and yet placed them in his account. As a bank, Farmers was aware that Allfirst would pay Check No. 2 out of its funds. Farmers Bank was also aware that First Equity was a title company, and, through the receipt of Check No. 1 which was sent directly to Farmers Bank, was on notice that the necessary payments to remove the liens on Shannahan's property were being made. Farmers Bank acknowledges that Shannahan's line of credit was included with his other business and personal debts that were all secured by the IDOT. Certainly, if Farmers Bank was aware that First Equity was attempting to perfect its title in Shannahan's property through its receipt of Check No. 1, it would be reasonable to assume that Farmers Bank's knowledge of the refinancing process would make them aware that Check No. 2 represented a payment in connection with Shannahan's refinancing as well. This knowledge supports both the Circuit Court's and the intermediate appellate court's conclusions that the requisite intimate nexus was created between Farmers Bank and First Equity.

We also note . . . that the drawer of the check was a title company in the business of insuring against title defects, including the priority of a lender's lien on real property. Shannahan's outstanding loans were secured by real property. Also, Farmers Bank had received a "payoff request" from Armada, the new lender (to whom First Equity would issue a lender's title policy). Farmers Bank had replied to that request identifying its two secured loans and stating the amount due. Cumulatively, these factors suggest that Farmers Bank knew, or should have known, that there was a risk that First Equity was expecting the proceeds of the check to pay off the line of credit secured by the IDOT. This conduct on the part of Farmers Bank, taken into consideration with all the other circumstances surrounding the transaction, represents conduct on the part of Farmers Bank that links it to First Equity, and evinces Farmers Bank's understanding of First Equity's reliance. Unlike the facts of *Ultramares*, our holding does not impose liability on Farmers Bank to an indeterminate class of people for an indeterminate time, but rather, addresses a specific entity, First Equity, for this specific transaction.

Conclusion

An action for negligence, where the damages are only economic, may be brought by a non-customer drawer against a depositary bank, where there is no violation of the provisions of the UCC, and where duty is established by a sufficient intimate nexus between the depositary bank and the non-customer, through privity or its equivalent. We affirm the judgment of the intermediate appellate court, and in so doing, remand this matter to the Circuit Court to consider the defense of contributory negligence as it applies to Allfirst. . . .

Questions and Problems 2.13. Does the "intimate nexus" identified in *Chicago Title* mean that a drawer of a check is always in the equivalent of contractual privity with the depositary bank that receives the check? In a cryptic footnote in the case, Justice Greene denied that the case would have that kind of contractual impact. As if it explains everything, Greene insisted, "Our holding applies to the specific facts of the instant case." *Chicago Title Ins. Co.*, 394 Md. at 299 n.22.

2.14. In *Chicago Title*, would it have made a difference to the outcome if the facts involved a check that was fraudulently altered? Note that Check No. 2 was neither fraudulently altered nor indorsed, and was "properly payable" under the UCC. *Cf. Sun 'n Sand, Inc. v. United California Bank*, 21 Cal.3d 671, 148 Cal. Rep. 329, 582 P.2d 920 (1978) (involving properly signed but fraudulently altered checks).

STATE SEC. CHECK CASHING, INC. V. AMERICAN GENERAL FINANCIAL SERVICES (DE)
409 Md. 81, 972 A.2d 882 (2009)

HARRELL, Judge.

In this case we are asked to determine which party, as between the issuer of a check and the check cashing business that cashed it, is liable under Md.Code, Commercial Law Art. § 3-404 (2002 Repl. Vol. & Supp. 2008) for the face amount of the check, when an imposter, posing successfully as another individual in securing a loan (the proceeds of which were represented by the check) from the issuer, subsequently negotiated the check at the check cashing business. We shall hold that, under the circumstances presented in this case, the issuer of the check is liable for the amount of the check.

I.

Factual and Procedural Background

On 20 June 2007, American General Financial Services, Inc., ("American General") was contacted by telephone by a man, later revealed to be an imposter posing as Ronald E. Wilder (we shall refer to this person as the "imposter", though he was not known to be so at most relevant times in this case). The imposter sought a $20,000.00 loan. Based on the information supplied by him over the telephone, American General ran a credit check on Ronald E. Wilder, finding his credit to be excellent. American General informed the imposter that it would need personal tax returns for the prior two years, and asked him what he intended to do with the proceeds of the desired loan. The imposter sent by electronic facsimile to American General the requested tax returns of Mr. Wilder and explained that he wanted the loan to renovate a property he owned. On Friday, 22 June 2007, American General's District Manager received the completed loan application and tax returns, performed a cash flow analysis, and obtained approval from senior management for an $18,000.00 loan.

On that same morning, American General informed the imposter that the loan was approved. The imposter appeared at noon at American General's Security Boulevard office in Baltimore County. He proffered an apparent Maryland driver's license bearing Mr. Wilder's personal information and the imposter's photograph. He remained in the loan office for approximately thirty minutes, meeting with the branch manager and a customer account specialist during the loan closing. After all the loan documents were signed, American General issued to the imposter a loan check for $18,000.00, drawn on Wachovia Bank, N.A., and payable to Ronald E. Wilder.

Later that afternoon, the imposter presented the check to State Security Check Cashing, Inc. ("State Security"), a check cashing business. At the time the imposter appeared in State Security's office, also on Security Boulevard in Baltimore County, only one employee was on duty, Wanda Decker. Decker considered the same driver's license that the imposter presented to American General, and reviewed the American General loan documents related to the check. She also compared the check to other checks issued by American General which had been cashed previously by State Security. Deeming the amount of the check relatively "large," Decker called Joel Deutsch, State Security's compliance officer, to confirm that she had taken the proper steps in verifying the check. Deutsch directed Decker to verify the date of the check, the name of the payee on the check, the address of the licensee, the supporting loan paperwork, and whether the check matched other checks in State Security's system from the issuer. Decker confirmed the results of all of these steps, and, upon Deutsch's approval, cashed the check, on behalf of State Security, for the imposter for a fee of 3-5% of the face value of the check.

On Monday, 25 June, the next business day after the imposter negotiated the check at State Security, the real Ronald E. Wilder appeared at the offices of American General indicating that he had been notified by the U.S. Secret Service that a person applied for a loan in his name. At that time, the true Ronald E. Wilder completed an Affidavit of Forgery. As a result of the Affidavit, Thurman Toland, the Branch Manager of American General's Security Boulevard branch, called Wachovia Bank to determine whether the $18,000.00 check had been presented for payment. Learning that the check had not been presented yet, Toland placed a "stop payment" on the check.

State Security filed a civil claim in the District Court of Maryland, sitting in Baltimore County, against American General for the face value of the check, plus interest, asserting that it was a holder in due course of American General's check, that it received the check in good faith, without knowledge of fraud, and that it gave value for the check. On 3 December 2007, the District Court conducted a bench trial. During the trial, the testimonies of Deutsch and Toland revealed three additional, potentially important points: (a) had State Security personnel called American General on 22 June 2007 to verify that American General issued a check to Ronald E. Wilder for $18,000.00, Toland would have confirmed that to be the case; (b) State Security employed a thumb print identification system for its check-cashing business, but, at the time the imposter cashed the check, it was unclear whether it was functional; and (c) although, as part of the loan application process, American General obtained names and telephone numbers of personal references from the imposter, it did not call any of the references before delivering the check.

On 19 December 2007, the District Court held in favor of American General. . . . The District Court concluded that, under Md.Code, Commercial Law Art. § 3-404(d), State Security had not exercised ordinary care in paying the imposter's check, and that its failure to exercise ordinary care contributed substantially to the loss.

. . . On 8 August 2008, the Circuit Court issued its Memorandum Opinion and Order affirming the judgment of the District Court. . . .

II.

Discussion

. . . State Security argued that, under Md.Code, Commercial Law Art. § 3-302, it was a holder in due course of the check issued by American General. ... In order to resolve the rights of the parties, it is necessary to address State Security's § 3-302 claim.

A. Commercial Law Art. § 3-302

The first prerequisite to being deemed a holder in due course is that the item held must be an "instrument." As used in Title 3 of the Commercial Law Article, " '[i]nstrument' means a negotiable instrument." Md.Code, Com. Law Art. § 3-104. . . .

The parties do not dispute that the check issued to the imposter by American General satisfies the definition of a negotiable instrument for the purposes of Title 3 of the Commercial Law Article.

Under subsection (a) of section 3-302 of the Commercial Law Article, there are multiple additional requirements that the holder of the instrument must satisfy in order to be a holder in due course. As iterated previously, those requirements are: the "instrument when issued or negotiated to the holder does not bear such apparent evidence of forgery or alteration or is not otherwise so irregular or incomplete as to call into question its authenticity"; and the holder took the instrument (1) for value, (2) in good faith, (3) "without notice that the instrument is overdue or has been dishonored or that there is an uncured default with respect to payment of another instrument issued as part of the same series," (4) without notice that the instrument contains an unauthorized signature or has been altered, (5) "without notice of any claim to the instrument described in § 3-306," and (6) " without notice that any party has a defense or claim in recoupment described in § 3-305(a)." State Security alleges that all of the requirements are satisfied in the present case. American General disputes State Security's allegations as to only one of the prerequisites-the good faith requirement.

American General argues that, because of the "suspicious circumstances" under which the imposter negotiated the check with State Security, State Security failed to satisfy the Title 3 requirement of good faith. In support of this position, American General advances five points, which, the company argues, when considered together, should defeat State Security's claim: (1) State Security's failure to develop any special procedures to validate the authenticity of large checks being presented at its check cashing business, as confirmed by the testimony of Decker and Deutsch that all checks are treated the same, regardless of amount, and that when Decker called Deutsch for assistance, Deutsch merely re-traced the steps Decker already had taken; (2) State Security "should have known that no competent businessman uses a check-cashing facility for an $18,000 check unless a stop payment order is likely" . . . ; (3) Wilder had not been a customer of State Security previously and was not a member of State Security's business . . . ; (4) State Security's failure to use its thumbprint identification system, even though the system may not have been functioning at the time of the transaction, was critical because "[h]ad State Security told the impostor that it would not complete the transaction without his thumbprint, he likely would not have proceeded and looked instead for a more careless victim"; and, 5) the imposter presented the check to State Security on a Friday afternoon, "just hours before most banks and businesses closed for the weekend."

State Security retorts that, under the circumstances of this case, its actions were sufficient to satisfy the good faith statutory requirement. . . .

The definition of "good faith," for the purposes of Title 3 of the Commercial Law Article, is found in Commercial Law Article § 3-103(a)(4): " 'Good faith' means honesty in fact and the observance of reasonable commercial standards of fair dealing." Md.Code, Com. Law Art. § 3-103. . . .

. . . Professors White and Summers explain this definition of "good faith," and the commentary provided in Comment 4, as follows:

> What does all of that mean? And what evidence is likely to be introduced to prove lack of reasonable commercial standards? Note that under section 3-308(b) a plaintiff confronted with defenses or claims

has the burden of proving "rights of a holder in due course," and thus the burden will be on the creditor plaintiff to show good faith.

Where might this arise? One can imagine many variations on this basic theme: a depositary bank takes a check, only to have other banks say they would not have taken such a check and that to do so violated commercial standards. For example, would it violate commercial standards for a bank to take a $100,000 check to open an account and later to allow the depositor to withdraw the funds? If not, the bank could be a holder in due course who might take free of a drawer's claim to that instrument even though the person with whom it dealt was a thief, not so? For reasons stated below we think the bank here would be in good faith. Can a payee violate commercial standards by demanding payment on a "demand note" where there has been no default in the underlying obligation?

Similar arguments might well arise at the closing of a kite, where one of the banks seeks to defend itself against a restitution claim by arguing it gave value in good faith and is protected by 3-418. That bank might be met with the argument that it was not a good faith holder of the checks passing through its hands because by observing reasonable commercial standards it should have understood the checks to be part of a kite. As we indicate elsewhere, we hope that few people are successful in asserting restitution causes of action after kites, but we anticipate that those arguments will be made.

Before one concludes that the banks described in the preceding paragraphs are not in good faith, return to the definition. A bank that fails to follow commercial standards is not in good faith only if it deviates from commercial standards of "fair dealing." Deviating from such standards on the side of generosity and gullibility rather than venality does not render one's act in bad faith. So beware, good faith does not require general conformity to "reasonable commercial standards," but only to "reasonable commercial standards of fair dealing." The issue is one of "unfairness" not of "negligence." If the Code is tilting back toward an objective standard, it is going only so far. We are clear on that point, but the courts are divided. As we see below, some courts insist on confusing negligence with unfairness. Some also find a duty for a depositary bank to consider the interests of all parties involved, including the drafter of the note with whom the banks has never had dealings.

2 JAMES J. WHITE & ROBERT S. SUMMERS, UNIFORM COMMERCIAL CODE § 17-6, at 191-92 (5th ed. 2008).

Both parties here find solace in *Any Kind Checks Cashed, Inc. v. Talcott*, 830 So.2d 160 (Fla.Dist.Ct.App.2002), a case from the Fourth District Court of Appeal of Florida, to support their respective positions regarding the "good faith" requirement. The issue before the Florida court was whether a check cashing store, Any Kind Checks Cashed, Inc., qualified as a holder in due course of a $10,000 check written by an elderly man, John G. Talcott, Jr., where Talcott was induced fraudulently to issue the check to the person who cashed it. . . .

On review, the Florida appellate court affirmed the judgment of the trial court, finding that Any Kind was not a holder in due course of the $10,000 check because the company did not act "in good faith," within the meaning provided in Florida's commercial law statute. Citing Drysdale and Keest's study[8] as support for the proposition that check cashing businesses are a "major source of traditional banking services for low-income and working poor consumers, residents of minority neighborhoods, and people with blemished credit histories" and businesses targeted to locations in which "traditional banks fear to tread", and noting on its own accord that check cashing businesses typically cash "small" checks, such as "a paycheck, child support, social security, or public assistance check" and are businesses whose "[a]ttractions ... are convenience and speed", the court concluded:

> [W]e cannot say that the trial court erred in finding that the $10,000 check was a red flag. The $10,000 personal check was not the typical check cashed at a check cashing outlet. The size of the check, in the context of the check cashing business, was a proper factor to consider under the objective standard of good faith in deciding whether Any Kind was a holder in due course. *See* [*Me. Family Fed. Credit Union v. Sun Life Assurance Co. of Can.*, 727 A.2d 335, 344 (Me.1999)]. . . .

Arguing that the policy rationale of *Talcott*, in particular the *Talcott* court's association that the need for speed in cashing a large business check "is consistent with a drawer who, for whatever reason, might stop payment," American General contends that the ersatz Wilder's negotiation of the $18,000 check for a 3-5% fee at a check cashing store should have put State Security on "inquiry notice that some confirmation or explanation should be obtained," and that because State Security applied the same level of scrutiny to checks presented, regardless of their amounts, State Security "makes itself a magnet for impostors," thereby shedding its ability to claim "good faith."

State Security responds by noting a factual distinction between the situation presented in *Talcott* and the situation here. It points out that in *Talcott* the appellate court affirmed the trial court's holding that the check cashing store was a holder in due course of the $5,700 check, but not the $10,000 check. State Security interprets the Florida court's opinion as indicating that the real issue was whether, under

---

[8] Lynn Drysdale & Kathleen E. Keest, *The Two-Tiered Consumer Financial Services Marketplace: The Fringe Banking System and its Challenge to Current Thinking About the Role of Usury Laws in Today's Society*, 51 S.C. L.REV. 589 (2000).

the circumstances presented there, the check cashing company should have verified with the maker of the $10,000 check that the $10,000 check was valid. Had the check cashing store asked Talcott whether the $10,000 check was valid when it was presented by Guarino, it would have learned that Talcott had placed a stop payment order on it. In contrast, by confirming with Talcott, the drawer, that the $5,700 check was valid at the time it was presented, the check cashing store satisfied the good faith requirement for a holder in due course.

Thus, not surprisingly, State Security reasons that the relevant inquiry in the present case is whether it took adequate steps before cashing the check to ensure that the $18,000 check issued by American General was valid. State Security posits that "[j]ust as [the check cashing store in *Talcott*] was not required to make sure that Mr. Talcott was not the victim of a scam, so too, State Security cannot be legally obligated to determine that American General should not have wanted to issue the check it issued." It points here to the testimony of Toland, American General's Branch Manager, who stated that, had State Security called him, he would have verified that the check represented the proceeds of a loan transaction American General had closed with someone it believed to be Wilder. Based on this distinction, State Security argues that *Talcott* actually supports a finding of good faith here because had State Security contacted American General regarding the validity of the check presented by the imposter, it would have learned only that the check was valid.

Professors White and Summers express some skepticism at how many courts have viewed check cashing businesses with regard to the good faith requirement for a holder in due course:

> Check cashing companies appear to be the pariahs of holder in due course law. In *Buckeye Check Cashing, Inc. v. Camp*, [159 Ohio App.3d 784, 825 N.E.2d 644 (2005),] a check cashing company sued drawer for payment after drawer contacted his bank and ordered the bank to stop payment. Drawer of check had negotiated with a contractor for services to be completed over the next three days and drawer drafted a post-dated check as payment. (The check bore the date of the projected date of completion of the services.) Contractor immediately cashed check with plaintiff, who submitted the check for payment. The drawer, fearing services would not be completed, contacted his bank the same day and ordered it to stop payment. The court held that the future date on the check should have put the check cashing company on notice that the check might not be good. The court also held that the company failed to act in a commercially reasonable manner, and did not take the check in "good faith," when it did not attempt to verify the check. We are less certain than the court is about the commercial practice with respect to postdated

checks. In some circumstances it might be commercially unreasonable to take a postdated check over-the-counter without some explanation from the customer, but that surely would not be true of a check presented to an ATM.

In *Any Kind Checks Cashed, Inc. v. Talcott*, a court held that the check cashing service did not act in good faith and should have verified a $10,000 check drawn on a 93 year-old's account when presented for cashing by a financial broker. "[The] procedures followed were not reasonably related to achieve fair dealing, ... taking into consideration all of the participants in the transaction." The court held that the financial broker was not the typical customer of a check cashing outlet because small businessmen rarely use a check cashing service that charges a 5% fee instead of a traditional bank. The business check is not the welfare or payroll check usually cashed at such an establishment. The court held that the need for speed in cashing a large business check is consistent with a drawer who might stop payment and fair dealing requires that the $10,000 check be approached with caution. "The concept of 'fair dealing' includes not being an easy, safe harbor for the dishonest."

Both the *Buckeye Check-Cashing* case and the *Any Kind Checks Cashed* case show courts that are quick to deny holder in due course status to check cashing facilities. We wonder how these courts would have handled these cases had the plaintiffs been banks and not check cashing facilities. In effect the courts are asking check cashers to adhere to a higher standard than might be required of a bank. Given the clientele of check cashing facilities, the courts' skepticism might be justified, but we would like to see a little more evidence that check-cashing facilities are a home for persons engaged in fraudulent behavior before we would subject them to higher standards than might be applied to a bank.

WHITE & SUMMERS, *supra*, § 17-6, at 197-98 (footnotes omitted).

Under § 3-308(b), the burden is on a plaintiff to prove "rights of a holder in due course," including situations such as the present, where the defense is that the plaintiff did not take the instrument in good faith. WHITE & SUMMERS, *supra*, § 17-6, at 191; *see* Md.Code, Com. Law Art. § 3-308 cmt. 2 ("Subsection (b) means only that if the plaintiff claims the rights of a holder in due course against the defense or claim in recoupment, the plaintiff has the burden of proof on that issue."). We conclude here that State Security is entitled to enforce the check because it has met its burden of proving that it took the check in good faith.

The core of the dispute between banking institutions over the good faith requirement most often distills to one banking institution taking a check, only to have another banking institution charge that, under the circumstances, it would not have taken that check, and that taking the check was a violation of commercial standards. *See* WHITE & SUMMERS, *supra*, § 17-6, at 191 ("Where might th[e good faith issue] arise? One can imagine many variations on this basic theme: a depositary bank takes a check, only to have other banks say they would not have taken such a check and that to do so violated commercial standards."). This is the dispute presented in the present case, albeit not between two banks.

Here, unlike in *Talcott* where the check presented to the check cashing business was a personal check sent via Federal Express, State Security took a check, issued by American General to the imposter in person, and relied on much of the same documentation and/or identification that American General had relied on in giving the imposter the loan proceeds check in the first place.[14] That the check presented in this case was a check drawn by American General, a financial institution, is a significant distinction from that of the personal check presented in *Talcott* for two reasons: the check itself was more likely to be valid, including the drawer's signature, as confirmed by State Security's comparing it to prior American General checks it had cashed; and the payee of the check was more likely to have been subjected to an examination of her or his personal identification, credit-worthiness, and purpose for taking out the loan, as confirmed by State Security's review of the driver's license presented and the loan documents before cashing the check.

American General's position that State Security did not take the check in good faith seems anomalous when State Security relied on the same document for personal identification, as well as the loan documents that American General generated in issuing the check to the imposter, when cashing the check. Because the check was issued by American General as the proceeds of a loan, a transaction verified by State Security, adoption of American General's position would require us to hold State Security, a check cashing business, to a higher commercial standard than American General, simply because the financial institution was duped into issuing the check to an imposter.

---

[14] Toland testified that American General required the following from the imposter in processing and approving his loan application: a paper application, personal tax returns for 2005 and 2006, a credit report, driver's license, references, and signed loan documents. Decker, State Security's teller, testified that State Security required the following in cashing the imposter's check: the check, which was verified for authenticity against other American General checks State Security had cashed, driver's license, and the American General loan documents, which were used to verify the name and signature with those on the check.

American General's desire that we hold the check cashing company here to a higher standard shall not carry the day. First, although it may be "unusual" for a person in the imposter's situation to use a check cashing business, instead of a traditional bank, *Talcott*, 830 So.2d at 168-69, whatever inhering "unusualness" does not inexorably negate good faith on State Security's part. State Security examined the same document of identification of the imposter (the forged driver's license), as well as the accompanying loan documents American General had prepared, to verify that the check presented by the imposter was the proceeds of a loan issued validly by American General, with the imposter as the intended payee, before cashing the check.

The other four points of concern advanced by American General are too speculative to alter our analysis. The fact that State Security "has no special procedures to validate large checks" is irrelevant for two reasons: a) the procedures State Security did utilize were quite similar to that of American General; and b) American General presented no evidence of any procedure State Security was "lacking" when it cashed the imposter's check that, if present, should have persuaded State Security to proceed other than as it did. Second, the fact that Ronald E. Wilder had not been a customer of State Security previously is irrelevant because of the verification steps State Security took before cashing the check, and because it does not appear from the record that American General itself was familiar with Wilder before the transactions in question. Third, we find American General's assertion that, had State Security asked the imposter to submit a thumbprint, the imposter likely would not have proceeded, to be the most speculative argument of all. . . . And fourth, the fact that the imposter presented the check at State Security on a Friday afternoon is equally likely to be coincidental, in light of the substantial identity theft actions undertaken, with the timing of his receipt of the check from American General – that same Friday afternoon – than with the conclusion that the timing was premeditated because the weekend was near.

We conclude therefore that State Security overcame American General's defense of a lack of good faith, as required under § 3-308(b), and, thus, that State Security took the check from the imposter in "good faith," defined as "honesty in fact and the observance of reasonable commercial standards of fair dealing." Md.Code, Com. Law Art. § 3-103. . . .

B. Commercial Law Art. § 3-404

Commercial Law Art. § 3-404 addresses the circumstances, among other situations, of imposters. . . . Regarding our imposter in the present case, the District Court ruled, under § 3-404(d), that State Security did not exercise ordinary care in paying the check presented by him, and that the failure to exercise such care contributed substantially to the loss. The Circuit Court, in affirming that judgment, concluded that there was substantial evidence to support the District Court's finding, and therefore the District Court's finding was not clearly erroneous. . . .

. . . In the present case, we find, for the reasons that follow, that the District Court erred as a matter of law in concluding that State Security did not meet the statutory standard of ordinary care, and that the failure to exercise ordinary care contributed substantially to the loss. Hence, the Circuit Court erred in affirming the judgment of the District Court.

The District Court determined initially and correctly that the imposter rule applies in this case because all of the pertinent requirements of Commercial Law Art. § 3-404(a) were present. . . .

. . . The District Court's ruling in favor of American General erred in two respects: a) the ruling is not in accord with the statutory definition of "ordinary care," in light of the uncontradicted testimony of Deutsch, State Security's compliance officer, and b) the ruling erred by shifting the default burden of loss in an imposter case to the subsequent holder, State Security, rather than the party who was in the best position to detect the fraud, the drawer, American General. . . .

. . . [T]he trial court's ruling in favor of American General is contrary to the position emphasized in Official Comment 3 of § 3-404 that "[i]f a check payable to an impostor ... is paid, the effect of subsections (a) and (b) is to place the loss on the drawer of the check rather than on the drawee or the Depositary Bank that took the check for collection." Md.Code, Com. Law Art. § 3-404 cmt. 3. This is due to the recognition that the "drawer is in the best position to avoid the fraud and thus should take the loss." Md.Code, Com. Law Art. § 3-404 cmt. 3. We found no evidence in the record of this case to suggest the application of this default rule would be inappropriate. . . .

Questions and Problems 2.15. Prompted by White and Summers, and given the clientele of check cashing facilities, judicial skepticism about the good faith and practices of check cashing firms might be justified, but one might like to see a little more evidence that check-cashing facilities are a home for persons engaged in fraudulent behavior before courts impose higher standards on these firms than might be applied to a bank. Do Drysdale and Keest have a better handle on the milieu of the typical check cashing operation? Would you be willing to bet that neither White nor Summers have ever entered a check cashing location?

2.16. *Thumb on the Scale*? In *State Security Check Cashing*, American General relied on *Messing* to support its argument that if State Security had asked the imposter for his thumbprint before cashing the check, it was likely that the imposter would not have proceeded. The *State Security Check Cashing* opinion rejected this argument, explaining:

> Although being asked for a thumbprint may serve as a powerful deterrent to those attempting to pass bad checks, we cannot accept American General's position here, without more support, that an imposter, who already went to the lengths of securing two years of Mr. Wilder's tax returns and much of his personal information for the forged driver's license and credit applications, likely would have stopped short of completing this theft by being asked for his thumbprint.

State Sec. Check Cashing, Inc., 409 Md. at 108 n.18. In light of all of this, would you recommend that Issuer Bank participate in the thumbprint program? Should it make a thumbprint a required part of the procedure for checking a check presented by a non-depositor?

MAINE FAMILY FED. CREDIT UNION V. SUN LIFE ASSURANCE CO.
727 A.2d 335 (Me. 1999)

SAUFLEY, J.

We are called upon here to address the concept of "holder in due course" as defined by recent amendments to the negotiable instruments provisions of the Maine Uniform Commercial Code. We conclude that, pursuant to those amendments, the Superior Court . . . did not err when it entered a judgment based on the jury's finding that the Maine Family Federal Credit Union was not a holder in due course. Because we find, however, that Sun Life Assurance Company was not entitled to raise a third party's defense of fraud to its liability as drawer of the instruments, we vacate that portion of the judgment entered in favor of Sun Life and against the Credit Union.

I. Facts

Daniel, Joel, and Claire Guerrette are the adult children of Elden Guerrette, who died on September 24, 1995. Before his death, Elden had purchased a life insurance policy from Sun Life Assurance Company of Canada, through Sun Life's agent, Steven Hall, and had named his children as his beneficiaries. Upon his death, Sun Life issued three checks, each in the amount of $40,759.35, to each of Elden's children. The checks were drawn on Sun Life's account at Chase Manhattan Bank in Syracuse, New York. The checks were given to Hall for delivery to the Guerrettes.

The parties have stipulated that Hall and an associate, Paul Richard, then fraudulently induced the Guerrettes to indorse the checks in blank and to transfer them to Hall and Richard, purportedly to be invested in "HER, Inc.," a corporation formed by Hall and Richard. Hall took the checks from the Guerrettes and turned them over to Richard, who deposited them in his account at the Credit Union on October 26, 1995. The Credit Union immediately made the funds available to Richard.

The Guerrettes quickly regretted having negotiated their checks to Hall and Richard, and they contacted Sun Life the next day to request that Sun Life stop payment on the checks. Sun Life immediately ordered Chase Manhattan to stop payment on the checks. Thus, when the checks were ultimately presented to Chase Manhattan for payment, Chase refused to pay the checks, and they were returned to the Credit Union.

The Credit Union received notice that the checks had been dishonored on November 3, 1995, the sixth business day following their deposit. By that time, however, Richard had withdrawn from his account all of the funds represented by the three checks. The Credit Union was able to recover almost $80,000 from Richard, but there remained an unpaid balance of $42,366.56, the amount now in controversy.

The Credit Union filed a complaint against Sun Life alleging that Sun Life was liable as drawer of the instruments, and that Sun Life had been unjustly enriched at the Credit Union's expense. Although it could have done so, the Credit Union did not originally seek any recovery from the Guerrettes. Sun Life, however, filed a third-party complaint against Daniel Guerrette and Paul Richard, whose signatures appeared on the back of one of the checks. The Credit Union then filed a cross-claim against third-party defendants Guerrette and Richard, alleging that they were liable as indorsers of the checks,[8] and Daniel Guerrette filed cross-claims against the Credit Union and against Sun Life. Finally, Sun Life eventually filed third-party complaints against Joel and Claire Guerrette.

The Credit Union moved for summary judgment. The Superior Court held, as a matter of law, that Daniel Guerrette had raised a "claim of a property or possessory right in the instrument or its pro-

---

[8] Paul Richard ultimately consented to judgment being entered against him on the Credit Union's cross-claim.

ceeds," 11 M.R.S.A. § 3–1306 (1995), and therefore that Sun Life was entitled to assert that claim as a "defense" against the Credit Union. *See* 11 M.R.S.A. § 3–1305(3) (1995). The court found, however, that a genuine issue of material fact remained as to whether the Credit Union had acted in "good faith" when it gave value for the checks—a fact relevant to determining whether the Credit Union was a holder in due course. *See* 11 M.R.S.A. § 3–1302(1)(b)(ii) (1995). Accordingly, the court denied the Credit Union's motion for summary judgment, and the matter proceeded to trial.

. . . The jury found that the Credit Union had not acted in good faith and therefore was not a holder in due course. Therefore, the Superior Court entered judgment in favor of Sun Life, Daniel, Joel, and Claire, and against the Credit Union. The court denied the Credit Union's renewed motion for judgment as a matter of law and motion to amend the judgment, and the Credit Union filed this appeal.

II. Obligations of the Parties

At the heart of the controversy in this case is the allocation of responsibility for the loss of the unpaid $42,366.56, given the fact that Paul Richard and Steven Hall, the real wrongdoers, appear to be unable to pay. . . .

Pursuant to Article 4 of the Maine U.C.C., the Credit Union, as a depositary bank, is a "holder" of the instruments, *see* 11 M.R.S.A. § 4–205(1) (1995),[12] making it a "person entitled to enforce" the instrument under Article 3-A. *See* 11 M.R.S.A. § 3–1301(1) (1995). Upon producing an instrument containing the valid signature of a party liable on the instrument, a person entitled to enforce the instrument is entitled to payment, unless the party liable proves a defense or claim in recoupment, *see* 11 M.R.S.A. § 3–1308(2) (1995), or a possessory claim to the instrument itself. *See* 11 M.R.S.A. § 3–1306.

Because their signatures appear on the backs of the checks, Daniel, Joel, and Claire are "indorsers" of the checks. *See* 11 M.R.S.A. § 3–1204(1), (2) (1995). As indorsers, they are obligated to pay the

---

[12] 11 M.R.S.A. § 4–205(1) provides that a depositary bank becomes a holder of an item if the item was deposited by a customer who was also a holder. The Credit Union's customer, Paul Richard, became a holder of the checks when Daniel, Joel, and Claire indorsed them in blank and transferred them to Richard and Hall. *See* 11 M.R.S.A. § 3-1201(1) (1995) (" 'Negotiation' means a transfer of possession, whether voluntary or involuntary, of an instrument by a person other than the issuer to a person who thereby becomes its holder."); 11 M.R.S.A. § 3-1202(1)(b) (1995) ("Negotiation is effective even if obtained ... [b]y fraud.").

amounts due on each dishonored instrument "[a]ccording to the terms of [each] instrument at the time it was indorsed." 11 M.R.S.A. § 3-1415(1)(a) (1995).[13] This obligation is owed "to a person entitled to enforce the instrument or to a subsequent indorser who paid the instrument under this section." *Id.*

As drawer of the checks, Sun Life is obligated to pay each dishonored instrument "[a]ccording to its terms at the time it was issued." 11 M.R.S.A. § 3-1414(2)(a) (1995). Again, this obligation is owed to a person entitled to enforce the instrument or to an indorser who paid the draft under section 3-1415. *See* 11 M.R.S.A. § 3-1414(2) (1995). Chase Manhattan, as drawee of these checks, was not obligated to accept them for payment, *see* 11 M.R.S.A. § 3-1408 (1995), and therefore has not been made a party to this action.

Unless the Credit Union is a holder in due course, its right to enforce the obligations of the drawer and indorsers of the instruments is subject to a variety of defenses, including all those defenses available "if the person entitled to enforce the instrument[s] were enforcing a right to payment under a simple contract." *See* 11 M.R.S.A. § 3-1305(1)(b) (1995). In addition, its right to enforce is subject to any claims in recoupment, *see* 11 M.R.S.A. § 3-1305(1)(c) (1995), or claims to the instruments themselves. *See* 11 M.R.S.A. § 3-1306. If, however, the Credit Union establishes that it is a "holder in due course," it is subject to only those few defenses listed in section 3-1305(1)(a). *See* 11 M.R.S.A. § 3-1305(2) (1995). None of those specific defenses is applicable here. Thus, the Credit Union argues that because it is entitled as a matter of law to holder in due course status, it is entitled to enforce the instruments against the Guerrettes and Sun Life.

III. Holder in Due Course

A. Burden of Proof and Standard of Review

A holder in due course is a holder who takes an instrument in good faith, for value, and without notice of any claims or defenses. *See* 11 M.R.S.A. § 3-1302(1) (1995). Once the persons who may be liable on the instruments have raised a recognized defense to that liability, the burden is on the holder to prove by a preponderance of the evidence that it is a holder in due course. *See New Bedford Inst. for Sav. v. Gildroy*, 36 Mass.App.Ct. 647, 634 N.E.2d 920, 925 (1994). If it fails in

---

[13] If, however, the instrument is accepted for payment, if the instrument is not presented for payment in a timely fashion, or if notice of dishonor is not given to an indorser in a timely fashion, her indorser's liability is discharged. *See* 11 M.R.S.A. § 3-1415(3)-(5) (1995).

that proof, the persons otherwise liable on the instruments may avoid liability if they prove a defense, claim in recoupment, or possessory claim to the instrument. *See* 11 M.R.S.A. §§ 3-1305(1)(b), 3-1308(2).

The issue of whether a party is a holder in due course is usually one of fact, although "where the facts are undisputed and conclusive, [a court] can determine ... holder in due course status as a matter of law." *See Triffin v. Dillabough*, 552 Pa. 550, 716 A.2d 605, 611 (1998). In this case, the Superior Court declined to decide the holder in due course issue as a matter of law, and submitted the question to the jury. The jury found that the Credit Union was not a holder in due course, implicitly because the Credit Union did not act in good faith.

The Credit Union argues that the court erred in failing to find, as a matter of law, that it was a holder in due course. . . . The question before us . . . is whether any reasonable view of the evidence, along with any justifiable inferences therefrom, can possibly support the jury's conclusion that the Credit Union did not act in good faith and therefore was not a holder in due course. Alternatively stated, the question is whether the evidence compelled a finding that the Credit Union was a holder in due course. If there is any rational basis for the jury's verdict, we must affirm the judgment.

B. Good Faith

We therefore turn to the definition of "good faith" contained in Article 3-A of the Maine U.C.C.15 In 1990, the National Conference of Commissioners on Uniform State Law recommended substantial changes in the U.C.C. The Maine Legislature responded to those recommendations in 1993 by repealing the entirety of Article 3 and enacting a new version entitled Article 3-A, which contains a new definition of "good faith." While the previous version of the good faith definition only required holder to prove that it acted with "honesty in fact," the new definition [requires "honesty in fact *and the observance of reasonable commercial standards of fair dealing.*" UCC § 3-103(1)(d) (emphasis added)]. Because the tests are presented in the conjunctive, a holder must now satisfy both a subjective and an objective test of "good faith."

1. Honesty in Fact

Prior to the changes adopted by the Legislature in 1993, the holder in due course doctrine turned on a subjective standard of good faith and was often referred to as the "pure heart and empty head" standard. *See* M.B.W. Sinclair, *Codification of Negotiable Instruments Law:*

A Tale of Reiterated Anachronism, 21 U. TOL. L.REV. 625, 654 (1990); *see also Seinfeld v. Commercial Bank & Trust Co.*, 405 So.2d 1039, 1042 (Fla.Dist.Ct.App.1981) (noting that the U.C.C. "seem[s] to protect the objectively stupid so long as he is subjectively pure at heart"). That standard merely required a holder to take an instrument with "honesty in fact" to become a holder in due course. . . .

Application of the "honesty in fact" standard to the Credit Union's conduct here demonstrates these principles at work. It is undisputed that the Credit Union had no knowledge that Richard obtained the Sun Life checks by fraud. Nor was the Credit Union aware that a stop payment order had been placed on the Sun Life checks. The Credit Union expeditiously gave value on the checks, having no knowledge that they would be dishonored. In essence the Credit Union acted as banks have, for years, been allowed to act without risk to holder in due course status. The Credit Union acted with honesty in fact. . . .

2. Reasonable Commercial Standards of Fair Dealing

We turn then to the objective prong of the good faith analysis. The addition of the language requiring the holder to prove conduct meeting "reasonable commercial standards of fair dealing" signals a significant change in the definition of a holder in due course. While there has been little time for the development of a body of law interpreting this new objective requirement, there can be no mistaking the fact that a holder may no longer act with a pure heart and an empty head and still obtain holder in due course status. The pure heart of the holder must now be accompanied by reasoning that assures conduct comporting with reasonable commercial standards of fair dealing. . . .

The new objective standard, however, is not a model of drafting clarity. Although use of the word "reasonable" in the objective portion of the good faith test may evoke concepts of negligence, the drafters attempted to distinguish the concept of "fair" dealing from concepts of "careful" dealing:

> Although fair dealing is a broad term that must be defined in context, it is clear that it is concerned with the fairness of conduct rather than the care with which an act is performed. Failure to exercise ordinary care in conducting a transaction is an entirely different concept than failure to deal fairly in conducting the transaction.

U.C.C. § 3–103 cmt. 4 (1991).

Unfortunately, the ease with which the distinction between "fair dealing" and "careful dealing" was set forth in the comments to the U.C.C. revisions belies the difficulty in applying these concepts to the facts of any particular case, or in conveying them to a jury. The difficulty is exacerbated by the lack of definition of the term "fair dealing" in the U.C.C. The most obvious question arising from the use of the term "fair" is: fairness to whom? Transactions involving negotiable instruments have traditionally required the detailed level of control and definition of roles set out in the U.C.C. precisely because there are so many parties who may be involved in a single transaction. If a holder is required to act "fairly," regarding all parties, it must engage in an almost impossible balancing of rights and interests. Accordingly, the drafters limited the requirement of fair dealing to conduct that is reasonable in the commercial context of the transaction at issue. In other words, the holder must act in a way that is fair according to commercial standards that are themselves reasonable.

The factfinder must therefore determine, first, whether the conduct of the holder comported with industry or "commercial" standards applicable to the transaction and, second, whether those standards were reasonable standards intended to result in fair dealing. Each of those determinations must be made in the context of the specific transaction at hand. If the factfinder's conclusion on each point is "yes," the holder will be determined to have acted in good faith even if, in the individual transaction at issue, the result appears unreasonable. Thus a holder may be accorded holder in due course status where it acts pursuant to those reasonable commercial standards of fair dealing – even if it is negligent – but may lose that status, even where it complies with commercial standards, if those standards are not reasonably related to achieving fair dealing.

Therefore the jury's task here was to decide whether the Credit Union observed the banking industries' commercial standards relating to the giving of value on uncollected funds, and, if so, whether those standards are reasonably designed to result in fair dealing.

The evidence produced by the Credit Union in support of its position that it acted in accordance with objective good faith included the following: The Credit Union's internal policy was to make provisional credit available immediately upon the deposit of a check by one of its members. In certain circumstances – where the check was for a large amount and where it was drawn on an out-of-state bank – its policy allowed for a hold to be placed on the uncollected funds for up to nine days. The Credit Union's general written policy on this issue was reviewed annually – and had always been approved – by the National Credit Union Administration, the federal agency charged with the duty of regulating federal credit unions. *See* 12 U.S.C.A. § 1752a (Law.Co-op. 1996). In addition, the policy complied with applicable banking laws, including Regulation CC. *See* 12 C.F.R. §§ 229.12(c), 229.13(b) (1998).

The Credit Union also presented evidence that neither Regulation CC nor the Credit Union's internal policy required it to hold the checks or to investigate the genesis of checks before extending provisional credit. It asserted that it acted exactly as its policy and the law allowed when it immediately extended provisional credit on these checks, despite the fact that they were drawn for relatively large amounts on an out-of-state bank.[22] Finally, the Credit Union presented expert testimony that most credit unions in Maine follow similar policies.

In urging the jury to find that the Credit Union had not acted in good faith, Sun Life and the Guerrettes argued that the Credit Union's conduct did not comport with reasonable commercial standards of fair dealing when it allowed its member access to provisional credit on checks totalling over $120,000 drawn on an out-of-state bank without either: (1) further investigation to assure that the deposited checks would be paid by the bank upon which they were drawn, or (2) holding the instruments to allow any irregularities to come to light.

The applicable federal regulations provide the outside limit on the Credit Union's ability to hold the checks. Although the limit on allowable holds established by law is evidence to be considered by the jury, it does not itself establish reasonable commercial standard of fair dealing. The factfinder must consider all of the facts relevant to the transaction. The amount of the checks and the location of the payor bank, however, are relevant facts that a bank, observing reasonable commercial standards of fair dealing, takes into account when deciding whether to place such a hold on the account. The jury was entitled to consider that, under Regulation CC, when a check in an amount greater than $5,000 is deposited, or when a check is payable by a nonlocal bank, a credit union is permitted to withhold provisional credit for longer periods of time than it is allowed in other circumstances. *See* 12 C.F.R. § 229.13(b), (h) (1998). Therefore, the size of the check and the location of the payor bank are, under the objective standard of good faith, factors which a jury may also consider when deciding whether a depositary bank is a holder in due course.

The Credit Union's President admitted the risks inherent in the Credit Union's policy and admitted that it would not have been difficult to place a hold on these funds for the few days that it would normally take for the payor bank to pay the checks. He conceded that the

---

[22] The Credit Union could also have withheld provisional credit under the law and its own internal policy if there were other reasons to doubt the validity of the checks. *See* 12 C.F.R. § 229.13(e) (1998).

amount of the checks were relatively large, that they were drawn on an out-of-state bank, and that these circumstances "could have" presented the Credit Union with cause to place a hold on the account. He also testified to his understanding that some commercial banks followed a policy of holding nonlocal checks for three business days before giving provisional credit.[23] Moreover, the Credit Union had no written policy explicitly guiding its staff regarding the placing of a hold on uncollected funds. Rather, the decision on whether to place a temporary hold on an account was left to the "comfort level" of the teller accepting the deposit. There was no dispute that the amount of the three checks far exceeded the $5,000 threshold for a discretionary hold established by the Credit Union's own policy.

On these facts the jury could rationally have concluded that the reasonable commercial standard of fair dealing would require the placing of a hold on the uncollected funds for a reasonable period of time and that, in giving value under these circumstances, the Credit Union did not act according to commercial standards that were reasonably structured to result in fair dealing. . . .

IV. Effect of Fraud Defense

A. The Guerrettes

Having failed to persuade the jury that it was a holder in due course, the Credit Union is subject to any defense of the Guerrettes or Sun Life "that would be available if the person entitled to enforce the instrument were enforcing a right to payment under a simple contract," 11 M.R.S.A. § 3-1305(1)(b), or any "claim of a property or possessory right in the instrument or its proceeds." 11 M.R.S.A. § 3-1306. Generally, fraud, such as that perpetrated by Paul Richard and Steven Hall, may be the basis for both a valid defense, *see Silber v. Muschel*, 190 A.D.2d 727, 593 N.Y.S.2d 306, 307 (1993), and a valid claim to the instrument itself. *See generally Bowling Green, Inc. v. State St. Bank & Trust Co.*, 307 F.Supp. 648, 651–52 (D.Mass.1969), aff'd, 425 F.2d 81 (1st Cir.1970).

Fraud is an affirmative defense to a contract. . . .To prevail on their fraud defense, the Guerrettes were required to prove, by clear and convincing evidence, that a fraudulent or material misrepresentation induced them to transfer the proceeds of their father's life insurance policy, in the form of the Sun Life checks, to Steven Hall and

---

[23] There was evidence that, on the second business day after he deposited the checks, Paul Richard notified the Credit Union that there may have been a problem with his deposit.

Paul Richard. In addition, they were required to prove they were justified in relying on the fraudulent misrepresentation. *See Kuperman v. Eiras*, 586 A.2d 1260, 1261 (Me.1991). The parties' stipulation that Hall and Richard fraudulently induced the Guerrettes to invest the checks in their company, HER, Inc., is sufficient to satisfy the Guerrettes' burden on this issue. The Guerrettes are not liable to the Credit Union for their indorsement of the Sun Life checks.

B. Sun Life

Sun Life, however, may not raise the fraud as a defense to its liability on the instrument. [The court quotes from UCC § 3-305(3).]

. . . Accordingly, a defense to liability on an instrument – such as fraud in the underlying transaction – raised by one party to an action may not be raised by another party to the action as its own defense to liability. Section 3-1305(3) provides, however, that "the other person's claim to the instrument may be asserted by the obligor if the other person is joined in the action and personally asserts the claim against the person entitled to enforce the instrument." *Id*. Therefore, only if the Guerrettes have made a claim to the instrument and are parties to the proceeding may Sun Life assert the fraud in defense of its own liability. *See* 11 M.R.S.A. 3-1305(3); *First Nat'l Bank of Nocona v. Duncan Sav. & Loan Ass'n*, 656 F.Supp. 358, 366 (W.D.Okla.1987), aff'd, 957 F.2d 775 (10th Cir.1992).

The Guerrettes, however, made no claim that they were entitled to possession of the instruments held by the Credit Union.[25] Instead, they merely argued that they were not liable as indorsers of the checks held by the Credit Union as a result of the fraud. The issue of fraud was therefore raised by the Guerrettes as a defense to their liability as indorsers of the instruments. *See Louis Falcigno Enters., Inc. v. Massachusetts Bank & Trust Co.*, 14 Mass.App.Ct. 92, 436 N.E.2d 993, 993–94 (1982). The Superior Court erred when it held that the issue of fraud had been raised as a "claim to the instruments."

Therefore, Sun Life may not raise the fraud against the Guerrettes as a defense to its own liability. Because Sun Life raises no other relevant defenses, it is liable to the Credit Union as the drawer of the instruments, *see* 11 M.R.S.A. § 3-1414(2)(a), and we vacate that portion of the Superior Court's judgment finding that Sun Life was not liable to the Credit Union.

---

[25] The Guerrettes were issued new checks for the same amounts by Sun Life after Sun Life stopped payment on the original instruments.

Questions and Problems 2.17. As *Maine Family* notes, the change in the definition of "good faith," adding an "objective" requirement, was intended to work a substantial effect on the way in which disputes about a payment are resolved – since denial of HDC status to a paying bank exposes it to a wider range of potential defenses. As a practical matter, of course, whether the objective requirement has been satisfied is often hotly disputed, and the requirement itself has been subjected to significant probing in the scholarly literature, focusing on the reason, meaning, and anticipated interpretations of the requirement. *See, e.g.,* Patricia L. Heatherman, Comment, *Good Faith in Revised Article 3 of the Uniform Commercial Code: Any Change? Should There Be?* 29 WILLAMETTE L. REV. 567 (1993); Kerry Lynn Macintosh, *Liberty, Trade, and the Uniform Commercial Code, When Should Default Rules be Based on Business Practices?* 38 WM. & MARY L. REV. 1465, 1466 (1997). If BayerCorp instructs Issuer Bank to place a stop payment on the check it issued to SallerCo, but in the interim SallerCo deposited the check in its account in Second Bank, which then credited SallerCo's account, how would you advise Second Bank when Issuer Bank refuses to pay? What issues should Second Bank be prepared to address if the dispute results in litigation?

2.18. The concept of good faith has other uses in commercial law. Assume that BayerCorp entered into a contract with SallerCo to purchase 100,000 motorized thingots for $600,000. With the delivery date still five weeks away, BayerCorp hires Hyram Lowe, a design engineer previously employed by SallerCo. Hy explains to a BayerCorp manager that, using a different design process, the company could produce thingots on their own at half the cost – they could install standard SallerCo motors in them for an additional cost of $80,000 for the motors and $20,000 in in-house labor. The BayerCorp supply manager writes to SallerCo cancelling the purchase order, "due to a change in our market commitments." When SallerCo's sales manager calls the BayerCorp supply manager complaining about the cancellation, BayerCorp offers to settle the dispute by purchasing 100,000 standard SallerCo motors for $80,000. BayerCorp then sends a letter to SallerCo outlining the terms of the settlement and encloses a check for $40,000 "as a deposit for the purchase of the [motors], in full satisfaction of our past contract undertaking. Final payment of $40,000 to be paid upon receipt and satisfactory inspection of the shipment" of 100,000 standard SallerCo motors. SallerCo deposits the enclosed check, completes delivery of the motors in accordance with the terms in BayerCorp's letter, and receives a second check from BayerCorp for $40,000. Four weeks later, SallerCo's sales manager discovers that BayerCorp has outbid it for a public contract to provide motorized thingots to the U.S. Coast Guard. SallerCo sues BayerCorp for breach of the original sales contract, claiming $500,000 in damages for the breach, along with $150,000 for other tort and trade secrets claims. BayerCorp's principal defense is that any previous contract liability was discharged as a result of the "accord and satisfaction" that it reached as a result of its letter. If you were advising SallerCo, what would you think is the likelihood that it would succeed in its suit against BayerCorp? In answering this question, consider the following case.

WEBB BUSINESS PROMOTIONS, INC. V. AMERICAN ELECTRONICS & ENTERTAINMENT CORP.
617 N.W.2d 67 (Minn. 2000)

LANCASTER, Justice.

This is an action for breach of contract between appellant, American Electronics & Entertainment Corp. (AE&E) and respondent, Webb Business Promotions, Inc. (Webb). Webb sued AE&E for breach of contract. AE&E asserted the affirmative defense of accord and satisfaction under Minn.Stat. § 336.3-311 (1998). [The court at this point quoted the Minnesota enactment of UCC § 3-311(a)-(b), Minnesota Statutes § 336.3-311(a)-(b), in a footnote.] Following a court trial, the district court found that there was no accord and satisfaction, concluding that there was an absence of good faith in the tender and no mutual agreement. The court of appeals affirmed, holding that mutual agreement is not required for an accord and satisfaction. We reverse the court of appeals and remand the matter to the district court.

We are presented in this case with two questions: First, did the district court err in imputing AE&E's bad faith in the underlying sales contract to AE&E's offer of an accord and satisfaction? Second, did the court of appeals err in holding that because mutual agreement is not explicitly enumerated in Minn.Stat. § 336.3-311, such agreement is not necessary to create an enforceable accord and satisfaction?

On May 16, 1995, AE&E entered into a contract with Target Corporation (Target). The agreement called for Target to purchase 300,000 units of three-pack MGM blank videotapes from AE&E, and AE&E was to provide 300,000 units of promotional merchandise (calendars, pencils and the like) as a "free gift with purchase" with each pack of videotapes. Subsequently, on May 24, 1995, AE&E executed a written contract with Webb in which Webb agreed to provide the 300,000 units of promotional merchandise to AE&E at a contract price of $684,000. In order to fulfill its part of the agreement between Webb and AE&E, Webb borrowed approximately $400,000 from First National Bank of Farmington, which in turn acquired a right of assignment of all funds due to Webb from AE&E. The contract between AE&E and Webb provided that AE&E would be responsible for any and all defects with respect to the MGM blank videotapes, that Webb would be expected to absorb $30,000 in advertising, packing, and shipping costs, and that delivery of the promotional merchandise was due on or before July 15, 1995.

On May 24, 1995, AE&E sent Webb purchase order # 604 for the 300,000 units of promotional merchandise. Purchase order # 604 specifically stated that it was "conti[n]gent upon Target['s] purchase order" with AE&E. Target's agreement with AE&E permitted Target to cancel its purchase order if the product was not up to Target's quality standards or at Target's sole convenience any time prior to shipping. AE&E never informed Webb of the conditions under which Target could cancel its purchase order with AE&E.

On May 4, 1995, more than two weeks before Webb entered into its contract with AE&E, Target requested that AE&E submit a sample of the MGM videotapes for quality testing. AE&E complied with the request. On May 31, 1995, approximately two weeks after Target issued its purchase order to AE&E, the quality testing service recommended that Target "stay away" from the MGM brand of videocassette "until they improve their quality." Target immediately notified AE&E that the tapes failed the quality test. On June 9, 1995, AE&E requested and Target agreed to re-test the videotapes at AE&E's expense. On June 23, 1995, the quality tester sent Target a second report, stating that the tapes were "satisfactory," but still had problems with consistency.

A few days prior to the July 15, 1995, delivery date for the promotional merchandise to AE&E from Webb, Target notified AE&E that it was canceling the transaction. In response, AE&E sent a representative to Target in an attempt to renegotiate the deal with Target. AE&E never notified Webb of the failed quality tests. AE&E was successful in renegotiating the deal but was only able to persuade Target to purchase 85,000 units of the videotape and promotional merchandise combination, instead of the 300,000 units originally agreed to. At trial, a Target representative testified that the primary reason for the reduction in the order was the poor test results of the MGM videotapes, but Target also considered the recent reduction in industry sales of blank videotapes.

On July 20, 1995, six days after the 300,000 units of promotional merchandise had arrived at the packaging location, AE&E sent a letter notifying Webb that based on Target's cancellation and renegotiation of its purchase order, AE&E was canceling its order with Webb and would thereafter place orders with Webb on a weekly basis. Alan Webb, [president and sole shareholder of Webb Business Promotions,] not knowing the terms of the arrangement between AE&E and Target, requested that AE&E cancel the order entirely and sue Target for breach. Alan Webb then contacted First National Bank of Farmington to let it know the status of the deal with AE&E. The bank directed him to follow through with the replacement order.

Webb ultimately agreed to deliver 85,000 units to AE&E based on Target's order to AE&E, although AE&E never issued an additional purchase order to Webb. Upon delivery, Webb submitted invoice # 11374 to AE&E for approximately $190,000 for payment by August 24, 1995. On September 20, 1995, because Webb had not yet received payment for invoice # 11374, Alan Webb placed a phone call to AE&E's vice president, Linda Tsai. Alan Webb requested immediate payment of the invoice. In response, Tsai asserted that the invoice was incorrect and that AE&E would deduct various costs from the payment, which would result in a payment of approximately $150,000 for the 85,000 units of promotional merchandise.

On September 20, 1995, AE&E sent a letter to Webb explicitly referencing purchase order # 604, referring to terms of the original May 24, 1995, agreement, and informing Webb that AE&E intended to deduct certain amounts for re-packaging and shipping from the total amount owed to Webb based upon the May 24 agreement. The letter also stated that AE&E intended to pay Webb on September 21, 1995, and that "[b]y accepting and cashing the check, Webb is assumed to agree that this is the final settlement and AE&E will owe nothing to Webb." On September 21, 1995, AE&E submitted a check as payment to Webb in the amount of $150,677. The check was accompanied by a letter stating in part, "[p]er our phone conversation * * * I am sending you the check as your favor [sic] * * *. Please be awared [sic] that this is a final check, AE&E will have no obligation to Webb as long as the check is cashed by Webb." After discussions regarding Alan Webb's concerns about accepting the check, First National Bank told him to accept the check. Alan Webb therefore accepted and deposited the check and gave the funds to the bank. In November 1995, AE&E sent a check for approximately $3,000 to Webb as a refund for unspent funds that it had withheld for shipping and packing costs.

Webb brought suit for breach of contract against AE&E seeking recovery of money due to him under the May 24, 1995, agreement as originally stated in purchase order # 604. AE&E asserted the affirmative defense of accord and satisfaction. At trial Webb asserted that the check for $150,677 was accepted to resolve the dispute surrounding the second agreement for delivery of the 85,000 units, and was not intended to resolve the claims relating to AE&E's breach of the first agreement for 300,000 units referenced by purchase order # 604. Further, Webb asserted that the check offering the accord and satisfaction was tendered in bad faith because AE&E had purposely withheld information from Webb with respect to the testing of the videotapes and because AE&E misinformed Webb about the terms of the contract between AE&E and Target. AE&E responded that the check and the accompanying communications clearly referenced purchase order # 604 and the May 24 agreement, and stated that the payment was intended to resolve all claims that Webb had against AE&E. AE&E argued that the original purchase order was expressly contingent on Target's order to AE&E and it was therefore entitled to reduce the amount of the order based on Target's change in its order to AE&E.

The district court found that AE&E breached its contract with Webb by anticipatory repudiation, that Webb did not know that Target's order with AE&E was cancelable at any time, and that AE&E's agent withheld the truth from Webb regarding the poor quality of the videotapes. The district court went on to find that if Webb had known of the quality failure of the videotapes when it first occurred, it could have ceased delivery as early as May 31, 1995. The district court concluded that AE&E acted in bad faith by wrongfully concealing material facts from Webb by failing to reveal: Target's request to test the tapes in early May 1995; the terms of sale and conditions of the contract between AE&E and Target; the true reason why Target cancelled its purchase order on July 14, 1995; and the results of the quality assurance tests. The court also found that AE&E acted in bad faith by affirmatively representing to Webb that the tape quality had never been questioned by Target. Finally, the court concluded that the parties did not mutually agree that Webb was accepting the payment in full satisfaction of all outstanding claims. The district court therefore held that Webb's acceptance of AE&E's check for $150,677 did not constitute an accord and satisfaction.

The court of appeals held that the district court did not err in concluding that there was no accord and satisfaction because AE&E tendered its check with the knowledge that there were "outstanding obligations in dispute," and therefore the accord and satisfaction check was not tendered in good faith. . . . The court of appeals also held that mutual agreement is not required for an accord and satisfaction.

I.

An accord is a contract in which a debtor offers a sum of money, or some other stated performance, in exchange for which a creditor promises to accept the performance in lieu of the original debt. . . . *See generally* Restatement (Second) of Contracts § 281 (1981). . . . The satisfaction is the performance of the accord, generally the acceptance of money, which operates to discharge the debtor's duty as agreed to in the accord. . . . The purpose of accord and satisfaction is to allow parties to resolve disputes without judicial intervention by discharging all rights and duties under a contract in exchange for a stated performance, usually a payment of a sum of money. *See* U.C.C. § 3-311 cmt. 3 (1990). . . .

An enforceable accord and satisfaction arises when a party against whom a claim of breach of contract is asserted proves that (1) the party, in good faith, tendered an instrument to the claimant as full satisfaction of the claim; (2) the instrument or an accompanying written communication contained a conspicuous statement to the effect that the instrument was tendered as full satisfaction of the claim; (3) the amount of the claim was unliquidated or subject to a bona fide dispute; and (4) the claimant obtained payment of the instrument. *See* Minn.Stat. § 336.3-311(a)-(b).[4] . . .

Whether there has been an accord and satisfaction is a question of fact. . . . However, "[f]indings of fact which are controlled or influenced by error of law are not final on appeal and will be set aside." *In re Holden's Trust*, 207 Minn. 211, 227, 291 N.W. 104, 112 (1940).

Good faith is demonstrated when the party tendering the instrument offers a check with the intent to honestly enter into an accord and satisfaction while observing reasonable commercial standards of fair dealing. *See* Minn.Stat. § 336.3-103(a)(4) (1998). The focus of the good faith inquiry is on the offer of the accord, and not on the actions of the parties in performing the underlying contract. *See* Minn.Stat. § 336.3-311(a)(i); *cf.* U.C.C. § 3-311 cmt. 4 (1990). ...

Bad faith is not necessarily established by a failure to disclose facts about the underlying dispute that would have led to rejection of the offer of an accord. By accepting a certain sum of money to discharge a debt, the creditor waives a cause of action relating to the original debt. . . . Therefore, part of the consideration for the accord is the creditor's waiver of claims that may entitle it to more than what the debtor is offering in the accord. Once the creditor accepts the accord and performs the satisfaction, the validity of the accord and satisfaction may not be challenged unless the party challenging the accord can demonstrate that the elements of the accord and satisfaction have not been satisfied. . . .

---

[4] In 1990 the common law doctrines of accord and satisfaction were codified into section 3-311 of the U.C.C. which, in turn, was adopted by the legislature in 1992. *Cf.* U.C.C. § 3-311 cmt. 3. . . ; Act of Apr. 24, 1992, ch. 565, § 39, 1992 Minn. Laws 1816, 1842, codified at Minn.Stat. § 336.3-311 (1998). . . .

In support of their arguments regarding good faith both parties rely on *McMahon Food Corp. v. Burger Dairy Co.*, 103 F.3d 1307 (7th Cir.1996). In Illinois, as in Minnesota, a party must prove that he or she acted in good faith in tendering an instrument in full satisfaction of a claim. . . . In *McMahon Food Corp.*, McMahon and Burger Dairy had an ongoing business relationship. . . . The debtor (McMahon), in tendering the instrument for the offer of the accord, purposely misled the creditor about the amount in dispute. . . . . In attempting to resolve a dispute regarding multiple transactions, McMahon purposely led Burger Dairy to believe that previous disputes had already been resolved, when in fact they had not. . . . As a result, the accord and satisfaction that was offered misrepresented the actual amount in dispute. The bad faith was directly related to the tender of the accord, and not purely related to McMahon's actions with respect to the underlying contracts, and the district court found accord and satisfaction to be unenforceable. . . .

The court in *McMahon* affirmed the district court's finding that McMahon had acted in bad faith and taken advantage of Burger Dairy by misinforming it about the total amount in dispute " 'at the time payment was tendered.' " . . . McMahon therefore failed to meet section 3-311(a)'s good faith requirement. ... In contrast, the district court here relied exclusively on AE&E's misrepresentations and concealment of facts related to the underlying sales contract. The district court made no findings relating specifically to AE&E's tender of the instrument offering the accord. Moreover, neither Webb nor the district court established a connection between AE&E's conduct as it related to the underlying sales contract and its offer of the accord. We conclude, therefore, that the district court erred as a matter of law in finding AE&E's tender of its check to Webb under Minn.Stat. § 336.3-311 was in bad faith. *See generally Shema v. Thorpe Bros.*, 240 Minn. 459, 62 N.W.2d 86 (1953). It may be possible that fraud or misrepresentation relating to an underlying contract is so pervasive that the fraud infects the good faith offer of an accord. However, where the district court fails to draw any connection between fraud in the underlying contract and the tender of the accord, such as in this case, those circumstances are not present. Because the district court's finding of bad faith was controlled by an error of law, we set the finding aside. ...

The court of appeals reasoned that because AE&E offered the accord with the knowledge that there were outstanding obligations in dispute, good faith was lacking. Section 336.3-311(a)(ii) requires that there be a bona fide dispute as to the amount of the claim or that the claim was unliquidated for an accord and satisfaction to be valid. The purpose of entering into an accord and satisfaction is to settle these disputed claims. Therefore, the existence of a dispute regarding the amount of the underlying claim cannot constitute bad faith for purposes of an accord and satisfaction.

We reverse the decision of the court of appeals and hold that the district court erred as a matter of law in finding that AE&E's offer of the accord to Webb was in bad faith based on the conduct relating to the underlying sales contract. Because the district court did not focus on the formation of the accord and satisfaction in determining good faith, we remand to the district court for that determination.

II.

We turn now to the second issue: Did the court of appeals err in holding that because mutual agreement is not explicitly enumerated in Minn.Stat. § 336.3-311, such agreement is not necessary to create an enforceable accord and satisfaction?

Under common law, accord and satisfaction may not be found where mutual agreement is lacking. . . . For an accord and satisfaction to be enforceable, the payment must be offered in full satisfaction of the debt, and the payment must be accepted as the same. . . .

As noted above, Minn.Stat. § 336.3-311 was intended to codify the common law elements of accord and satisfaction. . . . The common law elements include the basic contractual requirement of mutual agreement and therefore the court of appeals erred in holding that mutual agreement was not necessary for an accord and satisfaction under Minn.Stat. § 336.3-311.

AE&E argues that even if we conclude that mutual agreement is a separate element of an accord and satisfaction under the U.C.C., it is demonstrated here by the conduct of the parties. The district court made no specific factual findings with respect to the formation of the accord and satisfaction. The court simply concluded that the parties did not agree that Webb was accepting payment in full satisfaction.

The agreement necessary to form a contract need not be express, but may be implied from circumstances that clearly and unequivocally indicate the intention of the parties to enter into a contract. . . . Minnesota Statutes § 336.3-311(a) and (b) require a conspicuous statement that the tender of payment is offered as full satisfaction of the claim. By obtaining payment under that conspicuous statement, the creditor has communicated his agreement to the transaction. Performance of the statutory requirements therefore demonstrates a mutual agreement to effectuate a contract in which the creditor accepts payment from the debtor that serves to discharge claims against the debtor.

We hold that once the elements of section 336.3-311(a) and (b) are met, mutual agreement of the parties to enter into an accord and satisfaction is presumed as a matter of law. The presumption may be rebutted where the party challenging the accord and satisfaction can demonstrate, for example, some ambiguity in the language of the instrument or the accompanying communication such that a reasonable person would not have understood that payment was meant to discharge the obligation. . . .

Because the district court did not make findings regarding the formation of the accord and satisfaction, or determine whether ambiguity exists with respect to the offer of an accord that would defeat a finding of mutual agreement on the accord and satisfaction, we remand this case to the district court for findings as to whether any ambiguity existed sufficient to rebut the presumption of mutual agreement.

We hold that the district court erred in imputing bad faith to an accord and satisfaction from conduct relating only to the underlying contract. We also hold that mutual agreement is required for an enforceable accord and satisfaction.

C. PROPERTY CLAIMS

In § 2.A.3, *supra*, we saw that an instrument can be characterized as property, although our focus tends to be on the rights and obligations associated with negotiation, rather than the "bundle of rights" that is typically the focus of property law analysis. This section considers the extent to which property law concepts might influence the way in which the legal principles relevant to negotiable instruments are analyzed and applied.

Questions and Problems 2.19. In the following two cases, consider the extent to which property law concepts are in play, and the extent to which such concepts have any impact on the cases.

DIXON, LAUKITIS, AND DOWNING, P.C. V. BUSEY BANK
993 N.E.2d 580 (Ill. App. 2013)

Justice O'BRIEN delivered the judgment of the court, with opinion.

Plaintiff Dixon, Laukitis, & Downing, P.C. (DLD) filed this negligence action against defendant Busey Bank, alleging that Busey breached a duty of ordinary care it owed DLD regarding a fraudulent check DLD deposited and drew against, which was later determined to be uncollectible. The trial court dismissed the complaint on Busey's motion and DLD appealed. We affirm. . . .

Plaintiff Dixon, Laukitis & Downing, P.C. is a law firm that maintained its client trust account at defendant Busey Bank. On May 25, 2011, DLD deposited into its trust account a check from one of its clients in the amount of $350,000. The check was drawn on the account of Intact Insurance Company at Royal Bank of Canada in Toronto, Ontario. The check was marked, "US Funds" and "This Cheque contains a true security watermark—hold at an angle to view." On June 6, 2011, DLD transferred $210,000 from its trust account to the client who provided the $350,000 check. On June 8, 2011, DLD transferred $60,000 from the trust account to the client. On June 10, 2011, the check was returned to Busey uncollected, and Busey notified DLD and charged back $350,000 to DLD's account the same day.

DLD filed a complaint sounding in negligence in January 2012. After the complaint was dismissed without prejudice for failure to state a claim ..., DLD filed an amended complaint in April 2012. In its amended complaint, DLD alleged that Busey owed it "a duty to act with ordinary care by observing such reasonable commercial standards as prevail in the area where the Bank conducts business" and that the Bank breached its duty by failing to inquire as to the circumstances of how DLD acquired the check; to recognize the check as counterfeit and inform DLD; to advise DLD that funds should not be withdrawn until final payment given the nature of the check and the account; and to notify DLD at the "earliest time it knew or should have known that the Check would not be paid by the drawee bank."

Busey filed a motion to dismiss. . . . Attached to its motion to dismiss was the account agreement DLD executed with Busey when the law firm established the client trust account. The agreement provided that it was subject to all applicable state and federal laws, except where varied in the agreement, and that the account holders "agree to be jointly and severally (individually) liable for any account shortage resulting from charges or overdrafts." The agreement further stated, in pertinent part: "DEPOSITS—We will give only provisional credit until collection is final for any items, other than cash, we accept for deposit (including items drawn 'on us')." Also attached to Busey's motion to dismiss was the affidavit of Daniel Daly, executive vice president/market president of Busey Bank. He attested "[t]here was nothing on the face of this Check that gave any indication that it may not be genuine or that it may be dishonored"; the check complied with the requirements for a negotiable instrument under section 3-104 of the Uniform Commercial Code (UCC) . . . ; the Bank provided written and oral notice to DLD on June 10, 2011, the same day the Bank was informed the check was uncollectible; and the Bank charged back $350,000 against DLD's account per the account agreement.

A hearing took place on the Bank's motion to dismiss and the trial court issued a verbal ruling granting the motion. Thereafter, the trial court issued a written order. . . . The trial court stated the motion to dismiss was granted "for all the reasons stated by the Court in its verbal Ruling from the Bench." The record on appeal does not contain a transcript from the hearing. The trial court also issued a supplemental order in which it found that Busey did not owe DLD a duty under the common law because the UCC provides a comprehensive remedy for check processing which places the risk of loss on the depositor until final collection. In a supplemental order, the trial court also held that DLD's complaint was barred under the *Moorman* doctrine. DLD appealed.

ANALYSIS

The issue on appeal is whether the trial court erred when it granted Busey's motion to dismiss DLD's negligence complaint. . . .

. . . The existence of a duty is a question of law to be determined by the trial court. . . . The UCC governs the relationship between a bank and its customer. . . . The principles of law and equity supplement the UCC unless they are displaced by a particular provision in the UCC. [UCC § 1-103(b).] Article 4 of the UCC governs bank deposits and collections. It sets forth a bank's general duty to exercise ordinary care and states that "action or non-action approved by this Article * * * is the exercise of ordinary care and, in the absence of special instructions, action or non-action consistent * * * with a general banking usage not disapproved by this Article, is prima facie the exercise of ordinary care." [UCC § 4-103(c).]

A bank that takes an item is a "Depository Bank" and a bank that handles an item for collection and is not a drawee of the draft is a "Collecting Bank." [UCC § 4-105.] A collecting bank acts as an agent of an item's owner until final settlement of the item and "any settlement given for the item is provisional." [UCC § 4-201(a).] In addition, a collecting bank has a superior right over the item's owner to a setoff if an item does not settle. [*Id.*]

The UCC does not enumerate duties for a depository bank but section 4-202 sets forth the responsibilities for a collecting bank. . . .

Section 4–214(a) provides that a collecting bank may charge back a customer's account when the bank makes provisional settlement but does not receive final payment on an item if the collecting bank gives notice to its customer by midnight of the next banking day. [UCC § 4-214(a).]

Provisions such as section 4-202 of the UCC displace common law negligence principles; UCC compliance is nonnegligent as a matter of law. *Merrill Lynch, Pierce, Fenner & Smith, Inc. v. Devon Bank*, 702 F.Supp. 652, 665 (N.D.Ill.1988). The standards set forth in section 4-202 are "a restatement" of the common law negligence standard in that they define the applicable standard of care. . . . The UCC's provisions may also be varied by an agreement of the parties but a bank's responsibility for its failure to exercise ordinary care cannot be disclaimed. [UCC § 4-103(a).] An agreement between the parties may set forth the standards to measure the bank's responsibility so long as the standards are not manifestly unreasonable. . . . The relationship between a bank and its account holders is contractual in nature and one of creditor and debtor. *Continental Casualty Co. v. American National Bank & Trust Co. of Chicago*, 329 Ill.App.3d 686, 692, 263 Ill.Dec. 592, 768 N.E.2d 352 (2002). An account holder agreement executed between a bank and its customer creates a binding contract. . . . Under the common law, a collecting bank does not owe a duty to its customer to inspect a check later determined to be counterfeit. *Sibley v. Central Trust Co. of Illinois*, 226 Ill.App. 180, 186 (1922). . . .

We disagree with DLD's conclusion that Busey owed it a common law duty of reasonable care. Under the facts as set forth in DLD's amended complaint and available in the record, the duty owed to DLD by Busey was defined under the parties' account agreement and the UCC. The account agreement placed the risk of loss on DLD until final settlement of the $350,000 check. This provision applied whether Busey acted as a depository bank or a collecting bank. The language in the agreement tracks the risk of loss language of the UCC. DLD opted to write checks based on the $350,000 deposit before final settlement. The terms of the account agreement did not require Busey to investigate the genuineness of the check or specially warn DLD not to rely on the funds until the deposited check settled. Because DLD bore the risk of loss under the agreement, it cannot state a claim for the Bank's negligence based on its own withdrawal of funds before the check was finally settled. Moreover, as stated under the account agreement, applicable UCC provisions also governed the responsibilities between the parties. As a collecting bank, Busey's duties were enumerated in section 4-202 of the UCC. In its amended complaint, DLD did not allege that Busey breached any duties under section 4-202 in collecting or processing the counterfeit check. Rather, DLD alleged that Busey failed to exercise ordinary care in that it did not follow prevailing reasonable commercial banking standards, which it asserts includes investigating the circumstances regarding the check, recognizing it as counterfeit, advising DLD not to withdraw funds until final settlement, and notifying DLD at the earliest time that it was dishonored.

DLD maintains that the section 4-202 ordinary care standard only applies to the timeliness of the actions and not to whether they were performed in accordance with the ordinary care. We disagree. Under section 4-202, a collecting bank exercises ordinary care when it presents an item, sends notice of dishonor, finally settles an item, or timely notifies the transferor of any delay by performing such actions before midnight following receipt, notice or settlement of an item. DLD seeks to add an additional duty of ordinary care under the common law to supplement these specific standards. Contrary to DLD's claims, the UCC displaces common law duties for a collecting bank. As the trial court noted, the UCC provides a comprehensive plan for the processing of checks. Where, like here, its specific provisions set forth standards regarding particular banking practices, they displace the ordinary care standard under the common law. In the amended complaint, DLD does not assert that Busey failed to timely perform any section 4-202 duties of a collecting bank, including notifying DLD before the midnight deadline that the check was dishonored.

The cases offered by DLD do not compel a different determination. In *Mutual Service Casualty Insurance Co. v. Elizabeth State Bank*, 265 F.3d 601, 614 (7th Cir.2001), a customer's breach of contract claim against a bank that allowed the customer's employee to cash checks on an account on which he was not authorized was based on the bank's common law duty to its customer. In *Mutual Service*, neither the account agreement nor any specific provisions of the UCC governed the duty of the bank concerning the circumstances at issue. ... Here, in contrast, the account agreement and the UCC spelled out the standards constituting ordinary care. In *Greenberg, Trager & Herbst, LLP v. HSBC Bank USA*, 17 N.Y.3d 565, 934 N.Y.S.2d 43, 958 N.E.2d 77 (2011), a case on which Busey also relies, the plaintiff law firm fell victim to an international check scam similar to that in the instant case. The law firm filed an action alleging negligence, in part, against the depository/collecting bank and the payor. . . . As in *Mutual Service*, there were no specific provisions under the parties' account agreement or the UCC governing the circumstances at issue and the bank presented evidence that its action complied with the duty of ordinary care as defined through custom and practice of the banking industry. . . .

In our view, *Greenberg* supports Busey's position. The *Greenberg* court recognized that pursuant to section 2-214(a) of the UCC, the risk of loss remained with the law firm until the check was finally settled with the bank. . . . Both the UCC and the account agreement in the instant case place the risk of loss on DLD until the check finally settled. The Daly affidavit establishes that the check on its face did not indicate it was counterfeit and that the check satisfied the requirements necessary for a negotiable instrument. Daly also attested that DLD was notified the check was uncollectible the same day Busey learned it was dishonored. DLD did not offer any facts in its amended complaint or in response to Busey's motion to dismiss that dispute Daly's statements or that Busey did not timely satisfy the responsibilities of a collecting bank under the UCC, including notice before the midnight deadline that the check was dishonored.

We consider that DLD's common law negligence claim cannot be sustained. Busey owed DLD no other duties aside from those set forth in the account agreement and the UCC. The amended complaint fails to allege that Busey breached any duties under the account agreement or the UCC. On these facts, DLD cannot present allegations sufficient to establish any common law duty. Even if the account agreement and the UCC did not apply, there is no duty under the common law to inspect a check for genuineness or to remind customers that they bear the risk of loss before a deposited check is finally settled. We find that the trial court's dismissal of the complaint for failure to state a claim was not in error. Timely compliance with the section 4-202 responsibilities constitutes ordinary care per the UCC and is not negligent as a matter of law. The facts establish that Busey processed the check per its standard methods, received notice the check was uncollectible on June 10, and informed DLD the same day. In addition to complying with the terms of the agreement, Busey also timely complied with the UCC provisions concerning the responsibilities of a collecting bank. Contrary to DLD's assertions, Busey had no duty under the agreement or the UCC to investigate the genuineness of the check or to inform DLD that it could be counterfeit. Because DLD cannot allege that Busey failed to comply with the account agreement, it must establish that its terms are manifestly unreasonably, a claim it did not allege in its complaint and which these facts cannot sustain.

The trial court also dismissed DLD's complaint . . . , finding that the complaint was precluded by the *Moorman* doctrine. Under the *Moorman* doctrine, a plaintiff cannot recover for solely economic loss under a tort theory of negligence. *Moorman Manufacturing Co. v. National Tank Co.*, 91 Ill.2d 69, 91–92, 61 Ill.Dec. 746, 435 N.E.2d 443 (1982). The doctrine was extended to services, and claims against a service provider are barred where the "duty of the party performing the service is defined by the contract that he executes with his client." *Congregation of the Passion, Holy Cross Province v. Touche Ross & Co.*, 159 Ill.2d 137, 162, 201 Ill.Dec. 71, 636 N.E.2d 503 (1994). The reasoning behind the rule is that tort law provides a remedy for losses from personal injuries or property damages, and contract law and the UCC provide remedies for economic losses resulting from diminished commercial expectations without personal injury or property damage. *In re Illinois Bell Switching Station Litigation*, 161 Ill.2d 233, 241, 204 Ill.Dec. 216, 641 N.E.2d 440 (1994). An exception applies to service providers, such as attorneys or accountants, where their duty arises outside of the contract; under those circumstances the *Moorman* doctrine does not preclude a claim based solely on economic loss. *Congregation of the Passion*, 159 Ill.2d at 161, 201 Ill.Dec. 71, 636 N.E.2d 503.

PETERBORO TOOL CO., INC. PROFIT SHARING PLAN & TRUST V. PEOPLE'S UNITED BANK
848 F.Supp.2d 164 (D.N.H. 2012)

PAUL BARBADORO, District Judge.

Between 2007 and 2009, the fiduciary for the Peterboro Tool Co, Inc. Profit Sharing Plan and Trust ("the Plan") stole nearly $250,000 from the Plan's money market account at People's United Bank, successor in interest to Flagship Bank and Trust (collectively "the Bank"). The Plan brings suit against the Bank, asserting that the Bank should have detected its fiduciary's suspicious withdrawals and protected its funds from misappropriation. The Plan argues that the Bank is liable for (1) negligence; (2) breach of fiduciary duty; and (3) breach of a bailment agreement. The Bank moves to dismiss all claims, and for the reasons provided below, I grant the Bank's motion. . . .

In 1970, Peterboro Tool Company, Inc. ("the Company") established the Plan as a non-contributory profit-sharing plan for the benefit of its employees. Since 1996, the Plan has held assets in a money market account and several certificates of deposit at the Bank. For the relevant time period, Bernard R. Mullan was the Plan's fiduciary as well as the accountant for the Company and the Plan. In his capacity as fiduciary, Mullan had access to and signatory power over Plan assets, including bank accounts.

In a series of thefts dating as far back as 1992, Mullan misappropriated the Plan's funds for his personal use. The Plan estimates that it has lost $634,467 in total. At issue in this case is Mullan's theft of approximately $249,900 from the Plan's money market account with the Bank.

Between October 15, 2007 and November 2, 2009, Mullan made 23 separate withdrawals from the money market account, ranging in size from $1,000 to $40,000. He made one withdrawal in late 2007, four withdrawals in late 2008, and the remaining 18 withdrawals between June 29 and November 2, 2009. As with his prior thefts, Mullan concealed these 23 illicit withdrawals from the Company and the Plan by entering fraudulent information on the Plan's books. He recorded the withdrawals as transfers to a non-existent account at another financial institution. Mullan buttressed the illusion by making annual entries listing the additional interest that had accrued on the fictitious account, and he would list the account's value as having increased accordingly. The Plan finally discovered that Mullan had looted its funds in November 2009, when it replaced Mullan as fiduciary and investigated its assets.

The Plan asserts that the Bank knew that Mullan was the Plan's fiduciary. It also draws attention to the particular manner in which two of Mullan's withdrawals were made. On July 10, 2009, Mullan withdrew $40,000 from the Plan's account, taking $8,000 in cash and placing $32,000 into his own personal account at the Bank. Ten days later, Mullan withdrew $10,000 from the Plan's account, taking half in cash and placing the other half into the same personal account. The Plan indicates that other transactions were conducted in a similar manner, asserting that it is prepared to amend its pleading to "include elaborate details ... regarding how much of each withdrawal was cash and how much was deposited into Mr. Mullan's account at the Bank." ...

On November 12, 2009, the Company (acting on behalf of the Plan) brought suit against Mullan, and obtained an attachment in the amount of $225,000. Subsequently, Mullan filed for bankruptcy.

On August 2, 2011, the Plan filed suit against the Bank in New Hampshire Superior Court. Invoking this court's diversity jurisdiction, the Bank removed the case to federal court on September 15, 2011. . . .

III. ANALYSIS

The Plan brings claims against the Bank for negligence, breach of fiduciary duty, and breach of a bailment agreement. The Plan asserts that the Bank should have notified it of Mullan's transactions (and/or taken other protective steps) prior to late 2009 because a reasonably prudent bank should have been aware, in light of the suspicious circumstances surrounding the withdrawals, that Mullan may have been breaching his fiduciary duty to the Plan. . . . Additionally, the Plan faults the Bank for "failing to establish, maintain, update and follow internal procedures" that would have more quickly revealed Mullan's unauthorized conduct.

A. Negligence

1. Special Relationship

The Plan claims that the Bank's negligence in disbursing funds to Mullan breached a duty of care that it owed to the Plan. The Bank, relying on *Ahrendt v. Granite Bank*, 144 N.H. 308, 740 A.2d 1058 (1999), contends that it had no duty to protect the Plan from the fraudulent conduct of a third party. I agree with the Bank that *Ahrendt* is controlling on the facts of this case.

To prevail on a claim for negligence, a plaintiff must show that the defendant breached a duty of care that it owed to the plaintiff and that the breach proximately caused the plaintiff's claimed injury. . . . The existence of a duty is a question of law. In New Hampshire, the general rule is that an individual has no duty to protect another from the criminal acts of third parties. . . . A duty may arise, however, if a special relationship exists. . . .

In *Ahrendt*, the court considered whether a bank has the requisite special relationship with a depositor. 144 N.H. at 314, 740 A.2d 1058. In that case, the eighty-year-old plaintiff signed handwritten notes stating that she authorized a bank to disburse nearly $50,000 from her money market account to a man who had carried out repairs at her home. *Id.* at 309–10, 740 A.2d 1058. Bearing the notes, the man came in person to the bank four times, making a withdrawal exceeding $10,000 on each visit. *Id.* The employee who processed the first transaction noted that she felt "uncomfortable" about the situation, but wrote out a bank check after verifying the plaintiff's signature and calling her to confirm her intent. *Id.* at 310, 740 A.2d 1058. For two of the other three withdrawals, the bank verified the plaintiff's signature and called to confirm the transaction. *Id.* Shortly after the fourth transaction, the plaintiff's family discovered that the man had been cheating the plaintiff. *Id.*

The plaintiff sued the bank, alleging that its agents should have known that the man was exploiting her, and that it had failed to exercise due care to protect her. *Id.* at 314, 740 A.2d 1058. The court ruled in favor of the bank on the basis that it did not owe the plaintiff a duty: "We decline to hold that the relationship between a bank and its customer, under the facts of this case, gives rise to a special duty to protect the customer from the fraudulent conduct of third parties that the law would not otherwise impose." *Id.*[3]

---

[3] Courts in other jurisdictions have reached different conclusions, and I do not speak to the ultimate wisdom of the decision in *Ahrendt*. *See, e.g., Mut. Serv. Cas. Ins. Co. v. Elizabeth State Bank*, 265 F.3d 601, 618 (7th Cir.2001)

The Plan has failed to identify any material dissimilarity between the circumstances of this case and the circumstances in *Ahrendt*. The Plan's relationship with the Bank was the same typical bank-depositor relationship present in *Ahrendt*; none of the facts alleged tend to show any additional facets of the relationship that might otherwise bring it within the category of a special relationship. Moreover, the factual allegation at the heart of both claims is the same: an agent of the depositor defrauded the depositor while acting within the scope of his apparent authority. *Ahrendt* makes clear that a bank ordinarily has no duty to protect a depositor from the unauthorized acts of its agent under such circumstances. 144 N.H. at 314, 740 A.2d 1058.

2. Alternative Theories for Imposing a Duty

The Plan offers two alternative theories as to why a duty should be imposed. Both are unavailing.

The Plan asserts that the Bank voluntarily assumed a duty to protect its assets against fraudsters because the Bank established internal fraud-prevention procedures, albeit measures that turned out to be inadequate. . . . Although it is often true that "one who voluntarily assumes a duty thereafter has a duty to act with reasonable care," *Walls* [*v. Oxford Mgmt. Co.*, 137 N.H. 653, 659, 633 A.2d 103 (1993)], the Plan's attempt to apply the doctrine to this case is unpersuasive. First, despite specifically noting certain security and verification procedures taken by the bank in *Ahrendt*, the New Hampshire Supreme Court held that the bank nevertheless had no duty to protect its depositor from fraud. 144 N.H. at 310, 314, 740 A.2d 1058. Second, the Plan has not alleged with particularity any special procedures not mandated by federal banking regulations that could justify a duty based on voluntary assumption.[4]

("[A] bank's failure to observe ordinary care in handling its customer's transactions may support a tort claim[.]"); *Norwest Mortgage, Inc. v. Dime Sav. Bank of N.Y.*, 280 A.D.2d 653, 721 N.Y.S.2d 94, 95 (2d Dept.2001) ("Facts sufficient to cause a reasonably prudent person to suspect that trust funds are being misappropriated will trigger a duty of inquiry on the part of a depositary bank[.]"). I do note, however, that *Ahrendt* unequivocally states the current law in New Hampshire and that the Plan has not alleged that the law of any other jurisdiction should be applied to this case.

[4] Because certain fraud detection and prevention measures are mandated by the federal regulatory regime concerning banks, it cannot be that a bank that complies with required procedures loses the benefit of *Ahrendt* and "voluntarily" assumes a duty that it does not otherwise owe to its depositors.

The next alternative theory is that a duty arose because the Bank had constructive knowledge of Mullan's fraud.[5] The Plan relies on a number of decisions from the state courts of New York for the proposition that when a reasonably prudent person knows or should know that funds are about to be misappropriated, a duty arises to make reasonable inquiry to ascertain the true facts before permitting a withdrawal. . . . [See *Diamore Realty Corp. v. Stern*, 50 A.D.3d 621, 855 N.Y.S.2d 206, 207–08 (2d Dept.2008); *In re Bohenko's Estate*, 254 A.D. 140, 4 N.Y.S.2d 420, 423–24 (4th Dept.1938); *Ben Soep Co., Inc. v. Highgate Hall of Orange Cnty. Inc.*, 142 Misc.2d 45, 535 N.Y.S.2d 1018, 1021 (Sup.Ct.1988).] Regardless of whether the Plan has sufficiently pled facts showing that the Bank could be liable under New York law on the basis of its constructive knowledge of Mullan's misappropriation, a theory of liability premised on constructive knowledge is foreclosed in New Hampshire by *Ahrendt*.

B. Breach of Fiduciary Duty

The Plan contends that it had a fiduciary relationship with the Bank and that the Bank breached its fiduciary duty. The Bank responds that its relationship with the Plan was not a fiduciary one. I agree with the Bank.

A fiduciary relationship is a "comprehensive term and exists wherever influence has been acquired and abused or confidence has been reposed and betrayed." *Lash v. Cheshire Cnty. Sav. Bank*, 124 N.H. 435, 438, 474 A.2d 980 (1984) (per curiam) (quoting *Cornwell v. Cornwell*, 116 N.H. 205, 209, 356 A.2d 683 (1976)). "As a general rule, the relationship between a bank and a customer is not a fiduciary one unless the law otherwise specifies." *Ahrendt*, 144 N.H. at 311, 740 A.2d 1058. The relationship between an ordinary depositor and a bank is contractual in nature and does not create fiduciary obligations. Id. at 311–12, 740 A.2d 1058.

In this case, the Plan asserts that the suspicious nature of Mullan's transactions gave rise to a fiduciary duty by the Bank. Without more, however, an authorized agent's suspicious withdrawals from a bank account do not give rise to a fiduciary relationship between the bank and its depositor. *Id. Ahrendt* addressed precisely that situation, and found that no fiduciary obligations existed. Id. Furthermore, the cases where a bank was found to have a fiduciary duty to a customer all involved particular relationships of trust or confidence that have no

---

[5] Although the Plan frames its argument as based on the Bank's "actual or constructive knowledge," the Bank does not allege any facts that suggest actual knowledge. . . .

parallels to the facts of this case. *See, e.g., Appeal of Concerned Corporators of Portsmouth Sav. Bank*, 129 N.H. 183, 205–06, 525 A.2d 671 (1987) (trustees of mutual savings banks owe fiduciary obligations to prudently invest depositors' funds); *Murphy v. Fin. Dev. Corp.*, 126 N.H. 536, 541, 495 A.2d 1245 (1985) (bank acting as mortgagee had fiduciary duty to obtain fair and reasonable price under the circumstances for mortgagor); *Lash*, 124 N.H. at 437–39, 474 A.2d 980 (bank had fiduciary duty where customers obtained loan from bank and bank disbursed loan to third-party creditor of customers without customer authorization).

The Plan posits an additional argument in favor of the existence of a fiduciary duty by drawing attention to the court's statement in *Ahrendt* that "[a] fiduciary relationship ... can arise under certain facts if equity so requires." 144 N.H. at 311, 740 A.2d 1058. Taking this statement to mean that a fiduciary duty can arise simply out of a weighing of equitable considerations, the Plan regurgitates the basic facts of the case and asserts that "it would be inequitable to hold that the Bank has no duty to [the Plan] to prevent ... such a blatant misappropriation." . . . The Plan fails, however, to satisfactorily explain why equity requires an outcome in this case that it did not require in *Ahrendt*, and fails to point to any facts that would distinguish the nature of the relationship between the Bank and the Plan from the nature of the parties' relationship in *Ahrendt*. I therefore dismiss the Plan's claim for breach of fiduciary duty.

C. Bailment

The Plan's final claim is that the Bank is liable as a bailee for its failure to safeguard the Plan's funds. The relation between a bank and its depositor, however, is not a bailor-bailee relationship, but a contractual debtor-creditor relationship where title of the funds passes from depositor to bank. *Ahrendt*, 144 N.H. at 311, 740 A.2d 1058 (banks have "debtor-creditor" relationships with depositors); *see Dean Witter Reynolds, Inc. v. Variable Annuity Life Ins. Co.*, 373 F.3d 1100, 1107 (10th Cir.2004) ("Unlike a bailment, a general deposit passes title to the financial institution, which is required to repay the loan from its own funds upon demand."). In this case the Plan has not alleged the existence of anything other than a traditional bank-depositor relationship, and the Plan's citations to bailment cases involving banks' night depositories are inapposite. A bailment claim cannot be sustained on these facts.

Questions and Problems 2.20. Does the check constitute property in and of itself? A *claim* that gives rise to a payment certainly is property, though intangible. The payment itself is property. But what about the check? If the check is wrongly paid, could property law provide alternative theories that would justify allowing the payment to stand? The peculiar case that follows involved a failed building contract, under which a (subsequently bankrupt) contractor promised to build a house for Mr. and Mrs. Augustine (the property owners), and the owners apparently indorsed over to it a check they had received from their mortgagee, as an advance pursuant to the building contract. One of the owners – apparently Mrs. Augustine – had not indorsed the check. The contractor, being adjudicated bankrupt, did not perform its promise. However, the contractor had deposited the check (which was paid, despite the missing indorsement). The payor bank brought action against the depository bank to recover amounts which it paid on the check. The depository bank brought a third-party action against the Augustines. The trial court entered judgment in favor of the plaintiff bank on its claim and in favor of the defendant bank on its third-party claim, and the Augustines appealed. The Indiana Court of Appeals reversed. On petition for rehearing, the Court of Appeals held that: (*i*) the contractor was not entitled to keep payments made pursuant to the contract without performing its part, and the owners' promise under the contract never became a debt to the contractor (*i.e.*, property) and the contractor was not entitled to keep the proceeds of the check mistakenly credited to its account beyond the value of the work actually done; and (*ii*) Mr. Augustine did not waive any claim he had against the contractor by his indorsement of the disbursement check from the mortgagee. Does this seem to suggest that property law theories generally do not trump negotiable instruments law?

AMERICAN NAT. BANK & TRUST CO. V. ST. JOSEPH VALLEY BANK
391 N.E.2d 685, 180 Ind.App. 546 (1979)

YOUNG, Judge.

ON PETITION FOR REHEARING

The petitioner has raised two issues: first, whether there was sufficient evidence to support the judgment on the theory of unjust enrichment to the Augustines; and second, whether the judgment may be upheld on the theory of estoppel.

The petitioner directs our attention to evidence which it claims supports a finding that the Augustines were indebted to Hanover [the contractor] in the amount of the check mistakenly paid by the petitioner-Bank. This evidence would support a finding that under the contract the Augustines promised to pay such an amount. This is not the issue however. In *Angola Brick & Tile Co. v. Millgrove School Twp.*, (1920) 73 Ind.App. 557, 127 N.E. 855, 857, a debt is defined generally as "a specific sum of money due from one person to another, and denotes, not only the obligation of the debtor to pay, but *The* right of the creditor to receive and enforce payment." (emphasis added). In the present case, the Augustines promised to pay for, and Hanover promised to build, a house. These promises are consideration for each other and mutually dependent. For this reason the failure of one party to perform discharges the other. *Kroeger v. Kastner*, (1937) 212 Ind. 649, 10 N.E.2d 902. . . . This conditional aspect of mutual promises forming a contract prevents their being debt, since neither party can enforce the other's promise without performing his own. *Accord, Indian Refining Co. v. Taylor* (1924) 195 Ind. 223, 143 N.E. 682 (an oil inspector's fees became debt an obligation to pay a sum certain at the time of the inspection). A breaching party may recover, apart from the contract, in Quantum meruit. . . .

. . . Hanover was not entitled to keep payments made pursuant to the contract without performing its part. The evidence that Hanover did not perform its promise is undeniable, thus the Augustines' promise under the contract never became a debt to Hanover and Hanover was not entitled to keep the proceeds of the check mistakenly credited to its account beyond the value of the work actually done. It is this latter value for which the Augustines were indebted to Hanover and it is this latter value which has not been sufficiently established so as to support the judgment.

The petitioner argues that John Augustine waived any claim he had against Hanover by his indorsement of the check and admitted an indebtedness to Hanover in that amount. Waiver is an intentional relinquishment of a known right. *Lafayette Car Wash, Inc. v. Boes*, (1972) 258 Ind. 498, 282 N.E.2d 837. That which is alleged to have been waived must have been in existence at the time of waiver. *Doan v. City of Fort Wayne*, (1969) 253 Ind. 131, 252 N.E.2d 415. Mere silence, acquiescence or inactivity is not waiver unless there was a duty to speak or act. *Grenchik v. State ex rel. Pavlo*, (1978) Ind.App., 373 N.E.2d 189. The burden of proof lies on the party asserting the waiver. *Id*. There is no direct evidence as to what John knew or intended. Unless these elements can reasonably be inferred from the facts of John's admitted suspicions, his indorsement of the draw, and his knowledge that Hanover would attempt to deposit the draw without all necessary signatures, the judgment cannot be sustained on this theory. We believe it cannot. John's actions are no more than what was expected under the contract. There is no indication that he knew all construction would cease. There is no indication that he considered the check to represent the value of what had been done up to that time and that he would not demand its return if Hanover abandoned the contract. There is simply nothing to indicate otherwise than that John intended to perform his promise under the contract and hoped that Hanover would also, notwithstanding some anxiety on that point.

We find that the evidence does not support the judgment, under the theory of waiver.

Questions and Problems 2.21. There may be other theories for recovery of funds paid on fraudulently altered checks, some based on UCC provisions. Assume that a clerk in the Accounts Department of SallerCo prepared checks for signature by a corporate officer. Over a three-year period she made nine of such checks payable to Second Bank, each for a different, small amount. She obtained authorized signatures on these checks from an officer who believed they represented small sums that SallerCo owed to Second Bank. (No such debts were in fact owed.) The clerk then altered the checks, increasing the amount in each case to several thousand dollars, and presented them to Second Bank. Although the bank was the named payee, it permitted the proceeds of the checks to be deposited in the clerk's personal account at Second Bank. Second Bank presented each of these checks to Issuer Bank, where SallerCo maintains its accounts, and Issuer Bank paid them and charged SallerCo's account for their face amounts. The clerk concealed her actions by destroying some and manipulating other company records; as a result, SallerCo did not discover her fraudulent activity until three months after the clerk resigned and relocated to Argentina. On what theories, if any, could SallerCo recover the amounts from Issuer Bank and/or Second Bank? *See, e.g.,* UCC §§ 3-405 - 3-407, 3-417. *Cf. Sun 'N Sand, Inc., supra* (decided under prior version of UCC).

Chapter 3

Bank Deposits and Collections

UCC Article 3 provides us with a very specific set of transactional rules governing issuance, transfer, and payment of negotiable instruments. We must acknowledge, of course, that the banking system adds to the Article 3 payment system a highly detailed infrastructure for the processing and collection of payments, especially in the case of checks. As a practical matter, then, we need to understand the legal rules that apply to that infrastructure. For most purposes, UCC Article 4 provides us with those rules, [1] which are the subject of this chapter.

Questions and Problems 3.1. The transactional rules of Article 4 govern the bank collection process. They provide us with a road map of the route followed by an item like a check in the process of collection through the banking system. That map is laid out in rudimentary form on the following page. Study it, and consider what is expected to occur as an item proceeds along this route. Then answer the questions that follow.

---

[1] Note that, in addition to the detailed rules of Article 4 itself, UCC § 4-102 explicitly recognizes the possible applicability of Article 3 and Article 8 (governing investment securities). Under UCC § 4-102(a), Article 4 rules apply to collection and payment of instruments, and any inconsistent rules in Article 3 are superseded by Article 4 rules. However, in the case of conflict between applicable rules of Article 4 and Article 8, the rules of Article 8 govern. *Id.* UCC § 4-103(b) deals with a more typical problem in the collection process. It treats Federal Reserve regulations and operating circulars, as well as the rules of any other clearing-house through which payment may be effected, as agreements that supersede most generally applicable Article 4 rules. Action or non-action pursuant to Federal Reserve regulations or operating circulars is *per se* the exercise of ordinary care in the context of collection. UCC § 4-103(c).

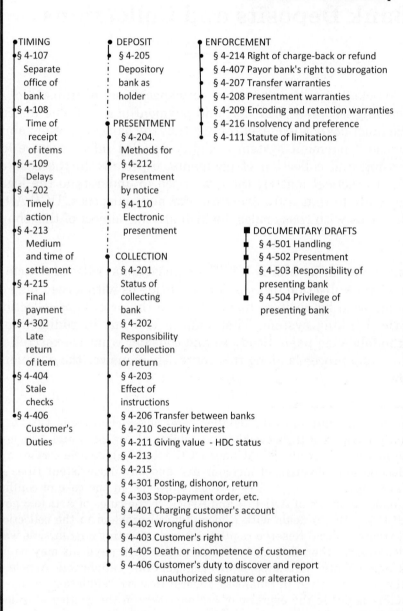

Article 4 Road Map

TIMING
§ 4-107
  Separate
  office of
  bank
§ 4-108
  Time of
  receipt
  of items
§ 4-109
  Delays
§ 4-202
  Timely
  action
§ 4-213
  Medium
  and time of
  settlement
§ 4-215
  Final
  payment
§ 4-302
  Late
  return
  of item
§ 4-404
  Stale
  checks
§ 4-406
  Customer's
  Duties

DEPOSIT
§ 4-205
  Depository
  bank as
  holder

PRESENTMENT
§ 4-204.
  Methods for
§ 4-212
  Presentment
  by notice
§ 4-110
  Electronic
  presentment

COLLECTION
§ 4-201
  Status of
  collecting
  bank
§ 4-202
  Responsibility
  for collection
  or return
§ 4-203
  Effect of
  instructions
§ 4-206 Transfer between banks
§ 4-210 Security interest
§ 4-211 Giving value - HDC status
§ 4-213
§ 4-215
§ 4-301 Posting, dishonor, return
§ 4-303 Stop-payment order, etc.
§ 4-401 Charging customer's account
§ 4-402 Wrongful dishonor
§ 4-403 Customer's right
§ 4-405 Death or incompetence of customer
§ 4-406 Customer's duty to discover and report
        unauthorized signature or alteration

ENFORCEMENT
  § 4-214 Right of charge-back or refund
  § 4-407 Payor bank's right to subrogation
  § 4-207 Transfer warranties
  § 4-208 Presentment warranties
  § 4-209 Encoding and retention warranties
  § 4-216 Insolvency and preference
  § 4-111 Statute of limitations

■ DOCUMENTARY DRAFTS
■   § 4-501 Handling
■   § 4-502 Presentment
■   § 4-503 Responsibility of
      presenting bank
■   § 4-504 Privilege of
      presenting bank

Questions and Problems 3.2. *Question(s) of Timing.* There are particular timing issues with respect to the passage of an item through the bank collection process. Consider the following questions:

(a) For the purpose of computing the time that SallerCo's bank, Depository Bank, has to process a transaction, does it matter if it contacts or visits a remote branch of Depository Bank, other than the office where its account is maintained? (*See* UCC § 4-107.)

(b) If a SallerCo clerk uses the ATM at a branch of Depository Bank late in the afternoon, when is that transaction considered to have taken place? (*See* UCC § 4-108.)

(c) If the branch's telephone lines go down during a blackout, does this affect the time that Depository Bank has to complete the transaction? (*See* UCC § 4-109.)

(d) If SallerCo deposits a check from BayerCorp that the SallerCo chief financial officer (CFO) indorsed for SallerCo, how long does Depository bank have to present that check for payment to Payor Bank, the bank on which it is drawn? (*See* UCC §§ 4-104(a)(10), 4-202.)

(e) How do you determine the appropriate manner and time in which Depository Bank settles an item by paying cash or crediting your account? (*See* UCC § 4-213.)

(f) What counts as final payment of the check? (*See* UCC § 4-215.)

(g) If Depository Bank presents the check to Payor Bank, how long does Payor Bank have to decide whether to pay the item or not? (*See* UCC §§ 4-104(a)(3), 4-302.)

(h) The check SallerCo deposited had been sitting in a drawer in the CFO's desk for seven months. Must Payor Bank pay the check when it is presented by Depository Bank? Can Payor Bank pay the check and debit its customer's account? (*See* UCC § 4-404.)

(i) If someone else found the check stuck in the CFO's drawer and took it, stamped SallerCo's indorsement on the back, and cashed the check at Payor Bank, can BayerCorp get its money back from Payor Bank? (*See* UCC § 4-406.)

3.3. *Deposit and Collection.* What happens when you deposit a check at the bank? A process begins to unfold, and rights and obligations are created. Consider the following questions:

(a) When Depository Bank receives the indorsed check for deposit in SallerCo's account and begins the process of collecting the proceeds from Payor Bank, what is its legal standing? Is it merely SallerCo's agent? Is it a "holder"? A "holder in due course" (HDC)? (*See* UCC §§ 3-302, 4-205, 4-210, 4-211.)

On HDCs, see Ch. 2, p. 100

(b) In collecting the proceeds of the item, is Depository Bank under any legal obligations or is collection entirely within its judgment and discretion? (*See* UCC §§ 4-204, 4-205.)

(c) Can Depository Bank present the check for collection electronically, or must it present the actual check? (*See* UCC § 4-110.)

(d) Would it make a difference if this were a BayerCorp note rather than a check that SallerCo asked Depository Bank to collect? (*See* UCC §§ 4-106, 4-212.)

(e) As the collecting bank, what is the responsibility of Depository Bank – and any other banks that might be involved in collecting the item from Payor Bank – as the check makes its way through the collection process? (*See* UCC §§ 4-104(a)(10), 4-201, 4-202, 4-203.)

(f) When it transfers the check to another bank in the collection process, what risks and responsibilities does Depository Bank – or any other bank that might be involved in collecting the item from Payor Bank – have, if any? What are SallerCo's risks and responsibilities, if any? (*See* UCC §§ 4-206, 4-207, 4-208, 4-210.)

(g) What counts as settlement of the obligation of Depository Bank – or any other bank that might be involved in collecting the item from Payor Bank – as a collecting bank in this process? (*See* UCC § 4-213.)

(h) What happens if Payor Bank decides to pay (settles) the check? What if it refuses (dishonors) the check? Can it dishonor if it has already settled? (*See* UCC §§ 4-301, 4-302, 4-401, 4-402.)

(i) Can BayerCorp instruct Payor Bank to refuse it? What if the bank pays it anyway? (*See* UCC §§ 4-303, 4-403.)

(j) What if the drawer of a check dies shortly after issuing the check to a payee? (*See* UCC § 4-405.)

(k) What if Payor Bank pays on the check, but BayerCorp later complains to the bank that the signature on the check was a forgery? (*See* UCC § 4-406.)

(*l*) What can Depository Bank – or any other collecting bank – do if the check is eventually refused (dishonored) by Payor Bank? (*See* UCC §§ 4-208, 4-210, 4-214, 4-215.)

3.4. *Enforcement.* Negotiable instruments law, and the collection process itself, revolves around identifying a person who is "entitled to enforce" the instrument. (*See, e.g.*, UCC §§ 3-301). What enforcement rules apply in the context of the collection process? Consider the following situations:

(a) Depository Bank gives SallerCo a "provisional settlement" for the BayerCorp check, which SallerCo draws on to pay some vendors, but later Payor Bank returns the BayerCorp check to Depository Bank stamped "**Non-Sufficient Funds**." Can Depository Bank charge SallerCo's account for the amount of the returned check? (*See* UCC § 4-214.)

(b) Recall the problem in 3.3(i). Does Payor Bank have any rights that can enforce against SallerCo if it has paid the check despite a valid stop payment order from BayerCorp? (*See* UCC § 4-407.)

(c) Recall the problem in 3.3(k). Does Payor Bank have any rights that it can enforce against SallerCo – or any other collecting bank – if it has paid the check before it discovered that the signature was a forgery? If one of these banks reimburses Payor Bank for the amount of the check, does that bank have any rights against SallerCo – or any other collecting bank? (*See* UCC §§ 4-207, 4-208.)

(d) Because of the high volume of checks that it issues to vendors and agents each month, SallerCo has an agreement with its bank, Banco Merca, that allows SallerCo to create and magnetically encode its own checks with the appropriate bank identification number, account number, and check amount. Unfortunately – as you can see from the sample check reproduced below – its encoding program has often mis-encoded check amounts. The result has been that a significant number of checks have been paid in amounts in excess of the written amount of the check. When Banco Merca dishonors any of these mis-encoded checks, who is liable for any resulting loss to a collecting bank? (*See* UCC § 4-209.)

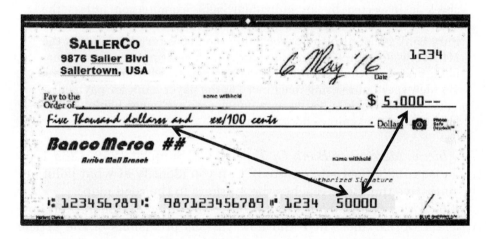

(e) What would happen to checks issued by SallerCo that are still in the process of collection if Banco Merca failed and was placed into an FDIC receivership? [*Not that this would **ever** happen, you understand – **never ever!**]* (*See* UCC § 4-216.)

(f) If any party sought to enforce any of the rights and obligations discussed in these questions, would the action be subject to the jurisdiction's generally applicable statute of limitations for contract actions? (*See* UCC § 4-111.)[2]

---

[2] It is possible that a more generous limitations would apply to an action brought by the FDIC on behalf of Banco Merca if the bank were in receivership, per 12 U.S.C. § 1821(d)(14), an FDIC "extender statute." *Cf. FDIC v.*

3.5. *Path of the Check.* Here is one court's description of the typical path of a check in the collection process:

> A drawer normally issues its check on a uniform standardized check stock form that bears magnetic ink character recognition ("MICR") encoding. The MICR encoding consists of a check number, the payor bank's American Bankers Association transit routing number, and the drawer's account number. The payee, after endorsing the check, presents the instrument to a bank for payment. The bank of first deposit, denominated a "depositary bank," examines the check and determines from a facial analysis whether the check is properly payable.
>
> Once the depositary bank cashes the check, the bank initiates payment of the instrument by adding the amount of the check to the MICR encoding line in electronically-recognized characters. This act completes the MICR encoding line. From that point forward, all processing of the check through various banking channels is effectuated through automatic electronic equipment. Thus, under the MICR encoding scheme, the depositary bank is the only situs at which the check is inspected by an individual sight examination unless the drawer requests "exception item processing." Assuming . . . the depositary bank is not also the payor bank, the depositary bank sends the MICR-encoded check to an automated bank clearinghouse (presumably a branch of the Federal Reserve System) which routes the check via high-speed processing machinery to the payor bank for payment. . . . Accordingly, while acting as a non-depositary payor bank . . . , [a bank] does not examine checks manually.

IBP, Inc. v. Mercantile Bank Of Topeka, 6 F.Supp.2d 1258, 1265-1266 (D.Kansas 1998) (footnote omitted). Can you identify at what points in the narrative the check reaches the markers in the road map?

3.6. *Which bank? What kind of bank?* In order to understand how Article 4 works, and when and how various provisions of the article apply to a particular situation, we need to keep track of the role played by the bank in the banking transaction at issue. While *bank* is defined broadly to include any "person engaged in the business of banking, including a savings bank, savings and loan association, credit union, or trust company,"[3] within the context of Article 4 there are a

---

First Horizon Asset Securities, Inc., --- F.3d ---, 2016 WL 2909338 (2d Cir. 2016) (holding that FDIC action within the limitations period of the extender statute was viable, despite expiration of otherwise applicable federal statute of limitations).

[3] UCC § 1-201(b)(4) (revised). *Cf.*UCC § 4-105(1) (pre-2002 version) (stating same definition).

variety of distinct legal characters that a bank may assume. Sort these out according to the "path of the check" in the process of collection:

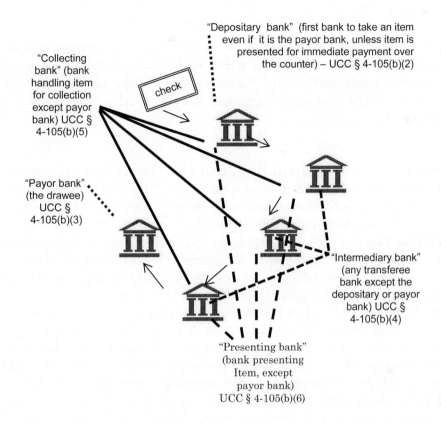

A. BANK-CUSTOMER RELATIONSHIP

In the last chapter, we saw several situations in which a court posited that there was no duty that inherently arose as a result of a non-customer's interaction with a bank.[4] That would seem to suggest that results might be different if we had a customer-bank interaction. What rights and duties are inherent in the bank-customer relationship, if any? The following case examines that relationship under very strained circumstances.

---

[4] *See Messing v. Bank of America, N.A., supra* at 106 (featuring non-customer payee and drawee bank); *Chicago Title Ins. Co. v. Allfirst Bank, supra* at 121 (featuring non-customer drawer and depositary bank).

IBP, INC. V. MERCANTILE BANK OF TOPEKA
6 F.Supp.2d 1258 (D.Kansas 1998)

VAN BEBBER, Chief Judge.

This case centers around a check cashed more than nine years after its issuance. Plaintiff, which wrote and delivered the check, commenced this action against the customer cashing the stale check, the bank at which the customer completed the transaction, and plaintiff's own bank. . . .

I. Background

. . .

On July 15, 1986, plaintiff IBP, Inc. ("IBP") issued and delivered to defendant Meyer Land & Cattle Company ("Meyer") a $135,234.18 check payable to both Meyer and defendant Sylvan State Bank ("Sylvan") for the purchase of cattle. IBP wrote the check on its account at Mercantile Bank of Topeka ("Mercantile"). IBP included Sylvan as a payee because Sylvan had a security interest in Meyer's cattle. Incredible as it may seem, officials at the closely-held family-run Meyer business apparently misplaced the check.

In the fall of 1995, Meyer president Tim Meyer found the 1986 undeposited check from IBP behind a desk drawer in his home. Although Mr. Meyer knew that the check was nine years old, he did not question its validity and assumed it reflected a payment for a previous sale of cattle.[1] Meyer, through its office manager, Jana Huse, later endorsed the check with the corporation's authorized and accepted endorsement stamp, which bore the name "MLC, Inc.," and presented the check for deposit at Sylvan. Sylvan's vice-president also endorsed the check on behalf of the bank (as payee) and accepted the instrument for deposit.

Sylvan then forwarded the check to an automated bank clearinghouse (presumably an office of the Federal Reserve System) which, in turn, routed the check to Mercantile. After Mercantile received the instrument and its computers noted the absence of any outstanding stop-payment order, it withdrew $135,234.18 from IBP's checking account and paid the check.

IBP issues thousands of checks on its Mercantile account every month. In the period of July 1995 through December 1995, IBP drew 73,769 checks on the account. In September 1995 alone, the month in which Mercantile processed the 1986 check to Meyer, IBP drew 14,852

---

[1] During the period 1986–1995, Meyer frequently presented checks for deposit at Sylvan involving amounts between $100,000 and $200,000. A $135,234.18 check, therefore, was not unusual.

checks. For IBP, a $135,234.18 check is not extraordinary as the company issues numerous checks each month for amounts well in excess of $100,000.

Upon learning that its account had been debited for the amount of the check to Meyer, IBP contacted Mercantile and insisted that the bank credit IBP's account. IBP claimed that Mercantile had improperly honored the stale instrument and had an obligation to return the funds to IBP. Mercantile refused. This lawsuit ensued. . . .

III. Discussion

A. Meyer's Summary Judgment Motion

IBP alleges that the $135,234.18 check given to Meyer in 1986 was voided two days after its issuance. IBP thus argues that Meyer's cashing of the check in 1995 amounts to conversion and unjust enrichment. The court finds insufficient evidence to support either claim.

1. Conversion

Meyer first insists that IBP's conversion claim is not cognizable under the Uniform Commercial Code ("UCC"). Clarifying prior ambiguities, the 1991 amendments to Kansas' version of the UCC state that "[a]n action for conversion of an instrument may not be brought by ... the issuer or acceptor of the instrument." K.S.A. 84–3–420(a). The rationale for precluding a drawer from maintaining a statutory conversion action is that "[t]he check represents an *obligation* of the drawer rather than the *property* of the drawer. The drawer has an adequate remedy against the payor bank for recredit of the drawer's account for unauthorized payment of the check." K.S.A. 84–3–420 official cmt. 1 (emphasis added).

IBP acknowledges that it has no valid claim for statutory conversion under the UCC. The company insists, however, that it does have an actionable conversion claim under common law. In response, Meyer avers that the UCC supersedes the common law as to the tort of conversion. The initial sentence of K.S.A. 84–3–420, which provides that the "law applicable to conversion of personal property applies to instruments," implicitly incorporates common law conversion. 2 James J. White & Robert S. Summers, Uniform Commercial Code § 18–4 at 216 (4th ed.1995). . . . Even if common law conversion survived the enactment of K.S.A. 84–3–420, IBP is unable to prevail on such a claim against Meyer.

Under Kansas law, conversion is defined as "the unauthorized assumption or exercise of the right of ownership over goods or personal chattels belonging to another to the exclusion of the other's rights." *Moore v. State Bank of Burden*, 240 Kan. 382, 386, 729 P.2d 1205, 1210 (1986) (citing *Carmichael v. Halstead Nursing Ctr., Ltd.*, 237 Kan. 495, Syl. ¶ 2, 701 P.2d 934 (1985)). Conversion in the banking context ordinarily involves stolen or forged checks that are forwarded through the stream of commerce and ultimately paid by the payor bank. *RPM Pizza, Inc. v. Bank One Cambridge*, 869 F.Supp. 517, 521 (E.D.Mich.1994). A drawer has no right to maintain a common law conversion action because a negotiable instrument is the property of the holder or payee—not the drawer. *Commercial Credit Corp. v. University Nat'l Bank*, 590 F.2d 849, 852 (10th Cir.1979) (citing *Stone & Webster Eng'g Co. v. First Nat'l Bank & Trust Co.*, 345 Mass. 1, 184 N.E.2d 358 (1962)). The drawer is not without a remedy. He may sue the payor bank for negligence or breach of the deposit contract. *See RPM Pizza*, 869 F.Supp. at 521 (citation omitted). Without valuable rights in the check itself, however, the drawer's conversion claim must fail.

In support of its common law conversion theory, IBP relies on *Carmichael*, 237 Kan. 495, 701 P.2d 934. In that case, the Halstead Nursing Center, which operated under the name "Halstead Nursing Center, Inc.," had been one of the prevailing plaintiffs in a class action lawsuit against the Kansas Department of Social and Rehabilitation Services. Prior to receiving payment on the judgment, the nursing center changed ownership. The new owners conducted business under a highly similar name—"Halstead Nursing Center, Ltd." The state, upon distributing the judgment funds to the prevailing litigants in the class action, sent a check to the nursing home made out to "Halstead Nursing Center." The new owners did not forward the check to the previous owners but instead deposited the funds into their own account.

The former shareholders of "Halstead Nursing Center, Inc." then filed suit against "Halstead Nursing Center, Ltd." for, inter alia, tortious conversion. Focusing on the intent of the issuer of the check, the Kansas Supreme Court held that the new owners of the nursing home had endorsed the instrument without authority, thereby exposing themselves to liability for conversion. *Id.* at 500–01, 701 P.2d at 938–39. Contrary to the representations of IBP, *Carmichael* did not establish that the drawer of a check may maintain a conversion action against a payor bank; nor has the court found a single Kansas case supporting IBP's position. Accordingly, Meyer's motion for summary judgment on IBP's conversion claim must be granted.

2. Unjust Enrichment

IBP also asserts an unjust enrichment claim against Meyer. IBP contends that its $135,234.18 debt to Meyer had been vitiated by the time Meyer cashed the check in 1995. IBP's claim, however, suffers from a fatal evidentiary deficiency.

The foundation for the unjust enrichment cause of action rests in a "promise implied in law that one will restore to the person entitled thereto that which in equity and good conscience belongs to him [or her]." *Haz–Mat Response, Inc. v. Certified Waste Servs. Ltd.*, 259 Kan. 166, 176, 910 P.2d 839, 846 (1996) (alteration in original) (citation omitted). The three requisite elements to such a claim are: "(1) a benefit conferred upon the defendant by the plaintiff; (2) an appreciation or knowledge of the benefit by the defendant; and (3) the acceptance or retention by the defendant of the benefit under such circumstances as to make it inequitable for the defendant to retain the benefit without payment of its value." *J.W. Thompson Co. v. Welles Prods. Corp.*, 243 Kan. 503, 512, 758 P.2d 738, 745 (1988).

IBP argues that it either issued the check erroneously to Meyer in 1986 or extinguished the debt shortly thereafter. IBP makes this form of alternative argument because the company has no accurate records of the circumstances surrounding the issuance or alleged voiding of the check. The only "evidence" IBP offers in support of its theory consists of several unauthenticated documents purportedly showing that the check was not outstanding at the time it was cashed. This does not create a genuine issue of material fact. . . .

Here, as Meyer correctly observes . . . , IBP articulates no foundation for the records attached to its response. In neither his affidavit nor deposition testimony did IBP vice-president Craig Hart give any indication that the records were made contemporaneous with the controverted transaction or were kept in the ordinary course of business. Moreover, Hart conceded that he is not responsible for issuing checks or maintaining records and had no knowledge of the $135,234.18 payment to Meyer prior to 1995. Although IBP may have officials who can authenticate the materials, the court is under no obligation at the summary judgment stage of proceedings to examine all the hypothetical ways in which evidence could be reduced to an admissible form by the time of trial. . . .

Even if IBP could prove with admissible documents that it voided the 1986 instrument within two days after issuance, that point would do little to bolster the company's claim. The fact that a plaintiff has voided a check does not mean, without more, that the plaintiff also eliminated the corresponding debt. If that were the case, dissatisfied business customers could avoid otherwise legitimate obligations merely by cancelling their outstanding checks.

IBP next argues that even in the absence of the records, "the age of the check alone would be sufficient evidence to require a jury trial on the issue of the existence of an underlying debt." The court disagrees. Without competent evidence that IBP had discharged the debt, the fact that Meyer waited an extraordinarily long period of time to cash the check is not sufficient to demonstrate that Meyer has been enriched unjustly. *See Hartsook v. Owens*, 236 Ark. 790, 370 S.W.2d 69, 70 (1963) (UCC policy relieving banks of liability for cashing stale checks in good faith was "adopted for the protection of the bank and plainly do[es] not have the effect of extinguishing a valid obligation" simply because it is stale).

IBP finally avers that Meyer's inability to explain the source of the check or IBP's continuing obligation for the debt mandates a denial of summary judgment. The court rejects this argument as an improper attempt to shift the burden of proof. The Supreme Court made unmistakably clear that the burden is not on the "party moving for summary judgment to produce evidence showing the absence of a genuine issue of material fact." *Celotex Corp.*, 477 U.S. at 325, 106 S.Ct. 2548. To the contrary, the movant need only show the district court "that there is an absence of evidence to support the nonmoving party's case." *Id.* Having satisfied this burden, Meyer is entitled to summary judgment.

B. Sylvan's Summary Judgment Motion

Turning downstream, IBP asserts conversion, unjust enrichment, and negligence claims against Sylvan, the depositary bank. Sylvan maintains that none of these claims has merit. The court concurs [for largely the same reasons the court granted summary judgment to Meyer on the identical claim]. . . .

3. Negligence

In its negligence claim against Sylvan, IBP alleges that Sylvan: (1) knew or should have known that IBP already had paid the $135,234.18 debt to Meyer; (2) knew or should have known that IBP's check was stale; (3) failed to require Meyer's proper endorsement; (4) neglected to inform IBP that Meyer had attempted to cash a stale check; and (5) failed to contact IBP prior to paying the check.

The first and third allegations are rejected outright. As noted above, IBP has advanced no evidence that its 1986 debt to Meyer had been discharged by the time Meyer cashed the check in 1995. In addition, IBP conceded in its response to Mercantile's summary judgment motion that "MLC, Inc." represented the proper endorsement for Meyer Land & Cattle Company. The improper payment of a stale check allegations require additional analysis.

No Kansas court has addressed whether a non-payor depositary bank owes a duty of care to the drawer of a check to examine the face of the instrument before accepting it for deposit. Neither has the court found a single case from any jurisdiction in which a non-payor depositary bank has been held liable for cashing a stale check. In analogous circumstances, however, nearly every court has reasoned that a bank owes no duty of care to a non-customer with whom it has no relationship.[3] *See Volpe v. Fleet Nat'l Bank*, 710 A.2d 661, 663–64 (R.I.1998) (collecting cases involving fictitious payees and forged indorsements). IBP contends that Sylvan's status as a co-payee on the 1986 check to Meyer puts Sylvan in a "unique relationship" with IBP, thereby implicating a duty of ordinary care. The court disagrees. IBP and Sylvan have no business relationship and have had no substantive communications with each other prior to this lawsuit. IBP placed Sylvan's name on its check to Meyer simply because Sylvan, as Meyer's secured creditor, had a lien on Meyer's cattle. Such a connection is too attenuated to impose upon Sylvan any duties toward IBP.

Further, even if Sylvan did owe a duty of ordinary care to IBP and breached that duty by failing to contact IBP prior to cashing the nine-year-old check to Meyer, IBP could not prevail on its negligence claim. To succeed on a negligence claim, a plaintiff must demonstrate that it suffered damages as a proximate result of the defendant's breach of duty. . . . Here, as repeatedly noted above, IBP is unable to establish with any competent evidence that it sustained harm as a result of Meyer's cashing the 1986 check in 1995. Duty and breach are irrelevant without a correlative injury. In the absence of such injury, the court grants Sylvan's motion for summary judgment on IBP's negligence claim.

---

[3] IBP cites *E.F. Hutton & Co. v. City Nat'l Bank*, 149 Cal.App.3d 60, 196 Cal.Rptr. 614 (1983), to support its depositary bank duty argument. That case, which relies on *Sun 'n Sand, Inc. v. United California Bank*, 21 Cal.3d 671, 148 Cal.Rptr. 329, 582 P.2d 920 (1978), has been repudiated by the UCC, see K.S.A. 84–3–417 official cmt. 2, as well as subsequent California state court decisions. *See Roy Supply, Inc. v. Wells Fargo Bank*, 39 Cal.App.4th 1051, 46 Cal.Rptr.2d 309, 325 (1995).

C. Mercantile's Summary Judgment Motion

At the terminus of the negotiable instrument stream sits the payor bank. IBP contends that the payor bank in this lawsuit—Mercantile—breached its contract of deposit and engaged in negligent conduct by honoring IBP's check to Meyer without first contacting IBP to verify the validity of the instrument. Mercantile insists that it is vulnerable to liability on neither cause of action. The court agrees. . . .

2. Negligence

IBP avers that Mercantile was negligent because Mercantile: (1) knew or should have known that IBP had extinguished its $135,234.18 debt to Meyer; (2) knew or should have known that IBP's check was stale; (3) failed to require Meyer's proper endorsement; (4) neglected to inform IBP that Meyer sought to cash the stale check; and (5) failed to contact IBP prior to paying the check.

For the same reasons articulated in the analysis of IBP's negligence claims against Sylvan, the court dismisses the first and third allegations without detailed discussion. As to the improper payment of a stale check allegations, the court finds that IBP's contentions must be rejected as well. . . .

b. Payment of Stale Check

A bank's obligations with respect to the payment of stale checks are governed by K.S.A. 84–4–404. This statute provides that "[a] bank is under no obligation to a customer having a checking account to pay a check, other than a certified check, more than six months after its date, but *it may charge its customer's account for a payment made thereafter in good faith.*" *Id.* (emphasis added). "Good faith" is defined as "honesty in fact and the observance of reasonable commercial standards of fair dealing." K.S.A. 84–3–103(a)(4) & 84–4–104(c).

The official UCC comment to K.S.A. 84–4–404, written more than thirty years ago, notes that the "time limit is set at six months because banking and commercial practice regards a check outstanding for longer than that period as stale, and a bank will normally not pay such a check without consulting the depositor." The 1996 Kansas comment to this provision further states that the greatest potential exposure for a bank paying a stale check is the statute's "good faith" language. The legislature heightened the exposure in 1991 by adding "the observance of reasonable commercial standards of fair dealing" to the definition of good faith as part of the incorporation of the 1990 UCC amendments.

IBP insists that Mercantile should have had a system in place by which the bank could detect all checks more than six months old at the time of presentment and verify the validity of such instruments before debiting customer accounts. IBP further contends that by relying on depositary banks such as Sylvan to detect stale instruments, Mercantile improperly delegated the duties it owes to customers. Mercantile responds that its check processing procedures adhere to reasonable commercial standards of fair dealing in the banking industry. Mercantile also avers that the only way to discern the staleness of negotiable instruments like IBP's 1986 check to Meyer would be to conduct manual examinations, an extraordinarily expensive and inefficient way of transacting business. The court concurs.

The 1990 UCC amendments explicitly acknowledged the need for automated check processing like the MICR encoding system to maintain efficiency in the banking industry.

> In 1950 at the time Article 4 was drafted, 6.7 billion checks were written annually. By the time of the 1990 revision of Article 4 annual volume was estimated by the American Bankers Association to be about 50 billion checks. The banking system could not have coped with this increase in check volume had it not developed in the late 1950's and early 1960's an automated system for check collection based on encoding checks with machine-readable information by Magnetic Ink Character Recognition (MICR). An important goal of the 1990 revision of Article 4 is to promote the efficiency of the check collection process by making the provisions of Article 4 more compatible with the needs of an automated system and, by doing so, increase the speed and lower the cost of check collection for those who write and receive checks. An additional goal of the 1990 revision of Article 4 is to remove any statutory barriers in the Article to the ultimate adoption of programs allowing the presentment of checks to payor banks by electronic transmission of information captured from the MICR line on the checks.

K.S.A. 84–4–101 official cmt. . . . Yet, the MICR system, upon which the entire banking system relies, provides no basis for detecting a check's date.

IBP argues that reasonable banking practices must include a disclosure to customers that the bank's check processing procedures have no mechanism to detect a stale check absent a stop-payment order. The only evidence IBP offers in support of this proposition is the affidavit of IBP vice-president Craig Hart. As Mercantile correctly points out, however, Hart conceded in his deposition that he has no personal knowledge of what constitutes "reasonable commercial standards" in the banking industry. Nor does Hart have any personal knowledge of IBP's dealings with Mercantile. In sum, Hart predicates his opinion exclusively on his status as a lay "consumer of banking services." The court does not credit such evidence on the issue of acceptable banking standards. See Fed.R.Evid. 602 (witness may not testify to a matter unless there is evidence that he has sufficient personal knowledge of the matter). The personal beliefs and preferences of a bank customer do not represent the standard for a negligence or breach of good faith claim.

Hart's opinions also run contrary to the UCC's definitions of "ordinary care" and "good faith" in the banking industry. Under the UCC,

> "[o]rdinary care" in the case of a person engaged in business means observance of reasonable commercial standards; prevailing in the area in which the person is located, with respect to the business in which the person is engaged. *In the case of a bank that takes an instrument for processing for collection or payment by automated means, reasonable commercial standards do not require the bank to examine the instrument if the failure to examine does not violate the bank's prescribed procedures and the bank's procedures do not vary unreasonably from general banking usage not disapproved by this article or article 4.*

K.S.A. 84–3–103(a)(7) (emphasis added). "Good faith," defined previously, must be read together with "ordinary care." K.S.A. 84–3–103 official Kansas cmt. "The reasonableness of the 'good faith' is in the entire transaction, while the reasonableness in 'ordinary care' will usually refer to individual events." *Id.* Mercantile's policies do not require the bank to examine all checks manually before debiting customer accounts. Nor do such policies contravene accepted banking procedures specifically outlined in the UCC.

The official commentary accompanying K.S.A. 84–4–404 contemplates that payor banks which honor stale checks often will incur no liability because they are unaware of the staleness.

> Several cases under the former definition of "good faith" in [K.S.A.] 84–1–201(19) held banks liable for paying stale checks under the former section.... Under these cases, a bank may be liable to its customer if it pays a check *known to be very stale* without making some inquiry, especially with the broader current definition of good faith. *Since most checks are run by computer, the drawee bank would be unaware of the staleness unless the check was large enough to merit individual inspection.*

K.S.A. 84–4–404 official Kansas cmt (emphasis added). Here, it is undisputed that Mercantile had no knowledge that the IBP check it honored in 1995 was more than nine years old. It is similarly uncontested that IBP frequently drafted checks of equal or greater value on its account. Furthermore, IBP was cognizant of Mercantile's procedures for seeking a stop-payment order, yet chose not to secure (or at least update) such an order. Under these circumstances, the court concludes that Mercantile exercised good faith and ordinary care in honoring the check without first consulting IBP. *See RPM Pizza*, 869 F.Supp. at 519–21. Mercantile's summary judgment motion on this claim, therefore, is granted.

3. Breach of Contract

IBP's final claim is that Mercantile breached its deposit contract with IBP by honoring the stale check to Meyer without verifying the validity of the instrument. The factual basis for this breach of contract claim is not altogether clear. The court concludes, however, that the claim has no merit.

The 1993 deposit agreement between IBP and Mercantile is silent as to Mercantile's obligations in the payment of stale checks. The only part of the agreement even remotely connected to this issue is a statement on stop-payment orders warning customers that such orders are valid for only six months and must be renewed at the end of each period to remain effective. This provision is consistent with K.S.A. 84–4–403. The official comment to that statute states, "When a stop-payment order expires it is as though the order had never been given, and the payor bank may pay the item in good faith under [K.S.A. 84–4–404] even though a stop-payment order had once been given." K.S.A. 84–4–403 official cmt. 6. Because IBP did not have a stop-payment order in effect at the time Mercantile honored the 1986 check, there was no breach of contract.

IBP properly notes that a bank is under an implied contract to disburse money from a customer's account only upon the customer's order and direction. *See, Chilson v. Capital Bank of Miami*, 237 Kan. 442, 444, 701 P.2d 903, 906 (1985). Mercantile did not breach this implied contract. The bank honored the 1986 check at IBP's request. A check, after all, is an order to a bank by a drawer to pay the check out of the drawer's account. See K.S.A. 84–3–104(a, f). Moreover, as noted above, Mercantile exercised the requisite good faith and ordinary care in honoring the check. Accordingly, Mercantile is entitled to summary judgment on IBP's breach of contract claim.

Questions and Problems 3.7. What, if anything, is missing in IBP's complaint that might have helped it withstand Mercantile's motion for summary judgment? Anticipating that motion, how would you have advised IBP in drafting its complaint?

3.8. Review the discussion of good faith in *IBP, Inc., supra* at 184-187. Do you agree that payment of a check, involving a substantial sum of money, nine years after it was issued could be done in good faith by the payor bank? Do you agree that Mercantile acted in good faith in paying the check?

3.9. In light of the previous discussion, consider whether the payor bank in the following case was acting in good faith in dishonoring the checks issued by its customer.

MARYOTT V. FIRST NATIONAL BANK OF EDEN
624 N.W.2d 96 (S.D. 2001)

GILBERTSON, Justice.

Ned Maryott (Maryott) sued First National Bank of Eden (Bank), its president and its branch manager under SDCL 57A-4-402 for the wrongful dishonor of three checks. A jury awarded Maryott $600,000 in damages for lost income, lost value of his business and emotional distress. On appeal, we affirm in part and reverse in part.

Facts and Procedure

Maryott has owned and operated a cattle-dealing business known as Maryott Livestock Sales near Britton, South Dakota, since 1973. In the cattle industry, Maryott had a reputation for honesty and integrity. Because of his respected reputation, he was considered one of the best dealers in the business. Maryott earned a commission of $.50 per hundred weight on the cattle he sold. In an average year, he would sell approximately 50,000 head of cattle, generating revenues of $175,000.

Maryott began doing business with Bank in 1977. Over the years, Maryott had borrowed substantial amounts of money from Bank. During that time, Maryott had never written a bad check, had never incurred an overdraft, and had never been late on a loan payment. On December 29, 1993, Maryott and his wife signed a promissory note in favor of Bank for $176,171.60. That note served as a line of operating credit and was secured by mortgages on Maryott's real estate and security interests on most of his personal property and inventory. Bank valued the property mortgaged by Maryott at $663,861. The note was due on December 29, 1999. On March 13, 1996, the Bank loaned Maryott an additional $100,000, due on November 1, 1996. That note was secured by a security agreement and real estate mortgage.

One of Maryott's major customers was the Oconto Cattle Company (Oconto), located in Custer County, Nebraska. Oconto was owned by Warren Bierman, [with whom] Maryott had been doing business . . . for more than twenty years. In the normal course of business, Oconto paid Maryott within six to seven days after shipping the cattle. Between July 16 and August 29, 1996, Maryott shipped 887 head of cattle to Oconto. The value of those cattle was approximately $480,000. After repeated attempts to collect payment from Bierman were unsuccessful, Maryott ceased shipping cattle to Oconto. Maryott did receive two sight drafts from Oconto, drawn on its line of credit. However, these drafts were returned because Oconto's lender had revoked the line of credit. Despite repeated assurances from Bierman that he "was good for it," Maryott never received payment on the 887 head of cattle shipped to Oconto.[1]

Bank first became aware of the Oconto situation when the two drafts were returned in mid-September. This situation caused concern to Tim Hofer, Bank's manager, and Peter Mehlhaff, its president. After visiting with Maryott regarding the situation on September 30, 1996, Mehlhaff and Hofer noticed that three large checks had been processed through Maryott's checking account. These checks were payable to Tri-County Livestock Auction for $30,544.38; to Tri-County Livestock (collectively "Tri-County") for $72,070.24; and to Schaffer Cattle Company (Schaffer) for $132,990. Each of these checks had been presented to Bank and paid in full on September 25, 1996. Maryott's checking account had been debited accordingly. In light of their concerns over the Oconto situation and after examining the physical checks, Hofer and Mehlhaff concluded Maryott was involved in or the

---

[1] There was evidence that Bierman was engaged in a check-kiting scheme unrelated to his transactions with Maryott. *Maryott v. Oconto Cattle Co.*, 259 Neb. 41, 607 N.W.2d 820, 824 (2000). [Note that "check-kiting," an illegal practice, involves "drawing checks on an account in one bank and depositing them in an account in a second bank when neither account has sufficient funds to cover the amounts drawn. Just before the checks are returned for payment to the first bank, the kiter covers them by depositing checks drawn on the account in the second bank." *United States v. Stone*, 954 F.2d 1187, 1188 n.1 (6th Cir. 1992).] Oconto eventually filed for bankruptcy protection after Farm Credit Services cancelled its line of credit. . . . [Since] Farm Credit's interest in the cattle was superior to Maryott's [and] Oconto's assets were insufficient to satisfy Farm Credit's claims, Maryott was unable to recover any cattle or receive payment thereon.

victim of "suspicious activity."[2] That afternoon, Bank decided to dishonor the three "suspicious" checks, even though Bank was aware such a dishonor was a potential violation of the "midnight deadline" rule found in SDCL 57A-4-302(1). Although Maryott had met with Hofer earlier in the day, he was not informed that Bank intended to dishonor his checks.

The next morning, October 1, 1996, Mehlhaff gave notice of dishonor for the three checks by filing a claim for late return with the Federal Reserve. Once the items were dishonored by the Federal Reserve, the funds were returned to Maryott's checking account. Bank immediately froze the assets in Maryott's checking account, meaning any additional checks drawn on his account would not be honored. That same day, Hofer received a call from Don Kampmeier, president of Central Livestock Company (Central). Kampmeier informed Hofer that Central was holding a check for $68,528 from Maryott. Hofer informed Kampmeier that the check would not be honored, despite the fact that Maryott's checking account contained nearly $300,000 at the time. Later that same day, Bank deemed itself insecure and used the proceeds of the dishonored checks to pay down the balance of Maryott's loans. . . .

[Because of claims against him by Central and Schaffer, Maryott was required to forfeit his dealer's license. Without that license, Maryott could not deal in livestock independently. That effectively shut down his business.]

The payees on the dishonored checks, Tri-County and Schaffer, subsequently sued Bank for the face value of the checks. Bank admitted that it had violated the midnight deadline rule and agreed to settle those claims for an aggregate amount of $168,534. The settlement amount was then applied against Maryott's line of credit. Maryott commenced this action against Bank on December 5, 1996, alleging breach of contract and conversion, later adding a claim for wrongful dishonor. Summary judgment was granted in favor of Bank as to the

---

[2] Hofer and Mehlhaff reached this conclusion because the two checks to Tri-County Livestock were endorsed by two different parties, one check was written in pencil, and one check was dated September 19, 1997, rather than September 19, 1996, the latter being the correct date. None of these suspicious markings were noticed by Bank officials until the re-examination on September 30, 1996, five days after they had been paid. Bank was also "suspicious" because Maryott was not keeping them up to date on the Oconto situation and in the words of Hofer, "we just did not know what was going on out there." Bank was unable to confirm that any "suspicious activity" actually occurred. Nor did it undertake any independent investigation into the Oconto situation to verify its suspicions before dishonoring the checks.

conversion claim, and Maryott abandoned the breach of contract claim at trial. A jury trial was commenced on March 27, 2000 on only the wrongful dishonor claim. On March 31, 2000, the jury returned a verdict in favor of Maryott in the amount of $250,000 for lost income, $200,000 for lost value of Maryott's business and $150,000 for emotional distress. With prejudgment interest, the total judgment came to $713,750. After the verdict, the trial court allowed a setoff in favor of Bank for $168,534, the amount of the settlement on the dishonored checks. . . .

Analysis and Decision

1. Whether the wrongful dishonor of the checks proximately caused Maryott's damages.

. . . SDCL 57A-4-402(b) provides that "[a] payor bank is liable to its customer for damages proximately caused by the wrongful dishonor of an item." Bank has not appealed the jury's determination that it wrongfully dishonored the three checks. Whether the wrongful dishonor proximately caused Maryott's damages is a question of fact for the jury to decide "in 'all but the rarest of cases.' " *Thompson v. Summers*, 1997 SD 103, ¶ 18, 567 N.W.2d 387, 394 (citing *Bauman v. Auch*, 539 N.W.2d 320, 325 (S.D.1995)). . . . Bank claims this is one of those rarest cases. After reviewing the evidence in a light most favorable to the verdict, we cannot agree. . . .

Maryott points to testimony that he informed Central on the day he issued the check that he did not have enough funds to cover the check. Central personnel agreed to work with Maryott and hold the check until Maryott had sufficient funds. When Maryott discovered Bank had dishonored his checks and frozen his checking account, he informed Central of the situation. The president of Central, Kampmeier, then telephoned Hofer, who informed Kampmeier that Bank would not honor the check. Because of the freeze put on Maryott's account, he was essentially out of business at that time, as no future checks would be honored. In the words of Kampmeier, "I had no recourse. I had nothing else I could do, I had to go against his bond at that time." When asked if he would have moved against the bond if the check had been honored, Kampmeier replied, "[m]ore than likely not because he would have–that would have meant he was still in business and can continue in business and he could have probably worked out of his indebtedness to us."

In addition, . . . the owner of Schaffer testified he would not have filed a claim against Maryott's bond if Bank had honored that check. Bank argues that Schaffer's claim on the bond is irrelevant, as the bond would have been lost because of the actions of Central. We have never endorsed such a restrictive view of proximate cause. Instead, we have stated that "[i]f the defendant's conduct was a substantial factor in causing the plaintiff's injury, it follows that he will not be absolved from liability merely because other causes have contributed to the result, since such causes, innumerable, are always present." *Leslie v. City of Bonesteel,* 303 N.W.2d 117, 120 (S.D.1981). The wrongful dishonor by Bank was clearly a substantial factor causing the actions taken by Schaffer. The jury was instructed that "[t]he proximate cause need not be the only cause, nor the last or nearest cause. It is sufficient if it concurs with some other cause acting at the same time, which in combination with it, causes injury." This instruction is mandated by our decision in *Leslie.* . . . Bank's actions clearly caused Schaffer to file a claim on the bond. In addition, Kampmeier testified that but for Bank's actions, Central would not have moved against Maryott's bond. After reviewing the evidence in a light most favorable to the verdict, there is sufficient evidence to support the jury's verdict. Bank has failed to carry its burden of showing that no reasonable minds could differ as to the existence of proximate cause. . . .

[Maryott also argued that damages for his emotional distress were recoverable under UCC § 4-402, which provides that a bank is liable for "actual damages proved and may include ... other consequential damages." He argued that damages for emotional distress were part of his consequential damages under § 4-402, and so he was not required to establish the elements of intentional or negligent infliction of emotional distress normally associated with a claim for emotional damages. (In the alternative, he claimed that he nevertheless met those requirements.) Neither the text of the section nor the official comment provided any assistance on this issue. In support of Maryott's interpretation was *Twin City Bank v. Isaacs,* 283 Ark. 127, 672 S.W.2d 651 (1984), involving a wrongful dishonor under § 4-402. To the contrary, *Farmers & Merchants State Bank of Krum v. Ferguson,* 617 S.W.2d 918, 921 (Tex.1981) held that "[d]amages for mental anguish [under § 4-402] cannot be recovered absent a showing of an intentional tort, gross negligence, willful and wanton disregard, or accompanying physical injury." *See also First Nat'l Bank of New Castle v. Acra,* 462 N.E.2d 1345, 1350 (Ind.App.1984) (allowing recovery of damages for emotional distress only when intentionally inflicted or accompanied by physical injury); *Lee v. Bank of America,* 218 Cal.App.3d 914, 267 Cal.Rptr. 387, 390 (1990) (requiring proof of either physical impact and resulting injury or intentional wrongdoing for damages for emotional distress under § 4-402). *Cf. Buckley v. Trenton Sav. Fund Soc.,* 111 N.J. 355, 544 A.2d 857, 864 (N.J.1988). (applying more stringent test requiring proof of intentional infliction of emotional distress for emotional damages under § 4-402). The court noted that UCC § 1-103 "provides that our common-law is effective in commercial transactions unless specifically displaced," and so it interpreted § 4-402 "in light of our precedent which requires a plaintiff to prove either intentional or negligent infliction of emotional distress to recover emotional damages." The court concluded that Maryott had not met these requirements. Otherwise, it did not find the jury's damage awards excessive, but it did reject Maryott's argument for punitive damages, finding the bank's violation of the midnight deadline statutory rule, on its own, to be insufficient to support punitive damages.]

SABERS, Justice (concurring in part and dissenting in part).

The citizens of South Dakota, represented by this Marshall County jury, found that the bank's wrongful dishonor was the cause of Maryott's mental anguish. The majority opinion jumps in the jury box and reverses the jury's award of $150,000 for Maryott's emotional damage which was clearly precipitated by the bank's wrongful conduct. In so holding, the majority opinion sidesteps the legislative pronouncement that when a bank chooses to wrongfully dishonor a properly payable item it is liable for any "actual damages." As the jury's determination is supported by law and fact, it should stand and not be overturned on a whim. . . .

The instructions to this jury properly stated that the Bank was liable for the foreseeable consequences proximately caused by its conduct. The jury was instructed that emotional distress "means mental suffering, mental distress or mental anguish. It includes all highly unpleasant mental reactions, such as fright, nervousness, horror, grief, shame, anxiety, humiliation, embarrassment, mortification, anger, worry and stress, as well as physical pain." Additionally, "the measure of damages is the amount which will compensate the party aggrieved for all detriment proximately caused thereby." The jury properly found that Maryott suffered emotional damages as a result of the Bank's wrongful conduct. . . .

In *Twin City Bank v. Isaacs*, 283 Ark. 127, 672 S.W.2d 651 (1984), the Supreme Court of Arkansas recognized that "the type of mental anguish suffered under § 4-402 does not need to rise to the higher standard of injury for intentional infliction of emotional distress." *Id.* at 654. It further compared these intangible injuries to those types of damages recognized in defamation actions. *Id.* In addressing this issue, we are faced with the economic reality that "embarrassment and humiliation" suffered from the bank's wrongful acts are very real, though sometimes intangible harms. See id. The damage to Maryott's reputation and the ensuing effect on his credit, a lifeline in his type of business, created very real and incredible damage. The jury recognized it based on proper instructions and so should we.

Leading commentators on the UCC have addressed the issue. "Might one argue that 'actual damages' excludes recovery for mental distress? We think not." White & Summers, Handbook of the Law Under the Uniform Commercial Code § 17-4 p. 675 (2d Ed 1980). Explaining further, White & Summers note: "It is inconsistent to allow recovery for embarrassment and mental distress deriving from arrest and prosecution and to deny similar recovery in other cases. Moreover, cases under the predecessor to 4-402, the American Banking Association Statute, held that 'actual damages' includes damages for mental distress." *Id.*

Questions and Problems 3.10. First National Bank officials Hofer and Mehlhaff were "'suspicious' because Maryott was not keeping them up to date on the Oconto situation. . . ." Did Maryott, as First National Bank's customer, have a duty to keep the bank informed about its problems with its buyer?

3.11. Did Hofer owe Maryott a duty to inform him that the bank intended to dishonor his three checks? Does it make a difference that in doing so, the bank was violating the midnight deadline rule of UCC § 4-302?

3.12. On the issue of damages for emotional distress, who has the more persuasive argument, the majority opinion or the dissent? Is the key issue whether or not "consequential damage," per § 4-402, includes emotional distress, or whether or not "consequential damage," per § 1-103, should include emotional distress only to the extent the common law allows it? Or is the key issue something else altogether?

3.13. Assuming that the *Maryott* majority is correct that a claim of emotional distress would require proof of the elements of "intentional or negligent infliction of emotional distress normally associated with a claim for emotional damages," what exactly would that entail? Do the facts of *Maryott* suggest that the plaintiff could have satisfied that requirement? In answering these questions, consider the following case.

FIX V. FIRST STATE BANK OF ROSCOE
807 N.W.2d 612 (S.D. 2011)

MEIERHENRY, Retired Justice.

This appeal involves Rita Fix's claim against First State Bank of Roscoe and Roscoe Community Bankshares, Inc. (Bank) for intentional infliction of emotional distress and abuse of process. The trial court dismissed Fix's intentional infliction of emotional distress claim; the abuse of process claim was tried to a jury. Fix claims that the trial court erred in dismissing the intentional infliction of emotional distress claim and erred in instructing the jury at trial. We reverse and remand for a new trial on the abuse of process claim.

Facts and Background

Part of the controversy between Fix and the Bank involves property Fix owned in Faulk County, South Dakota. In 1997, Fix signed a contract for deed selling the property to her son and daughter-in-law, Jeff and Marie Fix, but retained a life estate in the house located on the property. In 1999, Jeff and Marie obtained a loan from the Bank to finance their farming operation. To secure the loan, the Bank required Jeff and Marie to obtain a warranty deed for the property, including Fix's life estate in the house. Although hesitant to relinquish her house, Fix eventually executed a warranty deed to Jeff and Marie after the Bank assured her that she could retain possession of the house. In a letter from the Bank president, the Bank wrote:

> In the event that for any reason the bank becomes the owner of the described real estate, you will have full right of possession to the home on the premises as long as you are living.

In 2004, Fix filed for bankruptcy in federal court. Fix did not claim a homestead exemption for the house nor list her interest in the house as personal property. Fix retained possession of the house until 2005 when Jeff and Marie's financial problems forced them to convey the house and the property to the Bank in lieu of foreclosure. Later that same year, the Bank sold the property to a third party and then sought to remove Fix from the house.

While in federal bankruptcy court, Fix sued the Bank in state court for: (1) right to possession of the house; (2) breach of fiduciary duty; (3) intentional infliction of emotional distress; (4) deceit; and (5) fraudulent misrepresentation. In response, the Bank requested that the bankruptcy court enjoin Fix's state action. The Bank claimed that Fix's cause of actions belonged to the bankruptcy estate not Fix personally. The bankruptcy court agreed with the Bank that all five alleged causes of action could only be brought by Fix's bankruptcy trustee. Eventually, the issue was appealed to federal district court and to the Eighth Circuit Court of Appeals. The Eighth Circuit found that all of Fix's claims belonged to the bankruptcy estate with one exception: Fix's claim for intentional infliction of emotional distress. *See Fix v. First State Bank of Roscoe*, 559 F.3d 803, 810 (8th Cir.2009).

In addition to the bankruptcy and civil proceedings, Jeff, Marie, and Fix were indicted in June 2005 in state court on multiple criminal counts. The criminal counts involved an alleged criminal scheme where Jeff sold grain covered by the Bank's security interest in Fix's name; Fix would then endorse the grain checks, deposit them in her account, and write Jeff a check for the amount. Jeff ultimately pled guilty and the charges against Marie were dismissed. The criminal proceedings against Fix, however, were not dismissed but remained dormant for several months despite her attorney's requests to proceed or dismiss. Eventually in February 2006, Vaughn Beck, the Edmunds County State's Attorney who had brought the charges and who also represented the Bank civilly, contacted Fix's criminal attorney. Beck offered to dismiss the criminal charges against Fix if she would "deed the house back to the bank." This prompted Fix to amend her state court pleadings to include a claim of abuse of process against both the Bank and State's Attorney Beck and to proceed with her intentional infliction of emotional distress claim against the Bank. Her abuse of process claim alleged that the Bank conspired with Beck to use the criminal proceeding for the illegitimate purpose of removing her from the house.

Prior to trial, Beck settled with Fix for $50,000. Additionally, the trial court granted summary judgment against Fix on her intentional infliction of emotional distress claim against the Bank. The abuse of process claim was tried to a jury in February 2010. The jury returned a verdict finding the Bank liable but awarded no damages to Fix.

Issues

Fix raises several issues on appeal. (1) Fix claims that the trial court's instruction on emotional distress was improper and not a correct statement of the law. The trial court's instruction required Fix to prove "she suffered *extreme and disabling* emotional distress as a proximate result of the abuse of process." (Emphasis added.) She claims that she does not need to prove that her emotional distress was "extreme and disabling." (2) Fix also claims that the trial court erred in dismissing her claim of intentional infliction of emotional distress against the Bank. . . .

Analysis

1. Emotional distress damages resulting from an abuse of process claim need not be "extreme and disabling" in order to recover.

. . . Several of the trial court's jury instructions required the jury to find severe, extreme, and disabling emotional distress in order for Fix to recover damages.[1] We hold that Fix was not required to show that she suffered extreme and disabling emotional distress in order to recover damages for emotional distress caused by the abuse of process.

The Bank mistakenly relies on our prior decision in *Maryott v. First National Bank of Eden*, 2001 S.D. 43, 624 N.W.2d 96, 104. . . .

. . . The question was whether emotional damages were included and recoverable as "other consequential damages." Since the statute did not define "other consequential damages," this Court looked to other jurisdictions that had interpreted the same 402(b) language and followed those jurisdictions that required proof of intentional or negligent infliction of emotional distress. . . .

Maryott is distinguishable from the present tort case and should be read narrowly, mainly because the plaintiff's claim in *Maryott* was based on a U.C.C. statutory right to recover damages for a dishonored check. It did not involve a tort action. *Maryott* held that a plaintiff could not recover emotional damages under the statute unless the plaintiff met the requirements of the independent tort of negligent or intentional infliction of emotional distress. . . .

In South Dakota, tort damages are governed by SDCL 21–3–1, which provides: "For the breach of an obligation *not arising from contract*, the measure of damages, except where otherwise expressly provided by this code, is the amount which will compensate for *all* the detriment proximately caused thereby, whether it could have been anticipated or not." (Emphasis added.) We have consistently recognized emotional distress damages in tort actions. *Roth v. Farner–Bocken Co.*, 2003 S.D. 80, ¶ 70, 667 N.W.2d 651, 670 (upholding a jury award of

---

[1] Fix contends the following four jury instructions were an incorrect statement of the law:

    1. Jury Instruction No. 4 provided that the jury must find Fix "suffered an extreme and disabling emotional distress as a result of [the Bank] and Vaughn Beck's agreement to use, and their use of, a criminal prosecution primarily for an improper purpose."

    2. Jury Instruction No. 11 provided that Fix "may only recover damages for severe emotional distress."

    3. Jury Instruction No. 25 provided that if the jury decides for Fix on the question of liability, the jury "must then fix the amount of money which will reasonably and fairly compensate" Fix for "the pain and suffering, extreme emotional distress and loss of capacity of the enjoyment of life...."

    4. Special Verdict Question No. 4 directed the jury that they must find Fix "suffered extreme and disabling emotional distress as a proximate result of the abuse of process."

damages for the feelings of "anger, betrayal, and devastation" in an invasion of privacy action); *Carey v. Jack Rabbit Lines, Inc.*, 309 N.W.2d 824, 827 (S.D.1981) (upholding a trial court's award of damages in a negligence action as reasonable because "in addition to the painful injury, appellee ... suffered mental anguish"); *Bean v. Best*, 77 S.D. 433, 441–42, 93 N.W.2d 403, 408 (1958) ("A person who has a cause of action *for a tort* may be entitled to recover as an element of damages for that form of mental distress known as humiliation, that is, a feeling of degradation or inferiority...." (emphasis added) (quoting Restatement (First) of Torts § 905 cmt. d (1939))); *Davis v. Holy Terror Mining Co.*, 20 S.D. 399, 107 N.W. 374, 379 (1906) (reasoning that in determining damages "the jury should take into consideration the age and condition in life of the plaintiff, the physical injury inflicted, the bodily pain *and mental anguish endured*" (emphasis added)). Since an abuse of process claim is an intentional tort, a plaintiff can seek damages in the form of emotional distress without proving the independent tort of intentional infliction of emotional distress and without proving the heightened standard of "extreme and disabling" emotional distress.

This holding comports with other jurisdictions that recognize a plaintiff's right to recover damages for mental anguish in abuse of process actions without requiring the plaintiff to meet the heightened standard of "extreme and disabling." For example, in reviewing damages awarded by a jury in an abuse of process action, the North Dakota Supreme Court found that "[a] jury may properly consider wounded feelings, mental suffering, humiliation, degradation, and disgrace in fixing compensatory damages." *Stoner v. Nash Finch, Inc.*, 446 N.W.2d 747, 753 (N.D.1989). In a footnote, the North Dakota court distinguished damages in an abuse of process cause of action from those in a negligent infliction of emotional distress cause of action. The court noted that the "tort of abuse of process, unlike the tort of negligent infliction of emotional distress, does not require '[s]pecific proof of intangible damages [such as mental injury] ... as a prerequisite to an award if it is clear that such damages would accrue to a normal person.'" *Id.* at 753 n. 3 (alteration in original) (quoting Prosser & Keeton, The Law of Torts § 121, at 900 (5th ed.1984)).

In summary, we hold that to recover emotional distress damages sustained as a result of the tort of abuse of process, a plaintiff is not required to prove the elements of intentional or negligent infliction of emotional distress. The trial court erred by requiring Fix to prove that her emotional damages were "extreme and disabling." Because the jury was given the wrong legal standard for recovering emotional distress damages, we reverse and remand for a new trial.

2. Fix failed to show a genuine issue of material fact for her intentional infliction of emotional distress claim.

. . .

To survive the Bank's motion for summary judgment, Fix needed to demonstrate that there was an issue of material fact as to each of the elements of intentional infliction of emotional distress: "(1) an act by the defendant amounting to extreme and outrageous conduct; (2) intent on the part of the defendant to cause the plaintiff severe emotional distress; (3) the defendant's conduct was the cause in-fact of plaintiff's distress; and (4) the plaintiff suffered an extreme disabling emotional response to defendant's conduct." *Anderson v. First Century Fed. Credit Union*, 2007 S.D. 65, ¶ 38, 738 N.W.2d 40, 51–52.

[The court found that Fix had failed to satisfy the first element, which was a "rigorous benchmark."]

Because the trial court provided the jury with the incorrect legal standard for the recovery of emotional damages, we reverse and remand for trial.

Questions and Problems 3.14. Whatever the bank's obligations to its depositor, what obligations does the depositor owe the bank? Consider the following situation. SallerCo uses Pelleas & Associates, a large brokerage firm, for all of its real estate transactions. Pelleas recently contacted SallerCo's chief financial officer to inquire about unpaid fees owed to the firm. When the chief financial officer demonstrated that it had in fact paid in full, Pelleas uncovered what appears to have been a long-standing embezzlement scheme by its office manager, Melisande Golaud. Five years ago, she instructed Pelleas's bank, Banco Merca, to switch all Pelleas accounts to online banking. Among other things, this meant that no hard copies of monthly statements were mailed to Pelleas anymore. This enabled Melisande to transfer funds from Pelleas accounts to her own Cayman Islands account on the average of about $10,000 per month. No Pelleas employees except Melisande ever looked at the daily online statements, which would have given the reader the amount of each transaction in the account and the date on which the transaction was posted to the account. Melisande cannot be located, and Pelleas would like to demand that its bank restore the embezzled funds to its accounts, but should it be responsible to the bank for not discovering Melisande's scheme sooner? In analyzing whether Pelleas is likely to succeed in this demand, consider the following case.

C. NICHOLAS PEREOS, LTD. V. BANK OF AMERICA, N.A.
352 P.3d 1133 (Nev. 2015)

By the Court, HARDESTY, C.J.:

[Bank customer brought an action against a bank to recover losses sustained due to unauthorized activity in the customer's bank account. The District Court granted summary judgment in favor of the bank, and the customer appealed. The Nevada Supreme Court reversed and remanded, holding, among other things, that genuine issues of material fact existed as to the manner of delivery of the customer's account statements, whether the statements were sufficient to trigger the customer's duty to report unauthorized activity, and regarding the parties' fault with respect to the unauthorized activity.]

NRS 104.4406 regulates the relationship between a bank and its customers concerning losses sustained due to unauthorized activity in the customer's bank account. Generally, a customer "must exercise reasonable promptness" in examining a bank statement and within 30 days notify the bank of any unauthorized transactions. NRS 104.4406(3), 4(b). . . .

Mary Williams, a long-time employee of appellant, the C. Nicholas Pereos, Ltd., law firm, was a signator on the firm's operating account with respondent Bank of America. In September 2006, the firm's solo practitioner, C. Nicholas Pereos, removed Williams as a signator on the account, leaving Pereos as the sole signator. Pereos told Williams to let the Bank of America account "run itself out" to cover any outstanding checks, but he never took any action to affirmatively close the account.

In 2010, Pereos discovered that Williams had been embezzling money since 2006. Despite being removed as a signator on the account, Williams deposited checks made out to Pereos, Ltd. into the Bank of America account and would then write and sign checks for her own personal use. Pereos notified the bank of the unauthorized transactions on January 28, 2010. The next month, Pereos, Ltd. filed a complaint against Bank of America based on Williams' use of unauthorized signatures to withdraw funds from the account from 2006 to 2010. When it was discovered that Williams had enrolled the Pereos, Ltd. account in online banking and the bank statements had not been mailed, Pereos amended the complaint to include an allegation that Bank of America had failed to make Pereos, Ltd.'s statements available as required by NRS 104.4406(1).

Bank of America moved to dismiss the amended complaint, or alternatively for summary judgment, on the ground that Pereos, Ltd.'s claims for unauthorized transactions were time-barred either because they were not reported by Pereos, Ltd. within 30 days under NRS 104.4406(4)(b) or within the one-year period of repose under NRS 104.4406(6). The bank argued that, notwithstanding Pereos, Ltd.'s contention that the account statements were not mailed to it, Pereos' deposition testimony revealed that Pereos had on occasion personally picked up some of Pereos, Ltd.'s bank account statements from Bank of America in 2006, 2007, and 2008. The bank attached copies of the account's statements to its motion and argued that the "[u]nauthorized transactions ... were contained in the bank statements that were made available to [Pereos]". In opposition, Pereos, Ltd. argued that the statements he obtained were insufficient to provide it with notice of the unauthorized signatures as they "were only a single page or two-page document ... that showed check numbers and the amount of the check, and balances. Nothing more[.]" Moreover, he contended that the statements were insufficient because they did not contain a copy of the canceled checks. Pereos also argued that his claims for unauthorized checks cashed within the year preceding his notification to the bank were not time-barred. Conversely, Bank of America argued that, because the same wrongdoer committed all of the wrongful transactions, all claims were time-barred by Pereos, Ltd.'s failure to give the bank notice within 30 days after receiving the account statements. . . .

. . . NRS 104.4406 regulates the relationship between banks and bank customers concerning unauthorized activity in a customer's bank account. . . . Generally, the statute absolves a bank of liability for payment on an unauthorized transaction when it provides the customer with information that would allow the customer to identify any unauthorized transactions, such as an account statement, and the customer then fails to timely act in response to unauthorized transactions reflected therein. See Prestridge v. Bank of Jena, 924 So.2d 1266, 1270 (La.Ct.App.2006) (discussing analogous Louisiana statute).

Thus, once the customer is provided with the necessary account information, the customer must "exercise reasonable promptness" in examining the information and notifying the bank of any unauthorized transactions. NRS 104.4406(3). Failure to do so may limit the bank's liability for the unauthorized transactions contained in the information and also for any others made by the "same wrongdoer" that occur before the bank receives notice, depending on whether the bank exercised ordinary care in making the payments. NRS 104.4406(4), (5). Regardless of fault, however, a customer is barred from asserting any claims with respect to an unauthorized transaction more than one year after the bank made the information available to the customer. NRS 104.4406(6). . . .

To trigger a customer's duty to examine its account for unauthorized account activity, a bank may either (1) return or make available copies of the canceled checks to the customer, or (2) furnish an account statement to the customer. NRS 104.4406(1). If copies of canceled checks are not returned, the account statement must provide the customer with sufficient information for "the customer reasonably to identify the items paid" on the account. NRS 104.4406(1). This requirement is met "if the item is described by item number, amount and date of payment." Id.

This "safe harbor" rule permitting banks to furnish account statements to customers that contain the item number, amount, and date of payment in lieu of providing customers with copies of canceled checks was intended to reduce the costs associated with check collection. See U.C.C. § 4–406 cmt. 1 (2002). The drafters reasoned that this information is generally sufficient to notify "[a] customer who keeps a record of checks written" of any unauthorized signatures, while also recognizing that this information may be insufficient for a customer who does not "utilize [a] record-keeping method." Id. The drafters explained that "accommodating customers who do not keep adequate records is not as desirable as accommodating customers who keep more careful records," nor does it reduce the cost of the check collection system to all customers. Id. Therefore, the drafters placed the burden on the bank's customers to remain reasonably aware of the activity on their accounts. See id. Accordingly, if the customer "should reasonably have discovered the unauthorized payment" from the information provided, the customer must promptly notify the bank. NRS 104.4406(3).

Here, there are genuine issues of material fact as to the manner of delivery and the content of the "statements" that Bank of America contends were mailed to Pereos or delivered to him during his branch visits. Pereos, Ltd. disputes the fact that Bank of America mailed bank statements to its office location during the time in question. While Bank of America supplied copies of the bank statements to the district court, it appears from the record that the bank did not actually mail those statements to Pereos, Ltd., but rather, they were made available online at the direction of Williams. It is not clear from the record the extent of Williams' authority and when she converted delivery of the bank statements to an online format. Nonetheless, Bank of America continues to maintain that, regardless of the method of delivery, Pereos received some of the statements during his visits to the bank between September 2006 and January 2008, the contents of which would have put him on notice of the unauthorized activity. And even though Pereos concedes that the statements he received contained the item number and amount for each item paid, he maintains that they did not contain the date of payment. Because genuine issues of material fact remain as to the delivery method of the bank statements and whether the statements Pereos received during his visits to Bank of America contained the statutory safe harbor information to discover the unauthorized transactions, we conclude that the district court erred in granting summary judgment under the 30–day rule in NRS 104.4406(4)(b).

Pereos, Ltd. next argues that, even if the statements triggered its duty to identify and promptly notify Bank of America of the unauthorized activity, its claims for checks forged within the year preceding giving notice to the bank are not time-barred by the one-year deadline. Bank of America argues that all of Pereos, Ltd.'s claims are barred pursuant to NRS 104.4406(4)(b), because payment on all of the acts of forgery, committed by the same wrongdoer, occurred after Pereos, Ltd. had 30 days to examine the first account statement containing forged transactions and before Pereos, Ltd. reported the unauthorized transactions to Bank of America. To resolve this issue, we examine the interplay between NRS 104.4406's subsections 4, 5, and 6, to determine whether Pereos, Ltd.'s claims for unauthorized payments made from its bank account during the one-year period before January 2010 are statutorily barred.

Distinguishing between a single forgery and multiple forgeries by the same wrongdoer, subsection 4 provides that a customer who fails to exercise the reasonable diligence required in subsection 3 is precluded from asserting a claim against the bank for a single forged item if the bank "proves that it suffered a loss" from that failure, NRS 104.4406(4)(a), or for multiple forged items "by the same wrongdoer ... paid in good faith by the bank[,] if the payment was made before the bank received notice from the customer of the unauthorized signature or alteration," but after the customer had 30 days to review the account statement. NRS 104.4406(4)(b). These preclusions are subject to exception for the bank's failure to exercise due care, however: "[i]f ... the customer proves that the bank failed to exercise ordinary care in paying the item and that the failure substantially contributed to loss," the loss is to be divided between the bank and the customer. NRS 104.4406(5). And if the bank pays the item without good faith, subsection 4's prohibitions against the customer asserting a claim are inapplicable altogether. Id. But regardless of either the bank's or the customer's failure to exercise ordinary care, a customer is precluded from bringing any claim against the bank if it is not brought within one year of the account statement being made available. NRS 104.4406(6).

To the extent that Bank of America argues that all of Pereos' claims are barred by NRS 104.4406(4)(b) because the same wrongdoer was responsible for all of the embezzlements and Pereos did not report them within 30 days of receiving the first account statement reflecting the forgeries, we note that the one-year period of repose in NRS 104.4406(6) does not differentiate between a single forgery and multiple forgeries by the same wrongdoer. See NRS 104.4406(6). Because NRS 104.4406(6) does not expressly differentiate between a single forgery and multiple forgeries by the same wrongdoer, we conclude that a new limitations period under its one-year statute of repose begins to run with each successive forgery. See Sun'n Sand, Inc. v. United Cal. Bank, 21 Cal.3d 671, 148 Cal.Rptr. 329, 582 P.2d 920, 935 (Cal.1978) ("This failure to explicitly differentiate between one-time and repetitive forgeries and alterations in [the one-year statute of repose] leads us, in light of the express distinction in [the 'same wrongdoer' subsection], to conclude that a new one-year period begins to run with each successive check."); Associated Home & RV Sales, Inc. v. Bank of Belen, 294 P.3d 1276, 1283 (N.M.Ct.App.2012) (holding that the one-year statute of repose controls because there is "no natural connection between [the] 'same wrongdoer' rule and the more general wording in [the one-year statute of repose subsection]"). Thus, Pereos is permitted to bring claims consistent with the provisions in NRS 104.4406.

Moreover, if the customer sufficiently proves that the bank failed to exercise ordinary care in making the unauthorized payment, NRS 104.4406(4)(b)'s limitation period is negated. Here, Pereos, Ltd. has alleged, and Bank of America has not denied, that it paid on checks drawn from the account signed by Williams after Williams' authority over the account was removed. Thus, Pereos may be able to prove that Bank of America failed to exercise ordinary care in continuing to honor Williams' signature on checks despite the account owner's instructions otherwise. Accordingly, genuine issues of material fact exist regarding the parties' fault with respect to these transactions. Even if Pereos, Ltd.'s claims for unauthorized transactions before January 2009 are barred by NRS 104.4406(4)(b), Pereos, Ltd. is entitled to go forward with its claims against Bank of America for those unauthorized payments made during the year before Pereos notified the bank in January 2010. See NRS 104.4406(5); Associated Home, 294 P.3d at 1283 (holding that, even though the 30–day statutory limitation period had elapsed, because the one-year statute of repose had yet not expired, the customer could bring a claim against the bank if the customer could prove that the bank did not exercise ordinary care).

Questions and Problems 3.15. The preceding cases explored the customer-bank relationship. What about the payee-drawee bank relationship? In Chapter 2, the *Messing* case suggested that there were no legal consequences of the relationship *per se*. Are there legal consequences – rights and obligations between payee and drawee – if the bank honors the check upon presentment? Consider the following case in addressing that question.

GUARANTY BANK & TRUST V. SMITH
952 S.W.2d 787 (Mo.App. 1997)

BARNEY, Judge.

This action was brought by Guaranty Bank & Trust (Plaintiff bank) against Lawrence Lee Smith (Defendant Smith) and L.B. Smith Co., Inc. (Defendant L.B. Smith Company), to recover funds paid to L.B. Smith Company contrary to a stop-payment order. The trial court granted summary judgment to Plaintiff bank against both Defendants in the sum of $18,198.00 (the amount of the check), plus interest and costs. Defendants appeal.

On December 4, 1995, Defendant L.B. Smith Company received a check from Merit Construction Company, Inc. (Merit) in the sum of $18,198.00 as payment for work performed by Defendant L.B. Smith Company. The check issued to Defendant L.B. Smith Company by Merit was drawn on Merit's business bank account with Plaintiff bank. Defendant L.B. Smith Company deposited Merit's check in Defendant L.B. Smith Company's bank account on December 5, 1995.

The next day, December 6, 1995, Merit placed a "stoppayment" order on the check it issued to Defendants because of an error in the computation of the amount owed. Merit immediately notified Defendant L.B. Smith Company that it had issued a stoppayment order on the check and offered Defendant L.B. Smith Company a replacement check.

On December 15, 1995, Defendant Smith traveled to Kansas City, Kansas, to receive a replacement check from Merit in the sum of $18,171.75, drawn on the same account as the original check. Defendant Smith endorsed the new check and in turn received a cashier's check. This cashier's check was then deposited in Defendant L.B. Smith Company's bank account with another bank.

However, Plaintiff bank failed to promptly stop payment on the first check issued to Defendant L.B. Smith Company from Merit. Consequently, Plaintiff bank made payment to Defendant L.B. Smith Company on both checks issued from Merit, together totaling $36,369.75.

Plaintiff bank demanded that Defendant L.B. Smith Company reimburse it for the payment it made to Defendant L.B. Smith Company on the first check, *i.e.*, $18,198.00. Defendant L.B. Smith Company refused, claiming that Merit owed it additional money as represented by the first check, and thus it maintained that it was entitled to keep the money. Plaintiff bank filed suit for restitution and unjust enrichment.[1] The trial court granted Plaintiff bank's motion for summary judgment against both Defendants.

Defendants appeal, assigning two points of trial court error. First, Defendants aver that section 400.4–407 (Uniform Commercial Code) supplanted the common law remedies of unjust enrichment and restitution. Defendants maintain that under section 400.4–407 Plaintiff bank was subrogated to the rights of Merit and that Plaintiff bank failed to prove that Merit had a defense to payment of the check at issue. Thus, Defendants contend, the trial court erred in granting Plaintiff bank summary judgment. Second, Defendant maintains that it was trial court error to grant judgment against Defendant Lawrence Lee Smith, individually, because he was acting in his capacity as president for Defendant L.B. Smith Company when the check at issue was endorsed and deposited. . . .

II.

In Defendants' first point, they assign error to the trial court in granting summary judgment to Plaintiff bank because Defendants maintain that section 400.4–407 precluded the Plaintiff bank's recovery of damages under the common law theories of restitution and unjust enrichment. Defendants maintain that this is because the Plaintiff bank failed to establish that Merit had a defense to the payment on the check at issue. See § 400.4–407(3).

[The court quoted UCC § 4-407.] Additionally, "subrogation," as used in section 400.4–407, is defined as the substitution of one party in the place of another with reference to a lawful claim or right. *Estate of Griffitts*, 938 S.W.2d 621, 624 (Mo.App.1997).

Therefore, under sub-section 400.4–407(3), in order to achieve subrogation, the subrogor (Merit) must have some existing right or legal claim that can be subrogated to fulfill the claim of the subrogee (Plaintiff bank).

Our attention has not been called to nor has our independent research revealed a Missouri case on point. Defendants rely on *Bryan v. Citizens Nat'l Bank in Abilene*, 628 S.W.2d 761 (Tex.1982) as authority for the proposition that section 400.4–407 of the Uniform Commercial Code displaced the common law theories of restitution and unjust enrichment in the case at bar.

---

[1] Plaintiff bank did not charge Merit's bank account for the check that was paid contrary to Merit's stop-payment order.

In *Bryan*, Defendant Charlie Bryan received a check from B & G Construction Company in the sum of $10,000 as payment for a business Defendant Charlie Bryan sold B & G Construction Company. *Id.* at 761. Thereafter, B & G Construction Company placed a stop-payment order on the check; however, Plaintiff Citizens National Bank paid the check over the stop payment order. *Id.* The bank then sued Defendant Charlie Bryan under the common law theory of restitution to recover the funds it paid contrary to its customer's stop-payment order. At trial, neither party introduced evidence of any defense to payment of the check that B & G Construction Company may have had against Defendant Charlie Bryan. *Id.* at 762. Nonetheless, the trial court rendered judgment in favor of Citizens National Bank, and a court of appeals affirmed. *Id.*

The Texas Supreme Court reversed, holding that under the provisions of [section 400.4–407], a "bank recovers by stepping into the shoes of the party who was entitled to the funds represented by the check." *Bryan*, 628 S.W.2d at 762. Thus, the court commented, if Citizens National Bank had brought its suit against Defendant Charlie Bryan, under [section 400.4–407] it would have been required to assert whatever defenses to payment of the check the drawer, B & G Construction Company, may have had against Defendant Charlie Bryan. Id.

The Texas Supreme Court held that the common law right of restitution is available as a remedy to the extent that it does not conflict with the Uniform Commercial Code provisions. *Id.* at 764. Thus, a bank may recover under the common law theory of restitution, but only to the extent that it alleges and proves that the maker had a defense to the payment of the check as required by section 400.4–407. *Id.* The court then held that Citizen National Bank failed to prove that B & G Construction Company had a defense to the payment of the check.[4] *Id.*

We agree with the Texas Supreme Court in its holding that a bank may recover under either the common law theory of restitution or section 400.4–407 to the extent that a maker of a check has a defense to payment to a payee who received the funds over a stop-payment order.[5] *See Bryan*, 628 S.W.2d at 764; *see also* 9 C.J.S. Banks & Banking

---

[4] The Texas Supreme Court also held that Citizens National Bank showed no unconscionable loss. Bryan, 628 S.W.2d at 763. The supreme court stated that the purpose of restitution is to prevent unconscionable loss to the party paying out funds and unjust enrichment to the party receiving the payment. Id. . . .

[5] We note that section 400.1–103 expressly provides that the common law principles of law and equity (including restitution and unjust enrichment)

§§ 362–363 (1996). The common law theory of restitution may not be used, however, to circumvent the provisions of the Uniform Commercial Code. *See Bryan*, 628 S.W.2d at 764.

In the instant matter, Plaintiff bank may recover from Defendant L.B. Smith Company only to the extent that it alleges and proves that Merit was not liable to Defendant L.B. Smith Company "with respect to the transaction out of which the [check] arose." *See id.* at 763–764; *see also* § 400.4–407(3). Based on the record before us, however, we cannot make a determination as to what is the precipitating "transaction" giving rise to the issuance of the check. This constitutes an unresolved material fact.

In its petition, as well as its motion for summary judgment, Plaintiff bank seeks to limit the "transaction" out of which the check arose, to the first check ($18,198.00) given by Merit to L.B. Smith Company, for which a substitute check was provided after Merit's stop-payment order.[6] Defendants' answers to Plaintiff bank's interrogatories, however, suggest that the pertinent "transaction" is much broader, involving an on-going contractual relationship arising from work performed by L.B. Smith Company for Merit. In these answers Defendants claim that Merit owed Defendant L.B. Smith Company $79,512.47, of which $76,407.47 had been paid. The amount paid included payment on the check at issue, $18,198.00. Defendants also stated that Merit owed an additional $3,105.00, which had not been paid.

Therefore, under the "transaction" suggested by Defendants' answers to Plaintiff bank's interrogatories, in order for Plaintiff bank to prevail against Defendant L.B. Smith Company, Plaintiff bank had to show that Merit had a defense with respect to the contractual transaction between Merit and L.B. Smith Company. *See Bryan*, 628 S.W.2d at 762. However, in Plaintiff bank's motion for summary judgment, no proof was submitted showing that Merit had a defense to Defendants' claim.

Where, as here, the record reasonably supports any inference other than those necessary to support a judgment for the movant, a genuine

---

shall supplement the provisions of the Uniform Commercial Code "unless displaced by the particular provisions of this chapter...." § 400.1–103. The provisions of section 400.4–407 do not purport to displace any common law remedies. § 400.4–407; *Bryan*, 628 S.W.2d at 764. Indeed, section 400.4–407 seeks "to prevent unjust enrichment."

[6] In this connection, see *Dunnigan v. First Bank*, 217 Conn. 205, 585 A.2d 659, 663 (1991) (holding that in determining whether a customer suffered a "loss" under [section 400.4–403], the focus is on the check itself and on the transaction underlying it, and not on whether there were other prior, unrelated transactions between the maker and payee of the check).

issue of material fact exists and the movant's motion for summary judgment must be overruled. *See J.M. v. Shell Oil Co.*, 922 S.W.2d 759, 761 (Mo. banc 1996). Accordingly, we reverse and remand.

Questions and Problems 3.16. *Guaranty Bank* relied heavily on the Texas Supreme Court's decision in *Bryan*, which had raised similar issues under UCC § 4-407. Here is what the Texas Supreme Court said on the subject of a payor bank's options under the section:

> A bank that mistakenly pays a check over a stop-payment order has several remedies. The bank may simply charge the customer's account for the amount of the payment. If the customer claims against the bank for wrongful payment, then the bank may implead the payee under [section 400.4–407] of the Code and assert against him any defenses which the customer asserts against the bank. Also, the bank may decide not to debit the customer's account and instead file suit against the payee of the check either for restitution or for recovery on the underlying contract as subrogee to the customer's rights. Under either theory, the bank may recover only to the extent it proves the drawer of the check was not liable to the payee.

Bryan v. Citizens Nat'l Bank in Abilene, 628 S.W.2d 761, 764 (Tex.1982). Is the *Guaranty Bank* decision consistent with this statement?

3.17. Is a bank always obliged to pay its cashier's checks? It certainly has a right to insist upon proper identification and indorsement before it pays. Beyond those details – one is tempted to call them "formalities" – does the bank necessarily commit a wrongful dishonor if it refuses to honor a cashier's check that it issued? In a situation in which the bank had reason to believe that the holder of three cashier's checks had committed fraud to obtain the funds to purchase the checks, *EA Management v. JP Morgan Chase Bank, N.A.*, 655 F.3d 573 (6th Cir. 2011), held that the holder was not entitled to enforce the checks. Among other things, EA Management cites UCC §§ 3-305(a) (obligor's defenses to holder's claim), 4-403 (effect of stop payment order).

3.18. Can the bank's customer "build in" a stop payment when it issues the check? *See, e.g., Aliaga Medical Center, S.C. v. Harris Bank N.A.*, 21 N.E.3d 1203 (Ill. App. 2014), where the bank customer had placed a notation on its check notation "void after 90 days." The court found that the notation did not effectively stop payment on the check. The court also considered whether the notation could render the check "stale" after 90 days, consistent with UCC § 4-404. If the check *was* stale after that period, could the bank still pay the stale check? *See Aliaga Medical Center, supra* at *4. *Cf.* UCC § 4-404.

3.19. Reread *Guaranty Bank*, footnote 5. If UCC § 4-407 seeks "to prevent unjust enrichment and only to the extent necessary to prevent loss to the bank by reason of its payment of the item," why doesn't that "displace" the common law principle of unjust enrichment? If the UCC has a remedy for such situations, why doesn't that control such claims?

3.20. If a check is dishonored – whatever the reason for the dishonor might be – what are the rights of the holder of such a check? Against whom can these rights be asserted? Should it make a difference that the asserted reason for the dishonor is intentional misconduct like forgery? Consider the following case in answering these questions.

TRIFFIN V. THIRD FEDERAL SAVINGS BANK
--- N.J.Super. ---, 2008 WL 5233796 (App.Div.2008),
cert. denied, 199 N.J. 130 (2009)

PER CURIAM.

. . . Plaintiff Robert J. Triffin is in the business of purchasing dishonored checks. Plaintiff entered into separate assignment agreements with Richmond Financial Services, Inc., a check cashing company (Richmond), to purchase Richmond's rights and interests in five dishonored checks drawn on defendant Third Federal Savings Bank. More specifically, the checks at issue were drawn on the account of defendant's depositor, Veterans of Foreign Wars Post 22 (Veterans).

The five checks uttered[a] on Veterans' account were presented to Richmond, which cashed them. Richmond deposited the checks into its account at Wachovia Bank (Wachovia). Wachovia credited Richmond's account and presented the checks to the Federal Reserve Bank, Philadelphia, PA (the Fed) branch for transmittal to defendant. The Fed presented electronic images of the checks to defendant for payment. Defendant paid Wachovia through a debit of defendant's Fed account and also debited Veterans' depository account.

After Veterans informed defendant it executed affidavits attesting the checks were forgeries, defendant printed an electronic copy of each check. On the face of each check, defendant stamped, "RETURNED

---

[a] The court's use of the term "uttered" – rather than, for example, "issued" – is suggestive. "Utter" has been defined to mean "To put or send (a document) into circulation; esp., to circulate (a forged note) as if genuine." BLACK'S LAW DICTIONARY (9th ed. 2009), *utter*.

UNPAID," with the additional notation "OTHER FORGERY." A different stamp appears on the back of the electronic copy of each check, which states:

> This is a photographic facsimile of the original check, which was endorsed by the undersigned and reported lost, stolen or destroyed, while in the regular course of bank collection. All prior endorsements and any missing endorsements and the validity of this facsimile are hereby guaranteed, and upon payment hereof in lieu of the original check, the undersigned will hold each collecting bank and payor bank harmless from any loss suffered, provided the original check is unpaid and payment is stopped thereon. Third Federal Savings Bank 2313-7218-3.

Below the stamp is a signature of defendant's authorized representative, who appears to be Junita John. The checks were sent to the Fed to reverse the prior account debit. The Fed credited defendant's account and debited Wachovia's account. Defendant credited Veterans' account. It can be assumed Wachovia debited Richmond's account.

Plaintiff purchased the dishonored checks from Richmond, pursuant to the terms of an assignment agreement. Plaintiff filed this action, solely against defendant, seeking payment on the instruments. In his complaint, plaintiff alleges liability based on a "breach of contract/warranties." Plaintiff argues the copies of the checks returned to Richmond, plaintiff's assignor, "do not constitute legally enforceable dishonored checks" because the copies failed to include the legend: "THIS IS A LEGAL COPY OF YOUR CHECKS YOU CAN USE IT THE SAME WAY YOU WOULD USE THE ORIGINAL CHECKS ." Plaintiff also contends defendant received funds from Richmond's account in an amount equal to the amount of the dishonored checks, triggering warranties extended to depositors. Citing 12 C.F.R. 229.56(a), plaintiff claims defendant is obligated to satisfy the face amount of the dishonored checks, pay prejudgment interest, and reimburse the return check fees.

Plaintiff moved and defendant cross-moved for summary judgment. Plaintiff also filed a motion to amend his complaint, asserting that without defendant's provision of legally enforceable substitute checks, he cannot sue the forger for recovery. Finally, plaintiff voluntarily dismissed, with prejudice, the "Sixth Claim" of his action. . . . [The trial court denied Triffins' motion.]

On appeal, plaintiff states his assignor did not get what he paid for,

> namely[,] legally equivalent copies of dishonored checks from [defendant]. The focus of plaintiff's theory of liability is that, although

[defendant] received 'consideration'-and as defined in 12 C.F.R. 229.2(ccc)-... [defendant's] return of ... legally non-conforming facsimile check[ ] copies constitutes a material breach of ... statutory warranties to the depositor of the ... original check.

Plaintiff argues that he, standing in the shoes of the original depositor, may recover damages for breach of the warranties set forth in 12 C.F.R. 229.52. . . .

Defendant maintains it did not and had no obligation to issue substitute checks because the instruments were dishonored due to forgery. . . . [W]e affirm the Special Civil Part orders. . . .

The statute provides the circumstances under which a payor bank that has settled on an item may return the item, revoke settlement, and recover funds paid. [The court quotes UCC § 4-301(a)-(b).]

Plaintiff argues defendant's failure to revoke settlement and return the item before the midnight deadline results in an obligation for final payment. We are satisfied plaintiff's contention lacks merit.

Despite plaintiff's suggestions to the contrary, "the action pursued ... is not based on a contractual right," but a statutory one that "consequently [ ] is not assignable." *Triffin v. TD Banknorth, N.A.*, 190 N.J. 326, 329 (2007). Plaintiff took the checks, following their untimely return, with full knowledge of their dishonor due to forgery. He " 'has no vested interest in the timely payment or return of these checks.... It is a cause of action for a breach of statutory duty, not an action for collection of a negotiable instrument.' " *TD Banknorth, supra*, 190 N.J. at 329 (quoting *Triffin v. Bridge View Bank*, 330 N.J.Super. 473, 478 (App.Div.2000)).

Next, we turn to the plaintiff's argument suggesting defendant breached its obligation to return the original dishonored checks or provide legally enforceable electronic substitutes. The "Check Clearing for the 21st Century Act" (the Act), allows banks to "truncate," or "remove [ ] original paper check[s] from the check collection or return process and send to the recipient, in lieu of such original paper check, a substitute check or, by agreement, information relating to the original check." 12 U.S.C.A. § 5002(3)(18). The Act was passed:

(1) To facilitate check truncation by authorizing substitute checks.

(2) To foster innovation in the check collection system without mandating receipt of checks in electronic form.

(3) To improve the overall efficiency of the Nation's payments system.

[12 U.S.C.A. § 5001(2)(b).] Section 5003(4)(b) of the Act, states:

> A substitute check shall be the legal equivalent of the original check for all purposes including any provision of any Federal or State law, and for all persons if the substitute check-
>
> (1) accurately represents all of the information on the front and back of the original check as of the time the original check was truncated; and
>
> (2) bears the legend: "This is a legal copy of your check. You can use it the same way you would use the original check.

Here, the electronic check images at issue do not bear the requisite legend to constitute substitute checks, but were stamped to identify their return as forgeries.

We reject plaintiff's argument that defendant held an affirmative obligation to return the original documents pursuant to the regulations promulgated to effectuate the Act. First, the Act makes clear, although a bank may return the original documents, electronic substitutes may be used instead to facilitate expeditious commercial paper transactions. 12 U.S.C.A. § 5001(2)(b).5 The regulation on which plaintiff relies, 12 C.F.R. § 229.51, reiterates a substitute check is "the legal equivalent of an original check for all persons and all purposes...." *Ibid.* The regulation does not provide a cause of action available to plaintiff.

Second, in this matter, defendant never received the original checks. At all times it utilized electronic copies of the checks received from the Fed. The originals, if they exist, were in Wachovia's possession and may have been presented to the Fed. However, it is more likely the originals were destroyed when the electronic copies were made. Defendant has no responsibility to plaintiff or his assignor to return the original instruments, which it never possessed.

Third, notice of dishonor

> may be given by any commercially reasonable means, including an oral, written, or electronic communication; and is sufficient if it reasonably identifies the instrument and indicates the instrument has been dishonored or has not been paid or accepted. Return of an instrument given to the bank for collection is sufficient notice of dishonor.

[N.J.S.A. 12A:3-503(b).] The notation stamped on the front of all five checks adequately complies with the statutory requirements.

Finally, the regulations promulgated under the Act provide adequate alternatives when an original document is unavailable. Section 229.31(f) of Title 12 of the Code of Federal Regulations, entitled "Notice in Lieu of Return," provides:

If a check is unavailable for return, the returning bank may send in its place a copy of the front and back of the returned check, or, if no copy is available, a written notice of nonpayment containing the information specified in § 229.33(b). The copy or notice shall clearly state that it constitutes a notice in lieu of return. A notice in lieu of return is considered a returned check and is subject to the expeditious return requirements of this section and to the other requirements of this subpart.

The stamped notation on each of the five checks at issue adequately complies with this regulation. The bank guarantees the copies were used in lieu of the original. Nothing more is necessary.

Questions and Problems 3.21. Why doesn't 12 C.F.R. § 229.51, at issue in *Triffin*, "provide a cause of action available to" Triffin? *Triffin, supra* at 217.

3.22. Why do these regulations, issued by the Federal Reserve pursuant to the Check Clearing, control the issue of the proper return of dishonored checks, rather than UCC § 4-301?

3.23. Since *Triffin* essentially involves a claim that the bank failed to comply with UCC § 4-301, why does the court invoke UCC § 3-503(b) as authority?

B. THE COLLECTION PROCESS

Questions and Problems 3.24. The materials in the previous section focused primarily on the transactional implications of the bank-related payment system. That system has its own structural and process rules, however, and these have an impact on the transactions. In any transaction, there is always the risk of fraud or bad faith, but in the bank collection process there is also a risk that a party to a transaction may "game" or manipulate the process itself. Consider how the system was being gamed in the next cases, and assess the effectiveness and efficiency of the response to that risk.

FIRST NATIONAL BANK IN HARVEY
V. COLONIAL BANK
898 F.Supp. 1220 (N.D.Ill. 1995)

GRADY, District Judge.

Before the court are the parties' cross-motions for summary judgment. For the reasons explained, plaintiff First National Bank in Harvey's motion is granted in part and denied in part. Defendant Colonial Bank's motion is granted in part and denied in part. Defendant Federal Reserve Bank of Chicago's motion is granted.

BACKGROUND

Check kiting is a form of bank fraud.[1] The kiter opens accounts at two (or more) banks, writes checks on insufficient funds on one account, then covers the overdraft by depositing a check drawn on insufficient funds from the other account.

> To illustrate the operation, suppose that the defrauder opens two accounts with a deposit of $500 each at the First National Bank and a distant Second National Bank. (A really successful defrauder will have numerous accounts in fictitious names at banks in widely separated states.) The defrauder then issues for goods or cash checks totalling $3000 against the First National Bank. But before they clear and overdraw the account, he covers the overdrafts with a check for $4,000 drawn on the Second National Bank. The Second National account will be overdrawn when the $4,000 check is presented; before that happens, however, the defrauder covers it with a check on the First National Bank. The process is repeated innumerable times until there is a constant float of worthless checks between the accounts and the defrauder has bilked the banks of a substantial sum of money.

John D. O'Malley, "Common Check Frauds and the Uniform Commercial Code," 23 Rutgers L.Rev. 189, 194 n. 35 (1968–69). By timing the scheme correctly and repeating it over a period of time, the kiter can use the funds essentially as an interest-free loan. *Williams v. United States*, 458 U.S. 279, 281 n. 1, 102 S.Ct. 3088, 3090 n. 1, 73 L.Ed.2d 767 (1982) (quoting Brief for the United States).

Check kiting is possible because of a combination of two rules found in Article 4 of the Uniform Commercial Code. Under § 4–208(a)(1), a depositary bank may allow a customer to draw on uncollected funds, that is, checks that have been deposited but not yet paid.[3] Second, under §§ 4–301 and 4–302, a payor bank must either

---

[1] 18 U.S.C. § 1344; *United States v. LeDonne*, 21 F.3d 1418, 1426 (7th Cir.), *cert. denied*, 513 U.S. 1020, 115 S.Ct. 584, 130 L.Ed.2d 498 (1994).

[3] Regulation CC, issued by the Board of Governors of the Federal Reserve System, governs the availability of funds and the collection of checks. 12 C.F.R. pt. 229. Under Regulation CC, a depositary bank must make funds drawn on a local check available two days following the deposit. 12 C.F.R. § 229.12(b)(1). During this two-day period, the funds are "uncollected." The depositary bank may either return checks drawn on those funds or choose to

pay or dishonor a check drawn on it by midnight of the second banking day following presentment. Barkley Clark, The Law of Bank Deposits, Collections and Credit Cards ¶ 5.03 [5] (3d ed. 1990). Thus when a kite is operating, the depositary bank allows the kiter to draw on uncollected funds based on a deposit of a check. The depositary bank presents that check to the payor bank, which must decide whether to pay or return the check before the midnight deadline. The check may appear to be covered by uncollected funds at the payor bank, and so the payor bank may decide to pay the check by allowing the midnight deadline to pass.

A kite crashes when one of the banks dishonors checks drawn on it and returns them to the other banks involved in the kite. Clark, *supra*. Usually, such a dishonor occurs when one bank suspects a kite. *Id*. However, an individual bank may have trouble detecting a check kiting scheme. "Until one has devoted a substantial amount of time examining not only one's own account, but accounts at other banks, it may be impossible to know whether the customer is engaged in a legitimate movement of funds or illegitimate kiting." James J. White & Robert S. Summers, Uniform Commercial Code § 17–1 (3d ed. 1988 & Supp.1994). But each bank is usually able to monitor only its own account, and "[t]here is no certain test that distinguishes one who writes many checks on low balances from a check kiter." White & Summers, *supra*, § 17–2. Even if a bank suspects a kite, it might decide not to take any action for a number of reasons. First, it may be liable to its customer for wrongfully dishonoring checks. § 4–202. Second, if it reports that a kite is operating and turns out to be wrong, it could find itself defending a defamation suit. White & Summers, *supra*, § 17–1 (Supp.1994). Finally, if it errs in returning checks or reporting a kite, it may risk angering a large customer. *Id*.

FACTS

This case involves the fallout of a collapsed check kite. Two of the banks involved, First National Bank in Harvey ("First National") and Colonial Bank ("Colonial") are the parties to this litigation. The Federal Reserve Bank of Chicago (the "Reserve Bank"), through whose clearinghouse the relevant checks were processed, is also a party.

Shelly International Marketing ("Shelly") opened a checking account at First National in December 1989. . . . The principals of Shelly also opened accounts at the Family Bank (a nonparty) in the names of Shelly Brokerage and Crete Trading around December 1990. . . . On

---

pay the checks. After two days, the depositary bank's records show the check "collected" for Regulation CC purposes, although the check is not actually collected until it is paid by the payor bank. . . .

December 31, 1991, the principals of Shelly opened a checking account at Colonial Bank in the name of World Commodities, Inc. . . . . Shelly and World Commodities were related companies, with the same or similar shareholders, officers, and directors. . . . The principals of Shelly and World Commodities began operating a check kiting scheme among the accounts at the three banks in early 1991. . . .

The main events at issue in this case took place in February 1992. The checks that form the basis of this suit are thirteen checks totalling $1,523,892.49 for which First National was the depositary bank and Colonial was the payor bank (the "Colonial checks"). Also relevant are seventeen checks totalling $1,518,642.86 for which Colonial was the depositary bank and First National was the payor bank (the "First National checks").

On Monday, February 10, Shelly deposited the thirteen Colonial checks to its First National account. . . . First National then sent those checks through the check clearing system. . . . That same day, World Commodities deposited the seventeen First National checks to its Colonial account. . . .

The next day, Tuesday, February 11, the Colonial checks were presented to Colonial for payment, and the First National checks were presented to First National for payment. . . . That day, David Spiewak, an officer with First National's holding company, Pinnacle, reviewed the bank's records to determine why there were large balance fluctuations in Shelly's First National account. . . . Spiewak began to suspect that a kite might be operating. . . . He did not know whether Colonial had enough funds to cover the Colonial checks that had been deposited on Monday, February 10, and forwarded to Colonial for payment. . . . Later that day, First National froze the Shelly account to prevent any further activity in it. . . .

On the morning of Wednesday, February 12, Spiewak met with First National president Dennis Irvin and Pinnacle's chief lending officer Mike Braun to discuss the Shelly account. . . . Spiewak informed the others of what he knew, and the three agreed that there was a possible kite. . . . They concluded that further investigation was needed. . . . The First National officers decided to return the First National checks to Colonial. First National says that the decision was made at this meeting, but Colonial says the decision was actually made the day before. . . .

On Wednesday, First National returned the First National checks to Colonial. Under Regulation CC, a bank that is returning checks in excess of $2,500.00 must provide notice to the depositary bank either by telephone, actual return of the check, or Fed Wire before 4:00 p.m. on the second business day following presentment. . . . First National notified Colonial by Fed Wire that it was returning the seventeen

First National checks. . . . Initially, the large item return form indicated that the reason for the return was "uncollected funds," but Spiewak changed that reason to "refer to maker." . . .

Colonial received the Fed Wire notices at approximately 2:45 p.m. on Wednesday and routed them to its cashier, Joanne Topham. . . . Randall Soderman, a Colonial loan officer, was informed of the large return, and immediately began an investigation. . . . He realized that if the Colonial checks were not returned by midnight that same day, Colonial would be out the money. . . . Returning the Colonial checks before midnight would protect Colonial from liability, but it would risk disappointing the customer. . . . Anthony Schiller, the loan officer in charge of the World Commodities account, called World Commodities comptroller Charles Patterson and its attorney Jay Goldstein. . . . Both assured Schiller that the First National checks were good and should be redeposited. . . . Ultimately, Richard Vucich, Colonial's president, and Joanne Topham, Colonial's cashier, decided not to return the Colonial checks on Wednesday. They decided instead to meet on Thursday morning with Schiller to discuss the matter. ...

Schiller, Topham, and Vucich met on the morning of Thursday, February 13. . . . At the conclusion of the meeting, they decided to return the thirteen Colonial checks to First National. . . . At about 10:45 a.m., Colonial telephoned First National to say that it intended to return the Colonial checks. . . . Colonial sent the Colonial checks back through the Reserve Bank as a return in a return cash letter. . . . The Reserve Bank debited First National's Reserve Bank account in the amount of the Colonial checks. . . . First National received the returned Colonial checks on Friday, February 14. . . .

First National then resorted to the Fed's "challenge procedure" to contest the return of the Colonial checks after the midnight deadline. First National prepared and submitted to the Reserve Bank a "Sender's Claim of Late Return" form for each of the Colonial checks. . . . The Reserve Bank processed the claim forms and credited the Reserve Bank account of First National $1,523,892.49 and debited the Reserve Bank account of Colonial in the same amount. . . . On February 24, Colonial prepared and filed a "Paying Bank's Response to Claim of Late Return" form for each of the thirteen Colonial checks. . . . As a consequence of the processing of the response forms, the Reserve Bank reversed the credit given to First National and the debit made to Colonial. . . .

First National then filed this suit against Colonial and the Reserve Bank, alleging that Colonial wrongfully returned the Colonial checks after the midnight deadline and the Reserve Bank wrongfully accepted the late return.[6] Count I of First National's amended complaint against Colonial alleges breach of warranty under Regulation CC for the late return of the checks. 12 C.F.R. § 229.34. Count II against the Reserve Bank alleges breach of warranty under Regulations CC and J for accepting the late return. 12 C.F.R. § 210.6. Count III against Colonial alleges breach of a duty of ordinary care in Colonial's return of the Colonial checks. Count IV against the Reserve Bank alleges breach of a duty of ordinary care in processing the late return. Count V against Colonial alleges breach of UCC § 4–302 for Colonial's failure to return the checks by the midnight deadline. Count VI against the Reserve Bank and Count VII against Colonial allege breach of contract for each party's failure to comply with the terms of the Reserve Bank's Operating Circular No. 4 ("OC–4")....

DISCUSSION . . .

I. Count V: Breach of UCC § 4–302 Against Colonial

A. Accountability

Article 4 of the Uniform Commercial Code adopts a policy of "final payment"; that is, a check is considered to be finally paid at some spe-

---

[6] The court has subject matter jurisdiction over the claims against the Reserve Bank under 12 U.S.C. § 632, which deems a suit against any Federal Reserve bank to "arise under" the laws of the United States and therefore to fall within the district court's original jurisdiction. The court has jurisdiction over the claims against Colonial Bank under 28 U.S.C. § 1367(a), which gives district courts supplemental jurisdiction over claims (including those against additional parties) that form part of the same case as those claims that raise the federal question. In this case, the claims against Colonial Bank arise out of the same transactions and occurrences as those against the Reserve Bank.

We believe that federal jurisdiction exists even in light of *First Illinois Bank & Trust v. Midwest Bank & Trust Co.*, 30 F.3d 64 (7th Cir.1994), *cert. granted sub nom. Bank One Chicago v. Midwest Bank & Trust Co.*, 515 U.S. 1157, 115 S.Ct. 2607, 132 L.Ed.2d 852 (1995). In that case, the Seventh Circuit held that disputes between two depositary banks over Regulation CC were to be handled administratively before the Board of Governors of the Federal Reserve System. *Id.* at 65. *First Illinois* differs from this case, however, because jurisdiction in that case was premised on the Expedited Funds Availability Act. 12 U.S.C. § 4010. The Act conferred federal jurisdiction only over suits between a depositary institution and a person other than a depositary institution. There, the dispute was between two depositary banks. Here, in contrast, jurisdiction exists because the Reserve Bank is a party and the claims against Colonial form part of the same case as those claims against the Reserve Bank.

cific and identifiable point in time. § 4–215 Comment 1. Final payment is the "end of the line" in the check collection process. *Id.* Section 4–301 sets up the "midnight deadline" in the process: a payor bank which intends to return a check presented to it must do so before midnight of the next banking day following receipt of the check. §§ 4–301(a), 4–104(a)(10). If a payor bank fails to return a check before the midnight deadline, final payment occurs. *Los Angeles Nat'l Bank v. Bank of Canton*, 229 Cal.App.3d 1267, 280 Cal.Rptr. 831, 836 (1991); *see Rock Island Auction Sales, Inc. v. Empire Packing Co.*, 32 Ill.2d 269, 204 N.E.2d 721, 722–23 (1965); *Templeton v. First Nat'l Bank*, 47 Ill.App.3d 443, 5 Ill.Dec. 720, 724, 362 N.E.2d 33, 37 (1977).

. . . The operative word in [§ 4-302(a)] is "accountable." Courts interpreting this section have nearly unanimously concluded that § 4–302 imposes strict liability on a payor bank for failing to adhere to the midnight deadline, and makes the measure of damages the face amount of the check. In an early decision, the Illinois Supreme Court held that "accountable" means "liable" for the amount of the item. *Rock Island Auction Sales, Inc. v. Empire Packing Co.*, 204 N.E.2d 721, 723 (Ill.1965). The Rock Island court contrasted the "accountability" language in § 4–302 with the language used to specify the measure of damages in what is now § 4–103(e). Section 4–103(e) makes a bank liable for failing to exercise ordinary care in the handling of a check in "the amount of the item reduced by an amount that could not have been realized by the exercise of ordinary care." § 4–103(e). The Official Comment to this section explains: "When it is established that some part or all of the item could not have been collected even by the use of ordinary care the recovery is reduced by the amount that would have been in any event uncollectible." In other words, § 4–103(e) imposes liability in the amount of the loss caused by the negligence, while § 4–302(a) imposes strict liability in the face amount of the check.

The *Rock Island* court reasoned that the special role of the payor bank in the check collection system justifies the imposition of liability regardless of negligence. The midnight deadline requires the payor bank—the bank in the best position to know whether there are funds available to cover the check—to decide whether to pay or return the check:

> The role of a payor bank in the collection process ... is crucial. It knows whether or not the drawer has funds available to pay the item. The legislature could have considered that the failure of such a bank to meet its deadline is likely to be due to factors other than negligence, and that the relationship between a payor bank and its cus-

tomer may so influence its conduct as to cause a conscious disregard of its statutory duty.

Rock Island, 204 N.E.2d at 723.

The overwhelming majority of courts that have considered the meaning of § 4–302(a) have followed the *Rock Island* court in concluding that the liability of a payor bank that fails to return a check by the midnight deadline is strict and is in the face amount of the check. *See, e.g., Starcraft Co. v. C.J. Heck Co.*, 748 F.2d 982, 986 (5th Cir.1984); *Chrysler Credit Corp. v. First Nat'l Bank & Trust Co.*, 746 F.2d 200, 201 (3d Cir.1984); *American Title Ins. Co. v. Burke & Herbert Bank & Trust Co.*, 813 F.Supp. 423, 426 (E.D.Va.1993), *aff'd*, 25 F.3d 1038 (4th Cir.1994); *Bank Leumi Trust Co. v. Bank of Mid–Jersey*, 499 F.Supp. 1022, 1024 (D.N.J.1980), *aff'd*, 659 F.2d 1065 (3d Cir.1981); *Los Angeles Nat'l Bank v. Bank of Canton*, 229 Cal.App.3d 1267, 280 Cal.Rptr. 831, 838 (Ct.App.1991); *Citizens Fidelity Bank & Trust Co. v. Southwest Bank & Trust Co.*, 472 N.W.2d 198, 202–03 (Neb.1991); *State & Sav. Bank v. Meeker*, 469 N.E.2d 55, 58–59 (Ind.Ct.App.1984).[8]

Even where the damage suffered by the payee is not caused by the lateness of the return, the midnight deadline still has been strictly enforced. For example, in *Chicago Title Ins. Co. v. California Canadian*

---

[8] Commentators, too, have concluded that § 4–302 liability is strict. *See, e.g.*, Henry J. Bailey & Richard B. Hagedorn, Brady on Bank Checks ¶ 24.12 (7th ed. 1992) ("When a payor bank retains a check drawn on it for a period beyond its midnight deadline, the 1962 and 1990 UCCs both make the bank accountable for the amount of the item. This rule was first given effect in an Illinois decision [*Rock Island*] holding a bank liable for the amount of a check retained beyond the permitted time limits.") ¶ 24.9 ("If the bank does not act within that specified time limit, the bank is absolutely liable for the amount of the item."); Barkley Clark, The Law of Bank Deposits, Collections and Credit Cards ¶ 5.02[1][b] (3d ed. 1990) ("The Rock Island case seems completely correct. The drafters consciously drew a sharp contrast between the 'strict' accountability of the drawee bank for holding an item beyond the midnight deadline, and the liability of collecting banks, which turns on the existence of actual damages under § 4–103(5). If the drafters had intended to require a showing of actual loss before the drawee bank could be held liable, they could easily have said so."); 6 William D. Hawkland et al., Uniform Commercial Code Series § 4–302:04 (1984) ("The difference in liability under UCC subsection 4–103(5) for failure to use ordinary care and the 'accountability' under UCC subsection 4–302(a) are startling. The latter has been equated with liability for the face amount of the item without regard to whether the depositary holder has in fact suffered any loss."); James J. White & Robert S. Summers, Uniform Commercial Code § 17–4 (3d ed. 1988) ("[O]ne who makes final payment is accountable for the amount of the item irrespective of the loss that others may have suffered.").

Bank, 1 Cal.App.4th 798, 2 Cal.Rptr.2d 422, 424 (Ct.App.1991), the payor bank decided to return twenty-eight checks involved in a massive check fraud scheme. The checks left the bank before the midnight deadline, but did not arrive at the clearinghouse until the next day—after the midnight deadline had passed. *Id.* at 424. The court held that the bank's return was late. *Id.* at 425. It held the bank strictly accountable for the face amount of the checks, reasoning that the bank " 'may be held strictly liable for its failure to return the checks by the applicable deadlines, regardless whether [the other party] demonstrated it suffered actual damage solely as a result of [the Bank's] omission.' " *Id.* at 426–29 (quoting *Los Angeles Nat'l Bank v. Bank of Canton*, 229 Cal.App.3d 1267, 280 Cal.Rptr. 831, 838 (Ct.App.1991)); *see also American Title Ins. Co. v. Burke & Herbert Bank & Trust Co.*, 813 F.Supp. 423, 426 (E.D.Va.1993) ("[L]iability for the face amount of the check is imposed without regard to whether any damages have been sustained as a result of the payor bank's failure to make a timely return."), *aff'd*, 25 F.3d 1038 (4th Cir.1994).

Reading "accountable" to mean strictly liable for the face amount of the check finds further support in the Seventh Circuit's analysis in *Appliance Buyers Credit Corp. v. Prospect Nat'l Bank*, 708 F.2d 290, 293 (7th Cir.1983). In that case, the plaintiff depositor argued that § 4–212[9] imposed strict liability in the face amount of the check on a bank which fails to give the depositor timely notice of a check's dishonor and charges back the depositor's account. The court held that it did not because § 4–212 does not make the bank accountable. The court compared § 4–212 with other Article 4 provisions that use the term "accountable," including § 4–302(a). . . .

---

[9] At the time, § 4–212 provided:

    (1) If a collecting bank has made provisional settlement with its customer for an item and itself fails by reason of dishonor, suspension of payments by a bank or otherwise to receive a settlement for the item which is or becomes final, the bank may revoke the settlement given by it, charge back the amount of any credit given for the item to its customer's account or obtain refund from its customer whether or not it is able to return the items if by its midnight deadline or within a longer reasonable time after it learns the facts it returns the item or sends notification of the facts. These rights to revoke, charge back and obtain refund terminate if and when a settlement for the item received by the bank is or becomes final (subsection (3) of section 4–211 and subsections (2) and (3) of section 4–213).

. . . Under this reasoning, § 4–302 imposes absolute liability in the face amount of the check for a payor bank's failure to meet the midnight deadline.

But is it appropriate to enforce the accountability provision of § 4–302 where a check kiting scheme is involved? The Minnesota Supreme Court did in *Town & Country State Bank v. First State Bank*, 358 N.W.2d 387, 393–95 (Minn.1984). There, the court held that two payor banks that held kited checks beyond the midnight deadline made "final payment" on the checks and were therefore accountable for the amounts of those checks. *Accord Schwegmann Bank & Trust* Co. v. Bank of La., 595 So.2d 1185 (La.Ct.App.), *writ denied*, 598 So.2d 360 (La.1992); *Farmers & Merchants Bank v. Bank of America*, 20 Cal.App.3d 939, 98 Cal.Rptr. 381 (Ct.App.1971).

Colonial cites cases in which courts have declined to impose strict liability under other UCC provisions. However, none of these other provisions contains the "accountable" language found in § 4–302. *County of Pierce v. Suburban Bank*, 815 F.Supp. 1124, 1126 (N.D.Ill.1993) (§ 4–207); *Sanwa Business Credit Corp. v. Continental Ill. Nat'l Bank & Trust Co.*, 247 Ill.App.3d 155, 187 Ill.Dec. 45, 50, 617 N.E.2d 253, 258 (Ill.App.Ct. 1st Dist.1993) (§ 4–401). The reasoning of these cases, then, is simply not applicable here.

Therefore, we conclude that Colonial is absolutely liable in the face amount of the Colonial checks for missing the midnight deadline. This does not end the analysis, however, because Colonial raises the defenses of good faith and mistaken payment to defeat strict accountability.

[The court proceeded to reject Colonial's alleged "bad faith" defense under § 1–203, noting that "[e]ach bank made a business decision; First National's turned out to be the correct one."

[Alternatively, Colonial argued that it had mistakenly paid a negotiable instrument and that it could rely on the mistake and restitution provisions of UCC § 3–418 to override § 4–302 accountability. The Court ultimately rejected this argument as well, "because Colonial has not shown that it made a mistaken payment under subsection [3-418](b).]

D. Damages

. . . On this motion, First National has presented evidence showing that it has suffered a loss from the Shelly/World Commodities check kite.

At some point during the operation of the kite, the kiters siphoned funds out of the banking system, and because Colonial returned the

Colonial checks to First National, the loss fell on First National.[16] Specifically, the Reserve Bank debited First National's Reserve Bank account in the amount of the return, $1,523,892.49. This caused First National to make ledger entries reflecting the debit to the Reserve Bank account and a reduction in First National's assets. . . .[17] But as we have held, Colonial's return was improperly late, and § 4–302 directs that it bear the loss here.

The next question is the amount for which Colonial is liable. Section 4–302 makes Colonial liable in the face amount of the checks. However, where the payee has mitigated its damages (as in the case of a payee bank recovering from the drawer of the check), the payor's liability is reduced by the amount mitigated. *State & Sav. Bank v. Meeker*, 469 N.E.2d 55, 59 (Ind.Ct.App.1984). Otherwise, the payee would be unjustly enriched by the full recovery. § 1–103. In this case, then, First National is entitled to the face amount of the Colonial checks ($1,523,892.49) less any amount it recovered from Shelly, its customer.

The parties dispute how much First National recovered from its customer. In addition to the checking account, Shelly also maintained a line of credit with First National. During the months of March, April, and May 1992, First National received $676,757.30 in loan payments. . . . First National also applied to the loan balance $42,463.38 that remained in the Shelly checking account when it was closed on February 28. . . . The defendants say, then, that First National actually received $719,220.68 from Shelly after the kite crashed—the $676,757.30 in loan payments plus $42,463.38 that remained in the Shelly checking account. . . .

Colonial says that First National's recovery should be reduced by $719,220.68. But Colonial has presented no evidence to refute First National's evidence that it applied the $719,220.68 to pay off the loan. This being the case, First National will not be unjustly enriched by

---

[16] The defendants present evidence that the funds were siphoned from the system during the spring and summer of 1991, before the Colonial account was even opened. . .. But when the funds were siphoned is not the issue; such an inquiry would lead to questions about whether Colonial is at fault for the loss. As explained in the text, the relevant principles here are Colonial's liability in the face amount of the checks reduced by any amount by which First National would be unjustly enriched.

[17] Had the Shelly account still been open when the Reserve Bank debited First National's account, First National says that it would have charged the debit to the Shelly account, causing an overdraft in the account. . . . The defendants deny that First National could have charged the debit to the Shelly account because there were never any collected funds in that account. . . . But the result is the same either way—First National took the loss.

recovering the face amount of the checks from Colonial. However, First National submits a report of Arthur Andersen & Co. saying that the funds from Shelly were sufficient to pay off the loan and reduce the loss from the kite, leaving it with an actual loss of $1,425,970.61. . . .[18] If First National's recovery is reduced to avoid unjust enrichment, it is entitled to recover $1,425,970.61, plus interest, which represents the face amount of the Colonial checks offset by any recovery from Shelly that exceeded the amount necessary to pay off the loan. . . .

[In the second count of its complaint, First National alleged that Colonial breached its duty of ordinary care with respect to its return of the Colonial checks. The court granted Colonial summary judgment. "Because Colonial's late return did not cause First National's loss, First National cannot prevail on its claim for breach of the duty of ordinary care."

[First National also alleged breaches of warranty by Colonial and by the Federal Reserve Bank under § 229.34 of Regulation CC.[a] The court noted that the Commentary to Regulation CC, 12 C.F.R. pt. 229, app. E, indicated that the damages under § 229.34(d) were the warranty damages of UCC § 4–207(c), "an amount equal to the loss suffered as a result of the breach. . . ." However, the court concluded that "First National's loss was not caused by Colonial's late return of the checks."

[Likewise, First National's claims for breach of the duty of ordinary care against the Federal Reserve Bank and for breach of contract against the Federal Reserve Bank and Colonial—for their alleged failure to follow dispute resolution procedures contained in the Federal Reserve Bank's Operating Circular No. 4 ("OC–4")—were rejected by the court, because "First National has cited no authority holding a bank liable under an operating circular on a negligence or breach of contract theory."]

---

[18] The defendants submit the affidavit of Dennis Irvin, president of First National, which says that after the funds were applied to the loan balance, there remained unpaid principal and interest totalling $41,356.91. . . . However, this does not create a genuine issue of material fact. Defendants' submission of the Irvin affidavit creates the odd situation of the defendants saying that the plaintiff's loss is greater than the plaintiff contends it is: if there were no surplus after paying off the loan, First National would be entitled to a higher recovery.

[a] The warranty claim against the Federal Reserve Bank was brought through Regulation J, 12 C.F.R. § 210.6(a)(1), which incorporates by reference Regulation CC, including § 229.34.

Questions and Problems 3.25. Reread note 6 in the *First National Bank* case. The Supreme Court eventually reversed the Seventh Circuit's decision in *First Illinois Bank & Trust*, discussed in the footnote. *See Bank One Chicago, N.A. v. Midwest Bank & Trust Co.*, 516 U.S. 264 (1996) (holding that federal court had jurisdiction not only in suits between customers and banks under Expedited Funds Availability Act (EFAA) but also in cases initiated by one depository institution against another). On remand in *Bank One Chicago, N.A. v. Midwest Bank & Trust Co.*, 85 F.3d 631 (7th Cir. 1996), the Seventh Circuit dismissed the case pursuant to a settlement agreement between the parties. Even with the "stipulated reversal" in *Bank One Chicago*, this would seem to strengthen the result in *First National Bank* on this issue. However, the final outcome in *Bank One Chicago* does raise procedural difficulties as to the collateral estoppel effects for the parties in *Bank One Chicago* itself. On this procedural conundrum, see Steven R. Harmon, Comment, *Unsettling Settlements: Should Stipulated Reversals be Allowed to Trump Judgments' Collateral Estoppel Effects Under* Neary? 85 Cal. L. Rev. 479 (1997). *Cf. Neary v. Regents of the University of California*, 834 P.2d 119, 125 (Cal. 1992) (holding that, absent "extraordinary circumstances," courts of appeal should grant parties' request to reverse judgment, in order to effectuate settlement agreement and terminate litigation; establishing "strong presumption in favor of allowing stipulated reversals").

3.26. Reread note 9 and the accompanying text in the *First National Bank* case. The right of charge-back or refund is now covered by UCC § 4-214. Do you see any significant differences between pre-1990 §4-212 and the current § 4-214 that might have been pertinent in the context of the dispute in *First National Bank*?

3.27. Is enforcement of the accountability provision of UCC § 4–302 too harsh or too broad a response where a check kiting scheme is involved in the transaction? Are there feasible alternative approaches that the drafters of Article 4 might have adopted?

3.28. Circular OC–4, referred to in *First National Bank*, sets up the Federal Reserve Bank's *Disputed Return Procedure*. It provides that, if a depositary bank believes that the payor bank has returned a check after the midnight deadline, the depositary bank may dispute the return by sending the Federal Reserve Bank the returned check and a signed statement that the bank believes the payor bank did not return the check within the midnight deadline. When the Federal Reserve Bank receives the statement, it credits the amount of the returned check to the disputing bank's account. It also charges the payor bank's account the amount of the check, and sends the returned check and statement to the payor bank. OC–4, para. 48. Circular OC–4 also provides that the Federal Reserve Bank will *revoke* the credit given to the disputing bank and recredit the payor bank if it receives a form from the payor bank that (i) states that the paying bank returned the check within the midnight deadline; and (ii) shows the banking day of receipt and the date of return, and "explains any difference in dates exceeding one banking day." *Id.*, para. 49. How does this internal Federal Reserve procedure create a private right of action? While there is almost no case law on this issue, at least one other court besides *First National Bank* has concluded that operating circulars do not create any substantive private rights. *Continental Ill. Nat'l Bank & Trust Co. v. Sterling Nat'l Bank & Trust Co.*, 565 F.Supp. 101, 103 (S.D.N.Y. 1983**).**

3.29. *First National Bank* says that "under §§ 4–301 and 4–302, a payor bank must either pay or dishonor a check drawn on it by midnight of the second banking day following presentment." While that seems to be the practical effect of the two UCC sections, how do you get that conclusion from the text of the current sections? *Cf.* Fred H. Miller, *Benefits of new UCC articles 3 and 4*, 24 UCC L.J. 99, 114 (1991):

> Midnight deadline litigation continually clogs the courts under present law. Revised UCC § 4-214 clarifies that a collecting bank that goes beyond its midnight deadline does not lose chargeback rights but only is responsible for resulting loss and thus codifies *Appliance Buyers Credit Corp. v. Prospect National Bank.*[79] Of course, the right to chargeback is not lost even after funds availability is due under [Federal Reserve] Regulation CC.[80] Revised Article 4 also addresses the case of the payor bank. Revised UCC § 4-302 codifies the line of cases that excuse delay beyond the midnight deadline where the person presenting the item was attempting to defraud the bank.[81]

How does this affect the approach taken by *First National Bank* to determing damages in the case?

3.30. In reading the following case, consider whether the Oklahoma Supreme Court agrees with this approach to the effect of the midnight deadline and the measure of damages.

---

[79] 708 F.2d 290 (7th Cir. 1983).

[80] *See* 12 C.F.R. §§ 229.10-229.12 (1990); Regulation CC Commentary § 229.32(b).

[81] *See, e.g.,Bank Leumi Trust Co. v. Bally's Park Place, Inc.*, 528 F. Supp. 349 (S.D.N.Y. 1981) (holder of check known to be drawn on insolvent estate not entitled to enforce liability for late return of check).

LIBERTY BANK AND TRUST CO.
OF OKLAHOMA CITY, N.A. V. BACHRACH
916 P.2d 1377 (Ok. 1996)

HODGES, Justice.

The plaintiff, Liberty Bank and Trust Company of Oklahoma City (Liberty), brought suit against defendant, Osher Bachrach (Bachrach), as an indorser of a check returned for insufficient funds and as a depositor for reimbursement of an overdrawn account. Liberty filed a motion for partial summary adjudication in the trial court. Bachrach opposed the motion arguing material issues of fact were in dispute. The trial court granted judgment in favor of Liberty. The Court of Appeals affirmed. . . .

The issue in this case is whether summary judgment was proper. We find that the trial court erred in granting judgment in favor of the plaintiff. . . .

The undisputed material facts of this case are as follows. The defendant, Osher Bachrach, is a lawyer who maintains a trust account in Liberty. Bachrach signed the depositor's signature card of Liberty whereby agreeing to the terms of the depository agreement. The depository agreement provided that all deposits were provisionally credited to the account. The agreement further provided Liberty could charge back credits to the account even if an overdraft occurred.

On June 24, 1992, Bachrach deposited in his trust account a check of $15,000 from Janice K. Whitefield which was made to him. The check was for restitution in a criminal matter. On June 26, Bachrach purchased seven cashier's checks totaling $12,255.86 from the funds in his trust account.

Liberty first received notice on June 29, 1992 that there were insufficient funds in Whitefield's account to cover the check to Bachrach. It received the second notice on July 2. Liberty did not give Bachrach notice of the insufficient funds until July 3, when it mailed a notice of dishonor to Bachrach. He received the notice on July 7. On July 6, while attempting to withdraw funds for another cashier's check, Bachrach was orally informed of the dishonor of the $15,000 check. . . .

Liberty filed suit alleging Bachrach was liable as an indorser of the check and under the depository agreement. Bachrach answered that Liberty had failed to give him timely notice after the check was dishonored the second time, but he did not raise the defense that Liberty had failed to give notice after it learned of the dishonor on June 29. . . .

Liability as a Depositor

Section 4-214 of title 12A applies to deposits, defines the liability of banks for failure to give notice of dishonor of a check to a depositor, and allows for the provisional settlement of deposits made to an account. [The court quoted UCC § 4-214(a).]

The midnight deadline is defined in section 4-104(a)(10) as "midnight on [a bank's] next banking day following the banking day on which [a bank] receives the relevant item or notice...." In this case, Liberty learned that the check had been dishonored on June, 29, 1992. It is undisputed that Liberty did not give notice until July 3, 1992.

Liberty contends that it was not statutorily required to give notice of first dishonor because (1) there is a custom in the industry of not giving notice of dishonor to the depositor until after a bank resubmits the check for payment and receives a second notice of dishonor, and (2) the depository agreement supersedes the statutory requirement of giving notice of dishonor. We disagree.

As stated above, when a bank makes a provisional settlement and fails to give timely notice, it becomes liable for damages resulting from its failure. Okla.Stat. tit. 12A at § 4-214. Seasonable notice is notice given by "its midnight deadline or ... a longer reasonable time after it learns the facts." *Id*. An example of a reasonably longer time is found in comment 3 to section 4-202: "In the case of time items, action after the midnight deadline, but sufficiently in advance of maturity for proper presentation, is a clear example of a 'reasonably longer time' that is timely." Liberty does not argue that it falls under this provision.

The custom asserted by Liberty is repugnant to the statutory requirement that notice of dishonor be given by the midnight deadline. *See id*. at 4-214. "Custom or usage repugnant to expressed provisions of a statute is void." *Hull v. Sun Refining and Marketing Co.*, 789 P.2d 1272, 1278 (Okla.1989). When there is a conflict between a statute and a custom and usage, the statute governs. *Id*. Custom in the industry does not excuse Liberty's failure to give notice of the first dishonor.

Liberty also argues that under title 12A it may alter the statutory obligations imposed on it. Liberty continues that the depositor's agreement right of charge back controls over section 4-214. Liberty relies on section 1-102 which allows the effect of the provisions of title 12A to be altered by agreement. Section 4-103 specifically addresses the provisions of article 4 and allows the effect of the provisions in article 4 to be altered by agreement. Because section 4-103 specifically addresses article 4, it is controlling in this case. *State ex rel. Trimble v. City of Moore*, 818 P.2d 889, 899 (Okla.1991). [The court quoted UCC §§ 4-103 and 4-202.]

Because Liberty cannot disclaim its responsibility to exercise ordinary care and ordinary care requires timely notice of dishonor, Liberty cannot alter its statutory duty to give notice by its midnight deadline or with a reasonably longer time by an agreement. *See Clements v. Central Bank*, 155 Ga.App. 27, 270 S.E.2d 194, 199 (1980); *Broadway Nat'l Bank v. Barton-Russell Corp.*, 154 Misc.2d 181, 585 N.Y.S.2d 933, 939 (N.Y.Sup.Ct.1992).

In *Reynolds-Wilson Lumber Co. v. Peoples Nat'l Bank*, 699 P.2d 146 (Okla.1985), the payor bank failed to give notice of dishonor after the second presentment. This Court held that section 4-302(a) required a payor bank to give notice of dishonor after every presentment. Section 4-302(a) provides that a payor bank is accountable for [an] item when the bank fails to return the item or give notice of dishonor by the midnight deadline.

Even if the duty to give notice of dishonor could be disclaimed by agreement, nothing in the agreement waives Bachrach's right to notice of dishonor. The agreement merely is a restatement of Liberty's statutory option to provisionally credit an account. The restatement of this right in the depository in and of itself did not relieve Liberty of the responsibility to give notice of dishonor after it first received notice of insufficient funds on June 29, 1992.

Damages

Section 4-214(a) provides that a bank may charge back the amount of a provisional credit to a depositor's account "if by its midnight deadline or within a longer reasonable time after it learns the facts it returns the item or sends notification of the facts." A majority of courts have interpreted this provision as establishing a condition precedent, timely notice of dishonor, before a bank can exercise its right to charge back. *Smallman v. Home Federal Savings Bank*, 786 S.W.2d 954, 957 (Tenn.Ct.App.1989). This construction is inconsistent with the other provisions of article 4. *See Ross v. Peters*, 846 P.2d 1107, 1112 (Okla.1993). [Quoting UCC § 4-214(a) and (d), dealing with the effect of delay in the return or notice beyond the bank's midnight deadline on its right to revoke and charge back, the court indicated that the right is unaffected by the delay, but the bank is liable for any loss resulting from the delay. Citing UCC § 4-202(a), (b), the court explained that failure to exercise ordinary care "include[d] failure to give notice before the banks midnight deadline or, if it does not learn of the dishonor in time to act before the midnight deadline, within a reasonable time after it learns the facts."]

[Quoting UCC § 4-103(e), the court went on to state that] [t]he depositor must prove the damages caused by the bank's failure to give timely notice. *Appliance Buyers Credit Corp. v. Prospect Nat'l Bank of*

Peoria, 708 F.2d 290, 294 (7th Cir.1983). Pursuant to section 4-214, Liberty may charge back the provisional credit but is nonetheless liable for damages caused by its failure to give timely notice.

In *Reynolds-Wilson Lumber Co.*, 699 P.2d at 146, this Court held that section 4-302 imposed strict liability on the payor bank for failure to either return an item or give notice of its dishonor before its midnight deadline. This holding was based on Section 4-302 making the payor bank "accountable" for an item when the bank fails to comply with the notice requirements. Sections 4-103(e) and 4-214(a) and (c) only hold the bank liable for damages rather than making it "accountable" for the item. Thus, if a bank fails to give timely notice of dishonor to a depositor, it is liable for the amount of damages caused by its failure and not strictly liable for the amount of the instrument. . . .

. . . The case is remanded to the trial court for evidentiary proceedings consistent with this opinion.

SIMMS, Justice, dissenting:

Summary judgment in favor of defendant Liberty Bank was properly rendered by the trial court and affirmed by the Court of Appeals. The bank was not attempting to recover for the dishonored check, but under the depository agreement and it is entitled to judgment. There is no showing of any legal infirmity in the depository agreement. I would deny certiorari.

Questions and Problems 3.31. In light of *First National Bank* and *Liberty Bank and Trust*, it does not seem that Miller's optimism about easing the clog of midnight deadline litigation (Question 3.29, *supra*) was well founded. If you were advising First Bank in its review of its check-processing procedures, what steps would you recommend that it take to manage the risk of litigation over collections and charge backs?

3.32. One way to ameliorate the risk would be to hold up on the availability of funds in the process of collection. However, as a matter of *federal* law, the EFAA, enacted in 1987 as part of the Competitive Equality Banking Act,[5] shortened the period between the deposit of a check and the availability of deposited funds. This of course increases the risk of nonpayment for the depositary bank. In response to this risk, the EFAA authorizes the Federal Reserve Board to issue regula-

---

[5] 12 U.S.C. §§ 4001-4010. For further discussion of the EFAA, see § C, *infra*.

tions expediting the collection and return of checks.[6] The Board's Regulation CC, 12 C.F.R. pt. 229, deals with the availability of funds and collection of checks. How does Regulation CC affect a bank's obligations under Article 4? In answering this question, consider the following case.

VALLEY NATIONAL BANK V. HUDSON UNITED BANK
--- N.J. Super. ---, 2002 WL 32068153 (N.J. Super. 2002)

ARTHUR N. D'ITALIA, Assignment Judge.

Valley National Bank filed this action seeking to recover from Hudson United Bank $484,732, the face amount of five checks Valley received from a depositor that were provisionally credited to the depositor's accounts. Valley presented the checks to Hudson for payment. Hudson then gave notice of nonpayment and returned the checks. Both banks are victims of a check-kiting scheme in which the kiter deposited into his Valley account worthless checks drawn on Hudson accounts and then absconded with the funds provisionally credited. Valley predicates Hudson's liability on the latter's alleged untimely issuance of its notice of nonpayment and late physical return of the checks under the Uniform Commercial Code (hereafter 'U.C.C.') and federal banking regulations. The order of events is as follows.

On Wednesday, August 29, 2001, the check kiter[1] deposited at Valley five checks, totaling $484,732, drawn against the kiter's accounts at Hudson. Valley presented the checks to Hudson for payment on Thursday, August 30. Friday, August 31 was the last banking day of that week. Due to the Labor Day weekend, the next bank business day was Tuesday, September 4.

Some time after Valley made its August 30 presentation for payment, Hudson learned that the kiter's accounts contained insufficient funds to cover the checks. At 1:13 p.m. on September 4, Hudson provided Valley notice of check return via the Electronic Advance Return Item Notification System (hereafter 'EARNS'), an industry electronic

---

[6] 12 U.S.C. § 4008(c)(I). *See Bank One Chicago, N.A. v. Midwest Bank & Trust Co.*, 516 U.S. 264 (1996) (discussing bank obligations under EFAA); *Oak Brook Bank v. Northern Trust Co.*, 256 F.3d 638 (7th Cir 2001) (construing and applying term "banking day" in light of EFAA regulations).

[1] The check kiter is not a party to this case. Valley, Hudson, and a third plaintiff, Platinum Funding, Inc., maintain claims against the check kiter in a separate consolidated case, *Valley National Bank et al v. Levant, Inc. et al.* ...

notification system to which both banks have computer access. This information was, therefore, immediately available to Valley. At 10:00 p.m. on September 4, Hudson dispatched the unpaid checks by courier to the East Rutherford Operations Center (hereafter 'EROC') of the Federal Reserve Bank of New York, which functions, in part, as a regional check processing clearinghouse. The EROC received the checks at 10:19 p.m. that night. On Wednesday, September 5, the EROC returned the checks unpaid to Valley. Valley discovered Hudson's EARNS notice of return at 1:13 p.m. the same day. . . .

The Court is presented with the following legal issues: first, whether Hudson failed to comply with the midnight deadline requirement of N.J.S.A. 12A:4-301; second, whether Hudson complied with the expeditious return requirement of 12 C.F.R. § 229.30(a); third, whether the midnight deadline was extended by 12 C.F.R. § 229.30(c), and, if so, whether the extended deadline was met; fourth, whether Hudson's notice of nonpayment via EARNS at 1:13 p.m. on September 4 satisfied the requirements of 12 C.F.R. § 229.33(a); fifth, whether notice under § 229.33(a) was permissible in lieu of physical return of the checks; and sixth, what measure of damages applies in the event of defendant's noncompliance with the U.C.C., the federal regulations, or both.

I. The Midnight Deadline under the U.C.C. . . .

Hudson does not dispute that it failed to dispatch the checks prior to its midnight deadline. Instead, it argues that its return of the checks was timely under Regulation CC, 12 C.F.R. § 229.30(c), which operates to extend the midnight deadline under certain circumstances. In reply, Valley contends that § 229.30(c) did not extend the midnight deadline because Hudson failed to return the checks in an expeditious manner under 12 C.F.R. § 229.30(a).

II. Regulation CC, 12 C.F.R. § 229.30

Although the U.C.C. provides the basic framework for bank deposits and check collections, it has been supplemented by a body of federal law. . . . Subpart C of Regulation CC, 12 C.F.R. § 229.30, covers a paying bank's responsibility for return of checks, and 'supersedes any inconsistent provisions of the U.C.C. as adopted in any state... but only to the extent of inconsistency.' 12 C.F.R. § 229.41.

A. Section 229.30(a)

Under § 229.30(a), if a paying bank determines not to pay a check, 'it shall return the check in an expeditious manner as provided in... this section.' Thus, while the U.C.C. midnight deadline focuses on when a return check must be sent or dispatched, § 229.30(a) governs the manner of return. Its aim is to encourage paying banks to employ an expeditious mode or manner of return, *i.e.*, courier rather than mail, in order to accelerate actual return of checks to the depositary bank.

Section 229.30(a) describes two tests for satisfying the duty of expeditious return. The 'forward collection test' requires the paying bank to return the check in the same way that a bank in the position of the paying bank would normally forward a check drawn on the depositary bank deposited with the paying bank on the same day. § 220.30(a)(2). Stated more simply, this standard requires returning banks to treat return items with the same expedition that they treat checks forwarded for collection. Neither party has presented evidence nor argued the applicability of this test.

The determinative test for expeditious return, under § 229.30(a)(1), is the 'two-day/four-day test.' It provides:

> A paying bank returns a check in an expeditious manner if it sends the returned check in a manner such that the check would normally be received by the depositary bank not later than 4:00 p.m. (local time of the depositary bank) or:
> (i) The second business day following the banking day on which the check was presented to the paying bank, if the paying bank is located in the same check processing region as the depositary bank; or
> (ii) The fourth business day following the banking day on which the check was presented to the paying bank, if the paying bank is not located in the same check processing region as the depositary bank.

Section 229.30(a), by its express terms, 'does not affect a paying bank's responsibility to return a check within the deadlines required by the U.C.C.' Thus, the obligation of a payor bank upon dishonor of a check is twofold: (a) to dispatch the instrument by its U.C.C. midnight deadline; and (b) to return it in an expeditious manner in accord with § 229.30(a).

In this case, Hudson could have satisfied its midnight deadline by dispatching the checks before midnight on Friday, August 31 and satisfied its duty of expeditious return by dispatching the checks before or after its midnight deadline but in a manner such that they normally would have been received by Valley no later than 4:00 p.m. on September 4, the second business day following the presentment of the checks on August 30. Hudson could have satisfied both deadlines by mailing the checks before midnight on August 31 if, in the ordinary course of the mails, they would have been delivered to Valley before 4:00 p.m. on September 4. Hudson did not dispatch the checks for delivery to the EROC until 10:00 p.m. on September 4, and thus failed to meet its responsibilities under both state and federal law.

While not disputing the foregoing analysis, Hudson contends that it is relieved of liability under both the U.C.C. and § 229.30(a) because its midnight deadline was extended by § 229.30(c).

B. Section 229.30(c)

Section 229.30(c) does, in fact, permit a bank to extend the time for return of checks under the U.C.C. It provides:

> (c) Extension of deadline. The deadline for return or notice of nonpayment under the U.C.C. or Regulation J (12 CFR part 210), § 229.36(f)(2) is extended to the time of dispatch of such return or notice of nonpayment where a paying bank uses a means of delivery that would ordinarily result in receipt by the bank to which it is sent-
>
> (1) On or before the receiving bank's next banking day following the otherwise applicable deadline, for all deadlines other than those described in paragraph (c)(2) of this section: this deadline is extended further if a paying bank uses a highly expeditious means of transportation, even if this means of transportation would ordinarily result in delivery after the receiving bank's next banking day[. . . .]

The language of this provision is clarified in Barkley Clark and Barbara Clark. The Law of Bank Deposits, Collections, and Credit Cards ¶ 8.01[4] (Rev. ed. 4th ed. 1995):

> Although the duty of a paying bank to dispatch a return item by the UCC midnight deadline is not repealed by Regulation CC, it is extended, under § 229.30(c), if the paying bank, in an effort to expedite delivery of a returned check to a returing or depositary bank, 'uses a means of delivery that would ordinarily result in the returned check being received by the bank to which it is sent on or before the receiving bank's next banking day following the otherwise applicable deadline.' The deadline is extended further 'if a paying bank uses a highly expeditious means of transportation, even if this means of transportation would ordinarily result in delivery after the receving bank's next banking day.' They key is whether the check reaches the receiving bank within the extended time.

The example given in the Commentary is that of a paying bank that has a courier that leaves sometime after midnight to deliver its forward collection checks. If the midnight deadline is midnight on Tuesday but the return checks are not dispatched to a returning bank by courier until 3:00 A.M. on Wednesday, in the same bundles as the forward collection items, return within the midnight deadline is excused if the bundle reaches the returning bank by its cutoff hour on

Wednesday afternoon. This emphasis on receipt rather than dispatch is consistent with the policy of expediting the overall return time.

Applying § 229.30(c) to this case, Hudson's midnight deadline for return under the U.C.C. was extended to the time of dispatch of the return checks (10:00 p.m. on September 4) only if the means of delivery (courier) would ordinarily result in receipt by the bank to which the checks are sent (EROC) on or before the receiving bank's (EROC) next banking day following the otherwise applicable deadline. The 'otherwise applicable deadline' is midnight on August 31. The EROC's next banking day was September 4. The issue is whether the EROC's 'banking day' extended to 10:19 p.m. when the checks were delivered. Regulation CC defines 'banking day' as 'that part of any business day on which an office of a bank is open to the public for carrying on substantially all of its banking functions.' . . . [T]he check processing department at EROC remains open for the receipt of checks from depositary institutions twenty-four hours of every business day the [Federal Reserve Bank of New York] is open, with specific deadlines for different classes of checks. In March 2001, the New York Fed issued a check services advisory establishing a cut-off hour for the end of its business day with regard to cash items. The advisory provides as follows: '[o]ur business day ends at 2:00 p.m. Therefore, any cash items received after 2 p.m. will be treated as received the next day for purposes of our midnight deadline under the Uniform Commercial Code.' More relevant to the issues in this case, on July 2, 2001, the Reserve Bank issued 'Operating Circular 3' explicitly amending its check service policy. Section 20.1 of the Circular provides:

> For purposes of our midnight deadline under the Uniform Commercial Code, items received after 2:00 p.m. for collection or return are considered to be received on our next banking day. The 2:00 p.m. cut off hour does not extend or otherwise affect the deadlines in our schedules for credit availability or for the presentation of items drawn on the Reserve Bank.

Based on the proffered testimony, I find that the EROC's banking day for the purpose of receiving return checks ends at 2:00 p.m. Hudson's dispatch of a courier with the return checks at 10:00 p.m. on September 4 did not result in receipt of the checks on or before the EROC's September 4 banking day because that day ended at 2:00 p.m. Based on the New York Fed's published hours, the checks reached their destination on the EROC's September 5 banking day. . . .

III. Notice Under 12 C.F.R. § 229.33(a)

The final matter to be resolved concerns the application of the notice provision of Regulation CC to Hudson's September 4 EARNS notice to Valley. Two issues arise with regard to Hudson's notice of return. First, whether Hudson's notice was timely under § 229.33(a) and, second, whether this notice requirement is in addition to that of a timely physical return of checks or, as Hudson argues, may be made in lieu of a timely physical return.

Section 229.33(a) of the Code of Fed Regulations, Part 12 provides:

> (a) Requirement. If a paying bank determines not to pay a check in the amount of $2,500 or more, it shall provide notice of nonpayment such that the notice is received by the depositary bank by 4:00 p.m. (Local time) on the second business day following the banking day on which the check was presented to the paying bank. If the day the paying bank is required to provide notice is not a banking day for the depositary bank, receipt of notice on the depositary bank's next banking day constitutes timely notice. Notice may be provided by any reasonable means, including the returned check, a writing (including a copy of the check), telephone, Fedwire, telex, or other form of telegraph.

Hudson contends that because each check was over $2,500 and that it provided notice to Valley via EARNS at 1:13 p.m. on September 4, a banking day, it complied with its duty of notice under the foregoing section, which supersedes the U.C.C.

Hudson is correct that it provided timely notice of its determination not to pay the checks at 1:13 p.m. on September 4, and not at 12:43 p.m. on September 5, when Valley chose to retrieve the posted information from its computer. Section 229.33(a) requires only that notice be received by the depositary bank by 4:00 p.m. on the second business day following the banking day on which the check is presented to the paying bank. Notice may be provided by [any] reasonable means. *Ibid.* The EARNS notification system qualifies as the sort of mechanism contemplated by the Federal Reserve Board to provide a reasonable means of notice. The EARNS notice was available to Valley almost immediately after its posting. Valley has provided neither excuse nor explanation for why it did not access the EARNS notification system by 4:00 p.m. on September 4, a normal banking day, and the deadline hour for the posting of notices of nonpayment. Neither language nor logic permit the conclusion that § 229.33(a) is intended to supersede the requirement of timely return of checks of $2,500 or more. If notice were permitted in lieu of timely return, the return provisions of the U.C.C. and § 229.30 would be inapplicable to all checks in the amount of $2,500 or more.

It would be anomalous to require a payor bank to provide only notice of nonpayment for larger checks while requiring expeditious physical return of all checks for smaller amounts. Moreover, § 229.33(b), listing information that must be included in the notice, also provides that 'the notice may include other information from the check that may be useful in identifying *the check being returned. . . . '* (Emphasis added). Where the drafters of the regulation intended notice to be in lieu of return, they said so explicitly. *See, e.g.,* § 229.31(f).

. . . I have found that Hudson's dispatch of the dishonored checks at 10:00 p.m. on September 4 failed to comply with the midnight deadline requirement of the U.C.C. and that Hudson's return delivery of the checks to the EROC at 10:19 p.m. on September 4 was not completed in an expeditious manner under 12 C.F.R. § 229.30(a), and further, that the midnight deadline was not extended under 12 C.F.R. § 229.30(e). While Hudson complied with the notice provisions of 12 C.F.R. § 229.33(a), its notice did not relieve it of its obligation for timely physical return of the checks. Accordingly, Hudson is accountable to Valley for the face amount of the checks. Summary judgment is entered in favor of Valley and against Hudson in the amount of $484,732.

Questions and Problems 3.33. *Business day? Banking day?* From the outset, *Valley National Bank* raises one of those vexing practical questions that always leaves a chill in the room. How do we count the days – especially over a long weekend? Note that the court says "Friday, August 31 was the last *banking day* of that week. Due to the Labor Day weekend, the next *bank business day* was Tuesday, September 4." (Emphasis added.) Compare this statement with UCC § 4-104(a)(3), (10). Is the court's terminology correct when it refers to a "bank business day"? Would it make a difference to the calculation of the midnight deadline if Hudson United Bank were closed on Saturday, September 1, or open on that day?

3.34. *Mailbox rules?* Assume that checks to be returned unpaid are deposited in the mail before midnight of the next banking day, but are not received by the depositary bank until after the midnight deadline. Are they returned timely? What if the checks are handed over to a courier instead of being placed in the mail? What if they are transmitted as an email attachment? *See Union National Bank of Little Rocky Metropolitan National Bank,* 578 S.W.2d 220 (Ark. 1979) (holding item is timely returned provided it is dispatched, not received, before midnight deadline).

C. FUNDS AVAILABILITY

Questions and Problems 3.35. Recall the discussion in Problem 3.25, *supra*, discussing private rights of action under the Expedited Funds Availability Act (EFAA).[7] While intended as a regulatory initiative, the EFAA can figure prominently in private litigation. The EFAA shortens the period between the deposit of a check and the availability to the depositor of deposited funds. To understand the scope and effect of the act, one must consider not only the statutory provisions but also the provisions of Regulation CC, 12 C.F.R. pt. 229, the implementing regulations of the Federal Reserve Board issued pursuant to 12 U.S.C. § 4008(c)(I).[8] What is the impact of the EFAA and Regulation CC on bank collections? In answering this question, consider the following cases.

ESSEX CONSTRUCTION CORP. V.
INDUSTRIAL BANK OF WASHINGTON, INC.
913 F.Supp. 416 (D.Md. 1995)

MOTZ, Chief Judge.

Plaintiff Essex Construction Corporation (Essex) claims violations of the Expedited Funds Availability Act and District of Columbia banking laws. Essex alleges that Defendant Industrial Bank of Washington, Inc. (Industrial) failed to make the proceeds of a deposited check permanently available for withdrawal on a promised date and that Industrial failed to provide timely notice that the check had been dishonored. Plaintiff seeks the amount of the check as damages. . . .

The relevant facts are not in dispute. On March 31, 1995, plaintiff deposited into its account at Industrial a check in the amount of $120,710.70 from East Side Manor Cooperative Association (East Side). East Side's check was drawn against its account at Signet Bank (Signet). At the time of the deposit, Industrial provisionally credited Essex's account but provided written notice that all but $100 of the funds would not be available for withdrawal until April 6, 1995.

On April 6, Signet notified Industrial that East Side had stopped payment on the check. Industrial placed a permanent hold on the $120,710.70 deposit, effectively revoking the provisional credit to Es-

---

[7] 12 U.S.C. §§ 4001-4010.

[8] *See Bank One Chicago, N.A. v. Midwest Bank & Trust Co.*, 516 U.S. 264 (1996) (discussing bank obligations under EFAA).

sex's account. On April 7, Industrial mailed written notice (including the returned check itself) to Essex.

On April 7, Essex wrote two checks in the amount of $21,224.00 and $18,084.60 against the funds it thought were available in its account at Industrial. Essex received Industrial's written notice of dishonor on April 11. . . .

The Expedited Funds Availability Act (EFAA), 12 U.S.C. §§ 4001 *et seq.*, establishes specific time periods in which depository banks must make deposited funds available for withdrawal. For example, § 4002(b)(1) requires that deposited checks drawn against accounts at a local bank must be available not more than one business day after deposit. Section 4003(b)(1), however, allows the creation by regulation of reasonable exceptions in cases of deposits that exceed $5000. 12 C.F.R. § 229.13(g) accordingly prescribes the form and method of notice that a bank must employ to extend the time of availability of large deposits. Nothing in the record indicates that Industrial's notice on March 31 that the deposit would not be available until April 6 failed to comply with these requirements.[2]

Essex argues that it is entitled to recover because Industrial failed either to provide notice of dishonor or to make the funds available by April 6, the date specified in the notice it provided. Under 12 U.S.C. § 4006(b) the funds technically became available at the beginning of the April 6 business day. Thus, unless Industrial received notice from Signet before the start of business on April 6, Industrial could not have provided notice of dishonor prior to the time specified for funds availability. In fact, however, Industrial received the notice of stopped payment from Signet later in the day on April 6. Plaintiff's argument therefore amounts to a contention that a depositor's right to funds becomes absolute at the time a deposit is required to become available pursuant to the EFAA.

Plaintiff is correct that "[t]he purpose of the Expedited Funds Availability Act is to require banks to make funds available to depositors quickly. Thus, the depositor has rights, enforceable in court, while the banks have obligations." *First Ill. Bank & Trust v. Midwest Bank & Trust Co.*, 30 F.3d 64, 65 (7th Cir.1994), *cert. granted sub nom. Bank One Chicago, N.A. v. Midwest Bank & Trust Co.*, 515 U.S. 1157,

---

[2] Essex literally argues that "Industrial ... improperly provided this § 229.13(g) notice by providing an incorrect time period for the availability of funds and a time period that apparently could not be relied upon by the customer." . . . Because Essex offers no evidence that Industrial knew or should have known that it would not receive notice of any problem with the deposit until after April 6, I interpret this as an argument that Industrial failed to comply with the notice it gave, not that the notice itself was improper.

115 S.Ct. 2607, 132 L.Ed.2d 852 (1995). The absolute entitlement plaintiff asserts is not, however, one of the rights provided to depositors under the Act. Section 4006(c)(2) expressly provides: "No provision of this chapter shall be construed as affecting a depository institution's right ... (B) to revoke any provisional settlement made by the depository institution with respect to a check accepted by such institution for deposit; (C) to charge back the depositor's account for the amount of such check; or (D) to claim a refund of such provisional credit." Under § 4006(c)(2)(B), therefore, the EFAA placed no limit on Industrial's right under state law to revoke the provisional credit to Essex's account.[3] *See also* 12 U.S.C. § 4007(b) (preserving state provisions not inconsistent with EFAA). The EFAA requires that banks provide prompt access to valid deposits, not that banks assume liability for bad checks given to depositors. Plaintiff therefore is not entitled to relief under the EFAA. . . .

Although the EFAA preserves a depository bank's right to revoke or charge back an uncollectible deposit, such action must comply with applicable state law. The District of Columbia has adopted the Uniform Commercial Code's system for regulating check processing transactions. The U.C.C. observes a fundamental distinction between "payor" and "collecting" banks. A payor bank is the bank maintaining the account against which a check is drawn, in this case Signet. *See* D.C.Code Ann. § 28:4–105(3). A collecting bank is a bank handling a check for collection from the payor, in this case Industrial. *See* D.C.Code Ann. § 28:4–105(5).

Payor and collecting banks have distinct obligations. A payor bank must decide whether to reject a check by midnight on the day it receives a check for collection. Failure to respond by midnight constitutes "final payment," making the payor bank strictly liable for the amount of the check. *See First Nat'l Bank in Harvey v. Colonial Bank*, 898 F.Supp. 1220, 1226 (N.D.Ill.1995) (discussing U.C.C.'s "final payment" system and role of payor banks); *see also* D.C.Code Ann. § 28:4–302(a). A collecting bank, in contrast, retains the right to revoke or charge back funds that are provisionally credited to a customer until the collecting bank's settlement with the payor bank becomes final. *See* D.C.Code Ann. § 28:4–214(a). It is at the moment of "final payment" by the payor bank that the respective liabilities for a check become fixed: the payor bank is strictly liable to the collecting bank for the amount of the check, *see* D.C.Code Ann. § 28:4–302(a), and the collecting bank loses the ability to revoke a provisional settlement or

---

[3] Indeed, even had Essex temporarily accessed the funds on early in the day on April 6, § 4006(c)(2)(C) would have preserved Industrial's ability under state law to charge back the amount of the deposit.

charge back withdrawn funds. *See* D.C.Code Ann. §§ 28:4–215(d), 28:4–214(a). . . .

[The court concluded that Industrial gave appropriate notice to Essex under UCC § 4–214(a) and in accordance with UCC § 3–503(b), providing for notice of dishonor by "any commercially reasonable means, including an oral, written, or electronic communication."]

WELLS FARGO BANK, N.A. V. WILLOUGHBY
--- F.Supp.3d ---, 2015 WL 5665115 (D. Or. 2015)

ANN AIKEN, District Judge.

Plaintiff Wells Fargo Bank brings this action against Defendant LeRoy Willoughby to recover money lost because of a check-cashing scam. Defendant accepted an offer to work part-time as a "payment officer" for a business in Japan, but the job offer was actually a check-cashing scam, "in which the victim is asked to accept what appears to be a legitimate check on behalf of a foreign corporation, deposit the funds, then wire some or all of the proceeds to a foreign account before the victim's bank realizes that the check is, in fact, counterfeit." *Branch Banking & Trust Co. v. Witmeyer,* 2011 WL 3297682, at (E.D.Va.2011) (footnote omitted). The scam here followed the pattern: Defendant deposited a $150,000 check to open an account with Plaintiff. When Plaintiff made the funds available, Defendant wired more than $95,000 to a bank in Japan. A few days later the $150,000 check was dishonored as counterfeit, and the wired funds could not be recovered. Those responsible for the scam have not been identified.

Plaintiff now moves for summary judgment on its claims for breach of contract, breach of warranty, conversion, account stated, and statutory violations. Defendant responds that he was a victim of the scam and had no intent to defraud Plaintiff.

The most culpable party is not before the court, so the issue is whether Plaintiff or Defendant should bear responsibility for the loss. Because Defendant was the party best able to prevent the loss, the Uniform Commercial Code, which governs the transaction here, holds Defendant responsible. *See Ed Stinn Chevrolet, Inc. v.. Nat'l City Bank,* 28 Ohio St.3d 221, 226, 503 N.E.2d 524, 530 (Ohio 1986) (per curiam), *modified on other grounds,* 31 Ohio St.3d 150, 509 N.E.2d 945 (1987). I grant Plaintiff's motion for summary judgment. . . .

Factual Background . . .
On January 7, 2009, Defendant received an email ostensibly from

Itochu Corp., a large multinational business based in Japan, offering part-time work depositing checks and wiring funds in exchange for a 5% commission. Defendant states that he worked more than twenty-five years in Japan and "was very familiar with the companies and practices over there." . . . Furthermore, Defendant was "familiar with [Itochu Corp.] because he had taught English to some of their managers and executives." . . . Even though the job offer resembled a typical check-cashing scam, Defendant states that he was "more trusting of emails from this company and their needing a part time employee to help them with their overseas business." . . .

The initial email[1] to Defendant explained that because most of Itochu Corp.'s board members did not understand English, the company sought a "noble and trusted representative client from CANADA AND USA." . . . The email stated, "Most of our customers pay out in check and we do not have an account in your country that will clear this money. Again, this is the problem of language." . . .

The email described the work required: "Your tasks are Receive payment from Customers Cash Payments at your Bank. Deduct 5% which will be your percentage/pay on Payment processed. Forward balance after deduction of percentage/pay to any of the offices you will be contacted to send payment to." . . .

Defendant responded with an email expressing his interest in the work. Defendant stated that he "used to teach English to your staff in Japan and am familiar with Itochu Corp." . . .

On January 8, 2009, the false Itochu Corp. sent Defendant an email accepting him as a "payment officer." The email instructed Defendant to deposit checks and to notify the company when his bank made the funds available. Defendant would then be told where to transfer the funds. . . .

As shown by the email correspondence submitted by Defendant, the scam's success depended on Defendant believing that (1) a multinational corporation based in Japan would forfeit 5% of payments received from North American customers because its board members did not understand English; (2) the multinational corporation had no access to banks in North America, so it used blind email solicitations to hire payment officers whose only qualifications were access to a bank account and the ability to understand English; and (4) the corporation had no mechanism, other than "trust," to prevent a payment officer from keeping the entire amount of the payment rather than only the 5% commission.

---

[1] As Plaintiff notes, applicants were told to send information to a Yahoo.com webmail address based in Hong Kong, not a corporate email address based in Japan. . . .

On January 27, 2009, Defendant received the $150,000 check that gave rise to this action. . . . On its face, the check appeared legitimate, payable to Defendant, issued by a business called MDS in Ontario, Canada, and drawn on an account at the Canadian Imperial Bank of Commerce (CIBC).

After Defendant received the check, he was apparently instructed by email that he was working for CNOOC Oil Base Group Ltd. China, rather than Itochu Corp. Responding to this new development, Defendant stated that he did "not want to process [the check] until I know what this is all about. I didn't know I was working as a rep for CNOOC Oil." . . . Despite this discrepancy, and the other red flags, on January 28, 2009, Defendant endorsed and deposited the check in a newly opened account at a Wachovia Bank (Plaintiff's predecessor in interest) in Pueblo, Colorado.

Defendant states that when he opened the account, he told bank employees that he "was suspicious of the check and with [Plaintiff's] advice proceeded with the deposit." Defendant alleges that Plaintiff's employees told him "if the check clears, the funds were okay." . . . Defendant does not allege that he told anyone why he thought the check was suspicious.

On January 28, 2009, Defendant notified "boydbarrett@consultant.com," apparently another contact with his employer, that Plaintiff would make funds from the $150,000 check available to Defendant on February 5, 2009. . . .

On February 5, 2009, Plaintiff credited $150,000 to Defendant's account. Defendant withdrew $5,500, depositing $5,000 in a new account and taking $500 in cash.

That day, Defendant emailed "Boyd Barrett" again, stating that the check had cleared. He wrote, "I await further direction from you or CNOOC Oil Base Group Ltd China. I await the next transfer as well." . . .

Defendant then received an email supposedly from Eizo Kobayishi, the president of Itochu Corp., instructing Defendant to wire $96,905 to Resona Bank, in Hiroshima, Japan, to the account of Asako Tradings. Defendant wired the funds as instructed, and notified "Kobayishi-san."

As of February 6, 2009, Plaintiff had not received payment for the $150,000 check from CIBC, the "payor" bank. On February 9, 2009, CIBC returned the check as dishonored. Plaintiff promptly notified Defendant that the check had been dishonored. The next day, one of Plaintiff's employees told Defendant that his accounts were on hold and that Plaintiff suspected fraud.

Defendant states that Plaintiff's employees told him "not to worry about anything, since it had been turned over to their fraud department." . . . On February 10, 2009, Plaintiff's investigator spoke to Defendant about the fraudulent check. Defendant told the investigator he had been suspicious about the check.

On February 26, 2009, the Japanese bank that had received the wired funds notified Plaintiff that the transfer could not be reversed and the funds would not be returned. Asako Tradings was a fictional entity. The money was never recovered.

In April 2009, Plaintiff sent Defendant an account statement showing a negative balance of $97,448.99. That is the amount Plaintiff now seeks as damages. . . .

Indorser Liability

"[I]f an instrument is dishonored, an indorser is obliged to pay the amount due on the instrument (I) according to the terms of the instrument at the time it was indorsed." Colo. Stat. § 4–3–415(a) ("Obligation of indorser"). Here, Defendant endorsed and deposited the counterfeit check, and the check was later dishonored. Although the wired funds were lost, Plaintiff was able to prevent further losses after learning the check was dishonored. Defendant is not liable for the entire amount of check but for $97,448.99, the amount lost.

Defendant argues that he never intended to defraud Plaintiff. But intent to defraud is not relevant to Plaintiff's claims under the UCC. *See Vadde v. Bank of America,* 687 S.E.2d 880, 886 (Ga.App.2009) (rejecting argument that "ignorance of a fraud or counterfeit is a defense to a collecting bank's claim for recoupment"); *SunTrust Bank v. Bennett (In re Bennett),* 517 B.R. 95, 104 (Bankr.M.D.Tenn.2014) (bankruptcy court noted that debtor would have been liable for endorsing and presenting bad checks "regardless of any fraudulent intent").

Defendant argues he is also a victim of the scam. But when the true culprit behind a scam is not before the court, the Uniform Commercial Code assigns responsibility to the party who was best able to prevent the loss. . . .

Plaintiff was required by the Expedited Funds Availability Act (EFAA) to give its customers prompt access to deposited funds. *See Essex Constr. Corp. v. Indus. Bank of Wash., Inc.,* 913 F.Supp. 416, 418 (D.Md.1995) (construing EFAA, 12 U.S.C. § 4006). When Plaintiff made funds available to Defendant, Plaintiff was not vouching for the check's validity. *See id.,* 913 F.Supp. at 419 ("The EFAA requires that banks provide prompt access to valid deposits, not that banks assume liability for bad checks given to depositors."). Under the EFAA and the UCC, banks may make a "provisional settlement" on a deposit, crediting the customer's account with the amount of a deposited check even though the bank (called the "depositary bank") has not yet received payment from the "payor bank" on which the check was drawn. *See id.*, 913 F.Supp. at 418; UCC § 4–214(a). If, as here, the payor bank dishonors the check, the depositary bank (also called the "collecting bank" when it seeks payment) "retains the right to revoke or charge back funds that are provisionally credited to a customer until the collecting bank's settlement with the payor bank becomes final." 913 F.Supp. at 418. . . .

Questions and Problems 3.36. Is the *Wells Fargo* decision correct in its reading of the *Essex Construction* remark that a collecting bank "retains the right" of revocation or charge-back of provisional credits? As a practical matter, does the EFAA affect this right?

3.37. Litigants invoking the EFAA seem to be suggesting that the rules imposed by the act and its implementing regulations somehow alter the rights and obligations under UCC Article 4. Is there merit to that suggestion? What are the consequences of *not* complying with the EFAA? Note that 12 U.S.C. § 4010 imposes civil liability upon a bank that does not comply with the notice requirements of the act. However, 12 U.S.C. § 4003 does *not* limit a bank's right to charge back the depositor's account for the amount of a check that is dishonored by the payee bank or turns out to be counterfeit. *See JPMorgan Chase Bank, N.A. v. Freyberg,* --- F.Supp.3d ---, 2016 WL 2605209, at *12-*13 (S.D.N.Y. 2016); *Fischer & Mandell LLP v. Citibank, N.A,* --- F.Supp.3d ---, 2009 WL 1767621, at *5–6 (S.D.N.Y. 2009); *Lynch v. Bank of America, N.A.*, 493 F.Supp.2d 265, 268 (D.R.I. 2007).

Chapter 4

LETTERS OF CREDIT

Letters of credit (L/Cs) are another device by which payments move in commerce. In U.S. practice, they are governed primarily by UCC Article 5. Although that article makes no distinction among types of L/Cs, they are typically viewed as two basic varieties, commercial (or "documentary" or "trade") L/Cs, and standby (or "guaranty") L/Cs. As we shall see, these two varieties of L/C perform quite different functions. The commercial L/C is a method of payment *for* something, while the standby L/C is used for payment when some expected event does *not* occur. So one question that needs to be explored is whether these two types of L/Cs ought to be subject to the same transactional rules, or whether the rules should be tailored to suit the differing purposes of the two.

L/Cs are used in two different settings, domestic (*e.g.*, for transactions occurring within the United States) and transnational (*i.e.*, for transactions in which the parties are located in different nations). For domestic L/C/ transactions, there should be nothing remarkable about the use of local law governing L/Cs, although in a federal system there may still be choice of law questions about which individual state's L/C law should apply.[1] Transnational L/C transactions will of course be subject to international choice of law rules or contracting parties' choice of law. However, we may need to explore whether a distinctly *transnational* version of L/C law would be desirable.

---

[1] The adoption of UCC Article 5 has largely eliminated this issue in the United States, although the article as enacted, interpreted and applied in individual states may still be subject to some variation in practice from state to state.

And so the chapter pursues three basic themes. First, what is the nature of an L/C and how does it work? Second, are there materially different issues confronting commercial and standby letters of credit? Third, what rules and general practices apply to transnational L/C transactions? The following section gives an overall view of the various types of L/Cs used in banking practice.

A. THE L/C TRANSACTION

1. Introduction: Four Documents

The typical L/C transaction involves four basic elements. First, there is of course the contract between the parties – buyer and seller, customer and service provider – that allocates risks and costs. In the present context, contract is often referred to as "the underlying transaction" when the focus is on the L/C itself.

Second, if the contract is a sales contract for goods, there will be a bill of lading (BOL), a contract for the shipment of the goods between the *shipper* (*e.g.*, the seller) and the *carrier* (*e.g.*, the shipping company). The BOL will also serve as a receipt for the goods issued by the carrier. It will also serve as evidence of title to the goods specified in the BOL. A sample BOL (omitting any fine print on the reverse) is provided on the next page.

Third, there is the L/C itself, typically issued by a bank, which is a written promise to make a specified payment or payments under specifically defined circumstances. For example, it may – and usually does – require that any demand for payment must be accompanied by the original BOL and perhaps other specified documents.

Finally, there is the documentary draft is a payment instrument (like the checks and other negotiable instruments that we discussed in Chapter 2), by which the demand for payment is actually made to the bank or other issuer of the L/C.

Each of these elements plays a role in reducing the risks of the transaction for the parties. Like most contracting parties, they will use their contract to allocate risks and responsibilities and to anticipate issues that might arise during contract performance. The BOL is a way for the buyer to be able to rely on the shipping company, for information that goods have actually been shipped, rather than just relying on the seller's own statements. The L/C allows the seller to rely on a bank's reputation for creditworthiness, rather than just relying on the buyer's reassurances that "the check is in the mail." Finally, the draft permits integration of the payment process into the regular bank collection system. It can also be used by a seller to generate short-term credit by selling ("discounting") the draft in the secondary market for such instruments. Traditionally, the BOL, the L/C, and the draft would be actual paper documents. However, in contemporary practice increasingly these documents are virtual documents, electronic communications serving the same functions as the earlier paper documents.

An International Bill of Lading

Questions and Problems 4.1. The BOL is a receipt for the goods delivered to the carrier. However, the BOL is also a *contract* between the shipper and the carrier. SallerCo is planning to ship 100 cartons of motorized thingots to BayerCorp, pursuant to a sales contract between the two. SallerCo is arranging with Freight Services, Inc., to have the goods carried from SallerCo's main factory by trailer to the nearest port facility for transport by ship to a receiving port near BayerCorp's main warehouse, where it will be picked up by BayerCorp personnel or by a trucking firm selected by BayerCorp. In drafting the terms for this "through bill of lading," *i.e.*, one involving containerized goods, which is issued by an inland carrier (typically a railroad or trucking agency) to cover the entire voyage, including transshipment to a vessel, and perhaps carriage on another inland carrier from the ship's destination, what sort of provisions should you be focusing on?[2] Allocating responsibilities for damages? If SallerCo and BayerCorp are located in different countries, should there be specific provisions to cover problems of compliance with applicable domestic laws of different nations through which the goods pass? Multilateral treaties like the U.N. Convention on the Carriage of Goods by Sea,[3] which entered into force for the United States in 1992, would offer some basic default rules, but it remains within the power of the parties to decide on their own terms.

2. The L/C

A commercial L/C is a commitment by the issuer that it will make payment to an identified beneficiary on drafts drawn on the L/C under circumstances agreed upon by the parties in their contract and specified in the L/C. (A sample L/C is provided on the next page.) The customer of the bank who opens the L/C (the applicant) is usually the buyer of the goods. The L/C beneficiary is usually the seller of those goods, or a bank specified by the seller. The L/C typically conditions payment on the presentation to the issuer of a draft and any other documents agreed upon in the contract and specified in the L/C. These other documents may be, for example, include the BOL or other evidence of title, customs documents, and insurance certificates.

Some other bank, known as a confirmer, may be used to "confirm" the L/C, *i.e.*, to make payment to the beneficiary under the L/C, with subsequent presentation of demand to the issuing bank for reimbursement. A confirmer may be used where the issuer is unknown to

---

[2] *See, e.g., James N. Kirby, Pty Ltd. v. Norfolk Southern Railway Co.*, 300 F.3d 1300 (11th Cir. 2002) (examining legal issues arising in context of multimodal BOL).

[3] 1695 U.N.T.S. 3 (Mar. 31, 1978).

the seller, or where it is not convenient for the beneficiary to deal directly with an issuing bank in the buyer's home country.

It is also possible that some other bank may be used as an adviser, *i.e.*, a bank that informs seller that an L/C has been established in seller's favor. An adviser does *not* undertake any obligation to make payment under the L/C.

INTERNATIONAL BANKING GROUP   ORIGINAL

Megabank Corporation
P.O. BOX 1000, ATLANTA, GEORGIA 30302-1000
CABLE ADDRESS: MegaB
TELEX NO. 1234567
SWIFT NO. MBBABC 72

OUR ADVICE NUMBER: EA00000091
ADVICE DATE: 08MAR97   ****AMOUNT****
ISSUE BANK REF: 3312/HBI/22341   USD****25,000.00
EXPIRY DATE: 23JUN97

BENEFICIARY: APPLICANT:
THE WALTON SUPPLY CO.   HHB HONG KONG
2356 SOUTH N.W. STREET   34 INDUSTRIAL DRIVE
ATLANTA, GEORGIA 30345   CENTRAL, HONG KONG

WE HAVE BEEN REQUESTED TO ADVISE TO YOU THE FOLLOWING LETTER OF CREDIT AS
ISSUED BY:
THIRD HONG KONG BANK
1 CENTRAL TOWER
HONG KONG

PLEASE BE GUIDED BY ITS TERMS AND CONDITIONS AND BY THE FOLLOWING:
CREDIT IS AVAILABLE BY NEGOTIATION OF YOUR DRAFT(S) IN DUPLICATE AT
SIGHT FOR 100 PERCENT OF INVOICE VALUE DRAWN ON US ACCOMPANIED BY THE
FOLLOWING DOCUMENTS:

1. SIGNED COMMERCIAL INVOICE IN 1 ORIGINAL AND 3 COPIES.

2. FULL SET 3/3 OCEAN BILLS OF LADING CONSIGNED TO THE ORDER OF THIRD HONG KONG
   BANK, HONG KONG NOTIFY APPLICANT AND MARKED FREIGHT COLLECT.

3. PACKING LIST IN 2 COPIES.

EVIDENCING SHIPMENT OF: 5000 PINE LOGS – WHOLE – 8 TO 12 FEET
                        FOB SAVANNAH, GEORGIA

SHIPMENT FROM: SAVANNAH, GEORGIA   TO: HONG KONG
LATEST SHIPPING DATE: 02JUN97

PARTIAL SHIPMENTS NOT ALLOWED   TRANSHIPMENT NOT ALLOWED

ALL BANKING CHARGES OUTSIDE HONG KONG ARE FOR BENEFICIARYS ACCOUNT.
DOCUMENTS MUST BE PRESENTED WITHIN 21 DAYS FROM B/L DATE.

AT THE REQUEST OF OUR CORRESPONDENT, WE CONFIRM THIS CREDIT AND ALSO ENGAGE
WITH YOU THAT ALL DRAFTS DRAWN UNDER AND IN COMPLIANCE WITH THE TERMS OF THIS
CREDIT WILL BE DULY HONORED BY US.

PLEASE EXAMINE THIS INSTRUMENT CAREFULLY. IF YOU ARE UNABLE TO COMPLY WITH
THE TERMS OR CONDITIONS, PLEASE COMMUNICATE WITH YOUR BUYER TO ARRANGE FOR
AN AMENDMENT.

Standard Form of Letter of Credit

In the typical situation, buyer asks its bank to issue an L/C naming seller as beneficiary, and promises to pay when a BOL for the goods is presented to it. The bank will send the L/C to the seller. When seller ships the goods, it receives a BOL from the carrier, will negotiate it to the order of buyer, and transmit it to issuer, together with a draft and any other documents required by the L/C. After reviewing the documents for conformity to the requirements of the L/C, issuer will pay seller and transmit the documents to buyer, who must reimburse the issuer. Alternatively, buyer may present its draft and other required documents to a confirmer (possibly its own bank) for transmission to issuer, either directly or through other intermediary banks that may themselves be advisers or confirmers.

The L/C itself may be transmitted electronically. (Electronic transmittal in L/C practice is recognized by the 1995 revision of UCC Article 5.) So, for example, UCC § 5-104 expressly authorizes the L/C to be issued "in any form that is a *record*," which is defined to mean "information that is inscribed on a tangible medium, or that is stored in an electronic or other medium and is retrievable in perceivable form."[4] Any "document" involved in the transaction expressly may be "presented in a written *or other medium* permitted by the letter of credit."[5] Review the provisions of revised UCC Article 5 that appear in the Supplement before answering the following questions.

Questions and Problems 4.2. BayerCorp and SallerCo's sales contract provides for payment for the thingots by L/C, but the contract does not say anything about the method of presenting documents for payment under the L/C. SallerCo sends Issuer Bank a pdf.doc containing a draft and supporting documents that would clearly have satisfied the L/C conditions for payment if they had been paper documents. Issuer Bank's employee looks at the pdf.doc on screen, but does not process SallerCo's payment demand. The L/C eventually expires. Is Issuer Bank liable to SallerCo under revised UCC Article 5? To BayerCorp?

4.3. The BayerCorp–SallerCo contract provides for payment by L/C, and both the contract and the L/C condition payment on the presentation of "[t]he original and three copies of" the documents required for payment under the L/C. SallerCo sends Issuer Bank a pdf.doc containing a draft and supporting documents that would clearly have satisfied the L/C conditions for payment if they had been paper documents. Bank's employee looks at the pdf.doc on the computer screen, but does not process SallerCo's payment demand. The L/C eventually expires. Would Bank be liable to SallerCo under the revised UCC article 5? To BayerCorp?

4.4. The sales contract that BayerCorp and SallerCo signed provides for payment for the thingots via an L/C, and explicitly chooses

---

[4] UCC § 5-102(a)(14).

[5] UCC § 5-104.

"West Dakota Commercial Code art. V" as the law governing payment. (W.D.C.C. art. V is the locally enacted version of revised UCC Article 5.) SallerCo sends Issuer Bank an email with an attached electronic document containing a draft and supporting documents that would clearly have satisfied the L/C conditions for payment if they had been paper documents. Bank's employee cannot open the attachment, and closes the email with the intention of asking Bank's IT department to look at it. The L/C eventually expires. Would Bank be liable to SallerCo under the revised UCC article 5? To BayerCorp?

3. The Draft or Bill of Exchange

A draft or bill of exchange is an order in writing by one person (the drawer, typically the seller) to another person (the drawee, typically a bank), signed by the drawer and requiring the drawee to pay on demand, or at a fixed or determinable future time, a sum certain in money to, or to the order of, a specified person (the payee) or to bearer. (A sample draft is provided below.) As we know from Chapter 2, a drawee does not owe an obligation to the payee to pay the draft, unless drawee signs ("accepts") the draft, at which point drawee becomes an acceptor, with its own obligation to pay the instrument. Whether the instrument is accepted or not, it is likely to be negotiable. If you recall the Article 4 road map on page 182 of Chapter 3, you  will see that there are specialized provisions of Article 4 that deal with such a documentary draft, which is otherwise not generally covered by Article 4.

At Sight	Any City, Ks.	May 2, 1997

Pay to the order of **Seller**　　　　　**US $10,000.00**

Ten Thousand and no/100 U.S. Dollars

Through Banco di Roma

　　　　　　　　　　　　Seller

Buyer

Qualsiasi Città, Italia　　　　Exporter

Negotiable Draft

Questions and Problems 4.5. Issuer Bank has issued an L/C, per BayerCorp and SallerCo's sales contract, in SallerCo's favor. SallerCo's bank, Advisor State Bank (ASB), takes its documentary draft for collection and presents the draft and accompanying documents to Issuer Bank. Issuer Bank informs ASB that it will not pay on the draft, because it has "questions" about the accompanying documents. Does ASB have any responsibilities at this point? (*See* UCC §§ 4-501, 4-503, 4-504.) What if ASB had discounted the draft from SallerCo? (*See* UCC § 4-501.)

4.6. Consistent with language in the contract, Issuer Bank's L/C says that drafts are "payable on arrival of . . . shipment. SallerCo gives ASB a draft, a BOL, and other required documents to present for payment to Issuer Bank. The goods have not arrived yet, and Issuer Bank informs ASB that it is "not prepared to pay at this time." Is this a dishonor of the draft by Issuer Bank? What are ASB's responsibilities under these circumstances? (See UCC § 4-502.)

4.7. As you can see from the illustration below, there is a pattern to the typical L/C transaction – a round trip with several stops – with documents moving in one direction, and payment returning. Legal difficulties arise if there is a break in either leg of the trip.

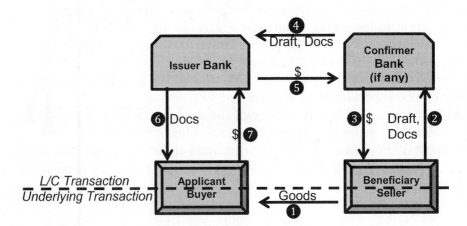

❶ Seller ships goods; obtains necessary documents ("docs") from shipper
❷ Seller submits draft and docs to Confirmer
❸ Confirmer pays Seller on draft
❹ Confirmer submits draft and docs to Issuer
❺ Issuer reimburses Confirmer
❻ Issuer makes docs available to Buyer
❼ Buyer reimburses Issuer in exchange for docs

Typical Documentary Letter of Credit[6]

---

[6] *Source*: MICHAEL P. MALLOY, PRINCIPLES OF BANK REGULATION § 9.20 (3d ed. 2011).

4.8. In the following case, do you see what went wrong with the L/C transaction? What could SallerCo and BayerCorp do to avoid such problems?

FERTICO BELGIUM S.A. V. PHOSPHATE CHEMICALS EXPORT ASS'N, INC.
100 A.D.2d 165 (N.Y. App. Div. 1984)

SULLIVAN, Justice.

On October 18, 1978 Phosphate Chemicals Export Association, Inc. (PhosChem), an American exporter of fertilizer products, agreed to sell 35,000 metric tons of phosphate fertilizer to Fertico Belgium S.A., a Belgium-domiciled, international trader of various commodities, including fertilizer. The fertilizer was to be shipped to Antwerp, . . . and delivered in two installments—15,000 metric tons between November 1 and 15, 1978 and the balance by November 30, 1978. Although the contract did not specify a date for the fertilizer's arrival in Antwerp, time was allegedly of the essence since Fertico was contractually obligated to ship 12,000 metric tons to Baghdad by November 25th. Fertico was required to open a confirmed irrevocable letter of credit in PhosChem's favor through a reputable United States bank no later than October 30, 1978. Shipment was to be within 15 days after receipt of the letter of credit.

On November 2, 1978, Fertico's bank, The Banque de Paris et des Pays-Bas Belgique S.A. (Paribas), notified the Irving Trust Company by telex that an irrevocable documentary credit in the amount of $1,725,000 was being opened in PhosChem's behalf. Irving Trust, in turn, advised PhosChem of the credit and the conditions thereof on November 6, 1978. Fertico, through Paribas, subsequently amended the conditions of the letter of credit and advised Irving Trust that no written confirmation would follow. On November 10, 1978, Irving Trust notified PhosChem of the amendments and confirmed the credit.

Irving Trust's confirmation specified shipment from an "East or Gulf U.S. Port" to Antwerp . . . and provided for payment against presentation to it of various documents including, "[f]ull set clean onboard ocean bills of lading ... dated onboard not later than November 8, 1978" and "[c]opy of your telex sent to Fertico Belgium S A advising name of ship, sailing date, weight and ETA Antwerp, the same date as end of loading, and certified true." . . .

After receiving Irving Trust's advice that an irrevocable credit had been issued in its favor, PhosChem chartered a cargo ship, the Scanspruce, and arranged for 15,000 metric tons of fertilizer to be promptly delivered onboard. Loading was completed by November 8th and onboard bills of lading, the accuracy of which is not in dispute, were issued bearing that date. That same day, PhosChem sent the following telex to Fertico:

> The M/V Scanspruce sailed from Tampa, Florida on November 8, 1978 carrying a total of 14805.580 metric tons granular triple super-phosphate and is due to arrive in Antwerp on December 4, 1978.
> We certify the above to be true and correct.

In fact, the Scanspruce took on other cargo and did not leave port until November 11th. PhosChem so advised Fertico, both orally and in writing, on November 16th.

Earlier, however, on November 3rd, Fertico, on learning that the Scanspruce was not due in Antwerp until December 4th, had complained to PhosChem that the fertilizer would arrive too late to complete the resale transaction to which it was committed. On November 13, 1978 Fertico reiterated this complaint and advised PhosChem that it was sending a representative to Baghdad in an effort to renegotiate the resale.

Notwithstanding its concern Fertico did not advise Irving Trust or Paribas of any problem with respect to the transaction; nor did it request either bank to withhold payment on the credit. PhosChem did not present its draft and the various documents required by the letter of credit to Irving Trust until November 17th. Payment was made on or about November 21st. Among the documents presented was PhosChem's November 8th telex to Fertico certifying a November 8, 1978 sailing. The Scanspruce did not arrive in Antwerp until December 17, 1978. Unloading of the fertilizer was undertaken on December 20, 1978. Fertico took possession of the goods, held them, and resold them to a customer in Antwerp at a gross profit of approximately $400,000.

Almost three years later, in October 1981, Fertico commenced an action against PhosChem, asserting, inter alia, causes of action in breach of contract and fraud and conversion.2 In the contract action, in which damages of $1,250,000 were sought, Fertico alleged that "[t]imely delivery by PhosChem of the [fertilizer] to plaintiff was essential, and was known to PhosChem to be essential to plaintiff, for it to fulfill its contractual obligations ...." Specifically, Fertico contends that PhosChem was contractually obliged to assure that the Scanspruce would arrive in Antwerp by a certain date and, as part of this obligation, agreed that it would set sail by November 8, 1978 and proceed directly to Antwerp. Instead, the Scanspruce made a stop at Hamburg before proceeding to Antwerp.

The fraud and conversion cause of action incorporated the contract allegations. Additionally, Fertico contends that PhosChem's November 8th telex contained fraudulent misrepresentations and that in reliance thereon it "[a]llowed Irving Trust Company to pay to PhosChem in excess of $1.7 million, to which PhosChem was not entitled." Thus, Fertico alleged that PhosChem's drawing on the letter of credit constituted actionable fraud and conversion.

PhosChem moved to dismiss the fraud and conversion cause of action for failure to state a cause of action. . . . Fertico cross-moved for partial summary judgment on the same cause of action on the issue of liability. While agreeing with PhosChem that "the alleged fraud is not an independent transaction but rather an integral part of defendant's alleged failure to timely perform the contract", Special Term nevertheless refused to dismiss the conversion claim, finding that "[t]he letter of credit is property of its maker plaintiff, Fertico, separate and apart from the underlying transaction...." Reasoning that the terms of the letter of credit were not met because "the sailing occurred after November 8th, and was not direct to Antwerp", Special Term concluded that "under such circumstances, [PhosChem] did not at the time of encashment have any entitlement to the funds", and awarded Fertico partial summary judgment on its conversion claim. An assessment of damages was directed.

Even assuming, arguendo, that a cause of action for either fraud or conversion is stated, the grant of summary judgment in Fertico's favor on the conversion claim was clearly erroneous since the factual premises underlying Special Term's determination either do not find support in the record or are, at the very least, in issue.

Special Term found that PhosChem did not comply with the terms of the letter of credit in two respects, one of which, direct shipment to Antwerp, was not even a specified condition. The letter simply specified "shipment from East or Gulf U.S. Port to Antwerpen C & F Antwerpen." Only transhipment, i.e., the transfer of goods from one ship to another, was prohibited, and only the Scanspruce transported Fertico's cargo.

In a C & F contract, a such as is involved here, the seller "must put the goods in the possession of ... a carrier and make such a contract for their transportation as may be reasonable ..." unless otherwise agreed. (Uniform Commercial Code, § 2–504[a].) The reasonableness of particular transportation arrangements turns on a review of the "circumstances of the case." (Uniform Commercial Code, § 2–504[a].) Although Fertico is obviously challenging the propriety of PhosChem's shipping arrangements, the letter of credit did not require that the vessel carry Fertico's cargo alone, that it proceed by any particular route or that Fertico's cargo be given any priority in unloading. These are matters totally extraneous to the text of the letter of credit and irrelevant to its interpretation.

A letter of credit is a commitment by a bank to pay under the terms of the credit upon presentation of specified documents, not upon occurrence of the events purportedly represented by the documents. (*United Bank v. Cambridge Sporting Goods Corp.*, 41 N.Y.2d 254, 258–259, 392 N.Y.S.2d 265, 360 N.E.2d 943. . . . An issuing or confirming bank presented with a demand for payment is concerned only with whether the description of the documents listed in the letter of credit has been met. Thus, Irving Trust was not obliged to look beyond the letter's specified conditions to check the particulars of shipping arrangements. (*See O'Meara Co. v. National Park Bank of N.Y.*, 239 N.Y. 386, 146 N.E. 636, reh. den. 240 N.Y. 607, 148 N.E. 725.)

Special Term also found that PhosChem failed to comply with the letter of credit because "the sailing occurred after November 8th." In so finding Special Term ignored the accepted meaning of a specified condition of the letter of credit and substituted its own interpretation. Irving Trust's confirmation of the letter of credit, in which it undertook to honor drafts drawn under the credit (*see Venizelos S.A. v. Chase Manhattan Bank*, 425 F.2d 461; [Uniform Customs and Practices (UCP)] Article 3; see, also, Uniform Commercial Code, § 5–107[2]), required only that shipment be effected by November 8th. More specifically, it conditioned payment upon presentation of, inter alia, onboard bills of lading dated no later than November 8, 1978, while the Paribas telex required "shipment from East or Gulf U.S. port to Antwerpen at latest 8th November 1978." No matter which clause is used as the operative text of the letter of credit the result is the same. November 8, 1978 was the date of shipment. . . .

Moreover, the term "sailing" appears only in the description of the telex PhosChem was to send to Fertico, a copy of which was to be presented to the bank, advising Fertico of, inter alia, the name of the ship and sailing date. Since this document was neither a shipping nor insurance document or commercial invoice, the contents of which a bank is obliged to scrutinize carefully, but rather a collateral document, it was subject only to cursory examination. (*Courtaulds North America Inc. v. North Carolina Nat. Bank*, 528 F.2d 802, 806. . . .) The bank was not required to demand more than that which was explicitly set forth in the description of the telex. PhosChem was merely required to advise Fertico of the sailing date. The telex description did not specify a particular date by which sailing had to occur. Thus, PhosChem's November 8th telex certifying that the Scanspruce sailed from Tampa on November 8th was neither false nor deceptive on its face. Finally, it should be noted that, contrary to Fertico's claim, the December 17th arrival of the Scanspruce was not violative of the terms of the letter of credit since the letter failed to specify a delivery date. Consequently, Fertico's cross-motion for summary judgment on the fraud and conversion action should have been denied in its entirety.

[The court went on to find that "the fraud and conversion claims are fatally deficient in stating a cause of action." It also concluded that Fertico's allegations "do not provide a basis for finding PhosChem liable in conversion, fraud or any other tort." Any lost profits that Fertico may have suffered should have been addressed as a breach of the underlying contract.]

Since PhosChem was required to ship C & F, the contract was a shipment, not a destination, contract, and delivery of the goods to the carrier was delivery to the buyer for purposes of risk and title. (Official Comment No. 1, McKinney's Consolidated Laws of New York, Book 62 ½, Uniform Commercial Code, § 2–320.) PhosChem was entitled to payment upon tender of the required documents of title. (Uniform Commercial Code, § 2–320[4]). The letter of credit was merely the mechanism to effect that payment.

A letter of credit represents a separate contract between the issuing or confirming bank and the beneficiary, independent of the contract for the sale of goods between the buyer and seller. (*United Bank v. Cambridge Sporting Goods Corp.*, supra, 41 N.Y.2d at 259, 392 N.Y.S.2d 265, 360 N.E.2d 943; *Foreign Venture Ltd. Partnership v. Chemical Bank*, 59 A.D.2d 352, 399 N.Y.S.2d 114; *Shanghai Commercial Bank Ltd. v. Bank of Boston International, supra*, 53 A.D.2d at 830, 385 N.Y.S.2d 548.) Thus, contrary to Special Term's finding, Fertico was not a maker of the letter of credit or even a party to the agreement embodied therein between Irving Trust and PhosChem.

Three distinct contracts are involved in a documentary letter of credit transaction: a contract between the bank and its customer by which the bank undertakes to issue a credit; the letter of credit itself, which is a commitment on the part of the issuing bank that it will pay a draft presented to it by a holder of a letter under the terms of the credit and upon presentation of the required documents of title; and the underlying contract of sale between the buyer who has procured issuance of the letter and the seller. (*United Technologists Corp v. Citibank, N.A.*, 469 F.Supp. 473.) "The question between the customer and the vendor is the one whether the goods comply with the contract and if they do not the former has his appropriate right of action." (*Laudisi v. American Exchange Nat. Bank, supra*, 239 N.Y. at 243, 146 N.E.2d 347; *see, also, O'Meara Co. v. National Park Bank of N.Y.*, supra, 239 N.Y. at 395-396, 146 N.E. 636.)

The only exception to the rule barring the customer's intervention in the separate letter of credit contract between the bank and the beneficiary is limited to instances where "fraud in the transaction" has been shown and the holder of the draft is not a holder in due course, in which event the customer may seek to enjoin the issuer of a letter of credit from honoring the demand for payment. (*Sztejn v. Schroder Banking Corp.*, 177 Misc. 719, 31 N.Y.S.2d 631; *see United Bank v. Cambridge Sporting Goods Corp., supra*, 41 N.Y.2d at 259, 392 N.Y.S.2d 265, 310 N.E.2d 943; *Bank of Montreal v. Recknagel*, 109 N.Y. 482, 17 N.E. 217; *see, also*, Uniform Commercial Code, § 5–114[2](b).) Fertico never took any steps to enjoin payment under the letter of credit. Even if an injunction had been sought, it is doubtful that Fertico would have been successful since PhosChem's alleged misdeeds clearly do not amount to "fraud in the transaction." At most, under Fertico's interpretation of the letter of credit, PhosChem shipped the fertilizer three days late. It was precisely this type of risk—a buyer's claims of non-compliance or late delivery—against which the irrevocable letter of credit was intended to hedge so as to assure prompt payment to the seller. (*See Foreign Venture Ltd. Partnership v. Chemical Bank, supra*, 59 A.D.2d 352, 399 N.Y.S.2d 114.)

Since Irving Trust was never put on notice of facts constituting "fraud in the transaction" it was obligated to honor the demand for payment once the demand complied with the terms of the relevant credit. (UCP Article 8; see Uniform Commercial Code, § 5–114[1].) . ...

Questions and Problems 4.9. In another part of the opinion, the court noted that the contract between the parties incorporated by reference the Uniform Customs and Practice for Documentary Credits (UCP). The UCP are a set of customary practices in international commerce that are maintained by the International Chamber of Commerce, based in Paris, and typically referenced in a letter of credit, thus becoming part of the terms. The UCP rules are regularly updated, the current version being UCP 600. What is the relationship between the UCP rules and UCC Article 5? The *Fertico* court states:

> Irving Trust's confirmation, as well as its original advice, further advised that the credit was subject to the Uniform Customs and Practice for Documentary Credits [1974 Revision], International Chamber of Commerce Publication 290 (UCP).1 Thus, since the letter of credit was subject to the UCP, Article 5 of the Uniform Commercial Code—Letters of Credit—does not apply. (Uniform Commercial Code, § 5–102[4].) The UCP, however, is by definition a recording of practice rather than a statement of legal rules. (Harfield, Practice Commentary,

McKinney's Consolidated Laws of New York, Book 62 ½, Uniform Commercial Code, § 5–114.)

If the UCC Article 5 does not apply to the L/C in *Fertico*, why does the court repeatedly cite to it as authority throughout its opinion?

B. STANDBY L/Cs

In U.S. banking practice, national banks do not have the authority to issue a guaranty on behalf of a customer for an obligation owed to a third party.[7] To remain competitive for the business of their commercial customers, banks developed a functional equivalent to the guarantee that was a "standby" or "guarantee" letter of credit.[8] The basic justification of this practice was that, since a standby L/C was in form an L/C subject to generally applicable rules like UCC Article 5, the fact that it might arguably be functionally equivalent to a third-party guarantee did not render it impermissible for U.S. banks.[9]

Questions and Problems 4.10. As you can see from the illustration on the following page, the standby L/C transaction follows much the same pattern as the documentary L/C transaction, at least superficially. A careful comparison between the two patterns may reveal some significant differences in implicit assumptions about the relationship between the L/C and its underlying transaction and in the way in which the two transactions proceed. Do you perceive any differences between the two types of L/Cs?

---

[7] *See, e.g., Federal Intermediate Credit Bank of Omaha v.L'Herrison*, 33 F.2d 841 (8th Cir. 1929). *See generally* MICHAEL P. MALLOY, PRINCIPLES OF BANK REGULATION § 5.18 (3d ed. 2011) (discussing rules applying to third-party guarantees).

[8] *See* MALLOY, *supra*, § 5.20 (discussing standby letters of credit).

[9] *See, e.g., Barclays v. Mercantile Nat'l Bank*, 481 F.2d 1224 (5th Cir. 1973) (accepting use of L/C to support transactions other than sales of goods). *Cf.* Henry Harfield, *Legality of Guaranty Letters of Credit*, [1974 Transfer Binder] Fed. Banking L. Rep. (CCH) ¶ 96,301 (July 1, 1974) (arguing that functional equivalence of standby L/C and third-party guarantee was "immaterial" to the permissibility of standby L/C).

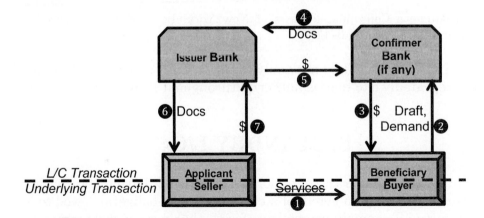

1. Seller of services allegedly breaches contract for services to Buyer
2. Buyer submits demand and draft to Confirmer
3. Confirmer pays Buyer on demand and draft
4. Confirmer submits demand and draft to Issuer
5. Issuer reimburses Confirmer
6. Issuer notifies Seller of demand and payment
7. Seller reimburses Issuer

Typical Standby Letter of Credit[10]

4.11. To what extent should standby L/Cs be treated like commercial L/Cs? Do the legal rules applicable to commercial L/Cs seem appropriate for standby L/Cs? In responding to these questions, consider the following cases.

AMERICAN INSURANCE ASS'N V. CLARKE
865 F.2d 278 (D.C.Cir. 1989)[a]

Buckley, Circuit Judge:

[The American Insurance Association (AIA) challenged the Comptroller of the Currency's approval of a proposal by Citibank to form a municipal bond insurance subsidiary, referred to in the opinion as "AMBAC". The D.C. Circuit agreed with the Comptroller's argument that issuing "standby credits" to ensure payment of municipal bonds

---

[10] *Source*: MICHAEL P. MALLOY, PRINCIPLES OF BANK REGULATION § 9.21 (3d ed. 2011).

[a] The court's original opinion, 854 F.2d 1405 (D.C. Cir. 1988), was withdrawn.

was an "incidental power" under the authority of the National Bank Act, 12 U.S.C. § 24(Seventh).]

. . . [W]e begin with a brief review of the operation of letters of credit, which come in two basic forms: commercial and standby. A basic function of the commercial letter of credit is to make it possible for a seller to ship goods to a buyer whose creditworthiness is unknown to him in confidence that the goods will be paid for.

> Stripped to its essentials, the [commercial letter of credit] transaction runs as follows: the buyer arranges for a bank– whose credit the seller will accept -- to issue a letter of credit in which the bank agrees to pay drafts drawn on it by the seller if, but only if, such drafts are accompanied by specified documents, such as bills of lading or air freight receipts, representing title to the goods that are the subject matter of the transaction between buyer and seller. The bank undertakes this obligation for a specified period of time.

Verkuil, *Bank Solvency and Guaranty Letters of Credit*, 25 Stan. L. Rev. 716, 718 (1973). The obligation created by the letter of credit is absolute. Upon the presentation of the stipulated documents by the seller, the bank is required to make the payment irrespective of any counterclaims the buyer might have against the seller.

A standby letter of credit represents the other side of the commercial letter of credit coin. Whereas the latter is used to guarantee payment upon performance, the former guarantees payment upon a failure to perform. Thus, by way of illustration, if a purchaser is concerned over the seller's ability to deliver the contracted goods on schedule, the seller may ask his bank to open a standby letter of credit in favor of the buyer. If the buyer subsequently presents documents showing that the seller has failed to deliver the goods, his bank is obliged to pay the buyer the amount specified in the standby letter. The bank will be reimbursed by the seller.

Although the two varieties of letters of credit differ, they serve the same essential purpose: to facilitate transactions by substituting the credit of the bank for that of one of the contracting parties. Banks have long been permitted to provide this form of credit. *See, e.g.*, 12 C.F.R. §7.7016 (1988) (letters of credit); *First Empire Bank-New York v. FDIC*, 572 F.2d 1361, 1367 (9th Cir.) (standby credits), *cert. denied*, 439 U.S. 919 (1978); 12 C.F.R. §32.2(e) (1988) (recognizing standby letters of credit as service provided by banks). As one commentator has explained:

The nature of the banking business implies the lawful power to make loans. A necessary incident of that power is the power to commit to make the loan at a future date. If that future commitment is made to a third party, it amounts to a present loan of credit. So long as the bank's promise is made for the account of its customer, and is a money promise, its characterization or form should be immaterial in determining its validity. . . .

H. Harfield, Bank Credits and Acceptances 165-66 (5th ed. 1974).

AMERICAN BELL INTERNATIONAL, INC. V. ISLAMIC REPUBLIC OF IRAN
474 F.Supp. 420 (S.D.N.Y. 1979)

MacMahon, District Judge.

Plaintiff American Bell International Inc. ("Bell") moves for a preliminary injunction . . . , enjoining defendant Manufacturers Hanover Trust Company ("Manufacturers") from making any payment under its Letter of Credit No. SC 170027 to defendants the Islamic Republic of Iran or Bank Iranshahr or their agents, instrumentalities, successors, employees and assigns. . . .

. . . Bell, a wholly-owned subsidiary of American Telephone & Telegraph Co. ("AT&T"), made a contract on July 23, 1978 (the "Contract") with the Imperial Government of Iran—Ministry of War ("Imperial Government") to provide consulting services and equipment to the Imperial Government as part of a program to improve Iran's international communications system.

The contract provides a complex mechanism for payment to Bell totalling approximately $280,000,000, including a down payment of $38,000,000. The Imperial Government had the right to demand return of the down payment at any time. The amount so callable, however, was to be reduced by 20% of the amounts invoiced by Bell to which the Imperial Government did not object. Bell's liability for return of the down payment was reduced by application of this mechanism as the Contract was performed, with the result that approximately $30,200,000 of the down payment now remains callable.

In order to secure the return of the down payment on demand, Bell was required to establish an unconditional and irrevocable Letter of Guaranty, to be issued by Bank Iranshahr in the amount of $38,800,000 in favor of the Imperial Government. The Contract provides that it is to be governed by the laws of Iran and that all disputes arising under it are to be resolved by the Iranian courts.

Bell obtained a Letter of Guaranty from Bank Iranshahr. In turn, as required by Bank Iranshahr, Bell obtained a standby Letter of Credit, No. SC 170027, issued by Manufacturers in favor of Bank Iranshahr in the amount of $38,800,000 to secure reimbursement to Bank Iranshahr should it be required to pay the Imperial Government under its Letter of Guaranty.

The standby Letter of Credit provided for payment by Manufacturers to Bank Iranshahr upon receipt of:

> Your [Bank Iranshahr's] dated statement purportedly signed by an officer indicating name and title or your Tested Telex Reading: (A) "Referring Manufacturers Hanover Trust Co. Credit No. SC170027, the amount of our claim $___ represents fund due us as we have received a written request from the Imperial Government of Iran Ministry of War to pay them the sum of ___ under our Guarantee No. ___ issued for the account of American Bell International Inc. covering advance payment under Contract No. 138 dated July 23, 1978 and, such payment has been made by us" . . . .

In the application for the Letter of Credit, Bell agreed – guaranteed by AT&T – immediately to reimburse Manufacturers for all amounts paid by Manufacturers to Bank Iranshahr pursuant to the Letter of Credit. . . .

. . . In the wake of [the overthrow of the Imperial Government and its replacement by the Islamic Republic of Iran], Bell was left with substantial unpaid invoices and claims under the Contract and ceased its performance in January 1979. Bell claims that the Contract was breached by the Imperial Government, as well as repudiated by the Islamic Republic, in that it owed substantial sums for services rendered under the Contract and its termination provisions. . . .

On July 25 and 29, 1979, Manufacturers received demands by Tested Telex from Bank Iranshahr for payment of $30,220,724 under the Letter of Credit, the remaining balance of the down payment. Asserting that the demand did not conform with the Letter of Credit, Manufacturers declined payment and so informed Bank Iranshahr. Informed of this, Bell responded by filing this action. . . . Following argument, we granted a temporary restraining order on July 29 enjoining Manufacturers from making any payment to Bank Iranshahr until forty-eight hours after Manufacturers notified Bell of the receipt of a conforming demand, and this order has been extended pending decision of this motion.

On August 1, 1979, Manufacturers notified Bell that it had received a conforming demand from Bank Iranshahr. . . .

Plaintiff has failed to show that irreparable injury may possibly ensue if a preliminary injunction is denied. Bell does not even claim, much less show, that it lacks an adequate remedy at law if Manufacturers makes a payment to Bank Iranshahr in violation of the Letter of Credit. It is too clear for argument that a suit for money damages could be based on such violation, and surely Manufacturers would be able to pay any money judgment against it.

Bell falls back on a contention that it is without any effective remedy unless it can restrain payment. This contention is based on the fact that it agreed to be bound by the laws of Iran and to submit resolution of any disputes under the Contract to the courts of Iran. Bell claims that it now has no meaningful access to those courts.

There is credible evidence that the Islamic Republic is xenophobic and anti-American and that it has no regard for consulting service contracts such as the one here. Although Bell has made no effort to invoke the aid of the Iranian courts, we think the current situation in Iran, as shown by the evidence, warrants the conclusion that an attempt by Bell to resort to those courts would be futile. . . . However, Bell has not demonstrated that it is without adequate remedy in this court against the Iranian defendants under the [Foreign] Sovereign Immunity Act which it invokes in this very case. 28 U.S.C. §§ 1605(a)(2), 1610(b)(2) (Supp. 1979). . . .

Even assuming that plaintiff has shown possible irreparable injury, it has failed to show probable success on the merits. . . .

In order to succeed on the merits, Bell must prove, by a preponderance of the evidence, that either (1) a demand for payment of the Manufacturers Letter of Credit conforming to the terms of that Letter has not yet been made, . . . or (2) a demand, even though in conformity, should not be honored because of fraud in the transaction, *see, e.g.,* N.Y. UCC § 5-114(2). . . . It is not probable, in the sense of a greater than 50% likelihood, that Bell will be able to prove either nonconformity or fraud.

As to nonconformity, the August 1 demand by Bank Iranshahr is identical to the terms of the Manufacturers Letter of Credit in every respect except one: it names as payee the "Government of Iran Ministry of Defense, Successor to the Imperial Government of Iran Ministry of War" rather than the "Imperial Government of Iran Ministry of War." . . . It is, of course, a bedrock principle of letter of credit law that a demand must strictly comply with the letter in order to justify payment. . . . Nevertheless, we deem it less than probable that a court, upon a full trial, would find nonconformity in the instant case. . . .

If conformity is established, as here, the issuer of an irrevocable, unconditional letter of credit such as Manufacturers normally has an absolute duty to transfer the requisite funds. This duty is wholly independent of the underlying contractual relationship that gives rise to the letter of credit. . . . Nevertheless, both the Uniform Commercial Code of New York, which the parties concede governs here, and the courts state that payment is enjoinable where a germane document is forged or fraudulent or there is "fraud in the transaction." N.Y. UCC § 5-114(2). . . . Bell does not contend that any documents are fraudulent by virtue of misstatements or omissions. Instead, it argues there is "fraud in the transaction."

. . . A demand which facially conforms to the Letter of Credit and which contains no misstatements may, nevertheless, be considered fraudulent if made with the goal of mulcting the party who caused the Letter of Credit to be issued. Be that as it may, we need not decide this thorny issue of law. For, even on the construction most favorable to Bell, we find that success on the merits is not probable. Many of the facts alleged, even if proved, would not constitute fraud. As to others, the proof is insufficient to indicate a probability of success on the merits.

Bell, while never delineating with precision the contours of the purported fraud, sets forth five contentions which, in its view, support the issuance of an injunction. Bell asserts that (1) both the old and new Governments failed to approve invoices for services fully performed; (2) both failed to fund contracted-for independent Letters of Credit in Bell's favor; (3) the new Government has taken steps to renounce altogether its obligations under the Contract; (4) the new Government has made it impossible to assert contract rights in Iranian courts; and (5) the new Government has caused Bank Iranshahr to demand payment on the Manufacturers Letter of Credit, thus asserting rights in a transaction it has otherwise repudiated. . . . Even if we accept the proposition that the evidence does show repudiation, plaintiff is still far from demonstrating the kind of evil intent necessary to support a claim of fraud. Surely, plaintiff cannot contend that every party who breaches or repudiates his contract is for that reason culpable of fraud. The law of contract damages is adequate to repay the economic harm caused by repudiation, and the law presumes that one who repudiates has done so because of a calculation that such damages are cheaper than performance. Absent any showing that Iran would refuse to pay damages upon a contract action here or in Iran, much less a showing that Bell has even attempted to obtain such a remedy, the evidence is ambivalent as to whether the purported repudiation results from non-fraudulent economic calculation or from fraudulent intent to mulct Bell.

Plaintiff contends that the alleged repudiation, viewed in connection with its demand for payment on the Letter of Credit, supplies the basis from which only one inference–fraud–can be drawn. Again, we remain unpersuaded.

Plaintiff's argument requires us to presume bad faith on the part of the Iranian government. It requires us further to hold that that government may not rely on the plain terms of the consulting contract and the Letter of Credit arrangements with Bank Iranshahr and Manufacturers providing for immediate repayment of the down payment upon demand, without regard to cause. On the evidence before us, fraud is no more inferable than an economically rational decision by the government to recoup its down payment, as it is entitled to do under the consulting contract and still dispute its liabilities under that Contract. . . .

If plaintiff fails to demonstrate probable success, he may still obtain relief by showing, in addition to the possibility of irreparable injury, both (1) sufficiently serious questions going to the merits to make them a fair ground for litigation, and (2) a balance of hardships tipping decidedly toward plaintiff. . . . Both Bell and Manufacturers appear to concede the existence of serious questions, and the complexity and novelty of this matter lead us to find they exist. Nevertheless, we hold that plaintiff is not entitled to relief under this branch of the *Caulfield* test[, *Caulfield v. Board of Education*, 583 F.2d 605, 610 (2d Cir. 1978) (providing test for appropriateness of preliminary injunction),] because the balance of hardships does not tip decidedly toward Bell, if indeed it tips that way at all.

To be sure, Bell faces substantial hardships upon denial of its motion. Should Manufacturers pay the demand, Bell will immediately become liable to Manufacturers for $30.2 million, with no assurance of recouping those funds from Iran for the services performed. . . .

But Manufacturers would face at least as great a loss, and perhaps a greater one, were we to grant relief. Upon Manufacturers' failure to pay, Bank Iranshahr could initiate a suit on the Letter of Credit and attach $30.2 million of Manufacturers' assets in Iran. In addition, it could seek to hold Manufacturers liable for consequential damages beyond that sum resulting from the failure to make timely payment. Finally, there is no guarantee that Bank Iranshahr or the government, in retaliation for Manufacturers' recalcitrance, will not nationalize additional Manufacturers' assets in Iran in amounts which counsel, at oral argument, represented to be far in excess of the amount in controversy here.

Apart from a greater monetary exposure flowing from an adverse decision, Manufacturers faces a loss of credibility in the international banking community that could result from its failure to make good on a letter of credit. . . .

Finally, apart from questions of relative hardship and the specific criteria of the *Caulfield* test, general considerations of equity counsel us to deny the motion for injunctive relief. Bell, a sophisticated multinational enterprise well advised by competent counsel, entered into these arrangements with its corporate eyes open. It knowingly and voluntarily signed a contract allowing the Iranian government to recoup its down payment on demand, without regard to cause. It caused Manufacturers to enter into an agreement whereby Manufacturers became obligated to pay Bank Iranshahr the unamortized down payment balance upon receipt of conforming documents, again without regard to cause.

Both of these arrangements redounded tangibly to the benefit of Bell. The Contract with Iran, with its prospect of designing and installing from scratch a nationwide and international communications system, was certain to bring to Bell both monetary profit and prestige and good will in the global communications industry. The agreement to indemnify Manufacturers on its Letter of Credit provided the means by which these benefits could be achieved.

One who reaps the rewards of commercial arrangements must also accept their burdens. One such burden in this case, voluntarily accepted by Bell, was the risk that demand might be made without cause on the funds constituting the down payment. To be sure, the sequence of events that led up to that demand may well have been unforeseeable when the contracts were signed. To this extent, both Bell and Manufacturers have been made the unwitting and innocent victims of tumultuous events beyond their control. But, as between two innocents, the party who undertakes by contract the risk of political uncertainty and governmental caprice must bear the consequences when the risk comes home to roost. . . .

Questions and Problems 4.12. Should the "fraud in the transaction" rule found in former UCC § 5-114(2)(a) (since recodified in UCC § 5-109[11]) be interpreted as narrowly in the standby L/C context as in the commercial L/C context? In a commercial L/C situation, the applicant and the beneficiary end up either with the money or the goods, but not both. In a standby L/C situation – like *American Bell International* – the applicant may end up with nothing but a cause of action for money damages, which may or may not be successful. On the issue

---

[11] The revision is discussed in Problem 4.16, *infra*.

of fraud in the transaction, should a distinct rule apply to standby L/Cs?[12]

4.13. Current L/C rules – originally developed on the basis of the scenario of the commercial letter of credit – emphasize the separability of the L/C obligations from the underlying contract between the applicant and the beneficiary. Exceptions like the "fraud in the transaction" rule are narrowly construed, in order to maintain that separability. The issuer – and, presumably, the applicant as well – will contain their respective risks, because each will have either the funds or the goods. Is that true in the situation of a standby L/C?

4.14. Former UCC § 5-114 was replaced in 1995 revision by UCC § 5-109. Review § 5-109, reproduced in the Supplement. Would Bell have had a stronger argument under the revised provision? In answering the question, consider the following case, which turns on Tex. Bus. & Com.Code Ann. § 5.109.

SAVA GUMARSKA IN KEMIJSKA INDUSTRIA d.d. V. ADVANCED POLYMER SCIENCES, INC.
128 S.W.3d 304 (Tex.App. 2004)

Opinion by Justice Moseley.

[Applicant on a standby L/C sought declaratory and injunctive relief to protect its advance deposit against the beneficiary's attempted draw on the L/C. The underlying transaction involved the purchase of equipment for a business to be operated by a Slovenian company owned by both. Applicant also claimed breach of the equipment agreement. Beneficiary counterclaimed for breach of the equipment agreement, breach of the agreement for formation of the company, and declaratory judgment. After a bench trial, the district court declared the L/C void, awarded damages and attorney fees to Applicant for breach of contract, conditionally awarded the Applicant attorney fees for appeals, and denied relief on Beneficiary's counterclaims. Beneficiary appealed. The Texas Court of Appeals held that (*i*) Applicant did not repudiate its obligations under the equipment agreement; (*ii*) the provision of the equipment agreement requiring each party to bear its own banking costs was enforceable; and, (*iii*) the evidence did not establish a material fraud by Beneficiary as a basis for voiding the L/C. The excerpts that follow deal with the issue of the validity of the L/C.]

---

[12] *Cf.* MICHAEL P. MALLOY, PRINCIPLES OF BANK REGULATION § 9.21 (3d ed. 2011) (arguing for distinct approach to "fraud in the transaction" in case of standby L/Cs).

The filament winding equipment was to be delivered within ten to fourteen months after the down-payment. Under the portion of the Equipment Agreement relating to the filament winding equipment, SAVA agreed to make an advance deposit to APS of $550,000, and provide a letter of credit to APS for the $2.2 million balance of the purchase price. To protect SAVA's advance deposit, APS agreed to put up a standby letter of credit for SAVA's benefit in the amount of $550,000. It is this standby letter of credit that is the main focus of this dispute.

On November 1, 1999, APS arranged for the standby letter of credit through Bank One Texas (the "Bank"). Under its terms, to draw on the letter of credit SAVA was required to present a sight draft and a signed statement that the delivery deadline under the Equipment Agreement had passed, SAVA had examined the equipment supplied by APS, and SAVA had refused acceptance of the equipment because:

> A. It does not meet the fabrication drawings or specifications presented by [APS] prior to manufacture, and/or
>
> B. It does not meet European Union/ANSI standards for safety and environmental protection, and/or
>
> C. It is not in accordance with the best available technologies, and/or
>
> D. It is not properly operational after a week-long performance test, and any defects in construction or installation of the equipment were not remedied within an agreed upon timeframe, and/or
>
> E. The delivery of equipment does not otherwise conform materially to the contract between SAVA and [APS] giving the buyer just cause to dispute payment.

As amended, the letter of credit expired on June 30, 2001.

In January 2000, SAVA made the $550,000 advance deposit to APS under the Equipment Agreement. On March 10, 2000, SAVA caused its bank to issue a letter of credit to APS in the amount of $2.2 million to secure payment of the balance of the purchase price for the filament winding equipment. APS used the $2.2 million letter of credit as collateral for a line of credit to manufacture the equipment.

From the inception of their relationship, both SAVA and APS had problems with various aspects of the transactions. . . .

. . . On October 10, 2000, SAVA notified APS that it was revoking the order for the filament winding equipment, and canceling the Company Formation Agreement and the Equipment Agreement. SAVA also indicated it would draw on the standby letter of credit to reimburse it for its $550,000 advance payment to APS for the filament winding equipment.

On November 6, 2000, SAVA presented documents to the Bank to draw the full amount of the standby letter of credit. APS filed this suit against the Bank seeking a temporary restraining order and a temporary injunction preventing the Bank from honoring the draw on the letter of credit. APS claimed SAVA committed a material fraud in presenting the documents in an attempt to draw on the standby letter of credit before shipment of the filament winding equipment was even due. In addition to an injunction, APS sought a declaratory judgment that the standby letter of credit was void and unenforceable and requested an award of its reasonable attorneys' fees under the declaratory judgment act.

APS obtained a temporary restraining order on November 8, 2000. SAVA intervened in the lawsuit. Following a hearing, the trial court entered a temporary injunction against payment of the letter of credit. . . .

The Bank requested and was granted leave to not participate in the trial pursuant to letter agreements between the parties. . . .[4]

SAVA asserts the evidence is legally insufficient to support the finding of material fraud that justifies the declaration that the letter of credit was void. SAVA asks us to render judgment against the Bank for the $550,000 amount of the letter of credit, and against APS for SAVA's attorneys' fees expended in seeking a declaratory judgment that it was entitled to payment under the letter of credit.

1. Introduction

. . . [P]ayment of a letter of credit does not determine the ultimate right to retain the funds as between the beneficiary and the applicant. *See CKB & Assocs., Inc. v. Moore McCormack Petroleum, Inc.*, 734 S.W.2d 653, 655 (Tex.1987). Contracting parties may use a letter of credit in order to "make certain that contract disputes [between the applicant and beneficiary] wend their way towards resolution with money in the beneficiary's pocket rather than in the pocket of the [applicant]." *Id.* The beneficiary's immediate right of possession of the funds on payment of the letter of credit does not decide the dispute over who will ultimately retain those funds. *Id.* "Without this rule, the beneficiary of the letter of credit would be the ultimate arbiter of compliance with the underlying contract and the commercial viability of the letter of credit would be destroyed." *Id.* Thus, the letter of credit determines the beneficiary's right to immediate possession of the

---

[4] The letter of credit expired shortly after trial. However, the Bank stipulated with the parties that it would abide by whatever order or judgment was entered by the court and would pay any proceeds of the letter of credit as directed by the court.

funds on presentation of conforming documents to the issuer, but not the right to ultimately retain those funds.

Payment of a letter of credit may not be enjoined, or similar relief granted, unless there is evidence of a material fraud by the beneficiary on the applicant or the issuer. Tex. Bus. & Com.Code Ann. § 5.109(b); *Philipp Bros., Inc. v. Oil Country Specialists, Ltd.*, 787 S.W.2d 38, 40-41 (Tex.1990). The standard of fraud necessary to warrant interference with the independence of the letter of credit is that "the wrong doing of the beneficiary has so vitiated the entire transaction that the legitimate purposes of the independence of the issuer's obligation would no longer be served." *Philipp Bros.*, 787 S.W.2d at 40 (quoting, *GATX Leasing Corp. v.. DMB Drilling Corp.*, 657 S.W.2d 178, 182 (Tex.App.-San Antonio 1983, no writ); *see* Tex. Bus. & Com.Code Ann. § 5.109 cmt. 2. The elements of a cause of action for fraud are: "(1) that a material representation was made; (2) the representation was false; (3) when the representation was made, the speaker knew it was false or made it recklessly without any knowledge of the truth and as a positive assertion; (4) the speaker made the representation with the intent that the other party should act upon it; (5) the party acted in reliance on the representation; and (6) the party thereby suffered injury." *In re FirstMerit Bank, N.A.*, 52 S.W.3d 749, 758 (Tex.2001). To warrant interference with payment of a letter of credit, the fraud must be "extreme, intentional, and unscrupulous." *SRS Prods. Co. v. LG Eng'g Co.*, 994 S.W.2d 380, 384 (Tex.App.-Houston [14th Dist.] 1999, no pet.).

2. Relevance of Analysis

[The court decided that, with the Bank's stipulation (*see* note 4, *supra*), and the agreement by SAVA and APS that "they neither seek now nor will seek any affirmative relief, including money damages, attorneys' fees, interest, or the imposition of costs or otherwise, against [the Bank] in this action," SAVA was not entitled to judgment against the Bank. The court also found that APS had established that SAVA repudiated and breached the Equipment Agreement. As a result the court held that SAVA would not be entitled to retain proceeds of the letter of credit, citing *Oil Country Specialists, Ltd. v. Philipp Bros., Inc.*, 762 S.W.2d 170, 179-80 (Tex.App. 1988), *writ denied*, 787 S.W.2d 38 (Tex.1990) (despite take-nothing judgment on applicant's breach of contract claim, beneficiary not entitled to retain proceeds of letter of credit because of its prior material breach of underlying agreement).]

However, both parties requested attorneys' fees in connection with their respective declaratory judgment actions regarding the letter of credit. Relevant to those claims for attorneys' fees is whether SAVA was entitled to draw on the letter of credit. Because of our disposition of the parties' claims for attorneys fees, as set forth herein, we conclude it necessary and appropriate to address SAVA's claims regarding the letter of credit.

3. Analysis

The trial court declared that the letter of credit was void. This declaration has the same effect as a permanent injunction against payment. *See* Tex. Bus. & Com.Code Ann. § 5.109 cmt. 5 (same principles apply when applicant tries to achieve same legal outcome as injunction against honor by other methods including declaratory judgment). Thus we apply the material fraud standard of section 5.109 to the trial court's declaration. *Id.* § 5.109(b). . . .

A. Breach of Underlying Agreement

The trial court found that SAVA breached the Equipment Agreement and "therefore forfeited any right to draw upon the letter of credit." Breach of the underlying agreement between the applicant and the beneficiary is not a ground for enjoining or canceling the letter of credit. *Philipp Bros.*, 787 S.W.2d at 40. Under the independence doctrine, the obligation of the issuer to the beneficiary on the letter of credit is independent of the "existence, performance, or *nonperformance* of a contract or arrangement out of which the letter of credit arises or which underlies it, including contracts ... between the applicant and the beneficiary." Tex. Bus. & Com.Code Ann. § 5.103(d) (emphasis added). "The purpose of a letter of credit is to assure payment when its own conditions have been met irrespective of disputes that may arise between the parties concerning performance or other agreements which comprise the underlying transaction." *Sun Marine Terminals, Inc. v. Artoc Bank & Trust Ltd.*, 797 S.W.2d 7, 10 (Tex.1990); *Synergy Ctr., Ltd. v. Lone Star Franchising, Inc.*, 63 S.W.3d 561, 566 (Tex.App.-Austin 2001, no pet.).

Thus even though SAVA's breach of the underlying agreement meant that it was not entitled to keep the proceeds of the letter of credit as against APS, *see CKB & Assocs.*, 734 S.W.2d at 655, that breach does not constitute material fraud permitting a court to enjoin payment of the letter of credit. Such a breach would only give APS the right to recover the proceeds of the letter of credit from SAVA after the letter of credit was paid; it would not be a basis to enjoin or void the letter of credit. *See CKB & Assocs.*, 734 S.W.2d at 655. The trial court's finding that SAVA breached the Equipment Agreement does not support its decision to declare the letter of credit void.

The trial court also found that SAVA attempted to draw on the letter of credit before permitting APS to perform under the Equipment Agreement, and that SAVA attempted to draw on the letter of credit after repudiating the Equipment Agreement without justification. Both of these findings go to the performance or nonperformance of the underlying contract between SAVA and APS, and do not constitute a basis for enjoining the payment of the letter of credit. Tex. Bus. & Com.Code Ann. § 5.103(d); *Synergy Ctr.*, 63 S.W.3d at 566; SRS Prods. Co., 944 S.W.2d at 386.

B. Failure to Disclose Incorrect Term in Letter of Credit

The letter of credit required a statement that the Equipment Agreement called for delivery of all equipment by September 9, 1999. The Equipment Agreement does not in fact call for delivery of all equipment by that date. Rather, the agreement called for delivery of the spray and heat curing equipment within fourteen weeks after receipt of SAVA's down-payment and delivery of the filament winding equipment ten to fourteen months after receipt of the down-payment. The trial court concluded SAVA committed fraud on APS and the Bank because it knew the delivery date in the letter of credit was incorrect and did not inform APS of the error.

However, APS, not SAVA, caused the letter of credit to be issued by its bank. The record does not indicate how the September 9, 1999 date was included in the letter of credit. The evidence shows APS delivered a copy of the Equipment Agreement to the Bank and the Bank drew up the letter of credit. APS never saw the letter of credit until after SAVA attempted to draw on it. There was also evidence that the terms of the letter of credit were acceptable between the Bank and SAVA.

The evidence does not support the trial court's finding of fraud based on the September 9 date specified in the letter of credit. As a general rule, a failure to disclose information does not constitute fraud unless there is a duty to disclose the information. *Ins. Co. of N. Am. v. Morris*, 981 S.W.2d 667, 674 (Tex.1998). Thus, silence is equivalent to a false representation only when the particular circumstances impose a duty on the party to speak and he deliberately remains silent. *Bradford v. Vento*, 48 S.W.3d 749, 755 (Tex.2001) (citing *SmithKline Beecham Corp. v. Doe*, 903 S.W.2d 347, 353 (Tex.1995), and *Smith v. Nat'l Resort Communities, Inc.*, 585 S.W.2d 655, 658 (Tex.1979)). Whether a duty to speak exists is a question of law. *Bradford*, 48 S.W.3d at 755.

The trial court did not find that SAVA had a duty to disclose material information. . . . Thus, there is no evidence to support the trial court's conclusion that SAVA's failure to advise APS of the delivery date stated in the letter of credit amounted to material fraud. See id.

C. False Statements in Presentation Documents

Several of the trial court's findings and the evidence cited by APS in support of the judgment relate to false statements in the presentment documents. For example, the trial court found that in order to draw on the letter of credit, SAVA had to represent to the Bank that the filament winding equipment had been delivered and found to be nonconforming. The trial court found that SAVA falsely represented to the Bank that APS had delivered the equipment in a nonconforming state and had failed to cure the defects within the specific delivery schedule. . . .

The evidence supports the trial court's findings that SAVA made false statements to the Bank in presenting the letter of credit. However, false statements in the presentment documents are insufficient to warrant enjoining payment of the letter of credit. *Philipp Bros.*, 787 S.W.2d at 40-41. Establishing material fraud or fraud in the transaction requires more than a showing of untruthful statements in the presentment documents. *See SRS Prods. Co.*, 994 S.W.2d at 384. Such false statements in making presentment would not amount to egregious fraud vitiating the transaction and warranting a declaration that the letter of credit is void. *See Philipp Bros.*, 787 S.W.2d at 40-41. The trial court's finding that the statements in the presentation documents were false does not support its conclusion that SAVA committed material fraud such that the letter of credit should be canceled and declared void. *Id.*

D. Second Presentment During Injunction

The trial court found that after the court temporarily enjoined the Bank from paying the letter of credit, SAVA made a second presentment where it again represented that the delivery deadline had passed. This constitutes another finding that the statements in SAVA's presentment documents were not true. As we discussed above, proof that the statements in the presentment documents are not true does not establish material fraud warranting cancellation of the letter of credit. *See Philipp Bros.*, 787 S.W.2d at 40-41. . . .

Questions and Problems 4.15. The court makes an extended argument justifying the rule that the L/C transaction is separate from the underlying transaction between the applicant and beneficiary of the L/C. Do you find the argument convincing?

4.16. How does the court's analysis and application of UCC § 5-109 compare with the *American Bell International* court's analysis and application of former UCC § 5-114? Since both cases decide that the court should not interfere with a demand under the standby L/C, is there really any significant difference between the two statutory provisions?

C. TRANSNATIONAL L/C TRANSACTIONS

Sava Gumarska, involving American and Slovenian co-owners of a Slovenian company and a standby L/C issued by a Texas bank, is a good example of a "transnational L/C transaction" – one in which rights and obligations traverse national boundaries. Naturally, such a situation raises potential issues concerning the law to be applied to any dispute between the parties. In another part of the opinion, the court discussed this issue, as follows:

. . . The Company Formation Agreement does not contain a choice of law provision, but the Equipment Agreement provides that the laws of England apply to any disputes under that agreement. Generally, the parties' contractual choice of law will be given effect if the contract bears a reasonable relationship to the chosen state and no countervailing public policy of the forum demands otherwise. . . . If a contractual choice of law fails, Texas will apply the law of the state or nation with the most significant relationship to the transaction and the parties. . . . However, we should first determine if the laws are in conflict. If the result would be the same under the laws of either jurisdiction, there is no need to resolve the choice of law question. . . .

The trial court's conclusions of law discuss some aspects of English contract law, but the trial court also concluded that under Texas choice of law principles, the law of England has no relation to this transaction and the court would not apply English law. SAVA does not argue this conclusion was incorrect. We agree that the laws of England do not bear a reasonable relationship to this transaction.

The parties have briefed Texas law and where they argue English law, they conclude the result would be the same as under Texas law. Neither party has shown that English law or any other law is materially different from Texas law on the issues before us, and in light of the trial court's finding that English law should not be applied in this case, we will apply Texas law to the issues presented.

The parties in *Sava Gumarska* might have breathed a big sigh of relief at this point, but the fact remains that they did not plan very carefully on the issue of the law that might apply to the L/C transaction. One well recognized and resilient device that has advanced harmonization of the rules applicable to transnational L/Cs is the Uniform Customs and Practice for Documentary Credits ("UCP"), referred to in *Fertico Belgium, supra*. Not a government-imposed set of mandatory rules, the UCP is a compilation of usages of trade for L/Cs.[13] It consists of rules negotiated by the International Chamber of Commerce (ICC), based in Paris, that are typically incorporated by reference in an L/C, thus becoming part of the terms. The UCP rules have been regularly updated since the ICC issued the first version in 1930. The L/C involved in *Bank of Cochin, infra*, was ostensibly governed by the UCP, pursuant to its own express terms. (footnote 3, *infra*.) In both cases, the assumption is that the L/C transaction is governed by Article 5 of the UCC unless the parties agree to apply the UCP. A similar approach is apparently taken in English commercial law.[14] The latest version of the UCP is the UCP 600, which became effective on July 1, 2007. The UCP appears in the Supplement.

BANK OF COCHIN LTD. V. MANUFACTURERS HANOVER TRUST
612 F. Supp. 1533 (S.D.N.Y. 1985),
affirmed, 808 F.2d 209 (2d Cir. 1986)

CANNELLA, Senior District Judge:

Bank of Cochin Limited ["Cochin"], an Indian corporation and the issuer of letter of credit BB/VN/41/80, commenced this diversity action against Manufacturers Hanover Trust Company ["MHT"], a New York corporation that acted as the confirming bank on the letter. Cochin seeks recovery of the amount paid by MHT, thereafter debited to Cochin's account at MHT, on drawings negotiated in New York between MHT and St. Lucia Enterprises, Ltd. ["St. Lucia"]. Codefendant St. Lucia, a purported New York corporation and the letter of credit beneficiary, has perpetrated a large fraud on both banks and nonparty customer Vishwa Niryat (Pvt.) Ltd. ["Vishwa"]. Unfortunately, St. Lucia has vanished and the Court must decide whose shoulders will bear the scam.

---

[13] *Banca Del Sempione v. Provident Bank of Maryland*, 75 F.3d 951, 954 (4th Cir. 1996).

[14] *See* Robert Wight & Alan Ward, *The Liability of Banks in Documentary Credit Transactions under English Law*, [1998] J. INT'L BANKING L. 387.

. . . On February 8, 1980, in Bombay, India, Vishwa requested Cochin to issue an irrevocable letter of credit covering up to $798,000 for the benefit of St. Lucia. The letter was to have expired on April 15, 1980 and covered the anticipated shipment and purchase of 1,000 metric tons of aluminum melting scrap consisting of aluminum beverage cans.

On February 14, 1980, Cochin requested MHT to supply financial information on St. Lucia. MHT responded by telex the following day that St. Lucia did not maintain an MHT account and that a thorough check of normal credit sources did not reveal any "pertinent" information. On February 22, Cochin conveyed the terms and conditions of the letter of credit to MHT by Telex and requested MHT to advise "St. Lucia Enterprises Ltd." of the establishment of the letter and to add MHT's confirmation. The letter of credit was issued subject to the Uniform Customs and Practice for Documentary Credits (1974 Revision), Int'l Chamber of Commerce, Pub. No. 290 ["UCP"].

On February 25, MHT mailed its written advice of the letter of credit establishment to St. Lucia and confirmed the amended letter on February 29. Cochin amended certain terms of the letter of four occasions in March and April 1980. MHT mailed its advices of these amendments to St. Lucia from March to May and sent copies to Cochin, which were received without comment. The final amended letter of credit contained the following relevant terms and conditions:

      a. Sight drafts of the invoice values;

      b. Six copies of the signed invoices;

      c. One set of clean shipped on board bills of lading;

      d. A west European certificate of origin;

      e. A certificate of analysis of the aluminum scrap from Lloyd's of London ["Lloyd's"] or another international testing agency;

      f. Shipment from a west European port to Bombay;

      g. A maritime insurance policy, covering note 429711, to be confirmed by St. Lucia's cable to Oriental Fire and General Insurance Co. ["Oriental"];

      h. A packing list in triplicate;

      i. One set of nonnegotiable documents to be sent to Vishwa and a confirming cable to Vishwa;

      j. A certification from Lloyd's or the shipping company that the ship was a first class or approved non-Pakistani vessel;

      k. St. Lucia's certification that it had complied with all terms of the letter of credit;

      l. Shipment by May 31, 1980; and

      m. Letter of credit expiration on June 15, 1980.

The aluminum was allegedly shipped in May 29, 1980 from Bremen, West Germany to Bombay on the M/V Betelguese. On June 2, St. Lucia established an account at a Manhattan office of Citibank, N.A. ["Citibank"], the collecting bank, in the name of St. Lucia Enterprises, Ltd. On June 9, St. Lucia presented MHT with documents required by the letter of credit and ten sight drafts amounting to $796,603.50, payable to St. Lucia Enterprises. The documents included five copies of the invoices, a clean shipped on board bill of lading, a St. Lucia certification that the aluminum was of west European origin, a certificate of analysis by an international Dutch materials testing agent, a telex confirmation of a telephone message to Oriental that the aluminum had been shipped to Bombay pursuant to covernote 4291, a packing list in triplicate, a St. Lucia certification that one set of nonnegotiable documents had been sent to Vishwa and that Vishwa had been advised by cable, certifications from the shipping company that the M/V Betelguese was an approved first class Panamanian vessel, and a St. Lucia cover letter specifying the documents submitted and requesting payment from MHT. The St. Lucia letter and certification were on the letterhead of "St. Lucia Enterprises" and were signed by "D Agney".

MHT compared the documents against the requirements of the letter and determined that they complied with all the terms and conditions. On June 13, MHT negotiated the drafts and issued a check for $798,000 payable to St. Lucia Enterprises. . . . MHT debited Cochin's account for $798,000 on June 13. MHT sent a copy of its payment advice, the drafts and documents to Cochin by registered air mail on June 13. Unfortunately, Cochin apparently did not receive these documents until June 21. As it turned out, St. Lucia shipped nothing to Vishwa. The documentation submitted to MHT was fraudulent in every regard; indeed, the bills of lading, quality certification and vessel certification were issued by nonexistent corporations. St. Lucia received payment on the letter of credit and Cochin has been unable to locate any party connected with the fraudulent scheme.

. . . On June 21, Cochin sent the following telex to MHT:

> We acknowledge receipt of the documentu [sic] Stop We find certain discrepencies [sic] in the same Stop kindly donot [sic] make payment against the same until we telex you otherwise Stop

On June 23, MHT replied to Cochin's telex as follows:

> Reference your telex June 21 credit BB VN 4180 our 500748 Stop We note your telex fails to give reason fro [sic] rejection documents as required UCP Article 8 Stop According our records documents fully

complied credit terms and beneficiary already paid therefore we cannot accept your refusal of documents.

By telex dated June 27, Cochin informed MHT of alleged defects in the documents apparently uncovered by Vishwa: (1) St. Lucia's cable to Oriental showed the wrong insurance covernote number of 4291 instead of 429711; (2) St. Lucia did not submit "proof" that a set of nonnegotiable documents and confirming cable had been sent to Vishwa; (3) only one set of documents showed the original certificate of origin whereas the rest included only photocopies; and (4) the invoice packing list and certificate of origin were not duly authenticated. Cochin also noted (5) the overpayment of $1,396.50. MHT credited Cochin's account for $1,396.50 and notified Cochin by telex on June 30.

By telex dated July 3, Cochin asked MHT to recredit its account for $796,603.50 and advised MHT that it was returning the letter of credit documents. Cochin also cited an additional discrepancy that (6) MHT had negotiated documents for St. Lucia Enterprises but that the letter of credit was established for St. Lucia Enterprises Ltd. On July 4, Cochin informed MHT by telex that the documents negotiated by MHT contained the following additional defects: (7) only five signed copies of the commercial invoices, rather than six, were forwarded and (8) documents were signed by "D Agney" without specifying his capacity at St. Lucia.

MHT responded by telex of July 14 that Cochin had failed to timely and properly specify the alleged documentary variances as required by article 8 of the 1974 UCP. The telex also noted that Cochin had failed to promptly return the documents or advise MHT that Cochin was holding the documents at MHT's disposal as required by the UCP. MHT asserted in a telex dated July 16 that it still had not received certain documents from Cochin. The parties exchanged additional telexes confirming and denying that payment was proper. Cochin[] . . . adds the additional allegations that (9) St. Lucia failed to indicate the documents submitted in drawing against the letter of credit, and (10) the shipping company certificate fails to indicate the vessel registration number. . . .

The central issue presented by this case is whether St. Lucia's demand for payment from MHT was in compliance with the conditions specified in the letter of credit. Cochin's action for wrongful honor is based upon its assertion that MHT's payment was improper because the documents submitted by St. Lucia did not comply with the letter. Neither the UCP nor the Uniform Commercial Code ["UCC"] specify whether a bank honoring a letter of credit should be guided by a standard of strict compliance with the terms of the letter.

The great weight of authority in this jurisdiction, and elsewhere, holds that an issuing or confirming bank is usually obligated to honor the beneficiary's draft only when the documents are in strict compliance with the terms of the letter of credit. . . . Thus, New York courts have traditionally held that letter of credit law requires a beneficiary to strictly comply with the conditions of the letter. . . . Additionally, this Court has previously held that "[a] bank's obligation in a letter of credit transaction is defined by the contract between the bank and its customer. It is obliged to pay only if the documents submitted strictly comply with the essential requirements of the letter of credit." *Corporacion de Mercadeo Agricola v. Pan American Fruit & Produce Corp.*, Memorandum Decision at 4-5, 75 Civ. 1611 (JMC) (S.D.N.Y. Apr. 13, 1976), quoted in *Corporacion de Mercadeo Agricola v. Mellon Bank*, 608 F.2d 43, 48 n. 1 (2d Cir. 1979). This principle of strict compliance has been recently reaffirmed by the Second Circuit and the New York Court of Appeals. *See Beyene v. Irving Trust Co.*, 762 F.2d 4, 6 (2d Cir. 1985) . . . ; *Voest-Alpine Int'l Corp. v. Chase Manhattan Bank, N.A.*, 707 F.2d 680, 682 (2d Cir. 1983) . . . ; *Marino Indus. v. Chase Manhattan Bank, N.A.*, 686 F.2d 1112, 114 (2d Cir. 1982) . . . ; *United Commodities-Greece v. Fidelity Int'l Bank*, 64 N.Y.2d 449, 455, 478 N.E.2d 172, 174, 489 N.Y.S.2d 31, 33 (1985). . . .

Courts and commentators have noted, however, that New York appears to maintain a bifurcated standard of compliance. . . . This approach calls for a strict compliance standard when the bank is sued by the beneficiary for wrongful dishonor but allows for a substantial compliance test when the bank is sued by the customer for wrongful honor. The stated rationale for the bifurcated standard is that it accords the bank flexibility in reacting to "a cross-fire of pressures . . . especially in times of falling commodity prices," . . . by limiting the liability burden on the bank, which might otherwise be caught between the "rock of a customer insisting on dishonor for highly technical reasons, and the hard place of a beneficiary threatening to sue for wrongful dishonor." . . .

MHT correctly asserts that Cochin was its "customer" in this transaction and therefore argues that a substantial compliance standard should be used to test its review of St. Lucia's documents. Although the ultimate customer, Vishwa, may be barred from a direct action against the confirming bank because of the absence of privity,[7]

---

[7] The UCP suggests the better view, however, that there is a duty running from the confirming bank to the ultimate customer. *See* UCP art. 12(a) (1974), art. 20(a) (1983) ("Banks utilizing the services of another bank for the purpose of giving effect to the instructions of the applicant for the credit do so

... it is undisputed that MHT owes a duty of care to Cochin, *see* UCP art. 7 (1974), art. 15 (1983). The question then is whether the bifurcated standard applies in a lawsuit by the issuing bank against the confirming bank.

The bifurcated standard is designed to permit the bank to retain flexibility in dealing with simultaneous customer pressure to reject and beneficiary pressure to accept. This discretion ostensibly preserves the bank's ministerial function of dealing solely with documents and the insulation of the letter of credit from performance problems. The difficulty with applying a bifurcated substantial compliance standard to actions against a confirming bank is reflected in the realities of commercial transactions. An issuing bank's good faith discretion is most required when its customer seeks to avoid payment by objecting to inconsequential defects. Although the bank should theoretically take comfort from a substantial compliance test if it honors the beneficiary's drafts over its customer's protests, the bank would usually not want to exercise its discretion for fear that its right to indemnity would be jeopardized or that its customer would break off existing banking relationships. Accordingly, the looser test of compliance does not in practice completely remove the issuer from its position between a rock and a hard place, but has a built-in safety valve against issuer misuse if the documents strictly comply with the letter.

A confirming bank, by contrast, is usually in relatively close geographical proximity with the beneficiary and typically chosen by the beneficiary because of past dealings. Although the confirming bank should not want to injure purposely its relationship with the issuing bank, the confirming bank would usually be somewhat biased in favor of the beneficiary. Additionally, the confirming bank is not in privity with the ultimate customer, who would be most likely to become dissatisfied if a conflict is resolved by the confirming bank. A biased issuing bank that in bad faith uncovers "microscopic discrepancies," . . . would still be forced to honor the letter if the documents are in strict compliance. A biased confirming bank, however, can overlook certain larger variances in its discretion without concomitant liability. A safety mechanism against confirming bank misuse is therefore not present and it would be inequitable to let a confirming bank exercise such discretion under a protective umbrella of substantial compliance. Moreover, the facts of this case do not warrant the looser standard. MHT was not faced with a "cross-fire of pressures" or concern that a disgruntled "customer" would refuse reimbursement because Cochin had sufficient funds on deposit with MHT. The Court also notes that

---

for the account and at the risk of [such applicant].") art. 12(c) (1974), art. 20(c) (1983) (customer indemnification of the confirming bank). . . .

the bifurcated substantial compliance standard is only a suggested approach by courts and commentators and has not actually been followed by New York courts.[8] Finally, in *Voest-Alpine Int'l Corp. v. Chase Manhattan Bank, N.A., supra*, the Court implied that confirming bank actions should be judged under a strict standard in wrongful dishonor as well as wrongful honor actions. It ruled that if the confirming bank waived discrepancies in the drafts, the confirming bank would not be entitled to reimbursement from the issuing bank, which timely discovered the mistakes, because "the issuing bank[] was entitled to strict compliance." 707 F.2d at 686. Accordingly, the Court finds that an issuing bank's action for wrongful honor against a confirming bank is governed by a strict compliance standard.

An analysis of the ten listed variances suggests that MHT failed to pick up two discrepancies not strictly complying with the letter of credit terms. The first alleged defect concerns St. Lucia's cable to Oriental using the wrong covernote number of 4291 instead of 429711. The insurance was procured by Vishwa and the cable was intended to give notice to Oriental of the shipment by quoting the proper covernote. The failure to provide the correct covernote was not inconsequential as the mistake could have resulted in Oriental's justifiable refusal to honor Vishwa's insurance policy. This mistake may appear immaterial on its face, but in *Beyene v. Irving Trust Co.*, ... the Second Circuit affirmed the dishonor of a letter of credit on the sole ground that the misspelling of Mohammed Sofan as Mohammed Soran on the bill of lading constituted a material discrepancy. . . .

The sixth defect is that the payment was made on documents presented by St. Lucia Enterprises despite the fact that the letter of credit was established for St. Lucia Enterprises, Ltd. The result is similar to that caused by the deviation of the Oriental covernote. Although there does not appear to be any difference between the two entities, it is not clear that the "intended" party was paid. The difference in names could also possibly be an indicia of unreliability or forgery. . . .

In the final analysis, only the variances as to the Oriental covernote and the name St. Lucia Enterprises, Ltd., appear not to comply strictly with the letter of credit conditions. The inquiry is not ended at this point because courts in this Circuit have applied concepts of equitable waiver and estoppel in cases of issuer dishonor. Application of estoppel has been premised upon discoverable nonconformities that could have been cured by the beneficiary before the expira-

---

[8] In discussing New York's bifurcated standard, courts and commentators have mistakenly cited each other . . . as support for the proposition that New York courts use a bifurcated approach. . . . A closer reading of these cases suggests otherwise. . . .

tion of the letter, but were not raised by the issuing bank until its dishonor. The banks were estopped from asserting the variances because of previous assurances to the beneficiary of documentary compliance or because of silence coupled with the retention of nonconforming documents for an unreasonably long time after the beneficiary had submitted its drafts for payment. . . .

Application of waiver has been predicated upon situations in which the issuer justifies dishonor on grounds later found to have been unjustified. In these instances, all other possible grounds for dishonor are deemed to have been waived. . . . Waiver of nonconforming documents can also be found from statements by officials of the issuing bank or from customer authorization. . . .

. . . The UCP expressly provides that an issuer has the obligation to immediately notify the beneficiary by "expeditious means" of any reason for noncompliance and the physical disposition of the disputed documents. UCP art. 8(e) (1974), 16(d) (1983). The UCP also implicitly invites cure of any documentary deficiencies apparent before the letter of credit expiration by issuer notification to the beneficiary. . . . In the context of this case, "[a]n equitable approach to a strict compliance standard demands that the issuer promptly communicate all documentary defects to the beneficiary [or confirming bank], when time exists under the letter to remedy the nonconformity." . . . The Court finds that Cochin is precluded from claiming wrongful honor because of its failure to comply with the explicit notice and affirmative obligation provisions of the UCP and its implicit duty to promptly cure discoverable defects in MHT's confirming advices to St. Lucia.

The issuing bank must give notice "without delay" that the documents received are (1) being "held at the disposal" of the remitting or confirming bank or (2) "are being returned" to the second bank. UCP art. 8(e) (1974), art. 16(d) (1983). An issuing bank that fails to return or hold the documents for the second bank is precluded from asserting that the negotiation and payment were not effected in accordance with the letter of credit requirements. UCP art. 8(f) (1974), 16(e) (1983). ... The UCP also directs that an issuing bank intending to claim noncompliance shall have a "reasonable time" to examine the documents after presentment and to determine whether to make such a claim. UCP art. 8(d) (1974), art. 16(c) (1983). The revised UCP allows explicitly for the imposition of the 16(e) sanction for failure to comply with the "reasonable time" provision as well; however, this interpretation is not clear under the parties' explicit choice of law, the 1974 UCP.

Neither the 1983 UCP nor the 1974 UCP defines what constitutes a "reasonable time" to determine if the documents are defective or notice "without delay" that the documents are being held or returned. When the UCP is silent or ambiguous, analogous UCC provisions may be utilized if consistent with the UCP. . . . The UCC provides for a period of three banking days for the issuer to honor or reject a documentary draft for payment. N.Y. U.C.C. § 5 112(1)(a) (McKinney's 1964) (issuer-beneficiary relationship). The letter of credit was issued subject to the 1974 UCP but it is silent as to what law governs its terms. Cochin cites to Indian statutes interpreting a "reasonable time" as a factual question depending on the nature of the negotiable instrument and the usual course of dealing. Under the circumstances of this case, however, it appears that under New York's comparative interest choice of law approach, New York UCC law would apply. . . .

Cochin's failure to promptly notify MHT that it had returned the documents or that it was holding them at MHT's disposal thus violates the UCP. Cochin's telex of June 21 states that there are certain discrepancies in St. Lucia's documents, but Cochin did not advise MHT that it was returning the documents to MHT until the July 3 telex. The "reasonable time" three-day period should be the maximum time allowable for the notification "without delay" requirement. Because June 21, 1980 was a Saturday, Cochin should have complied with its notice obligations no later than June 26. The passage of an additional week before compliance precludes Cochin from asserting its wrongful honor claim. Moreover, it was not until June 27 that Cochin first specified any reason for its dishonor argument, and the St. Lucia Enterprises, Ltd. omission was not noted until July 4.

Cochin proposes that its failure to timely notify MHT was not violative of UCP or letter of credit policy because it caused no additional loss to MHT. Cochin argues that the defects were in any case incurable by the time Cochin received the documents, because St. Lucia had disappeared with the letter of credit proceeds. Although the UCP is not explicit, the Court finds that these provisions should be applied identically to an issuing bank's obligations to a confirming bank after the latter's honor of a demand for payment. Cochin's contention ignores the expectation in the international financial community that the parties will live up to their statutory obligations and is at odds with the basic letter of credit tenet that banks deal solely with documents, not in goods. Cochin's argument would defeat the letter of credit's function of being a swift, fluid and reliable financing device. ...

Finally, the two documentary discrepancies could have been anticipated by Cochin and were curable before the demand for payment. Cochin received a copy of MHT's incorrect March 31 advice to St. Lucia, which mistakenly listed the insurance covernotes as 4291. Similarly, Cochin received copies of all of MHT's advices to St. Lucia, which omitted the "Ltd." from the corporate name. Cochin had sufficient notice and time to correct MHT's confirming defects to St. Lucia and is therefore estopped from asserting them. Although MHT failed to strictly comply with the letter requirements, Cochin's failure to perform its affirmative obligations precludes an action for wrongful honor under the UCP and by letter of credit estoppel.

Questions and Problems 4.17. *Bank of Cochin* takes the position that UCP 290, the 1974 version that applied to the L/C transaction in that case, required strict compliance of the documents with the terms of the L/C. What would be the outcome in the case if the current version of the UCP applied? The following case illustrates the application of one of the later versions of the UCP. How does its analysis compare with that of the previous case?

BLONDER & CO., INC. V. CITIBANK, N.A.
28 A.D.3d 180, 808 N.Y.S.2d 214 (N.Y. App. Div. 2006)

Andrias, J. . . .

In this action, plaintiff claims, inter alia, that defendant, the [letter of credit] issuer, improperly paid a $540,225 letter of credit covering a shipment of nickel scrap from Nicaragua to the Netherlands. Plaintiff claims that the goods, which it and a joint venturer, Moav International, contracted to purchase, were never received in Rotterdam; that the supporting documents were fake; and that defendant failed to examine the documents presented with reasonable care so as to ensure that they were in substantial compliance with the terms and conditions of the letter of credit.

. . . [T]he motion court granted defendant's motion to dismiss the complaint . . . on the basis of a defense founded upon documentary evidence or, in the alternative, for summary judgment . . . , to the extent of dismissing plaintiff's first cause of action for wrongful honor on the basis of the letter of credit itself and the supporting documents presented to defendant. Examining such evidence, the court found that the supporting documents presented to defendant substantially complied with the terms of the letter of credit, in accordance with the Uniform Customs and Practice for Documentary Credits (UCP), a set of universally accepted rules on documentary credits established by the International Chamber of Commerce. The UCP, which is intended to make it easier for companies in different countries to trade with each other, has been used worldwide for more than 60 years and, by the terms of the letter of credit, specifically governs the transaction.

. . . In this case, the motion court properly relied upon the unambiguous terms of the letter of credit, as amended, which specifically provided that it was subject to the UCP and, as to matters not addressed by the UCP, it was to be governed by and construed in accordance with New York law and applicable federal law.

A letter of credit is governed by the same general principles of law applying to all other written contracts, and it is fundamental that courts enforce contracts, not rewrite them. "[W]here the intention of the parties is clearly and unambiguously set forth in the agreement itself effect must be given to the intent as indicated by the language used without regard to extrinsic evidence (Schmidt v. Magnetic Head Corp., 97 A.D.2d 151, 157 [468 N.Y.S.2d 649] [1983] [citation omitted])" such as the opinion of plaintiff's expert.

Plaintiff does not question the motion court's action in deciding defendant's motion on the evidence before it, but contends that the court erred by substituting its own interpretation of what constitutes international standard banking practice for that of plaintiff's expert with 30 years' experience in the field. It claims that while international standard banking practice cannot contradict the UCP, the UCP does not exclude those items of custom and practice in international banking that are consistent with the UCP but not specifically spelled out therein. Plaintiff relies, for this proposition of law, on the opinion of its document expert that, based upon "International Standard Banking Practice," such discrepancies were material and should have alerted defendant not to make payment on the letter of credit without first seeking a waiver of discrepancies from plaintiff. However, just as a court cannot impose upon the parties to a letter of credit any conditions not contained in the letter, neither can plaintiff do so in the guise of expert testimony. . . .

As the motion court noted in its opinion, "[a]lthough plaintiff and its expert capitalize 'International Standard Banking Practice,' as if it were a separate document or agreement, it is not." The UCP requires that banks must examine documents "with reasonable care" in order to determine whether the documents "on their face" appear to comply with the letter of credit. As correctly found by the motion court, "[t]hat determination must be made in accordance with 'international standard banking practice *as reflected in these Articles*' (emphasis added [by the motion court])." . . .

In addition, opinions issued by the International Chamber of Commerce Banking Commission, the body that promulgated the UCP, reject the notion that all of the documents should be exactly consistent in their wording. They state that a common sense, case-by-case approach would permit minor deviations of a typographical nature because such a letter-for-letter correspondence between the letter of credit and the presentation documents is virtually impossible. The Banking Commission has also stated that "consistency," as that term is used in the UCP, means that the "whole of the documents must obviously relate to the same transaction, that is to say, that each should bear a relation (link) with the others on its face" (International Chamber of Commerce Banking Commission Publication No. 371, Decisions [1975-1979] of the ICC Banking Commission R. 12 [1980]). Moreover, as previously noted, and correctly found by the motion court, an issuing bank is not required to ascertain whether the documents are false or whether the goods were delivered, only that the documents substantially comply with the letter of credit on their face.

Obviously recognizing that defendant's examination was limited to the face of the documents presented, plaintiff, which claimed many other discrepancies in the documents at nisi prius, limits its appeal to claims that the required bill of lading was incomplete because it failed to name any consignee, that there was a discrepancy between the typed date on the bill of lading (January 11, 2000) and the "Clean on Board" stamp on the same document (January 11, 2001), and that there are two different ports of loading on the required inspection certificate.

Despite plaintiff's expert's opinion that the bill of lading was incomplete because it failed to name the consignee, there was no such requirement in the letter of credit, which merely required "1 copy of the bill of lading evidencing freight prepaid and shipment from Corinto Port, Nicaragua to Rotterdam, Netherlands." The motion court aptly noted that "[w]hether a consignee is named or not goes only to the issue of whether the bill of lading is negotiable or not, and the failure of a bill of lading to name a consignee does not, as plaintiff's expert suggests, make the bill of lading so defective that it is no longer even a bill of lading."

Likewise, as found by the motion court, the claimed discrepancy between the dates on the bill of lading ignores the "Clean On Board 11 ENE 2001" stamp on the bill of lading (ENE being the Spanish abbreviation for January). The typed date of "January 11, 2000" on the document, which is an understandably common mistake at the beginning of a new year, not only predates the issuance of the letter of credit by more than ten months but, as noted by defendant, loading on board may be indicated pursuant to UCP article 23(a)(ii) by preprinted wording on the bill of lading or by a notation of the date on which the goods have been loaded on board. The "Clean on Board 11 ENE 2001" stamp clearly meets the UCP requirement.

Finally, on the second page of the preprinted inspection certificate, in the only place in the four-page document calling for the "Port of Loading," "Corinto Port, Nicaragua" is specifically so designated, as required by the terms of the letter of credit. Whether the "Location" referred to on the first page of the document as "Almacen General de

Occidente S.A. Zona Franca, Carretera Leon, Nicaragua" reflects the name and address of the local company inspecting the goods or some other information is unclear and unexplained by the parties; nevertheless, there is no basis for any conjecture that it designates a different port of loading. As the motion court correctly found, the documents presented by the beneficiary substantially complied with the terms and conditions of the letter of credit. ...

Tom, J.P. (dissenting). . . .

In the instant matter, the documentary evidence fails to clearly negate any essential element of plaintiff's first cause of action. The reimbursement agreement provides that defendant is to make payment only if the documents presented are in "substantial compliance" with the terms and conditions of the letter of credit. As noted, plaintiff's expert has opined, based on his years of experience, that "the documents did not 'substantially comply' with the letter of credit" and that the material discrepancies in the documents should have alerted defendant not to make payment without seeking a waiver from plaintiff.

The motion court's decision indicates only that, upon a probing analysis on the merits, the court was persuaded that the evidence adduced thus far is insufficient to support judgment in favor of plaintiff. This, however, is not the test established by the Court of Appeals in Rovello [v. Orofino Realty Co.,] 40 N.Y.2d 633, 389 N.Y.S.2d 314, 357 N.E.2d 970, which warrants dismissal only if the complaint fails to set forth a cognizable claim on its face. . . . As the Court of Appeals stated, "a complaint should not be dismissed on a pleading motion so long as, when the plaintiff is given the benefit of every possible favorable inference, a cause of action exists" (Rovello, 40 N.Y.2d at 634, 389 N.Y.S.2d 314, 357 N.E.2d 970). Here, [the] Supreme Court, rather than deciding whether the pleadings sufficiently set forth a cognizable claim . . . , instead drew all factual inferences in favor of defendant–in particular, resolving questions concerning the bank's duties under international standard banking practice as a matter of law–to render judgment on the merits in favor of defendant. The court's disposition is unsupportable, even in the absence of material questions of fact. As Rovello cautions, "Although absent further evidence, the dispute may be finally resolved on the more embracive and exploratory motion for summary judgment, disposition by summary dismissal under CPLR 3211 (subd. [a], par. 7), is premature" (*id.*). . . .

On the instant motion, plaintiff submitted the affidavit of an expert who concluded that defendant failed to review the documents tendered by the beneficiary for payment in accordance with accepted international standard banking practices. He noted that the failure to designate a consignee was unique in his 30 years of experience, stating, "Without a consignee, a bill of lading is incomplete because it lacks . . . 'evidence of title.' " He found numerous deficiencies in the documents tendered by the beneficiary, particularly in the bill of lading, including conflicting ports of loading on the shipping documents and anomalies in the weight of the shipping containers in the certificate of weighing, sampling and assay, that "plainly required Citibank to refuse payment on the Letter of Credit on the ground of substantial noncompliance." This conclusion is uncontroverted by any opposing expert opinion offered by defendant. Thus, even if the complaint can be regarded as facially insufficient, which it is not, the expert's affidavit supports a "potentially meritorious" claim sufficient to defeat defendant's dismissal motion (Rovello, 40 N.Y.2d at 635, 389 N.Y.S.2d 314, 357 N.E.2d 970).

. . . The penultimate issue to be decided in this case is inherently factual: Whether defendant bank fulfilled its duty, as imposed by the parties' reimbursement agreement and the UCP, to examine the documents presented for payment "with reasonable care" and "in conformity with . . . letter of credit practices." While a court may take judicial notice of statutes and regulations . . . , it may not apply its own knowledge to decide matters requiring expert testimony. A court is only permitted to take judicial notice of matters "of common and general knowledge, well established and authoritatively settled, not doubtful or uncertain. The test is whether sufficient notoriety attaches to the fact to make it proper to assume its existence without proof. If there is any doubt either as to the fact itself or as to its being a matter of common knowledge, evidence will be required" (Ecco High Frequency Corp. v. Amtorg Trading Corp., 81 N.Y.S.2d 610, 617 [1948], affd. 274 App.Div. 982, 85 N.Y.S.2d 304 [1948]).

Contrary to these settled rules, Supreme Court decided this controversy by applying its own belief or understanding of what constitutes accepted international banking practice to find that, pursuant to the parties' reimbursement agreement, the bank properly accepted the proffered documents as conforming to the conditions of the letter of credit. However, where a question of fact is raised with respect to the existence or extent of a usage of trade, summary dismissal is inappropriate. . . .

. . . [T]he record raises numerous questions of fact relating to whether defendant conducted a competent review of the documents presented for payment. The certificate of weighing, sampling and assay, in particular, contains some glaring inconsistencies. Anomalously, it asserts that "[w]eighing was carried out under our constant supervision on 100% of the cargo chosen at random." The first page of the four-page document states:

> PACKING: The nickel scrap will be stuffed, bulk, into 20 foot sea-going containers. The gross weight of each container, including the tare weight, will not exceed 20,000 kgs.
> LOADED TO THE VESSEL: M/S Tophas-Voyage No. 0048
> LOCATION: Almacen General de Occidente S.A. Zona Franca, Carretera Leon, Nicaragua

The second page, by contrast, identifies the "port of loading" as "Corinto Port, Nicaragua." Plaintiff's expert explained, "Something is clearly amiss and should have been flagged as a discrepancy. Either the load port has been stated incorrectly on one of the locations in the Inspection Certificate or, the goods were moved in a manner inconsistent with any of the transaction documents." The weight of the cargo is stated to have been determined "over weighscale by weighing loaded." Incredibly, each of the nine containers into which the nickel scrap had been loaded tipped the scales at precisely 44,100 pounds (20,000 kgs.). The complaint also identifies several facial irregularities in the certificate, asserting that its "sloppy appearance, mangled language" and "poorly drawn logo" should have resulted in its rejection by defendant. Plaintiff's expert concluded that all such discrepancies constitute grounds for dishonor of the letter of credit. Even if the materiality of the discrepancies had been disputed by opposing expert testimony, which it was not, these irregularities merely present questions of fact. The motion court's resolution of the factual issues on its own knowledge is clearly improper. . . .

Questions and Problems 4.18. What would have been the outcome in this case if a strict compliance standard had been required for the documents presented?

4.19. Both the majority and Judge Tom in dissent seem to accept as a starting point that the standard in the case is substantial compliance. What, then, divides the two sides? A difference of opinion about the compliance of the documents? Or a difference in application of procedural standards?

4.20. Judge Tom is quite insistent on the significance to be given to the opinion of the plaintiff's expert on the issue of the conformity of the document review to "International Standard Banking Practice." In another portion of their opinion, the majority offered the following response:

The conclusory affidavit of plaintiff's expert, that in his 30 years of experience in the field he had never seen a bill of lading without a named consignee and that the document at issue "does not constitute a 'Bill of Lading' as that term is used in the International Standard Banking Practice," is insufficient to create an issue of fact as to whether such a usage of trade exists. The expert cited no authority, including the UCP, or any treatise, standard, article or other corroborating evidence to support his conclusory assertions (*see Buchholz v. Trump 767 Fifth Ave.*, 5 N.Y.3d 1, 8-9, 798 N.Y.S.2d 715, 831 N.E.2d 960 [2005]). While the existence and scope of such a usage ordinarily present factual issues, where such a usage is embodied in a trade code such as the UCP or other writing, "the interpretation of the writing is for the court" (UCC 1-205[2]). Thus, any interpretation of the UCP was properly made by the motion court, which properly refused to allow the expert to usurp its function as the sole determiner of law (*see Buchholz v. Trump 767 Fifth Ave., LLC*, 4 A.D.3d 178, 179, 772 N.Y.S.2d 257 [2004], *affd.* 5 N.Y.3d 1, 798 N.Y.S.2d 715, 831 N.E.2d 960 [2005]).

Blonder & Co., Inc., 808 N.Y.S.2d at 217. Which side has the better argument?

Transnational commerce obviously gains efficiencies from modern electronic transmittal of L/C documents. Electronic transmittal was facilitated by the 1995 revision of UCC Article 5. Treatment of electronic transmittal of L/C documents is handled somewhat differently under UCP practice. In April 2002, the ICC issued the eUCP (version 1.0), originally an electronic supplement to the ICC's UCP 500 and now to the current UCP 600. The eUCP is available in the Supplement. Review that text in considering the problems posed that follow.

Questions and Problems 4.21. BayerCorp and SallerCo, headquartered in different countries, sign a contract for the sale of 100 digital thingots with payment via a letter of credit (L/C). The contract does not say anything about the method of presenting documents for payment under the L/C. SallerCo sends Issuer Bank a pdf.doc containing a draft and supporting documents that would clearly have satisfied the L/C conditions for payment if they had been paper documents. Issuer Bank's employee looks at the pdf.doc on the computer screen, but does not process SallerCo's payment demand. The L/C eventually expires. Would Issuer Bank be liable to SallerCo under the UCP?

4.22. The contract between BayerCorp and SallerCo specifies that the L/C is subject to UCP 600. SallerCo sends Issuer Bank a pdf.doc containing a draft and supporting documents that would clearly have satisfied the L/C conditions for payment if they had been paper documents. Issuer Bank's employee looks at the pdf.doc on the computer screen, but does not process Seller's payment demand. The L/C eventually expires. Is Issuer Bank liable to Seller?

4.23. BayerCorp and SallerCo specify that the L/C is subject to "the eUCP to the extent that its provisions are different from those of the Uniform Commercial Code article 5," which is the L/C law in the U.S. jurisdiction where BayerCorp has its principal place of business. Does UCP 600 or UCC art. 5 apply to this transaction?

Chapter 5

Funds Transfers

A. INTRODUCTION

What if we dispensed with documents as the medium of payment (both physical and electronic) and opted instead for a fully ideated payments system? What would such a system look like? It would involve direct transfers of funds, with or without the assistance of an institution specializing in such transfers, by means of electronic communication or instructions. Since the system ostensibly would not use documents, there would be some serious doubt whether the rules that govern negotiable instruments or documentary drafts, discussed in Chapter 2-4, would apply to these transfers at all, except through some purblind analogy that neglected the many differences between these payment media.

In fact, however, we *do* have such systems for payment outside the medium of documents. Cryptocurrencies, discussed in Chapter 1, represent one contemporary example of such a system. Historically, however, banks and other institutional actors have transferred funds denominated in official currencies through instructions sent to correspondent firms "over the wire," *i.e.*, by telegraphic or other electronic means of communication. At the retail level, individuals and smaller firms routinely make electronic transfers of funds, now that electronic communication is available to them as well. This chapter examines the state and federal rules that govern funds transfers undertaken at

what we might call the retail level – electronic funds transfers (EFTs,) and at the wholesale level – so-called wire transfers.

B. ELECTRONIC FUNDS TRANSFERS

First things first. Today the most prevalent form of EFT is the debit card transaction – typically, an ATM card linked to a consumer's checking or savings account, but also such things as payment cards, gift cards, and the like.[1] How does this transaction work? The following case excerpt offers a straightforward tour of EFTs. (We shall return to this case later, to discuss controversies over appropriate regulation of these transactions under the Electronic Funds Transfer Act (EFTA), 15 U.S.C. §§ 1693 *et seq.*)

NACS V. BOARD OF GOVERNORS
OF FEDERAL RESERVE SYSTEM
746 F.3d 474 (D.C.Cir. 2014)
cert. denied, --- U.S. ---, 135 S.Ct. 1170 (2015)

TATEL, Circuit Judge:

. . .

Combining features of credit cards and checks, debit cards have become not just the most popular noncash payment method in the United States but also a source of substantial revenue for banks and companies like Visa and MasterCard that own and operate debit card networks. In 2009 alone, debit card holders used their cards 37.6 billion times, completing transactions worth over $1.4 trillion and yielding over $20 billion in fees for banks and networks. . . .

I.

Understanding this case requires looking under the hood—or, more accurately, behind the teller's window—to see what really happens when customers use their debit cards. . . .

A.

We start with the basics. For purposes of this case, the term "debit card" describes both traditional debit cards, which allow cardholders to deduct money directly from their bank accounts, and prepaid cards, which come loaded with a certain amount of money that cardholders can spend down and, in some cases, replenish. Debit card transactions are typically processed using what is often called a "four party sys-

---

[1] For federal consumer protection provisions with respect to general-use prepaid cards, gift certificates, and store gift cards, see 15 U.S.C. § 1693*l*-1. On regulation of "," see *id.* § 1693o-1.

tem." The four parties are the cardholder who makes the purchase, the merchant who accepts the debit card payment, the cardholder's bank (called the "issuer" because it issues the debit card to the cardholder), and the merchant's bank (called the "acquirer" because it acquires funds from the cardholder and deposits those funds in the merchant's account). In addition, each debit transaction is processed on a particular debit card "network," often affiliated with MasterCard or Visa. The network transmits information between the cardholder/issuer side of the transaction and the merchant/acquirer side. Issuers activate certain networks on debit cards, and only activated networks can process transactions on those cards.

Virtually all debit card transactions fall into one of two categories: personal identification number (PIN) or signature. PIN and signature transactions employ different methods of "authentication"—a process that establishes that the cardholder, and not a thief, has actually initiated the transaction. In PIN authentication, the cardholder usually enters her PIN into a terminal. In signature authentication, the cardholder usually signs a copy of the receipt. Most networks can process either PIN transactions or signature transactions, but not both. Signature networks employ infrastructure used to process credit card payments, while PIN networks employ infrastructure used by ATMs. Only about one-quarter of merchants currently accept PIN debit. Some merchants have never acquired the terminals needed for customers to enter their PINs, while others believe that signature debit better suits their business needs. More about this later. And merchants who sell online generally refuse to accept PIN debit because customers worry about providing PINs over the Internet. Merchants who do accept both PIN and signature debit often allow customers to select whether to process particular transactions on a PIN network or a signature network.

Whether PIN or signature, a debit card transaction is processed in three stages: authorization, clearance, and settlement. Authorization begins when the cardholder swipes her debit card, which sends an electronic "authorization request" to the acquirer conveying the cardholder's account information and the transaction's value. The acquirer then forwards that request along the network to the issuer. Once the issuer has determined whether the cardholder has sufficient funds in her account to complete the transaction and whether the transaction appears fraudulent, it sends a response to the merchant along the network approving or rejecting the transaction. Even if the issuer approves the transaction, that transaction still must be cleared and settled before any money changes hands.

Clearance constitutes a formal request for payment sent from the merchant on the network to the issuer. PIN transactions are authorized and cleared simultaneously: because the cardholder generally enters her PIN immediately after swiping her card, the authorization request doubles as the clearance message. Signature transactions are first authorized and subsequently cleared: because the cardholder generally signs only after the issuer has approved the transaction, the merchant must send a separate clearance message. This difference between PIN and signature processing explains why certain businesses, including car rental companies, hotels, and sit-down restaurants, often refuse to accept PIN debit. Car rental companies authorize transactions at pick-up to ensure that customers have enough money in their accounts to pay but postpone clearance to allow for the possibility that the customer might damage the vehicle or return it without a full tank of gas. Hotels authorize transactions at check-in but postpone clearance to allow for the possibility that the guest might trash the room, order room service, or abscond with the towels and robes. And sit-down restaurants authorize transactions for the full amount of the meal but postpone clearance to give diners an opportunity to add a tip.

The final debit card payment processing step, settlement, involves the actual transfer of funds from the issuer to the acquirer. After settlement, the cardholder's account has been debited, the merchant's account has been credited, and the transaction has concluded. Rather than settle transactions one-by-one, banks generally employ companies that determine each bank's net debtor/creditor position over a large number of transactions and then settle those transactions simultaneously.

THE EFTA

The EFTA was enacted in November 1978 as a new consumer credit protection initiative.[2] Originally administered by the Federal Reserve, since 2010 the act has been administered by the Consumer

---

[2] Pub. L. No. 95–630, § 2001, 92 Stat 3641, 3728-3741 (Nov. 10, 1978) (codified at 15 U.S.C. §§ 1693-1693r). *See Wachter v. Denver Nat. Bank*, 751 F.Supp. 906 (D.Colo. 1990) (noting that EFTA was enacted "to create rights for consumers in an era in which banking could be conducted almost exclusively through machines"). The act does not have preemptive effect over state laws, except to the extent such laws are inconsistent with the EFTA. 15 U.S.C. § 1693q. *See also id.* § 1693r (providing for regulatory exemption of state regulation).

Financial Protection Bureau (CFPB),[3] except for regulation of auto dealers[4] and supervision of reasonable fees and rules for payment card transactions,[5] both of which remain subject to the authority of the Federal Reserve.

At the heart of the EFTA is a principal of disclosure. In accordance with CFPB regulations, a financial institution must disclose terms and conditions of EFTs involving a consumer's account at the time that the consumer contracts for EFT service.[6] The disclosures must be "in readily understandable language."[7] If there is any change in any of those terms or conditions that would result in greater cost or liability for the consumer or decreased access to the account, the financial institution must notify the consumer in writing at least twenty-one days prior to the effective date of the change.[8]

Mandated disclosure continues as an on-going obligation. The financial institution must, at the time a transfer is initiated, make available to the consumer written documentation of each electronic fund transfer initiated by the consumer from an electronic terminal.[9] Furthermore, the financial institution must provide positive notice to the consumer when preauthorized EFTs from the same payor is made as scheduled, or negative notice to the consumer when the credit is *not* made as scheduled.[10] It must also provide the consumer with periodic statements for each account the consumer may access by means of an EFT.[11]

The act also imposes certain substantive requirements as well. Issuance to a consumer of "any card, code, or other means of access to such consumer's account for the purpose of initiating an electronic fund transfer" generally requires a request or application from the consumer or must be a renewal or replacement of an accepted card, code, or other means of access.[12] Preauthorized EFTs from consumer accounts must be authorized by the consumer in writing, and a copy of

---

[3] 15 U.S.C. § 1693b(a)(1). On the origins and authority of the CFPB, see 1 Michael P. Malloy, Banking Law and Regulation § 1C.10[E] (2d ed. 2011).

[4] 15 U.S.C. § 1593b(b)(2)(A).

[5] *Id.* §§ 1593b(b)(2)(B), 1693o-2.

[6] *Id.* § 1593c(a).

[7] *Id.*

[8] *Id.* § 1593c(b).

[9] *Id.* § 1593d(a).

[10] *Id.* § 1593d(b).

[11] *Id.* § 1593d(c).

[12] *Id.* § 1593i(a). A consumer cannot be required to establish an account for receipt of EFTs with a particular financial institution as a condition of employment or as a condition to receive a government benefit. *Id.* § 1593k(2).

the authorization must be provided to the consumer *when made*.[13] There are also detailed rules for investigation of alleged errors in EFTs, determining whether an error has occurred, and reporting results to the consumer.[14]

Most famously, perhaps, from the consumer perspective, the act limits consumer liability for unauthorized EFTs to carefully delineated circumstances.[15] Generally, consumer liability is limited to the *lesser* of $50.00 or the amount of money or value of property or services obtained in the unauthorized electronic fund transfer prior to the time when the financial institution is notified or otherwise becomes aware of the relevant circumstances.[16] Liability of the financial institution to the consumer generally extends to "all damages proximately caused" by its failure to make an authorized EFT as instructed, in the correct amount and in a timely manner.[17] Note that the act specifically provides that no right conferred by the act can be waived or restricted by a writing or agreement between a consumer and any other person.[18]

Questions and Problems 5.1. What is the purpose of the requirements imposed by the EFTA? When are they triggered? In answering these questions, consider the following case.

PUGLISI V. DEBT RECOVERY SOLUTIONS, LLC
822 F.Supp.2d 218 (E.D.N.Y. 2011)

JOSEPH F. BIANCO, District Judge.

[A debtor sued a debt collector, alleging among other things a violation of the EFTA disclosure notice requirements. The district court granted the defendant's summary judgment motion on the EFTA

---

[13] *Id.* § 1593e(a). A consumer cannot be required to utilize preauthorized EFTs as a condition of receiving credit. *Id.* § 1593k(1). For preauthorized consumer transfers to the same person that may vary in amount, the financial institution (or the designated payee) must provide reasonable advance notice to the consumer of the amount to be transferred and the scheduled date of the transfer prior to each transfer. *Id.* § 1593e(b).

[14] *Id.* § 1593f.

[15] *Id.* § 1593g.

[16] *Id.* § 1593g(a)(1)-(2).

[17] *Id.* § 1593h(a). On civil liability generally for noncompliance with the act, see *Id.* § 1693m. *See also id.* §§ 1693n (providing for criminal liability for intentional violations of EFTA), 1693o (concerning administrative enforcement of EFTA by various federal regulatory agencies).

[18] *Id.* § 1693*l*.

claim because the disputed withdrawal from plaintiff's account was not the sort of "preauthorized electronic fund transfer" covered under the EFTA. The excerpted opinion deals with the EFTA issues raised by the dispute.]

Plaintiff and defendant have cross-moved for summary judgment with regard to plaintiff's claim that defendant violated the EFTA, [15 U.S.C. § 1693e(b)], by failing to give advanced written notice to plaintiff for the preauthorized electronic fund transfer [from plaintiff's checking account]. . . .

The EFTA is a consumer law aimed at "provid[ing] a basic framework [to] establish[ ] the rights, liabilities, and responsibilities of participants in electronic fund transfer systems." 15 U.S.C. § 1693. . . . An "electronic fund transfer" is defined as "any transfer of funds other than a transaction originated by check, draft, or similar paper instrument, which is initiated through an electronic terminal, telephonic instrument, or computer or magnetic tape so as to order, instruct, or authorize a financial institution to debit or credit an account. Such term includes, but is not limited to, point-of-sale transfers, automated teller machine transactions, direct deposits or withdrawals of funds, and transfers initiated by telephone." 15 U.S.C. § 1693a(6). A "preauthorized electronic fund transfer" is defined as "an electronic fund transfer authorized in advance to recur at substantially regular intervals." 15 U.S.C. § 1693a(9).

[The court quoted 15 U.S.C. § 1693e(b), which provides for "reasonable advance notice to the consumer" of an amount to be transferred from the consumer's account and the date scheduled for the transfer.]

. . . The statute's implementing regulation, known as "Regulation E," states:

> Preauthorized electronic fund transfers from a consumer's account may be authorized only by a writing signed or similarly authenticated by the consumer. The person that obtains the authorization shall provide a copy to the consumer.

12 C.F.R. § 205.10(b)[, since transferred to the CFPB and codified as 12 C.F.R. § 1005.10.]

As a threshold issue, it is clear from defendant's papers that defendant is disputing whether its attempted withdrawal of plaintiff's funds on December 17, 2007 was a "preauthorized electronic funds transfer" which is "an electronic fund transfer authorized in advance *to recur at substantially regular intervals*," under 15 U.S.C. § 1693a(9) (emphasis added). . . . [T]he undisputed evidence demonstrates that there were no recurring automatic payments and, thus, defendant was not statutorily obligated to provide notice to plaintiff. The Court agrees.

It is undisputed that plaintiff agreed to make two payments in full settlement of his debt and he authorized defendant to make only two withdrawals. . . . In short, there is no evidence that plaintiff's authorization was designed to allow for deductions at substantially regular intervals. *See Okocha v. HSBC Bank USA, N.A.*, No. 08 Civ. 8650 (MHP), 2010 WL 5122614, at *2 (S.D.N.Y. Dec. 14, 2010) ("Although the deposit account agreement authorizes defendants to use funds in the deposit account to pay off debts owed to HSBC, such authorization is not designed 'to recur at substantially regular intervals' [pursuant to 15 U.S.C. § 1693a(9)]. HSBC may have debited plaintiff's account on several occasions to offset the balance on his overdraft account, but plaintiff has provided no evidence that these offsets occurred, for example, at weekly, monthly, or annual intervals."); *see also In re DirecTV Early Cancellation Litigation*, 738 F.Supp.2d 1062, 1091 (C.D.Cal.2010) ("The authorization DirecTV obtains for a one-time charge of the Cancellation Fee does not fit within [the] definition [of 15 U.S.C. § 1693a(9)]. . . . [T]here are no allegations of recurring automatic payments in violation of EFTA.") In sum, after drawing all reasonable inferences in favor of plaintiff, the Court concludes that a rational jury could only conclude that there was no preauthorized electronic funds transfer. Accordingly, plaintiff's EFTA claim cannot survive summary judgment.

Questions and Problems 5.2. What if the EFT is not only *not* preauthorized, but *not authorized* at all? What if the EFT is "authorized," but not by the purported customer? In cutting through these knotty problems, consider the following case.

MARQUESS V. PENNSYLVANIA STATE EMPLOYEES CREDIT UNION
427 Fed.Appx. 188 (2011)

TASHIMA, Circuit Judge.

The Electronic Fund Transfers Act (EFTA) and its implementing regulations impose, in certain situations, liability on banks for unauthorized electronic fund transfers (EFTs) drawn against their customers' accounts. 15 U.S.C. § 1693 *et seq.*; 12 C.F.R. § 205.6 *et seq.* The question is whether the EFTA applies to bank accounts opened through forgery.

After a bench trial, the District Court made factual findings that neither party challenges. William Marquess, now deceased, opened a bank account at Pennsylvania State Employees Credit Union (PSECU) in the name of his adult son, Jason, by forging Jason's signature. William never told Jason about the forgery or the account. William used his own Philadelphia address for the account instead of Jason's Florida address. Later, William made himself a joint holder of the account by forging Jason's signature on another form. Later still, William authorized electronic transfers from the joint Jason/William account to an account in the name of David Marquess, William's other son, by forging Jason's signature on yet another form.

When William died, the joint Jason/William account held over $25,000, although Jason still had no idea that the account existed. David, however, learned of the account through a letter that PSECU sent to William's home. David then called PSECU, impersonated Jason, obtained the account's PIN number and on-line banking password, and stole the $25,000 balance. When Jason finally learned what had happened after receiving notice that he owed inheritance tax on the joint account, PSECU refused to refund the stolen money.

William's estate and Jason sued PSECU for violation of the EFTA and breach of contract. The district court found for Jason on the EFTA claim, but found for PSECU on all other claims. PSECU appeals. . . .

Under the Federal Reserve Board's official staff interpretation, the EFTA does not apply unless the consumer has entered an agreement for EFT services:

> 1. Accounts covered. The requirements of the regulation apply only to an account for which an agreement for EFT services to or from the account has been entered into between:
>
> i. The consumer and the financial institution (including an account for which an access device has been issued to the consumer, for example);
>
> ii. The consumer and a third party (for preauthorized debits or credits, for example), when the account-holding institution has received notice of the agreement and the fund transfers have begun.

12 C.F.R. Pt. 205, Supp. I § 205.3. . . . Only subsection (i) of the interpretation applies to this case, because the unauthorized transfer did not involve preauthorized debits or credits by a third party.

No agreement for EFT services existed between PSECU and either Jason or William. Obviously Jason never entered any such agreement; he did not even know that the account existed until after David stole the money. As for William, he purported to establish an EFT agreement by forging Jason's signature on the PSECU form, but this agreement—like the antecedent account-opening agreement—was forged and is therefore void. *See Tonkin v. Tonkin*, 172 Pa.Super. 552, 94 A.2d 192, 196 (1953) ("[T]he legal effect of [forgery] is to void the instrument."); *FDA Packaging Inc. v. Advance Personnel Staffing, Inc.*, 73 Pa. D. & C.4th 420, 430 n. 4 (Ct.Com.Pl.2005) ("Void contracts generally arise in cases of forgery of a party's name or unauthorized execution of an agreement on behalf of another party.").

Plaintiffs argue, incorrectly, that PSECU somehow created an agreement with Jason by treating him as the account owner after William's death. One cannot, however, ratify a contract that never existed. *Long v. Sears Roebuck & Co.*, 105 F.3d 1529, 1535 n. 10 (3d Cir.1997).

Because no agreement existed between any plaintiff and PSECU, the EFTA does not apply. *See* 12 C.F.R. Pt. 205, Supp. I § 205.3(1)(i).

Questions and Problems 5.3. What if the customer authorizes – or at least *tries* to authorize – but something goes wrong, or nothing happens at all? To what extent should we allocate this risk to the bank? Or to the customer? Consider the following case.

PORTER V. CITIBANK, N.A.
123 Misc.2d 28, 472 N.Y.S.2d 582 (N.Y. Civ.Ct. 1984)

EDWARD H. LEHNER, Judge:

To withdraw funds from your Citibank account at any time all you need do is place your card in their machine, enter your secret code, and then push a button. So the advertisement goes. But, complains the plaintiff, on two occasions this was done, no money was received, and yet his account was charged. Thus the Court is faced with another type of dispute between man and machine, for which no precedent has been found.

Plaintiff testified that on August 23, 1983 he sought to withdraw $100 from his checking account. When no money was dispensed from the machine after the necessary buttons were pushed, he reported the fact to a bank official who stated that the matter would be investigated. A few weeks later, on September 5, plaintiff took the requisite steps to make a $200 withdrawal. When no money appeared, he then repeated the process with the same result, which he thereupon reported to management. As a result of the foregoing plaintiff's account showed one withdrawal of $100 and two of $200 (for a total of $500), which amount he seeks to recover in this action.

The witnesses employed in the branch of the bank where the machine involved was located testified that in examining it on the day after the first of the two occurrences they found the account in balance, while on the latter date there was a cash overage of $90. They further indicated that, on the average, the cash machines were out of balance once or twice per week, but never for a sum in excess of $100.

Although no reported decision has been found dealing with this type of situation, *McEvans v. Citibank, N.A.,* 96 Misc.2d 142, 408 N.Y.S.2d 870 (Civil Ct., N.Y.Co., 1978) involved a somewhat analogous problem. There, a customer, who admitted failing to supply the bank with a deposit slip, claimed to have made a deposit by placing cash in an envelope in the cash machine. However, she received no credit because the bank denied receipt. The Court ruled in favor of the customer, but only because it found the bank negligent in failing to follow its own publicized procedures of having one person open the deposit envelopes, with a second employee observing the opening.

In *Employers Insurance of Wausau v. Chemical Bank,* 117 Misc.2d 601, 459 N.Y.S.2d 238 (Civil Ct., N.Y.Co., 1983), the undersigned[a] was confronted with a situation where the plaintiff claimed to have made a deposit in the night depository for which the bank had no record. Believing the testimony of the plaintiff's witness, judgment was rendered in its favor through application of the rules of bailment. *See also*: *Judd v. Citibank,* 107 Misc.2d. 526, 435 N.Y.S.2d 210 (Civil Ct., Queens Co., 1980) and *Ognibene v. Citibank, N. A.,* 112 Misc.2d 219, 446 N.Y.S.2d 845 (Civil Ct., N.Y.Co., 1981); where bank customers who were tricked into permitting others to use their bank cards were granted recovery.

As indicated in the discussion in *Employers Insurance of Wausau v. Chemical Bank, supra*, a minority of the few courts in the nation that have considered the question have declined to grant a recovery against a bank solely on the testimony of a customer that a deposit was made. This reluctance is based on the fear of fraudulent suits against these public institutions. The policy underlying this view is illustrated by the dicta in *Roscoe v. Central National Bank of Canajoharie,* 96 Misc.2d 517, 409 N.Y.S.2d 189 (Sup.Ct., Schenectady Co.1978), where it was said that it would be "sheer folly" to "permit unrestrained and unlimited suits against banks simply on the bare assertion of an individual that he made a deposit. Without subsequent discovery, there would be no way of actually knowing whether the claimed deposit was in fact made, and in such a situation, frought [*sic*] with limitless opportunities for fraud, banks should not be held answerable or liable."

However, the preferable majority view is to permit recovery where the Court is convinced that the deposit was in fact made and the bank

---

[a] *I.e.,* the same Judge Lehner. Was this a trend?

could not explain its absence. Although the bailment presumptions applicable to night deposit cases cannot be said to be applicable to the opposite situation at bar where the claim is that the withdrawal was not received, the cases are pertinent in their holdings that a Court may give credence to testimony of an undocumented deposit. Similar to the night depository customer, who is not in a position to produce any documentary evidence to establish that he made the deposit, the cash machine customer can produce nothing to show that the money was not dispensed to him.

Here we are dealing with machines which defendant's witnesses acknowledged were out of balance one or two nights a week (although not to the extent involved in this case). Such witnesses also stated their belief that at times a subsequent machine customer received money properly belonging to the prior user of the machine. Plaintiff was a rather credible witness who had no record of banking problems although he had used the machines numerous times.

Under the circumstances, the Court holds that plaintiff established by a fair preponderance of the evidence that he did not receive the money for which he was charged as a result of the abovementioned transactions. Therefore, he is entitled to judgment for $500, plus interest from September 5, 1983.

Questions and Problems 5.4.   Is the professed fear of "unrestrained and unlimited suits against banks" realistic? Particularly in electronic or online banking situations, we may assume that there would be some sort of digital trail to corroborate the customer's claim. What if anything corroborated Mr. Porter's claim?

5.5. *I'd like to buy a Vowell, Pat.* When someone illicitly gains access to your bank account – by stealing and forging one of your checks, by stealing your ATM card, or by hacking into the account digitally – there are obviously consequences under UCC Article 4. Article 4 applies not just to checks and notes governed by Article 3, but to any "item." UCC § 4-102(a), But there are also ambiguities – UCC § 4-104(a)(9) defines "item" to mean "an instrument or a promise or order to pay money handled by a bank for collection or payment. *The term does not include . . . a credit or debit card slip.*" (Emphasis added.) Presumably, debit card transfers will be picked up by the EFTA. Before we turn to the possible impact of the EFTA, review the following case and consider the UCC implications of unauthorized debits or withdrawals from a bank account.

MERCANTILE BANK OF ARKANSAS v. VOWELL
117 S.W.3d 603 (Ark. App. 2003)

JOHN F. STROUD, JR., Chief Judge.

[A bank and its customers, Dr. and Mrs. Vowell, sued over who was to bear the losses for forgeries and other unauthorized transactions by the customers' daughter involving their checking and savings accounts. In a bench trial, the trial court found neither the bank nor the customers failed to exercise ordinary care, and that they should share the losses. The bank appealed.]

　. . . We hold that there is no clear error in the trial court's finding that Dr. Vowell's conduct did not substantially contribute to the forgeries and unauthorized transactions. Neither do we find clear error in the trial court's finding that the appellant bank did not fail to exercise ordinary care. Where we do find error, however, is in the trial court's determination of which items appellee is precluded from recovering from appellant and the trial court's allocation of the loss between appellant and appellee. We therefore affirm in part and reverse and remand in part so that the trial court can enter a new judgment in accordance with this opinion.

　Appellee and his wife, now deceased, . . . signed the customer-account agreements with respect to each account. Each agreement contained a provision immediately above the signature line, which provided:

　　SIGNATURE(S)—THE UNDERSIGNED AGREE(S) TO THE TERMS STATED ON THE FRONT AND BACK OF THIS FORM, AND ACKNOWLEDGE(S) RECEIPT OF A COMPLETED COPY ON TODAY'S DATE. THE UNDERSIGNED ALSO ACKNOWLEDGE(S) RECEIPT OF A COPY OF OUR ACCOUNT INFORMATION BROCHURE[.]

The agreements also contained the following provision:

　　STATEMENTS—You must examine your statement of account with "reasonable promptness." If you discover (or reasonably should have discovered) any unauthorized payments or alterations, you must promptly notify us of the relevant facts. If you fail to do either of these duties, you will have to either share the loss with us, or bear the loss entirely yourself (depending on whether we exercised ordinary care and, if not, whether we substantially contributed to the loss). The loss could be not only with respect to items on the statement but other items forged or altered by the same wrongdoer. You agree that the time you have to examine your statement and report to us will depend on the circumstances, but that such time will not, in any circumstance, exceed a total of 30 days from when the statement is first made available to you.

You further agree that if you fail to report any unauthorized signatures, alterations, forgeries or any other errors in your account within 60 days of when we make the statement available, you cannot assert a claim against us on any items in that statement, and the loss will be entirely yours. This 60 day limitation is without regard to whether we exercised ordinary care. The limitation in this paragraph is in addition to that contained in the first paragraph of this section.

Appellant's policy regarding bank statements is to mail monthly bank statements on any account that has deposit or withdrawal activity. The bank statement covers the previous month's activity for the time frame that appears on the statement. The statements were usually sent to the account holder two days after the cutoff day listed on the statement and were generally considered as received two days thereafter. Appellee received bank statements at the Little Rock, Arkansas, address provided in the customer-account agreements. Appellee testified at trial that his wife had been responsible for reviewing the bank statements and balancing the checkbooks. Appellee did not personally review the accounts.

In June of 1997, appellee and his wife allowed their daughter, Suzan Vowell, now also deceased, and her boyfriend to move in with them at their home. At that time, they knew that Suzan and her boyfriend had been involved with drugs, alcohol, writing bad checks, and stealing. They also knew that Suzan had stolen checks from them in the past and forged either appellee's or his wife's signatures. The trial court found that appellee and his wife took precautions against future theft and forgeries by Suzan by hiding Mrs. Vowell's purse, which contained their checkbook, under the kitchen sink. Furthermore, appellee's wife suffered from diabetes mellitus and alcoholism, conditions that forced her to stay in bed either all or most of the time.[a] Appellee, however, continued to rely on his wife to review the bank statements and to balance the checkbooks.

[During June-September 1997, Suzan forged Mrs. Vowell's signature on forty-two checks and made nine unauthorized ATM withdrawals, in a total amount of $12,028.75. She found Mrs. Vowell's purse and stole the checkbooks and ATM card from it. While it is not clear from the opinion, she either had access to or otherwise guessed Dr.

---

[a] No, this is not a missing episode from AMC's *Breaking Bad*. Please ignore the faint resemblance and concentrate on the legal aspects of the situation.

Vowell's ATM personal identification number (PIN). (It was identical to the Vowells' home security-system code.)

[The first unauthorized banking transaction appeared on the June 1997 bank statement for the checking account, covering transactions occurring June 6 through July 7, 1997. It was sent to Dr. Vowell on July 9, 1997, and deemed by the trial court to be received July 11, 1997. This statement contained unauthorized payments totaling $230.00. The pattern quickly escalated over the following months – unauthorized payments totaling $1,235.25 in the July checking account statement, $5,140.00 in the July saving account statement, $1,423.50 in the August checking account statement, $4,000.00 in the August savings account statement.]

. . . The trial court specifically found that appellee did not notify appellant of the unauthorized transactions appearing on the June and July checking-account statements within thirty days from the date each was either sent or deemed received. Finally, on September 15, 1997, appellee discovered a receipt for an unauthorized credit-card transaction and notified appellant about his discovery at a meeting with Bill Eldridge, branch manager of appellant's Geyer Springs branch. Immediately, appellant froze appellee's and his wife's accounts, alerted its tellers and computer system, and began investigating the alleged forgeries and other unauthorized transactions pursuant to its policy.

As a result of the alert on appellee's account, Suzan was arrested on September 16, 1997, after she attempted to obtain an unauthorized cash advance at appellant's Riverfront branch. No more unauthorized transactions occurred after the alert was issued. Appellant prepared eight separate "Forged or Altered Check Affidavits of Loss," setting forth the forty-two forged checks and nine unauthorized ATM withdrawals. Appellee's wife signed the affidavits and Bill Eldridge notarized her signature on each affidavit.

Based on the facts before it, the trial court concluded that appellee and his wife "attempted to take proper precautions to safeguard their checkbooks, ATM cards and PIN" and that Dr. Vowell's conduct did not "substantially contribute to the forgeries and unauthorized transactions by Suzan Vowell which were paid in good faith by Firstar." Thus, the trial court determined that appellee was not precluded from asserting any of the forgeries and unauthorized transactions against appellant under Ark.Code Ann. § 4–3–406.

The trial court concluded, however, that appellee failed to exercise reasonable promptness in the examination and reporting of the forged checks and other unauthorized transactions on the June checking-account statement and the July checking-account statement. Therefore, the court found that appellee was precluded from asserting against appellant the forgeries contained on both of those checking-account statements. The trial court also found that appellee was entitled to an allocation of loss as between him and appellant. The trial court ordered appellant to pay $6,014.38, without going into any detailed explanation of how this allocation was calculated.

The trial court further found that appellant had not failed to exercise ordinary care and that it did not substantially contribute to the losses. Specifically, the court found that appellee was precluded from asserting against appellant the unauthorized payments in the June 1997 checking statement totaling $230.00, as well as the payments contained in the July 1997 checking statement totaling $1,235.25. . . .

Arkansas Code Annotated section 4–3–406

Appellant first argues that the trial court (1) erred in finding that appellee's conduct did not substantially contribute to the forgeries and unauthorized transactions, and (2) therefore erred in concluding that appellee was not precluded from asserting the forgeries and unauthorized transactions against appellant pursuant to Arkansas Code Annotated section 4–3–406. We find no error and affirm. . . .

Arkansas Code Annotated section 4–4–406(e)

For its second point of appeal, appellant contends that the trial court erred in its application of Arkansas Code Annotated section 4–4–406(e). We agree and point out that, generally, section 4–3–406 applies to a customer's conduct before a forgery and section 4–4–406 applies to a customer's conduct after a forgery. . . .

According to Arkansas Code Annotated section 4–4–406(e), if a bank customer can prove that the bank failed to exercise ordinary care in paying the forged item, even though the customer failed to exercise reasonable promptness in examining the bank statements, the loss is allocated between the bank and the customer according to the extent of the customer's failure to comply with the duties of § 4–4–406(c) and the bank's failure to exercise ordinary care in paying the item. In order to prove a bank's failure to exercise ordinary care, a customer must prove that the bank's conduct does not fall within the statutory definition of ordinary care, as found in Arkansas Code Annotated section 4–3–103(a)(7) [revised UCC § 3-103(a)(9)]. . . .

In the instant case, the trial court's findings contain no suggestion that appellant was negligent or otherwise failed to exercise ordinary care when it made the payments. To the contrary, the trial court specifically stated that the "Court does not find that Firstar failed to exercise ordinary care and that Firstar substantially contributed to the loss." For purposes of this issue, it is significant that appellant made its last payment pursuant to Suzan Vowell's unauthorized transactions and forgeries on September 4, 1997, eleven days before it received notification from appellee that there was a problem. Appellant could not have known that the transactions were the result of forgery or other unauthorized conduct. Subsection (e) requires proof that appellant failed to exercise ordinary care. Such proof was missing here, and therefore, we reverse the trial court's allocation of loss.

Arkansas Code Annotated section 4–4–406(d)(2)

The fact that appellant exercised ordinary care in paying the items presented to it does not resolve the question of whether appellee is precluded from asserting some or all of those items against appellant. Arkansas Code Annotated subsections 4–4–406(c) and (d) explain a customer's duties with respect to examining his or her bank statements and the consequences of failing to do so. [The court quotes the provisions, and proceeds to review and analyze the account statements in detail.]

Appellee is precluded from recovering on any of the items contained in the June and July checking account statements because of the thirty-day time limit contained in the customer-account agreement, which was quoted previously. According to the agreement, if the customer fails to examine his or her statement and notify the bank of any unauthorized transactions within thirty days of the date that the statement is deemed to be received, and the bank is not at fault, then the customer is precluded from recovery. . . . Appellee did not notify the bank until September 15, 1997, which was outside the agreed-upon time limits.

The terms of the customer-account agreement do not preclude appellee from recovering on the items contained in the other three bank statements, *i.e.,* the July savings, the August checking, and the August savings statements, because the bank was notified before thirty days had elapsed following the deemed-receipt dates of those statements, to wit September 24, October 11, and October 26, 1997.

However, the preclusion provision of Arkansas Code Annotated section 4–4–406(d)(2) does affect the July savings, the August checking, and the August savings statements because "the same wrongdoer," Suzan Vowell, was involved in all of the unauthorized transactions contained in these statements. This section precludes appellee from recovering on any unauthorized transactions that occurred after August 10, 1997, which is thirty days from the deemed receipt-date of the first statement, *i.e.,* the June checking account statement. This totally precludes appellee's recovery under the August checking and

the August savings statements. However, the July savings account statement contains seventeen items, some of which are precluded and some of which are not. The last ten items have transaction dates after August 10, 1997, and are therefore precluded. The first seven items, however, precede the August 10 date and are therefore not precluded.
. . .

These seven transactions total $1,725.

Allowing recovery for the items that the bank paid before August 10, 1997, but precluding recovery for those items that were paid after August 10 is in keeping with the purpose of section 4–4–406 [explaining that payment of an additional item by the same wrongdoer is a loss suffered by the bank traceable to the customer's failure to exercise reasonable care in examining statements and notifying the bank.]

Effect of the Customer–Account Agreements on Loss Apportionment

Appellant alternatively argues that the trial court erred in apportioning the loss between appellee and appellant pursuant to the Customer–Account Agreements. Generally, Arkansas Code Annotated section 4–4–103 (Repl.2001) permits certain changes from the requirements set forth in title 4, chapter 4 of the Arkansas Code by means of private agreements between banks and customers. However, in the instant case, we conclude that the language contained in the applicable provisions, quoted previously, does not substantially vary from the requirements under Arkansas Code Annotated section 4–4–406, but rather virtually tracks the statute's language. In addition, the trial court, when addressing that contractual argument below, expressly referred to its finding concerning the allocation of loss under Arkansas Code Annotated section 4–4–406(e), the one it had "previously noted." Therefore, we need not address this argument further because, as we have pointed out previously, we find no error in the trial court's findings of fact that appellee did not substantially contribute to the forgery, that appellant did not fail to use ordinary care in paying the forged items, and that appellee did fail to timely examine and report the forgeries reflected in the bank statements. Thus, there is no basis in this case for allocation under section 4–3–406, section 4–4–406, or the customer-account agreements.

WENDELL L. GRIFFEN, Judge, concurring.

I concur, because I agree in the outcome of this case, but write separately to express that I would have found additional error in the trial court's analysis of Ark.Code Ann. § 4–3–406—incidentally, a matter quite distinct from our analysis under Ark.Code Ann. § 4–4–

406(d)(2), with which I agree. Concerning the analysis under § 4–3–406, the trial court specifically found that appellee's conduct did not substantially contribute to the forgeries and unauthorized transactions even though the facts of the case, as reflected in the trial court's findings, appear to suggest otherwise, as I shall explain below. Thus, I disagree with the majority's view that there were not enough facts for the trial court to find that appellee failed to exercise ordinary care and substantially contributed to his daughter's unauthorized transactions and forgeries under the purview of Ark.Code Ann. § 4–3–406. . . .

Appellant correctly points out that Arkansas courts have not had many opportunities to provide guidance as to what constitutes negligence under Ark.Code Ann. § 4–3–406(a). The policy behind U.C.C. § 3–406, which is essentially what our State chose to codify under § 4–3–406, appears to be to shift the loss for negligence to the party who was in the best position to have prevented it. *Guardian Life Ins. Co. of America v. Chemical Bank*, 94 N.Y.2d 418, 705 N.Y.S.2d 553, 727 N.E.2d 111 (2000). Courts in other jurisdictions have concluded that the bank customer's failure to promptly discover and report a forgery or unauthorized transaction after it has occurred may also constitute negligence under U.C.C. § 3–406, even though such negligence does not directly contribute to the *making* of a forgery or an alteration. The rationale generally appears to be that such failure to report contributes to the making of subsequent forgeries. *See, e.g., Fundacion Museo de Arte Contemporaneo de Caracas—Sofia Imber v. CBI–TDB Union Bancaire Privee*, 996 F.Supp. 277 (S.D.N.Y.1998) (noting that customer's negligence in maintaining and controlling blank checks along with failure to advise bank of the first forgery substantially contributed to the loss); *Kramer v. Chase Manhattan Bank, N.A.*, 235 A.D.2d 371, 653 N.Y.S.2d 546 (1997) (holding that a bank should not be held responsible for losses caused by a customer's failure to safeguard his or her ATM card and PIN and to timely examine statements); *Gulf States Section, PGA, Inc. v. Whitney Nat'l Bank of New Orleans*, 689 So.2d 638 (La.1997) (finding that checks stolen from unsecured box under printer desk coupled with customer's failure to account for breaks in check numbering and failure to notice employee's substitution of forged account statements supported a finding of negligence on part of customer); *Five Towns College v. Citibank, N.A.*, 108 A.D.2d 420, 489 N.Y.S.2d 338 (1985) (finding that a prolonged delay by a customer in discovering and reporting a forgery may constitute negligence under § 3–406).

In light of this case law, I think we should hold that the trial court applied Ark.Code Ann. § 4–3–406 incorrectly. First, neither appellee, as plaintiff below, nor the trial court reasoned that appellant bank failed to exercise ordinary care in paying or taking the checks, pursuant to Ark.Code Ann. § 4–3–406(b). Second, there is ample evidence that appellee and his wife, as joint account holders, failed to exercise ordinary care and thus substantially contributed to the forgeries. In fact, the trial court found that appellee left the monitoring of all account activities to his very ill wife, that both he and his wife knew of the propensities of their daughter, and that their entire attempt to protect their check books consisted in hiding the purse and the books under the kitchen sink. In addition, appellee's PIN consisted of the same number used for his burglary alarm system, a fact that appears striking when one ostensibly tries to safeguard his ATM cards from unauthorized use by the daughter who is known to try to obtain any means possible to make unauthorized transactions—and when the ATM cards in question are hidden only within a purse under the kitchen sink. Finally, appellee failed to notify appellant of any problem until September 15, 1997. Appellant had no knowledge and, consequently, was unable to do anything about Suzan's forgeries and unauthorized transactions until that date solely because appellee and his wife failed to examine the bank statements and timely notify appellant about the unauthorized transactions that they reflected. Thus, appellee's conduct falls squarely under the scope of the cases cited *supra,* holding that a customer's failure to safeguard check books, cards, and PIN, can constitute failure to exercise ordinary care under U.C.C. § 3–406. . . .

ANDREE LAYTON ROAF, Judge, concurring in part and dissenting in part.

I would reverse this case because I do not believe that the appellee, John G. Vowell, is entitled to recover any of his losses from appellant Mercantile Bank of Arkansas with regard to the forged checks, and [I would] reverse and remand with respect to the unauthorized cash withdrawals. . . .

Accordingly, Vowell should be precluded from asserting his losses regarding any of the forged instruments against Mercantile Bank pursuant to § 4–3–406(a). Because the bank did not fail to exercise ordinary care, Vowell is not entitled to allocation of any of his losses pursuant to § 4–3–406(b). Moreover, there is no need to further consider the applicability of Ark.Code Ann. § 4–4–406 (Repl.2001) pertaining to Vowell's duty to discover and report any unauthorized signatures or alteration of instruments. This is because the two statutes are alternative in nature. . . .

It is clear to me that the Vowells' conduct before the forgery played a "substantial part" in making the deception possible. Consequently, Mercantile Bank should be absolved from any liability with regard to the forged checks, and I dissent from the majority's decision to the contrary.

However, the cash withdrawals that were accomplished using the Vowells's ATM card and pin number compel a different analysis. This is because such transfers are governed by federal law. Indeed, Ark.Code Ann. § 4–4A–108 (Repl.2001), "Exclusion of consumer transactions governed by federal law," provides:

> This chapter [Chapter 4][b] does not apply to a funds transfer any part of which is governed by the Electronic Fund Transfer Act of 1978 (Title XX, Public Law 95–630, 92 Stat. 3728, 15 U.S.C. 1693 et seq.) As [sic] amended from time to time.

15 U.S.C. § 1693a(6) defines "electronic fund transfer" as follows:

> [T]he term "electronic fund transfer" means any transfer of funds, other than a transaction originated by check, draft, or similar paper instrument, which is initiated through an electronic terminal, telephonic instrument, or computer or magnetic tape so as to order, instruct, or authorize a financial institution to debit or credit an account. Such term includes, but is not limited to, point-of-sale transfers, *automated teller machine transactions,* direct deposits or withdrawals of funds, and transfers initiated by telephone. (Emphasis added.)

Neither Vowell nor Mercantile Bank raised to the trial court the applicability of the federal statute to the cash withdrawals, and the trial court's judgment treats the forged checks and cash withdrawals alike in its analysis of Vowells's right to recover from the bank pursuant to Ark.Code Ann. §§ 4–3–406 and 4–4–406. Clearly, section 4–3–406 pertains to forged instruments and alteration of instruments only, and has no application to cash withdrawals, and section 4–4–406, contained in Chapter 4, excludes funds transfers from its purview.

This court may generally affirm the trial court where it has reached the right result for the wrong reason. *Jegley v. Picado,* 349

---

[b] Judge Roaf inserted this bracketed language into the quotation, not your editor. Notice anything wrong with this? *See* Question 5.8, *infra.* This confusion over the difference between UCC Article 4 and UCC Article 4A is apparently more common than one might expect. *See, e.g., Gilson v. TD Bank, N.A.,* --- F.Supp.2d ---, 2011 WL 294447 at *3 (S.D.Fla. 2011) (noting amendment of plaintiff's complaint substituting Article 4A claim for Article 4 claim).

Ark. 600, 80 S.W.3d 332 (2002). However, in this instance, it would be impossible to discern the "right result" without reviewing the federal statute. . . .

It is worth noting that there is no Arkansas appellate case construing this statute. However, at least one state court has held that a bank customer's failure to notify the bank of an initial unauthorized withdrawal of funds using the customer's ATM card releases the bank of liability for unauthorized transfers some months later. *Kruser v. Bank of America*, 230 Cal.App.3d 741, 281 Cal.Rptr. 463 (1991). In *Kruser,* the California Court of Appeal held that the customers were put on notice when the first transfer appeared on their bank statement, that the wife's illness did not excuse her failure to notify the bank of the unauthorized transfer, and that the husband's understanding that his wife would review the bank statements did not excuse him from the obligation to notify the bank of any such transfer. These facts are remarkably similar to the case before us.

Questions and Problems 5.6. In another part of his concurring opinion, Judge Griffen asks rhetorically, "If the facts in this case do not demonstrate failure to exercise ordinary care under section 4–3–406, what set of facts would ever do so?" *Mercantile Bank of Arkansas v. Vowell*, 117 S.W.3d at 443. Who is right on this point, the majority or Judge Griffin? did Dr. Vowell fail to exercise ordinary care under UCC § 3-406? What about under UCC § 4-406?

5.7. In a footnote elsewhere in its opinion, the majority explains:

> Judge Roaf's dissenting opinion mentions a federal statute that pertains to electronic-fund transfers, including ATM transactions, 15 U.S.C. § 1693 *et seq*. The applicability of this statute and the manner in which it affects this case were not raised before the trial court by either party below nor were they raised to this court on appeal. With no Arkansas appellate cases construing this statute and without the benefit of argument from counsel for the parties involved in this case, we decline to address the issue.

Mercantile Bank of Arkansas v. Vowell, 117 S.W.3d at 428 n.1. If the *Mercantile Bank* court *had* considered the effect of the EFTA on the ATM transactions in dispute – or had remanded to the lower court for such analysis – what would the likely outcome have been? (*See* 15 U.S.C. § 1693(g), which generally limits a customer's liability for unauthorized EFTs to the *lesser* of $50 or the amount of money obtained prior to the time the financial institution was notified of such unauthorized transfer.)

5.8. Judge Roaf argues that UCC §§ 3-406(b) and 4-406 do not apply to the ATM transactions because of UCC § 4A-108. He is, of course, screamingly wrong about this. Why? Could you still argue, however, that the outcome he favors would be correct – but for other legal reasons?

5.9. Both the majority and Judge Roaf are aware of the existence of Federal Reserve regulations that implement the EFTA. Since the enactment of the Dodd-Frank Act in 2010, most of these responsibilities have been reassigned to the Consumer Financial Protection Bureau, technically an office within the Federal Reserve. 15 U.S.C. § 1693b(a)(1). The Federal Reserve continues to regulate fees and rules for payment card transactions. 15 U.S.C. §§ 1693b(a)(2)(B),1693o-2. But what is the role of these regulations, and how much discretion does the Federal Reserve have in regulating fees? Consider the following case.

<h2 style="text-align:center">NACS V. BOARD OF GOVERNORS
OF FEDERAL RESERVE SYSTEM</h2>

746 F.3d 474 (D.C.Cir. 2014)
cert. denied, --- U.S. ---, 135 S.Ct. 1170 (2015)

TATEL, Circuit Judge:

[A lobbying trade association of convenience stores brought an action against the Board of Governors of the Federal Reserve System challenging final rule issued pursuant to the EFTA. The rule sets transaction interchange fees that debit card issuers can charge to merchants' banks and imposes network anti-exclusivity requirements. The district court granted summary judgment to the merchants, on the grounds that the Board had exceeded its statutory authority in promulgating the rule. The Board appealed the judgment.]

. . . Concerned that these fees were excessive and that merchants, who pay the fees directly, and consumers, who pay a portion of the fees indirectly in the form of higher prices, lacked any ability to resist them, Congress included a provision in the Dodd–Frank financial reform act[a] directing the Board of Governors of the Federal Reserve System to address this perceived market failure. In response, the Board issued regulations imposing a cap on the per-transaction fees banks receive and, in an effort to force networks to compete for merchants' business, requiring that at least two networks owned and operated by

---

[a] Dodd-Frank Wall Street Reform And Consumer Protection Act, Pub.L. 111-203, Title X, § 1075(a)(2), 124 Stat. 1376, 2068 (July 21, 2010) (codified at 15 USCA § 1693o-2).

different companies be able to process transactions on each debit card. . . . Applying traditional tools of statutory interpretation, we hold that the Board's rules generally rest on reasonable constructions of the statute, though we remand one minor issue—the Board's treatment of so-called transactions-monitoring costs—to the Board for further explanation. . . .

[The court's description of the EFT transaction and networks is excerpted at the beginning of this section of the casebook.]

Along the way, and central to this case, the parties charge each other various fees. The issuer charges the acquirer an "interchange fee," sometimes called a "swipe fee," which compensates the issuer for its role in processing the transaction. The network charges both the issuer and the acquirer "network processing fees," otherwise known as "switch fees," which compensate the network for its role in processing the transaction. Finally, the acquirer charges the merchant a "merchant discount," the difference between the transaction's face value and the amount the acquirer actually credits the merchant's account. Because the merchant discount includes the full value of the interchange fee, the acquirer's portion of the network processing fee, other acquirer and network costs, and a markup, merchants end up paying most of the costs acquirers and issuers incur. Merchants in turn pass some of these costs along to consumers in the form of higher prices. In contrast to credit card fees, which generally represent a set percentage of the value of a transaction, debit card fees change little as price increases. Thus, a bookstore might pay the same fees to sell a $25 hardcover that Mercedes would pay to sell a $75,000 car.

Before the Board promulgated the rules challenged in this case, networks and issuers took advantage of three quirks in the debit card market to increase fees without losing much business. First, issuers had complete discretion to decide whether to activate certain networks on their cards. For instance, an issuer could limit payment processing to one Visa signature network, a Visa signature network and a Visa PIN network, or Visa and MasterCard signature and PIN networks. Second, networks had complete discretion to set the level of interchange and network processing fees. Finally, Visa and MasterCard controlled most of the debit card market. According to one study entered into the record, in 2009 networks affiliated with Visa or MasterCard processed over eighty percent of all debit transactions. Steven C. Salop, et al., *Economic Analysis of Debit Card Regulation Under Section 920*, Paper for the Board of Governors of the Federal Reserve System 10 (Oct. 27, 2010). Making things worse for merchants, these companies imposed "Honor All Cards" rules that prohibited merchants from accepting some but not all of their credit cards and signature debit cards. Merchants were therefore stuck paying whatever fees Visa and MasterCard chose to set, unless they refused to accept any Visa and MasterCard credit and signature debit cards—hardly a realistic option for most merchants given the popularity of plastic.

Exercising this market power, issuers and networks often entered into mutually beneficial agreements under which issuers required merchants to route transactions on certain networks that generally charged high processing fees so long as those networks also set high interchange fees. Many of these agreements were exclusive, meaning that issuers agreed to activate only one network or only networks affiliated with one company. Networks and issuers also negotiated routing priority agreements, which forced merchants to process transactions on certain activated networks rather than others. By 2009, interchange and network processing fees had reached, on average, 55.5 cents per transaction, including a 44 cent interchange fee, a 6.5 cent network processing fee charged to the issuer, and a 5 cent network processing fee charged to the acquirer. Debit Card Interchange Fees and Routing, Notice of Proposed Rulemaking ("NPRM"), 75 Fed.Reg. 81,722, 81,725 (Dec. 28, 2010).

B.

Seeking to correct the market defects that were contributing to high and escalating fees, Congress passed the Durbin Amendment as part of the 2010 Dodd–Frank Wall Street Reform and Consumer Protection Act. . . . The amendment, which modified the Electronic Funds Transfer Act (EFTA), Pub.L. No. 95–630, 92 Stat. 3641 (1978), contains two key provisions. The first, EFTA section 920(a), restricts the amount of the interchange fee. Specifically, it instructs the Board of Governors of the Federal Reserve System to promulgate regulations ensuring that "the amount of any interchange transaction fee ... is reasonable and proportional to the cost incurred by the issuer with respect to the transaction." 15 U.S.C. § 1693o–2(a)(3)(A); *see also id.* § 1693o–2(a)(6)–(7)(A) (exempting debit cards issued by banks that, combined with all affiliates, have assets of less than $10 billion and debit cards affiliated with certain government payment programs from interchange fee regulations). To this end, section 920(a)(4)(B), in language the parties hotly debate, requires the Board to "distinguish between ... the incremental cost incurred by an issuer for the role of the issuer in the authorization, clearance, or settlement of a particular debit transaction, which cost shall be considered ..., [and] other costs incurred by an issuer which are not specific to a particular electronic debit transaction, which costs shall not be considered." *Id.* § 1693o–2(a)(4)(B)(i)–(ii). Like the parties, we shall refer to the costs of "authorization, clearance, and settlement" as "ACS costs." In addition, section 920(a) "allow[s] for an adjustment to the fee amount received or charged by an issuer" to compensate for "costs incurred by the issuer in preventing fraud in relation to electronic debit transactions involving that issuer," so long as the issuer "complies with the fraud-related standards established by the Board." *Id.* § 1693o–2(a)(5)(A).

The second key provision, EFTA section 920(b), prohibits certain exclusivity and routing priority agreements. Specifically, it instructs the Board to promulgate regulations preventing any "issuer or payment card network" from "restrict[ing] the number of payment card networks on which an electronic debit transaction may be processed to ... 1 such network; or ... 2 or more [affiliated networks]." *Id.* § 1693o–2(b)(1)(A). It also directs the Board to prescribe regulations that prohibit issuers and networks from "inhibit[ing] the ability of any person who accepts debit cards for payments to direct the routing of electronic debit transactions for processing over any payment card network that may process such transactions." *Id.* § 1693o–2(b)(1)(B). Congress anticipated that these prohibitions would force networks to compete for merchants' business, thus driving down fees.

C.

In late 2010, the Board proposed rules to implement sections 920(a) and (b). . . .

After evaluating thousands of comments, the Board issued a Final Rule that almost doubled the proposed cap [of, at most, 12 cents per transaction]. The Board abandoned its proposal to define "incremental" ACS costs to mean average variable ACS costs, deciding instead not to define the term "incremental costs" at all. Debit Card Interchange Fees and Routing, Final Rule ("Final Rule"), 76 Fed.Reg. 43,394, 43,426–27 (July 20, 2011) [(codified at 12 C.F.R. §§ 235.1-235.10; App. A)]. Observing that "the requirement that one set of costs be considered and another set of costs be excluded suggests that Congress left to the implementing agency discretion to consider costs that fall into neither category to the extent necessary and appropriate to fulfill the purposes of the statute," the Board allowed issuers to recover all costs "other than prohibited costs." *Id.* Thus, in addition to average variable ACS costs, issuers could recover: (1) what the proposed rule had referred to as "fixed" ACS costs; (2) costs issuers incur as a result of transactions-monitoring to prevent fraud; (3) fraud losses, which are costs issuers incur as a result of settling fraudulent transactions; and (4) network processing fees. *Id.* at 43,429–31. The Board prohibited issuers from recovering other costs, such as corporate overhead and debit card production and delivery costs, that the Board determined were not incurred to process specific transactions. *Id.* at 43,427–29. Accounting for all permissible costs, the Board raised the interchange fee cap to 21 cents plus an ad valorem component of 5 basis points (.05 percent of a transaction's value) to compensate issuers for fraud losses. *Id.* at 43,404.

[As to the unaffiliated networks requirement, the Board had proposed two possible alternative approaches. (A) Issuers would have to activate at least two unaffiliated networks on each debit card, regardless of method of authentication (PIN or signature). (B) Issuers would have to activate at least two unaffiliated networks for *each* method of authentication.]

In the Final Rule the Board chose Alternative A. Acknowledging that "Alternative A provides merchants fewer routing options," the Board reasoned that it satisfied statutory requirements and advanced Congress's desire to enhance competition among networks without excessively undermining the ability of cardholders to route transactions on their preferred networks or "potentially limit[ing] the development and introduction of new authentication methods." Final Rule, 76 Fed.Reg. at 43,448.

D.

. . . The merchants argued that both rules violate the plain terms of the Durbin Amendment: the interchange fee cap because the statute allows issuers to recover only average variable ACS costs, not "fixed" ACS costs, transactions-monitoring costs, fraud losses, or network processing fees; and the anti-exclusivity rule because the statute requires that all merchants—even those who refuse to accept PIN debit—be able to route each debit transaction on multiple unaffiliated networks. . . .

The district court granted summary judgment to the merchants. The court began by observing that "[a]ccording to the Board, [the statute contains] ambiguity that the Board has discretion to resolve. How convenient." NACS v. Board of Governors of the Federal Reserve System, 958 F.Supp.2d 85, 101 (D.D.C.2013). Rejecting this view, the district court determined that the Durbin Amendment is "clear with regard to what costs the Board may consider in setting the interchange fee standard: Incremental ACS costs of individual transactions incurred by issuers may be considered. That's it!" *Id.* at 105. The district court thus concluded that the Board had erred in allowing issuers to recover "fixed" ACS costs, transactions-monitoring costs, fraud losses, and network processing fees. *Id.* at 105–09. The court also agreed with the merchants that section 920(b) unambiguously requires that all merchants be able to route every transaction on at least two unaffiliated networks. *Id.* at 109–14. The Board's final anti-exclusivity rule, the district court held, "not only fails to carry out Congress's intention; it effectively countermands it!" *Id.* at 112. . . .

The Board now appeals, arguing that both rules rest on reasonable constructions of ambiguous statutory language. . . . Because the Board has sole discretion to administer the Durbin Amendment, we apply the familiar two-step framework set forth in *Chevron U.S.A. Inc. v. Natural Resources Defense Council, Inc.*, 467 U.S. 837, 104 S.Ct. 2778, 81 L.Ed.2d 694 (1984). At *Chevron*'s first step, we consider whether, as the district court concluded, Congress has "directly spoken to the precise question at issue." *Id.* at 842, 104 S.Ct. 2778. If not, we proceed to *Chevron*'s second step where we determine whether the Board's rules rest on "reasonable" interpretations of the Durbin Amendment. *Id.* at 844, 104 S.Ct. 2778. . . .

II.

. . .

The parties' competing arguments present us with two options. Were we to agree with the merchants that the statute allows recovery only of "incremental" ACS costs, we would have to invalidate the rule without considering the particular categories of costs the merchants challenge given that the Board expressly declined to define the ambiguous statutory term "incremental," let alone determine whether those particular types of costs qualify as "incremental" ACS costs. . . . Were we to determine that the Board's reading of section 920(a)(4)(B) is either compelled by the statute or reasonable, we would have to go on to consider whether the statute allows recovery of "fixed" ACS costs, transactions-monitoring costs, fraud losses, and network processing fees. We must therefore first decide whether section 920(a)(4)(B) bifurcates the entire universe of costs the Board may consider, or whether the statute allows for the existence of a third category of costs that falls outside the two categories specifically listed.

A.

The Board may well have been able to interpret section 920(a)(4)(B) as the merchants urge. Such a reading could rely on the statutory mandate to "distinguish between" one set of costs and "other costs," and could interpret section 920(a)(4)(B)(i) as referring to variable costs and section 920(a)(4)(B)(ii) as referring to fixed costs. But contrary to the merchants' position, and consistent with the Board's Chevron step two argument, we certainly see nothing in the statute's language compelling that result. The merchants' preferred reading requires assuming that the phrase "incremental cost incurred by the issuer for the role of the issuer in the authorization, clearance, and settlement of a particular electronic debit transaction" describes all issuer costs "specific to a particular electronic debit transaction." For several reasons, however, we believe that phrase could just as easily, if not more easily, be read to qualify the language of section 920(a)(4)(B)(i) such that it encompasses a subset of costs specific to a particular transaction, leaving other costs specific to a particular transaction unmentioned.

To begin with, as the Board pointed out in the Final Rule, the phrase "incremental cost" has a several possible definitions, including marginal cost, variable cost, "the cost of producing some increment of output greater than a single unit but less than the entire production run," and "the difference between the cost incurred by a firm if it produces a particular quantity of a good and the cost incurred by the firm if it does not produce the good at all." Final Rule, 76 Fed.Reg. at 43,426–27. As a result, depending on how these terms are defined, the category of "incremental" costs would not necessarily encompass all costs that are "specific to a particular electronic debit transaction." . . .

Second, the phrase "incurred by an issuer for the role of the issuer in the authorization, clearance, or settlement of a particular electronic debit transaction" limits the class of "incremental" costs the Board must consider. So even if the word "incremental" were read to include all costs specific to a particular transaction, Congress left unmentioned incremental costs other than incremental ACS costs. See Final Rule, 76 Fed.Reg. at 43,426 n. 116 ("The reference in Section 920(a)(4)(B)(i) requiring consideration of the incremental costs incurred in the 'authorization, clearance, or settlement of a particular transaction' and the reference in section 920(a)(4)(B)(ii) prohibiting consideration of costs that are 'not specific to a particular electronic debit transaction,' read together, recognize that there may be costs that are specific to a particular electronic debit transaction that are not incurred in the authorization, clearance, or settlement of that transaction."). For example, in the proposed rule the Board determined that "cardholder rewards that are paid by the issuer to the cardholder for each transaction" and "costs associated with providing customer service to cardholders for particular transactions" are "associated with a particular transaction" but "are not incurred by the issuer for its role in authorization, clearing, and settlement of that transaction." NPRM, 75 Fed.Reg. at 81,735. Moreover, in the Final Rule the Board explained that fraud losses "are specific to a particular transaction" because they result from the settlement of particular fraudulent transactions, but are not incurred by the issuer for the role of the issuer in the authorization, clearance, or settlement of particular transactions. Final Rule, 76 Fed.Reg. at 43,431 (describing fraud losses as "the result of an issuer's authorization, clearance, or settlement of a particular electronic debit transaction that the cardholder later identifies as fraudulent"); see also Appellant's Br. 67 (defending the Board's decision to allow issuers to recover some fraud losses on the ground that fraud losses fall outside section 920(a)(4)(B)).

Third, as the Board pointed out, had Congress wanted to allow issuers to recover only incremental ACS costs, it could have done so directly. . . . Instead, in section 920(a)(3)(A) Congress required the Board to promulgate regulations ensuring that interchange fees are "reasonable and proportional to the cost incurred by the issuer with respect to the transaction" and separately instructed the Board, when determining issuer costs, to "distinguish between" incremental ACS costs, which the Board must consider, 15 U.S.C. § 1693o–2(a)(4)(B)(i), and "other costs ... which are not specific to a particular electronic debit transaction," which the Board must not consider, *id.* § 1693o-2(a)(4)(B) (ii). . . .

. . . Here, Congress introduced the clause at issue with the word "which" but failed to set it aside with commas. Word choice thus suggests a descriptive reading of the clause [explaining the term, not limiting it], while punctuation suggests a restrictive reading [defining the term and limiting it as such]. . . .

In this instance, the absence of commas matters far more than Congress's use of the word "which" rather than "that." Widely-respected style guides expressly require that commas set off descriptive clauses, but refer to descriptive "which" and restrictive "that" as a style preference rather than an ironclad grammatical rule. . . .

Next, the merchants assert that the Board, by inferring the existence of a third category of costs, improperly reads a delegation of authority into congressional silence. . . . But section 920(a)(3)(A) clearly grants the Board authority to promulgate regulations ensuring that interchange fees are reasonable and proportional to costs issuers incur. The question then is how section 920(a)(4)(B) limits the Board's discretion to define the statutory term "cost incurred by the issuer with respect to the transaction," not whether that section affirmatively grants the Board authority to allow issuers to recover certain costs. . . .

Given the Durbin Amendment's ambiguity as to the existence of a third category of costs, we must defer to the Board's reasonable determination that the statute splits costs into three categories: (1) incremental ACS costs, which the Board must allow issuers to recover; (2) costs specific to a particular transaction, other than incremental ACS costs, which the Board may, but need not, allow issuers to recover; and (3) costs not specific to a particular transaction, which the Board may not allow issuers to recover. . . .

B.

Because the Board reasonably interpreted the Durbin Amendment as allowing issuers to recover some costs in addition to incremental ACS costs, we must now determine whether the Board reasonably concluded that issuers can recover the four specific types of costs the merchants challenge: "fixed" ACS costs, network processing fees, fraud losses, and transactions-monitoring costs. Much like agency ratemaking, determining whether issuers or merchants should bear certain costs is "far from an exact science and involves policy determinations in which the [Board] is acknowledged to have expertise." *Time Warner Entertainment Co. v. Federal Communications Commission*, 56 F.3d 151, 163 (D.C.Cir.1995) (internal quotation marks omitted). We afford agencies special deference when they make these sorts of determinations. See, e.g., *BNSF Railway Co. v. Surface Transportation Board*, 526 F.3d 770, 774 (D.C.Cir.2008) ("In the rate-making area, our review is particularly deferential, as the Board is the expert body Congress has designated to weigh the many factors at issue when assessing whether a rate is just and reasonable."); *Time Warner*, 56 F.3d at 163. With that caution in mind, we address each category of costs.

"Fixed" ACS Costs

Microeconomics textbooks draw a clear distinction between "fixed" and "variable" costs: fixed costs are incurred regardless of transaction volume, whereas variable costs change as transaction volume increases. *E.g.*, N. GREGORY MANKIW, PRINCIPLES OF MICROECONOMICS 276–77 (3d ed.2004). . . .

We think the Board reasonably declined to read section 920(a)(4)(B) as preventing issuers from recovering "fixed" costs. As the Board pointed out, the distinction the merchants urge between what they refer to as non-includable "fixed" costs and includable "variable" costs depends entirely on whether, on an issuer-by-issuer basis, certain costs happen to vary based on transaction volume in a particular year. For example, in any given year one issuer might classify labor as an includable cost because labor costs happened to vary based on transaction volume over that year, while another issuer might classify labor as a non-includable cost because such costs happened to remain fixed over that year. . . . Moreover, the Board pointed out, the distinction between variable and fixed ACS costs depends in some instances on whether an issuer "performs its transactions processing in-house" or "outsource[s] its debit card operations to a third-party processor that charge[s] issuers a per-transaction fee based on its entire cost." . ... In any event, the Board concluded, requiring issuers to segregate includable "variable" costs from excludable "fixed" costs on a year-by-year basis would prove "exceedingly difficult for issuers ... [because] even if a clear line could be drawn between an issuer's costs that are variable and those that are fixed, issuers' cost-accounting systems are not generally set up to differentiate between fixed and variable costs." ... The Board therefore determined that any distinction between fixed and variable costs would prove artificial and unworkable.

Instead, pointing out that the statute requires interchange fees to be "reasonable and proportional" to issuer costs, the Board interpreted section 920(a)(4)(B) as allowing issuers to recover costs they must incur in order to effectuate particular electronic debit card transactions but precluding them from recovering other costs too remote from the processing of actual transactions. . . . In our view, the Board reasonably distinguished between costs issuers could recover and those they could not recover on the basis of whether those costs are "incurred in the course of effecting" transactions. . . .

Network Processing Fees

This is easy. Network processing fees, which issuers pay on a per-transaction basis, are obviously specific to particular transactions. ...

Fraud Losses

The merchants nowhere challenge the Board's conclusion that fraud losses, which result from the settlement of particular fraudulent transactions, are specific to those transactions. The only question is whether a separate provision of the Durbin Amendment—section 920(a)(5)'s fraud-prevention adjustment, which allows issuers to recover fraud-prevention costs if those issuers comply with the Board's fraud-prevention standards—precludes the Board from allowing issuers to recover fraud losses as part of section 920(a)(2)'s "reasonable and proportional" interchange fee. The merchants claim that it does. ...

. . . The Board determined—reasonably in our view—that because fraud losses result from the failure of fraud-prevention, they do not themselves qualify as fraud-prevention costs. . . .

. . . Even assuming the merchants' policy argument has some merit—allowing recovery of fraud losses regardless of compliance with fraud-prevention standards might well decrease issuers' incentives to invest in fraud prevention—the Board rejected it, reasoning that "[i]ssuers will continue to bear the cost of some fraud losses and cardholders will continue to demand protection against fraud." . . . Such policy judgments are the province of the Board, not this Court. . . .

Transactions–Monitoring Costs

The Board acknowledged in the Final Rule that transactions-monitoring costs, unlike fraud losses, are the paradigmatic example of fraud-prevention costs. . . . The Board then distinguished between "[t]ransactions monitoring systems [that] assist in the authorization process by providing information to the issuer before the issuer decides to approve or decline the transaction," which the Board placed outside the fraud-prevention adjustment, and "fraud-prevention activities ... that prevent fraud with respect to transactions at times other than when the issuer is effecting the transaction"—for instance the cost of sending "cardholder alerts ... inquir[ing] about suspicious activity"—which the Board determined should be "considered in connection with the fraud-prevention adjustment." . . .

As an initial matter, we agree with the Board that transactions-monitoring costs can reasonably qualify both as costs "specific to a particular ... transaction" (section 920(a)(4)(B)) and as fraud-prevention costs (section 920(a)(5)). Thus, the Board may have discretion either to allow issuers to recover transactions-monitoring costs through the interchange fee regardless of compliance with fraud-prevention standards or to preclude issuers from recovering transactions-monitoring costs unless those issuers comply with fraud-prevention standards. That said, "an agency must cogently explain why it has exercised its discretion in a given manner." *Motor Vehicle Manufacturers Association of the United States v. State Farm Mutual Automobile Insurance Co.*, 463 U.S. 29, 48, 103 S.Ct. 2856, 77 L.Ed.2d 443 (1983). We agree with the merchants that the Board has fallen short of that standard. . . .

[T]the Board may well be able to articulate a reasonable justification for determining that transactions-monitoring costs properly fall outside the fraud-prevention adjustment. But the Board has yet to do so. . . .

III.

Having resolved the merchants' challenges to the interchange fee rule, we turn to the anti-exclusivity rule. . . .

The merchants believe that the Durbin Amendment unambiguously requires that all merchants have multiple unaffiliated network routing options for each debit transaction. . . . [W]e must determine whether the statute requires that all merchants—even those who voluntarily choose not to accept PIN debit—have the ability to decide between unaffiliated networks when routing transactions.

The merchants have a steep hill to climb. Congress directed the Board to issue rules that would accomplish a particular objective, leaving it to the Board to decide how best to do so, and the Board's rule seems to comply perfectly with Congress's command. Under the rule, "issuer[s] and payment card network[s]" cannot "restrict the number of payment card networks on which an electronic debit transaction may be processed" to only affiliated networks—exactly what the statute requires. 15 U.S.C. § 1693o–2(b)(1)(A). . . .

. . . Given that the Board's rule advances the Durbin Amendment's purpose, we decline to second-guess its reasoned decision to reject an alternative option that might have further advanced that purpose. . . .

In sum, far from summiting the steep hill, the merchants have barely left basecamp. We therefore defer to the Board's reasonable interpretation of section 920(b) and reject the merchants' challenges to the anti-exclusivity rule.

C. WIRE TRANSFERS

UCC Article 4A provides the rules for a specialized payment method as a "funds transfer,"[19] but known in commercial practice as a wholesale "wire transfer." This terminology may be somewhat confusing, since the EFTs that we discussed in the last section are "funds transfers" as well, but they are not covered by Article 4A.[20] A funds transfer governed by Article4A is made by means of a "payment order."[21] The funds transfer follows a pattern that may seem similar to

---

[19] For purposes of Article 4A, the term *funds transfer* is defined to mean

> the series of transactions, beginning with the originator's payment order, made for the purpose of making payment to the beneficiary of the order. The term includes any payment order issued by the originator's bank or an intermediary bank intended to carry out the originator's payment order. A funds transfer is completed by acceptance by the beneficiary's bank of a payment order for the benefit of the beneficiary of the originator's payment order.

UCC § 4A-104(a).

[20] *See* UCC § 4A-108(a) (excluding from Article 4A any funds transfer governed by EFTA). *Cf.* Problem 5.8, *supra* (discussing § 4A-108).

[21] The term *payment order* is defined to mean

> an instruction of a sender to a receiving bank, transmitted orally, electronically, or in writing, to pay, or to cause another bank to pay, a fixed or determinable amount of money to a beneficiary if:
> (i) the instruction does not state a condition to payment to the beneficiary other than time of payment,
> (ii) the receiving bank is to be reimbursed by debiting an account of, or otherwise receiving payment from, the sender, and

that of a letter of credit,[22] but in fact it follows its own, distinctly linear pattern. (*See* the illustration *infra*.)

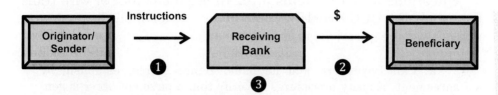

① Originator/sender transmits payment instruction to receiving bank. (There may be other intermediate senders and receiving banks)
② Receiving bank pays (or causes another, intermediate bank to pay) fixed or determinable amount of money to beneficiary
③ Receiving bank debits sender's account or receives payment from sender

Typical Wire Transfer

Prior to Article 4A, there was no comprehensive body of law that defined the nature or formal requirements of a wire transfer or the rights and obligations pertaining to them. Wire transfers were largely governed by practice and custom among participants, with some improvisation of contract and commercial law analogies to handle any unresolved disputes.[23] Even under Article 4A, and unlike negotiable instruments, the instruction of the sender to the receiving bank does not require any particular documentation; it can be oral, electronic, or in writing.[24] As with negotiable instruments, however, the instruction should not be subject to any condition for payment to the beneficiary except for time of payment.[25] For the most part, the rules contained in

---

    (iii) the instruction is transmitted by the sender directly to the receiving bank or to an agent, funds-transfer system, or communication system for transmittal to the receiving bank.

UCC § 103(a)(1)(i)-(iii).

    [22] *See* figure, *supra* at 260 (representing pattern of letter of credit payment).

    [23] On the mechanics of wire transfers and the role of Article 4A, see generally *Delbrueck & Co. v. Manufacturers Hanover Trust Co.*, 609 F.2d 1047, 1048 n. 1 (2d Cir. 1979); *Sheerbonnet, Ltd. v. American Express Bank, Ltd.*, 951 F.Supp. 403, 406–07 (S.D.N.Y. 1995); *Banque Worms v. BankAmerica Int'l*, 77 N.Y.2d 362, 568 N.Y.S.2d 541, 570 N.E.2d 189 (1991).

    [24] UCC § 4A-103(a)(1).
    [25] UCC § 4A-103(a)(1)(i).

Article 4A try to balance the competing interests and expectations of senders and beneficiaries and of receiving banks.

Questions and Problems 5.10. To begin our tour of wire transfers, study the UCC Article 4A road map[26] set forth on the next page, and answer the questions that follow.

a. Can BayerCorp and its bank, Banco Merca, establish, by agreement, security procedures to verify that a payment order is genuine? If so, what kind of procedures? (*See* UCC § 4A-201.)

b. How is a transfer authorized and how is it verified as an order authorized by BayerCorp? (*See* UCC §§ 4A-202, 4A-203.)

c. If there is an unauthorized payment order, what is the receiving bank's responsibility? What is the BayerCorp's responsibility? (*See* UCC § 4A-204.)

d. If there is an authorized payment order, but it is erroneously accepted or paid by Banco Merca, who bears the risk of loss from the error, the bank or BayerCorp? (*See* UCC § 4A-205.) What if Banco Merca erroneously pays the wrong amount to the right beneficiary? (*See* UCC § 4A-303.) What is BayerCorp's responsibility in this situation? (*See* UCC § 4A-304.)

e. If a funds-transfer system or other third-party communication system is used to transmit BayerCorp's order to Banco Merca, and an error or discrepancy occurs, is the bank or the customer responsible for the risk of loss from the error? (*See* UCC § 4A-206.)

f. BayerCorp gives Banco Merca a payment order to transmit $100,000 to the account of SellerCorp at Issuer Bank, but it had intended the payment for SallerCo. If Issuer Bank credits SellerCorp's account, who is responsible for the misdirected payment? (*See* UCC § 4A-207.) What are Banco Merca's responsibilities once it accepts the payment order? Has it "executed" the order? Has Issuer Bank? (*See* UCC §§ 4A-301, 4A-302, 4A-305.)

g. What if BayerCorp got SallerCo's name right, but transmitted the payment order to Banco Marcoa instead of Banco Merca? (*See* UCC § 4A-208.)

h. In the course of any of these preceding transactions, when is it that the receiving bank has accepted the payment order? Has rejected the payment order? When is it liable for the value of the payment order? (*See* UCC §§ 4A-209, 4A-210, 4A-212.)

i. Having discovered the error in its payment order in the situation in **f.** or **g.**, *supra*, can BayerCorp personnel telephone to the bank and cancel the payment order effectively? (*See* UCC § 4A-211.)

---

[26] At this late date, still the most useful introduction to Article 4A is Ernest T. Patrikis, Thomas C. Baxter, Jr. & Raj Bhala, *Article 4A: The new law of funds transfers and the role of counsel*, 23 UCC L.J. 219 (1991).

j. Payment is a separate event from accepting or executing. When would BayerCorp be obligated to pay Banco Merca for the payment order in favor of SallerCo? (*See* UCC §§ 4A-401, 4A-402, 4A-403.)

k. When Issuer Bank accepts the payment order from Banco Merca, what is its responsibility to SallerCo? (See UCC §§ 4A-404, 4A-405.)

l. Once Issuer Bank credits SallerCo's account with the wire transfer, is BayerCorp's contractual obligations to SallerCo discharged? (*See* UCC § 4A-406.)

5.11. Assume that BayerCorp instructs Issuer Bank to pay SallerCo $100,000 dollars through SallerCo's account at Banco Merca, and debit its account at Issuer Bank for the transfer. Under Article 4A terminology, what is BayerCorp? What is Issuer Bank? SallerCo? Banco Merca?

5.12. How exclusive is the wire transfer payment system? In the wire transfer situation described in the last problem, could Issuer Bank ignore the instruction and debit BayerCorp's account for an outstanding, unrelated loan that has not been repaid to the bank? In answering the question, consider the case beginning on page 339.

FFTA ROAD MAP

WIRE TRANSFER ROAD MAP

ISSUE & ACCEPTANCE

§ 4A-201
Security procedure

§ 4A-202
Authorization & verification

§ 4A-203
Unenforceable but verified payment

§ 4A-204
Refund & duty to report

§ 4A-205
Erroneous payment order

§ 4A-206
Funds-transfer or other communication system

§ 4A-207
Misdescribed beneficiary

§ 4A-208
Misdescribed intermediary or beneficiary bank

§ 4A-209
Acceptance of payment order

§ 4A-210
Rejection of payment order

§ 4A-211
Cancellation and amendment of payment order

§ 4A-212
Liability of Receiving bank

EXECUTION OF ORDER

§ 4A-301
Execution & execution date

§ 4A-302
Obligation of receiving bank

§ 4A-303
Erroneous execution of payment order

§ 4A-304
Duty of sender

§ 4A-305
Liability for late or improper execution

PAYMENT

§ 4A-401
Payment date

§ 4A-402
Obligation of sender to pay receiving bank

§ 4A-403
Payment by sender to receiving bank

§ 4A-404
Obligation of beneficiary's bank to pay and give notice to beneficiary

§ 4A-405
Payment by beneficiary's bank to beneficiary

§ 4A-406
Payment by originator to beneficiary discharge of underlying obligation

■ **MISCELLANEOUS PROVISIONS**

§ 4A-501 Variation by agreement and effect of funds-transfer system rule

§ 4A-502 Creditor process served, setoff by beneficiary's bank

§ 4A-503 Injunction or restraining order with respect to funds transfer

§ 4A-504 Order of charges to and withdrawals from account

§ 4A-505 Preclusion of objection to debit of customer's account

§ 4A-506 Rate of interest

§ 4A-507 Choice of law

BANCO DE LA PROVINCIA DE BUENOS AIRES
V. BAYBANK BOSTON N.A.
985 F.Supp. 364 (S.D.N.Y. 1997)

ROBERT J. WARD, District Judge.

[Banco de la Provincia (BP) made a loan to Banco Feigin (BF), both Argentine banks, and the loan proceeds were credited to BF's account maintained at BP's New York branch. BF was failing, and it instructed BP to transfer funds from the account to an account at BayBank. BP disregarded the instructions and applied the funds to pay BF's debt to BP. BP then sought declaratory relief against BayBank's claim to the funds.]

Disputes arising from wire transfers are now governed by Article 4A of the Uniform Commercial Code. Article 4A was enacted in the wake of technological advances allowing the electronic transfer of funds, a means by which up to a trillion dollars is shifted daily. *Sheerbonnet, Ltd. v. American Express Bank, Ltd.*, 951 F.Supp. 403, 407 n. 1 (S.D.N.Y.1995). At the time Article 4A was drafted, "there was no comprehensive body of law-statutory or judicial-that defined the juridical nature of a funds transfer or the rights and obligations flowing from payment orders." N.Y. U.C.C. § 4-A-102, Official Comment, p. 559. The statute reflects "[a] deliberate decision ... to use precise and detailed rules to assign responsibility, define behavioral norms, allocate risks and establish limits on liability, rather than to rely on broadly stated, flexible principles." *Id.*

The electronic transfer of funds is accomplished through the use of one or more payment orders. A payment order is sent by the "sender" to the "receiving bank," for ultimate payment to the "beneficiary" or the "beneficiary's bank." In the instant case, Banco Feigin is both the sender and the beneficiary, BPBA is the receiving bank, and BayBank is the beneficiary's bank. The first step in a funds transfer is the sender's transmission of a payment order to a receiving bank. Before the transfer proceeds, the receiving bank must accept the sender's payment order.

A. BPBA properly rejected the payment order under
    N.Y. U.C.C. § 4-A-209(1)

Under § 4-A-209(1), "a receiving bank other than the beneficiary's bank accepts a payment order when it executes the order." This provision has been interpreted to give receiving banks other than the beneficiary's bank general discretion in choosing whether to accept or reject payment orders. *Sheerbonnet*, 951 F.Supp. at 413. BPBA contends that its refusal to execute the payment order constituted a rejection of the payment order that was within its discretion.

According to BayBank, BPBA does not have absolute discretion in deciding whether to accept or reject payment orders.[3] . . .

In examining the circumstances under which BPBA rejected the payment order, however, it becomes clear that BPBA's rejection was neither an abuse of discretion nor in bad faith. At the time BPBA rejected the payment order, Banco Feigin's BPBA account—which consisted solely of proceeds of BPBA's January 1995 loan to Banco Feigin—was under an administrative freeze, and Banco Feigin's banking activities had been suspended as part of an Intervention by the Central Bank of Argentina. . . . . BPBA knew that the Intervention gave it an immediate right of set-off under N.Y. Debt. and Cred. Law § 151. Moreover, Banco Feigin's debt to BPBA exceeded the balance in the account. Under those circumstances, it was not unreasonable for BPBA to refuse to wire the entire balance of the account to Banco Feigin's BayBank account. Therefore, BPBA's rejection of the payment order was a proper exercise of its discretion under § 4-A-209.

B. Since BPBA properly rejected the payment order, it incurred
no duty to Banco Feigin or BayBank

Liability of receiving banks arises only if the receiving bank accepts a payment order, or if there is an express agreement between the sender and the receiving bank which requires the receiving bank to execute payment orders. [The court quotes UCC § 4A-212, concerning the obligation of a receiving bank under an express agreement to accept instructions.]

BPBA incurred no liability since there was no acceptance under § 4-A-209 and there was no agreement between BPBA and Banco Feigin requiring BPBA to accept the payment order. . . .

---

[3] BayBank also argues that "the critical issue in this litigation ... is whether BPBA acted in bad faith in failing to accept the payment order." . . . There is no support, however, for the imposition of such a good faith obligation. BayBank cites *dicta* in *Sheerbonnet, Ltd. v. American Express Bank, Ltd.,* . . . for the proposition that a bank acts in bad faith by retaining a debtor's funds to use as a set-off. In *Sheerbonnet*, however, the district court merely denied a motion to dismiss, holding that Article 4A was not exclusive, and that the plaintiff in that case had stated a prima facie claim for conversion. The court did not hold that AEB had acted in bad faith, but merely observed that AEB had at least been in a position to unfairly capitalize on the seizure of one of the intermediary banks in that funds transfer. *Sheerbonnet*, 951 F.Supp. at 413

Questions and Problems 5.13. As in Problem **5.11.**, assume that BayerCorp instructs Issuer Bank to transfer $100,000 to Inter-Media Bank with instructions that InterMedia transfer those funds to SallerCo's account at Banco Merca, and debit its account at Issuer Bank for the transfer. Issuer Bank makes the transfer to InterMedia Bank with the indicated instructions, but in the meantime, Banco Merca has failed and has been placed in receivership. BayerCorp has asked Issuer Bank to cancel the transfer and reverse the debit to its account. Unfortunately, InterMedia Bank has seized the funds to settle an outstanding indebtedness that SallerCo owes. Does BayerCorp, as sender, have a viable cause of action against InterMedia Bank under Article 4A in these circumstances? Under the common law? In answering the question, consider the following case.

GRAIN TRADERS, INC. V. CITIBANK, N.A.
160 F.3d 97 (2d Cir. 1998)

JOHN M. WALKER, Jr., Circuit Judge.

Grain Traders, in order to make a payment of $310,000 to Claudio Goidanich Kraemer ("Kraemer"), initiated a funds transfer on December 22, 1994, by issuing a payment order to its bank, Banco de Credito Nacional ("BCN"), that stated

> WE HEREBY AUTHORIZE YOU DEBIT OUR ACCOUNT NR.509364 FOR THE AMOUNT OF US $ 310,000.00 AND TRANSFER TO:
> BANQUE DU CREDIT ET INVESTISSEMENT LTD. ACCOUNT 36013997 AT CITIBANK NEW YORK IN FAVOUR OF BANCO EX-TRADER S.A. ACCOUNT NR. 30114—BENEFICIARY CLAUDIO GOIDANICH KRAEMER—UNDER FAX ADVISE TO BANCO EX-TRADER NR. 00541–318 0057/318–0184 AT. DISTEFANO/M. FLIGUEIRA.

Thus the transfer, as instructed by Grain Traders, required BCN to debit Grain Traders's account at BCN in the amount of $310,000, and then to issue a payment order to Citibank. That payment order, in turn, was to require Citibank to debit $310,000 from BCN's account at Citibank and to credit that amount to the account that Banque du Credit et Investissement Ltd. ("BCIL") maintained at Citibank. Citibank, in turn, was to issue a payment order to BCIL instructing it to transfer, by unspecified means, $310,000 to Banco Extrader, S.A.

("Extrader"). Extrader was then to credit the $310,000 to the account maintained at Extrader by Kraemer.

BCN duly carried out Grain Traders's instructions. Citibank, in turn, executed BCN's payment order by debiting $310,000 from BCN's account at Citibank, crediting that amount to BCIL's account at Citibank, and issuing a payment order to BCIL concerning the further transfers.

Both BCIL and Extrader suspended payments at some point after Citibank executed the payment order. BCIL apparently began closing its offices on December 31, 1994, and its banking license was revoked in July of 1995. Similarly, Extrader became insolvent sometime in late December of 1994 or early January of 1995. On December 28, 1994, apparently at Grain Traders's request, BCN contacted Citibank and requested cancellation of its payment order and return of the amount of the payment order. . . .

Citibank sought authorization from BCIL to debit the amount that had been credited to its account on December 22, 1994, and, after several unsuccessful attempts to contact BCIL, received a message on January 3, 1995, from BCIL that purportedly authorized the debit. Citibank asserts that it was at this juncture that it determined that BCIL had exceeded its credit limitations and placed the account on a "debit no-post" status, meaning no further debits would be posted to the account. Citibank refused BCN's request to cancel the payment order, stating:

> RE: YOUR PAYMENT [ORDER] ... WE ARE UNABLE TO RETURN FUNDS AS BNF [SIC] BANK HAS AN INSUFFICIENT BALANCE IN THEIR ACCOUNT. FOR FURTHER INFORMATION WE SUGGEST THAT YOU CONTACT THEM DIRECTLY. WE CLOSE OUR FILE.

In November of 1995, Grain Traders filed this action seeking a refund from Citibank pursuant to U.C.C. §§ 4–A–402(4), 4–A–209, 4–A–301, 4–A–305, and 1–203, as well as common law theories of conversion and money had and received. Grain Traders alleges that the transfer was never completed—i.e., Extrader never credited Kraemer's account for the $310,000. Grain Traders further claims that the reason the transfer was not completed was because Citibank had already placed BCIL's account on a "hold for funds" status before it credited the $310,000 intended for Kraemer to BCIL's account. By making the credit to BCIL's allegedly frozen account, Grain Traders contends, Citibank improperly used the funds to offset BCIL's indebtedness to it and prevented BCIL from withdrawing the funds to complete the transfer.

. . . The district court denied summary judgment to Grain Traders and granted summary judgment in favor of Citibank. Grain Traders now appeals.

DISCUSSION

In its opinion, the district court held that (1) Section 402 of Article 4–A established a cause of action only by a sender against its receiving bank, thus Grain Traders, who was a sender only with respect to BCN, had sued the wrong bank; (2) Sections 4–A–209, 4–A–301, 4–A–305, and 1–203 of the U.C.C. did not create causes of action; and (3) Grain Traders could not establish elements necessary to its common law claims of conversion and money had and received. . . . For the following reasons, we affirm the district court's judgment.

II. Article 4–A Claims

Article 4–A of the U.C.C. governs the procedures, rights, and liabilities arising out of commercial electronic funds transfers. . . .

. . . [A]s noted by the district court, "funds are 'transferred' through a series of debits and credits to a series of bank accounts." . . . For any given funds transfer, there can be only one originator, originator's bank, beneficiary, and beneficiary's bank, but there can be several senders and receiving banks, one of each for every payment order required to complete the funds transfer. See N.Y.U.C.C. § 4–A–103.

1. Grain Traders's Refund Claim under § 4–A–402

Section 4–A–402 ("Section 402") covers the obligation of a sender of a payment order to make payment to the receiving bank after the order has been accepted as well as the obligation of a receiving bank to refund payment in the event the transfer is not completed. . . .

. . . Thus, under Section 402(3), the sender's obligation to pay the receiving bank is excused in the event that the transfer is not completed. If payment has already been made, a sender can seek a refund from the bank it paid under Section 402(4). It was this so-called "money-back guarantee" provision that Grain Traders invoked to obtain a refund from Citibank.

The district court held that Grain Traders's refund action against Citibank, an intermediary bank for the purposes of Grain Traders's funds transfer, was barred because a Section 402 refund action could only be maintained by a "sender" against the receiving bank to whom the sender had issued a payment order and whom the sender had paid. Thus, because Grain Traders was a "sender" only with respect to the payment order it issued to BCN, Grain Traders could look only to BCN, the receiving bank, for a refund.

In reaching its conclusion, the district court relied on the plain language of Section 402(4) as well as other provisions of Article 4–A. It found that the language of Section 402(4) establishes a right of refund only between a sender and the receiving bank it paid. BCN, not Grain Traders, was the sender that issued the payment order to Citibank and paid Citibank by having its account debited in the amount of $310,000. Grain Traders argues that the fact that Section 402(4) does not use the words "receiving bank" but instead refers to "the bank receiving payment" means that the sender can sue any bank in the chain that received payment. We agree with Citibank that because the words "receiving bank" are defined as the bank that receives a payment order, Section 402(4)'s use of the words "bank receiving payment" simply clarifies that the right to a refund arises only after the sender has satisfied its obligation to pay the receiving bank. . . .

The district court also relied on the express right of subrogation created by Section 402(5), which applies when one of the receiving banks is unable to issue a refund because it has suspended payments. . . .

Where a right to refund has been triggered because a transfer was not completed, but one of the banks that received payment is unable to issue a refund because it has suspended payments, the orderly unraveling of the transfer is prevented and the risk of loss will be borne by some party to the transfer. Article 4–A allocates that risk of loss to the party that first designated the failed bank to be used in the transfer. See N.Y.U.C.C. § 4–A–402, cmt. 2 (where "Bank A [the sender] was required to issue its payment order to Bank C [the insolvent bank] because Bank C was designated as an intermediary bank by Originator[,].... Originator takes the risk of insolvency of Bank C"). Under Section 402(5), all intervening senders are entitled to receive and retain payment and the party that designated the failed bank bears the burden of recovery by being subrogated to the right of the sender that paid the failed bank. We agree with the district court that

> the subrogation language of § 4–A–402(5) demonstrates that the originator does not, as a general matter, have a right to sue all the parties to a funds transfer.... [and] makes clear ... that under § 4–A–402(4) no right to a refund otherwise exists between the originator and an intermediary bank. This is evident because there would be no need for the subrogation language of subsection (5) if the originator (as the first sender) already had a right to assert a refund claim directly against all intermediary banks.

960 F.Supp. at 790.

B. Common Law Claims

The district court also granted summary judgment to Citibank on Grain Traders's common law claims for conversion and money had and received, finding that Grain Traders could not establish essential elements of those claims. We do not address the district court's holding, however, because we agree with Citibank's argument, raised below but not reached by the district court, that even assuming Grain Traders could establish its claims, they are precluded by Article 4–A.

Whether and to what extent Article 4–A precludes common law actions is a matter of first impression for this court. Article 4–A was enacted to correct the perceived inadequacy of " 'attempt[ing] to define rights and obligations in funds transfers by general principles [of common law] or by analogy to rights and obligations in negotiable instruments law or the law of check collection.' " *Banque Worms v. BankAmerica Int'l*, 77 N.Y.2d 362, 369, 568 N.Y.S.2d 541, 570 N.E.2d 189 (1991) (quoting Official Comment to N.Y.U.C.C. § 4–A–102). . . .

Similarly, Section 4–A–212 states, in relevant part,

[l]iability based on acceptance arises only when acceptance occurs as stated in Section 4–A–209, and liability is limited to that provided in this Article. A receiving bank is not the agent of the sender or beneficiary of the payment order it accepts, or of any other party to the funds transfer, and the bank owes no duty to any party to the funds transfer except as provided in this article or by express agreement.

We agree with those courts that have interpreted the above language to preclude common law claims when such claims would impose liability inconsistent with the rights and liabilities expressly created by Article 4–A. . . .

CONCLUSION

We hold that Section 402 of Article 4–A imposes a privity requirement such that a sender seeking a refund for an uncompleted funds transfer may look only to the receiving bank to whom it issued a payment order and payment. As a result, Grain Traders may look only to BCN for a refund. We also hold that Grain Traders's common law claims are precluded because they seek to impose liability on Citibank that would be inconsistent with the provisions of Article 4–A.

Questions and Problems 5.14. Both in the context of bank accounts and in the context of letters of credit, there are provisions to protect parties to a transaction from fraud. In the cases of EFTs as well, customers have a fairly significant degree of protection from fraudulent transfers. What sort of protection from fraud do the participants in a wire transfer enjoy? In answering this question, consider the following two cases and the problems that follow each

CHAVEZ V. MERCANTIL COMMERCEBANK, N.A.
701 F.3d 896 (11th Cir. 2012)

BATTEN, District Judge:

[A bank customer sought to recover $329,500 that was transferred from his account as a result of an allegedly fraudulent payment order. The district court entered summary judgment for the bank, and the customer appealed. The central question raised on appeal was whether a procedure requiring that payment orders delivered in person be delivered by the customer was a "security procedure" within meaning of UCC §§ 4A-201, 4A-202, which provide a safe-harbor for payment order that complied with agreed-upon security procedure.]

Generally speaking, under Florida's version of the Uniform Commercial Code ("UCC"), if a bank and its customer agree upon a "security procedure," as that phrase is defined by Fla. Stat. § 670.201, and the procedure is commercially reasonable, a bank is absolved of liability for a fraudulent transfer of the customer's funds if the bank, when processing an order to transfer the customer's funds, follows the security procedure in good faith. See FLA. STAT. §§ 670.201 & 670.202(2). We conclude that the parties' agreed-upon security procedure does not satisfy [the definition of "security procedure" in] § 670.201 and consequently § 670.202(2) does not apply. Accordingly, we reverse.

I. BACKGROUND

In September 2002, Chavez, a resident of Venezuela, opened an account with the bank, which is located in Miami, Florida. Chavez contends that when he opened his account, the bank created and maintained an electronic file that had a copy of his passport and that included his address and phone number.

Chavez's account was subject to the bank's funds transfer agreement ("FTA"). Relevant to the current dispute is § 5 of the FTA, which details the security procedure for the account. . . . Section 5 of the FTA provides in pertinent part:

(i) The parties shall comply with the security procedure selected on Annex 1 to this Agreement (the "Security Procedure") ....

(ii) The use of the Security Procedure is hereby accepted and authorized by the Client and, unless and until any writing that is signed by the Bank and made a part of this Agreement, the use of the Security Procedure in the manner set forth in this Agreement shall be the sole security procedure required with respect to any Order, and the Client acknowledges and agrees that: (a) the Bank offers various procedures affording differing degrees of security; (b) the Security Procedure is sufficient to protect the interests of the Client in light of the Client's needs, and no special circumstances exist with respect to the Client that would require any other security procedure; and (c) the Security Procedure is a method of providing security against unauthorized Orders that is commercially reasonable under the circumstances of the Client and in light of the size, type, frequency and volume of Transfers the Client contemplates undertaking.

(iii) The Bank may execute any Payment Order and act on any other instruction relating to the Payment Order and the Payment Order or instruction shall be effective as the Client's Order, whether or not authorized *898 by the Client and regardless of the actual transmitter, provided that the Bank accepts the Payment Order or instruction in good faith and in compliance with the Security Procedure. At its option, the Bank may use, in addition to the Security Procedure selected by the Client, any other means to verify any Payment Order or related instruction.

(iv) The Client shall preserve the security and confidentiality of the Security Procedure and any related devices or materials, and shall promptly notify the Bank of any suspected compromise of the integrity of the Security Procedure.

(v) The Client acknowledges that the sole purpose of the Security Procedure is to determine the authenticity of Orders, and not to determine their accuracy ....

As indicated above, § 5(i) incorporates by reference a document entitled Annex 1, which lists three different options for security procedures that the bank will use when processing a customer's payment orders. Depending on the option, customers can select one option and at most two options.

Chavez selected only the first option, "Written Payment Orders." It provides:

Written Payment Orders shall be delivered by an Authorized Representative . . . to the Bank either in original form, in person or by mail, or by facsimile transmission. Each written Payment Order must be signed by at least one Authorized Representative or, if the terms of the account to which the Payment Order relates (the "Affected Account") require signature by more than one Authorized Representative, by the number of Authorized Representatives so required. Each written Payment Order not delivered to the Bank in person by an Authorized Representative must be confirmed by the Bank by telephone callback to any person who identifies himself or herself to the Bank's satisfaction as one of the Authorized Representatives, (irrespective of whether the terms of the Affected Account require more than one Authorized Representative to sign Payment Orders) ....

For Chavez's account, he was the only authorized representative. Thus, for written payment orders delivered in person, Chavez had to sign the payment order.

On February 4, 2008, Chavez flew to Miami and visited the bank's Doral branch. He inquired about why he had not been receiving monthly statements, and he made a large cash deposit. The next day, he returned and made a smaller cash deposit. On February 6, he returned his rental car to the Miami airport around 6:40 a.m. and flew back to Venezuela.

On February 6, someone purporting to be Chavez went to the Doral branch with a written payment order for $329,500. Chavez contends that he had already departed for Venezuela at the time the payment order was delivered to the bank. The order was processed by bank employee Rossana Gutierrez, who was a greeter at the bank, but she occasionally performed the responsibilities of a customer service representative, the type of employee who would typically process a payment order.

According to the district court, Gutierrez confirmed (1) the information on the payment order, (2) the customer's identity via an identification document provided by the customer, (3) the sufficiency of funds in the account, (4) the existence of an FTA for the account, and (5) the authenticity of the signature on the payment order. She then obtained written approval from two branch officers, Talia Pina and Lolita Peroza, who then performed additional steps to verify the authenticity of the payment order. After Pina and Peroza signed off on the order, Gutierrez submitted the payment order for completion, and on February 7 the funds were transferred from Chavez's account to a beneficiary in the Dominican Republic.

The bank's security cameras were not working on the day the payment order was delivered, and Gutierrez did not make a copy of the ID she was shown. As a result, the identity of the person allegedly impersonating Chavez cannot be determined. The bank does not concede that the person presenting the payment order was not in fact Chavez or someone acting on his behalf.

On April 14, 2008, over two months after the payment order was processed, Chavez checked his account online from Venezuela. He claims that this is when he first learned that his balance was considerably lower than expected. He called the bank and allegedly learned for the first time of the February 7 payment order and transfer of the $329,500. . . .

The bank filed a motion for summary judgment in which it argued that its third affirmative defense, premised upon the safe-harbor provision in § 202, shifted the risk of loss to Chavez. Chavez filed a motion for partial summary judgment in which he contended that the bank's safe-harbor defense failed as a matter of law.

The district court entered an order granting the bank's motion and denying Chavez's. The district court ruled that the safe-harbor provision in § 202(2) shifted the risk of loss from the bank to Chavez because the parties' agreed-upon security procedure satisfied the statutory definition of a "security procedure" contained in § 201, the bank's security procedure was commercially reasonable, and the bank complied with its security procedure in good faith. . . .

III. DISCUSSION

We divide our discussion into three parts. We begin with a brief overview of Article 4A of the UCC, which has been adopted in Florida. We then address the safe-harbor defense and what the bank must show to shift the risk of loss from the bank to Chavez. Lastly, we address what the parties' agreed-upon security procedure actually was and whether that procedure satisfied § 201.

A. Article 4A of the Uniform Commercial Code . . .

Ordinarily, the bank receiving a payment order bears the risk of loss of any unauthorized funds transfer. FLA. STAT. § 670.204. However, pursuant to § 202 the bank may shift the risk of loss to the customer by showing one of two things: (1) the "payment order received ... is the authorized order of the person identified as sender if that person authorized the order or is otherwise bound by it under the law of agency," id. § 670.202(1), or (2) the parties agreed to a security procedure that is commercially reasonable and that the bank followed in good faith, id. § 670.202(2). . . .

Thus, § 202(2) imposes three requirements: (1) the bank and the customer must have agreed on a security procedure for verifying payment orders; (2) the agreed-upon security procedure must be a "commercially reasonable method of providing security against unauthorized payment orders"; and (3) the bank must have accepted the payment order in good faith and in compliance with the security procedure and any relevant written agreement or customer instruction. With respect to the first requirement, the agreed-upon security procedure must satisfy the definition of that term in § 201. With respect to the second requirement, the commercial reasonableness of a security procedure is a question of law for the court. Id. § 670.202(3).

B. Safe Harbor

The bank based its third affirmative defense on § 202(2), asserting that the parties' agreed-upon security procedure was commercially reasonable, it accepted the payment order in good faith, and consequently the safe-harbor provision shifted the risk of loss to Chavez. The district court agreed and granted the bank summary judgment based on this defense. . . .

. . . It is undisputed that the parties agreed to a security procedure for verifying payment orders. However, the parties disagree as to the scope of the agreed-upon security procedure. Thus, we first identify the security procedure to which the parties agreed. We then assess whether the agreed-upon procedure satisfies the definition of "security procedure" contained in § 201.

1. The Agreed–Upon Security Procedure

Chavez contends that the district court misinterpreted the FTA and the security procedure identified therein. He asserts that § 5 of the FTA "expressly provides that the sole agreed security procedure is set forth in Annex 1 and shall remain exclusively so unless and until amended by a writing signed by the bank and made a part of the contract." Chavez argues that no such writing exists, and as a result the security procedure is limited to the annex option selected by Chavez, *i.e.*, a written payment order signed and delivered by an authorized representative.

The bank responds that Chavez misconstrues the FTA by ignoring § 5(iii), which provides in part, "At its option, the Bank may use, in addition to the Security Procedure selected by the Client, any other means to verify any Payment Order or related instruction." The bank contends that this language allows it to add additional procedures— which it actually used—and which, when coupled with the security procedure set forth in the annex, combine to provide for a security procedure that satisfies §§ 201 & 202. In other words, the bank asserts that the agreed-upon security procedure included both the procedure in the annex and the "other means" referenced in § 5(iii). . . .

Section 201 defines a security procedure as a "procedure established by agreement of a customer and a receiving bank for the purpose of: (1) Verifying that a payment order or communication amending or canceling a payment order is that of the customer; or (2) Detecting error in the transmission or the content of the payment order or communication." Thus, the security procedure must be one established by agreement of the parties. To determine what Chavez and the bank agreed to, we turn to the FTA and the annex.

Section 5(i) of the FTA provides, "The parties shall comply with the security procedure selected on Annex 1 to the Agreement (the 'Security Procedure')." Thus, the FTA makes the phrase "Security Procedure" a defined term, and through Chavez's selection of option one on the annex, limits its meaning to a written payment order delivered and signed by an authorized representative. The remainder of § 5 refers solely to "the Security Procedure," which further shows that the parties consistently used the limited term in its defined sense. In addition, § 5(ii) states that "the use of the Security Procedure in the manner set forth in this Agreement shall be the *sole* security procedure required with respect to any Order." (Emphasis added.) This unambiguous language shows that the parties agreed upon only the security procedure selected by Chavez in the annex.

The district court's holding that the parties agreed in § 5(iii) that the bank could use other procedures, in addition to the one selected by Chavez, to satisfy § 201 was error. Section 5(iii) provides that the bank "*may* use ... any other means to verify any Payment Order or related instruction." (Emphasis added.) Relying on *Filho* [*v. Interaudi Bank*, --- F.Supp. ---, 2008 WL 1752693, at *4 (S.D.N.Y. Apr. 16, 2008)], the district court interpreted § 5(iii) as broadening the parties' agreed-upon security procedure to include an identification verification before execution of payment orders. However, the language of § 5 does not support the district court's holding.

As discussed above, §§ 5(i) & (ii) of the FTA explicitly limit the agreed-upon security procedure to the procedure selected by Chavez. Section 5(iii) does not change that. It provides that the bank "may use, in addition to the Security Procedure selected by the Client, any other means" to verify payment orders. This language does not show that the "any other means" is a security procedure. In fact, it shows just the opposite, as § 5(iii) intentionally sets "any other means" apart from the defined "Security Procedure." In addition, the bank—which drafted the FTA and therefore will have any ambiguities construed against it—defined "the Security Procedure" in § 5(i) and chose not to include within that definition the language in § 5(iii). Consequently, "any other means" is not synonymous with "additional security procedures agreed upon by the parties," as the district court held.

Filho, upon which the district court relied, is inapposite. There, the plaintiffs signed an agreement that explicitly provided that their bank would "select security procedures for accepting instructions that are commercially reasonable," 2008 WL 1752693, at *4, and the court understandably held that in so doing the plaintiffs had agreed that they would be bound by whatever commercially reasonable security procedure the bank selected. The court reasoned that as long as the selected procedure was commercially reasonable, the plaintiffs could not complain about what the bank selected. What was important was that the agreement, signed by the plaintiffs, explicitly granted to the bank the right to select the security procedure.

Section 5(iii) does not do this. Its language that the bank may use "any other means to verify any Payment Order" does not constitute an agreement by Chavez that the bank had the power, at its sole discretion, to select any security procedure as long as the procedure was commercially reasonable. It appears that the bank drafted § 5(iii) to enable but not require it to use other means when processing payment orders, and Chavez could not be heard to complain if the bank failed to employ those additional security procedures—because the parties never agreed that the bank would use such additional security procedures. As a result, in § 5(ii)(c) the parties agreed that only "the Security Procedure [from the annex] is a method of providing security against unauthorized Orders that is commercially reasonable." Conspicuously absent from this provision is incorporation of the "any other means" provided for in § 5(iii). . . .

2. "Security Procedure" as Defined in § 201

The security procedure selected by Chavez requires only that payment orders delivered in person be in writing and delivered and signed by Chavez. Chavez asserts that this procedure does not satisfy § 201's definition of a security procedure because § 201 explicitly disavows the adequacy of the parties' agreed-upon security procedure. We agree.

Section 201 states that "[c]omparison of a signature on a payment order or communication with an authorized specimen signature of the customer is not by itself a security procedure." Consequently, the parties' agreed-upon procedure must have at least this and one other step in order to qualify as a § 201 "security procedure."

IV. CONCLUSION

For the foregoing reasons, we hold that the bank and Chavez did not have an agreed-upon security procedure as that term is defined in § 201. Consequently, § 202(2) does not apply to this case, and the bank was not entitled to summary judgment on its affirmative defense premised thereon.

Questions and Problems 5.15. BayerCorp is also a customer of Mercantil Commercebank, and there is a similar agreement between the two with respect to BayerCorp's wire transfers. In light of *Chavez*, how should the bank seek to modify the agreement with BayerCorp to avoid such conflicts in the future?

5.16. On remand, the district could found for Chavez, would was awarded a judgment in the amount of $329,500.00, with post-judgment interest but no prejudgment interest.[27] On appeal, the 11th Circuit reversed and remanded on the prejudgment interest issue.[28]

GILSON V. TD BANK, N.A.
--- F.Supp.2d ---, 2011 WL 294447 (S.D.Fla. 2011)

PAUL C. HUCK, District Judge.

Plaintiffs, Ms. Gilson and the entities LAZ Development Corporation and G & C Investment Joint Venture, contend that Defendant TD Bank's negligence caused Gilson's financial injury. More specifically, Plaintiffs allege that TD Bank's negligence permitted Edward T. Stein, Gilson's investment adviser, to open three bank accounts at TD Bank and transfer Gilson's money into and out of these accounts, all without her authorization. In addition to their claim for negligence, Plaintiffs originally brought another claim under UCC Article 4 as adopted by Florida law. TD Bank, on the other hand, argues that Plaintiffs' own actions and inactions, as well as the actions of Plaintiffs' agent, Edward Stein, caused their loss. TD Bank pleads Stein's actual and apparent agency as affirmative defenses. In these defenses, TD Bank alleges that Plaintiffs entrusted Stein to invest funds and conduct financial transactions on their behalf, gave him access to and control over their funds and that, pursuant to the Partnership Bank Agreement and For Profit Corporate Banking Resolution of the accounts at issue, he acted within the scope of his actual and apparent agency by, among other things, opening bank accounts at TD Bank. TD Bank also pleads multiple, additional affirmative defenses based upon the alleged agency relationship between Stein and Plaintiffs.

II. FACTUAL BACKGROUND
Carolyn Travis Gilson met Edward Stein through a long-time personal friend. Following the death of her parents, Gilson requested Stein's assistance with four financial transactions, some of which related to her late parents' estate. Gilson's attorney, Barry Nelson, suggested that Stein recommend annuities for Gilson's purchase and

---

[27] *Chavez v. Mercantil Commercebank, N.A.,* --- F.Supp.3d ---, 2014 WL 2158417 (S.D.Fla. 2014).

[28] *Chavez v. Mercantil Commercebank, N.A.* --- F.3d ---, 601 Fed.Appx. 814 (11th Cir. 2015).

Stein received funds for this intended purchase. Nelson also requested that Stein facilitate the liquidation of an overfunded private equity fund, and a third company, NYPPEX, liquidated this fund. Finally, Gilson asked Stein to invest money on her behalf in a legal services company, and she asked Stein to hold on her behalf for a short period of time certain Bank of America brokerage funds.

G & C Investment Joint Venture, a partnership, and LAZ Development Corporation are investment entities established by Gilson's late father. In November 2008, Stein opened three bank accounts at TD Bank, two in the name of G & C and one in the name of LAZ. The account opening documents gave Stein signatory authority on these accounts; however, Stein testified that Gilson did not authorize him to add his name as an account signatory. The record is unclear with regard to whether the accounts were opened via e-mail and also as to whether Stein provided TD Bank's branch manager, Mark Gusinov, with originals of the account opening documents. Stein testified that he previously had referred various accounts to the TD Bank branch of which Gusinov was the manager.

Gusinov testified that the documentation required to open a commercial bank account at TD Bank, whether for a corporation, LLC or partnership included, among other things, a filing receipt, proof of tax I.D., and certificate of incorporation or partnership agreement. Gusinov does not dispute that TD Bank's files do not contain a filing receipt for G & C, and Gusinov testified that he did not recall taking additional, standard steps to verify the entity G & C's existence. . . .

Following the account openings and through March 2009, Stein transferred approximately $ 3.5 million of Plaintiffs' funds into, and then out of, these TD Bank accounts. The accounts were funded exclusively through six wire transfers. Stein had access to the money he used to fund the TD Bank accounts because of the transactions for which he was purportedly providing assistance to Gilson, detailed above. Plaintiffs also contend, and TD Bank does not contest, that Stein transferred the funds out of the accounts for his own purposes and that these outgoing transfers were effectuated via wire.

Plaintiffs moved for partial summary judgment on TD Bank's agency-based affirmative defenses, arguing that the undisputed record shows that no agency relationship, whether actual or apparent, existed between Plaintiffs and Stein regarding the opening of the accounts in question and the activity in those accounts. TD Bank similarly moved for summary judgment on both counts asserted against it, arguing that Plaintiffs' UCC count should be brought under Florida law's adoption of UCC Article 4A, not Article 4, and that UCC Article 4A displaces or preempts Plaintiffs' negligence claim. Thereafter Plaintiffs sought, and the Court granted, Plaintiffs leave to file a Second Amended Complaint. This Second Amended Complaint, filed on January 18, 2011, removes the UCC Article 4 Count and replaces it with two counts asserted in the alternative, Count IV under Florida law's adoption of UCC Article 4A and Count V under Federal Regulation J, 12 C.F.R. §§ 210.25–32. Therefore, this Second Amended Complaint moots one of the two grounds for summary judgment advanced in TD Bank's motion. The Court now turns to Plaintiffs' Motion for Partial Summary Judgment . . . and the remaining portion of TD Bank's Motion for Summary Judgment. . . .

III. ANALYSIS

[The court concluded that a genuine issue of material fact existed regarding whether Gilson consented to Stein acting as plaintiffs' actual agent for purposes of opening the three TD Bank accounts at issue, and for purposes of transferring money into the TD bank accounts, and for purposes of being added as a signatory to plaintiffs' bank accounts The court therefore denied plaintiffs' summary judgment motion as to an alleged actual agency relationship. However, the court did find as a matter of law that plaintiffs' alleged grant of actual authority to Stein did not include implied authority to transfer money *out* of the TD Bank accounts other than for Gilson's benefit.

[As to apparent agency, the court found that genuine issues of material fact existed as to TD Bank's claims of an apparent agency relationship between Gilson and Stein.]

B. TD Bank's Motion for Summary Judgment

. . .

Article 4A of the UCC, as adopted by Florida law, "governs a specialized method of payment referred to in the Article as a funds transfer but also commonly referred to in the commercial community as a wholesale wire transfer." Fla. Stat. § 670.102, Official Comment. The Eleventh Circuit has spoken on the scope of UCC Article 4A and, more specifically, the scope of its preemption of common law claims. In *Regions Bank v. Provident Bank Inc.*, 345 F.3d 1267, 1274–75 (11th Cir.2003), the court concluded that, while Article 4A was intended as a comprehensive body of law regarding funds transfers, it "is not the exclusive means by which a plaintiff can seek to redress an alleged harm arising from a funds transfer."

> [T]he only restraint on a plaintiff [seeking to redress an alleged harm arising from a funds transfer] is that resort to principles of law or equity outside of Article 4A is not appropriate to create rights, duties and liabilities *inconsistent* with those stated in this Article.

Regions Bank v. Provident Bank Inc., 345 F.3d 1267, 1275 (11th Cir.2003) (emphasis in original) (internal quotations omitted).

Regions involved the fraudulent activity of [an] independent mortgage lender named Morningstar. Morningstar had a warehouse loan agreement with Provident Bank, who had demanded repayment of Morningstar's outstanding loans due to suspicions of Morningstar's criminal conduct. 345 F.3d at 1270–71. Around the same time, Morningstar entered into a separate warehouse loan agreement with a second bank, *Regions*. *Id*. at 1271. Pursuant to this agreement, Morningstar requested that Regions wire funds to the account of third-party closing attorneys at Fleet Bank. *Id*. Morningstar's President and CEO later fraudulently claimed that these wire transfers were made in error and instructed Fleet to wire the money into Morningstar's personal account at Provident Bank. *Id*. Provident applied the wire-transferred funds against Morningstar's outstanding debt to the bank; although shortly after doing so, it received notice of Morningstar's possible fraud. *Id*. at 1272. After Provident refused to return and/or repay to Regions the funds that were wired into Morningstar's account, Regions sued Provident asserting state law claims for among others, conversion and unjust enrichment. *Id*. at 1273. Provident defended on the theory that UCC Article 4A preempted Regions state law claims, and the district court agreed. *Id*. On appeal, the Eleventh Circuit came to a different conclusion regarding preemption. The Court found that Article 4A was silent with regard to claims based on Regions' theory–that is, the theory that a beneficiary bank accepted funds when it knew or should have known that the funds were fraudulently obtained. *Id*. at 1275. Therefore, under the test that rights and liabilities not inconsistent with those set out in Article 4A survive preemption, "Article 4A does not preempt a state law claim if money is transferred by wire to a party that knows or should have known that the funds were obtained illegally." *Id*. at 1279.

Plaintiffs argue that this case is analogous to *Regions* because their negligence claim is based on the TD Bank's constructive knowledge of the fraudulent nature of the wire transfers. Had TD Bank followed its security procedures, Plaintiffs claim, the Bank would have known that Stein was not authorized to open the subject bank accounts, much less wire transfer money in and out of them. While the Court agrees with Plaintiffs' argument on this point, it finds that they advance an even stronger argument for denying Article 4A preemption. As Plaintiffs point out, the basis for their negligence claim extends beyond TD Bank's conduct with regard to the wire transfers into and out of the accounts. Indeed, Plaintiffs' negligence claim centers on the Bank's allegedly negligent and reckless conduct with regard to opening the accounts. Plaintiffs' Second Amended Complaint alleges that TD Bank acted with gross negligence and recklessness in numerous ways during the account openings, and the record shows a genuine issue of material fact on this issue. Plaintiffs have come forward with evidence that TD Bank deviated from its standard account opening procedures by not receiving a filing receipt or partnership agreement for G & C. Moreover, Plaintiffs evidence shows that TD Bank failed to notice inconsistencies on the account opening documentation for the G & C accounts, such as the discrepancy between the account address and phone number, which were Stein's, and Stein's professed limited role as investment adviser. Because the crux of Plaintiffs' negligence claim is TD Bank's lack of care during the account openings, not the wire transfers, the Court finds that the negligence claim does not create rights, duties and liabilities inconsistent with those stated in Article 4A, which governs only wire transfers. For the same reasons, the Court finds that Plaintiffs' negligence claim extends beyond the scope of Florida Statute § 670.204 (a portion of Article 4A), which defines liability regarding unauthorized wire transfers. Therefore, the Court holds that UCC Article 4A as adopted by Florida law does not preempt Plaintiffs' negligence claim.

The Court notes that Plaintiffs' Second Amended Complaint adds a claim in the alternative under Federal Regulation J, 12 C.F.R. §§ 210.25–32. Regulation J applies UCC Article 4A to wire transfers conducted using Fedwire, the Federal Reserve Banks' funds transfer system. *Grossman v. Nationsbank, N.A.*, 225 F.3d 1228, 1228, 1232 (11th Cir.2000). TD Bank's Reply Memorandum argues that to the extent Regulation J, not Florida law, applies because the wire transfers at issue are Fedwire transfers, Regulation J, like Florida's codification of UCC Article 4A, would preempt Plaintiffs' negligence claim. For the same reasons that the Court finds that Florida's codification of Article 4A does not preempt Plaintiffs negligence claim, discussed above, it similarly finds that Regulation J does not preempt Plaintiffs' negligence claim. Indeed, the Court notes that Regions Bank v. Provident Bank Inc., the Eleventh Circuit case regarding UCC Article 4A preemption, involved UCC Article 4A's codification by Regulation J, not state statute. See 345 F.3d 1267, 1274 (11th Cir.2003).

Questions and Problems 5.17. Is the *Gilson* case based on the wrong theory? The parties accepted the fact that the transfers were subject to UCC Article 4A – but are they? In a footnote elsewhere in the court's opinion the court explains:

Because Plaintiffs' Second Amended Complaint concedes the applicability of UCC Article 4A, the Court will not address Plaintiffs' argument in its opposition memorandum that Article 4A does not apply because the wire transfers at issue are debit transfers, not credit transfers, as those concepts are defined by the Official Comment to Fla. Stat. § 670.104 and TD Bank's response to this argument. . . .

Gilson v. TD Bank, N.A., --- F.Supp.2d ---, 2011 WL 294447 at *7 n.7 (S.D.Fla. 2011). This is correct if by "credit transfer" and "debit transfer" the court means only a distinction, respectively, between an originator/sender who is instructing that a payment be credited to someone else, and an originator/sender who is also the recipient. *See* UCC § 4A-104, Official Comment 4 (explaining distinction between two types of wire transfers, each subject to Article 4A). If, however, what we have here is a consumer transfer effected by debit card or other electronic transfer subject to the EFTA, then as a matter of law Article 4A does *not* apply to them. UCC 4A-108(a).

5.18. Would it make a difference to the analysis and the outcome of the case if the transfer in question was mistakenly made rather than fraudulently made? In answering this question, consider the following case.

QATAR NAT. BANK V. WINMAR, INC.
650 F.Supp.2d 1 (D.D.C. 2009)

GLADYS KESSLER, District Judge.

[Qatar National Bank (QNB) brought action against a construction company that had been hired by the Al-Jazeera news agency to remodel its offices, alleging that the company had retained funds that were mistakenly transferred to it by the bank, on behalf of the news agency, and that the company was unjustly enriched. The company filed third-party complaint against agency. The bank moved for summary judgment.]

It is not disputed that QNB's duplicate payment of $474,677 resulted from an honest mistake of fact, that it conferred a benefit on Winmar, or that Winmar retained this benefit. Therefore, the only issue in dispute is whether Winmar's retention of this benefit is unjust. As the beneficiary of money paid as the result of a mistake of fact, Winmar bears the burden of proving that restitution would be unjust.

Winmar argues that it is entitled to retain the mistakenly-transferred funds in accordance with the discharge-for-value defense.[a] According to Winmar, summary judgment is not appropriate because factual disputes remain as to whether Winmar rightfully retained the mistaken payment in order to discharge a portion of the debt owed it by Al–Jazeera. . . .

The discharge-for-value defense is defined in the official comment to Section 4A–303 of the Uniform Commercial Code ("UCC"). The defense has been adopted in the District of Columbia as Section 28:4A–303 of the D.C.Code. *See In re Calumet Farm, Inc.*, 398 F.3d at 559 (stating that U.C.C. § 4A–303(a) "incorporates the discharge-for-value defense"); *In re Calumet Farm, Inc.*, 1997 WL 253278, at *4 (6th Cir.1997) ("[A] wire transfer effected via FedWire is covered by the provisions of U.C.C. § 4A–303(a) and its official commentary, and is therefore subject to the discharge-for-value rule."). In the Code of Federal Regulations, the text of Section 4A–303[7] is construed in light of the discharge-for-value defense. See 12 C.F.R. § 210.25, Appendix A to Subpart B ("The official comments to Article 4A are not incorporated in subpart B of this part or this Commentary to subpart B of this part, but the official comments may be useful in interpreting Article 4A.").

In describing the discharge-for-value defense, Section 4A–303 states that a bank that makes a mistaken payment to a beneficiary would "normally have a right to recover the overpayment" from that beneficiary. D.C.Code § 28:4A–303. However, it goes on to state that "in unusual cases the law of restitution might allow Beneficiary to keep all or part of the overpayment." *Id.*[8] The comment provides one example of an unusual case: if the bank's client "owed $2,000,000 to Beneficiary and Beneficiary received the extra $1,000,000 in good faith in discharge of the debt, Beneficiary may be allowed to keep it." *Id.*

---

[a] The discharge-for-value defense to unjust enrichment claim allows a beneficiary to keep mistakenly transferred funds if the payment discharges the obligation of a third party to the beneficiary, but only when it has received no notice of the mistake and has made no misrepresentations. The defense is discussed by the court in the paragraphs that follow.

[7] Section 4A–303 is located in Appendix B to Subpart B of 12 C.F.R. § 210.25.

[8] The comment adds one clarifying statement about the rights of the bank that made the error vis-a-vis the rights of the beneficiary: "[i]n this case Originator's Bank has paid an obligation of Originator and under the law of restitution, ... Originator's Bank would be subrogated to Beneficiary's rights against Originator on the obligation paid by Originator's Bank." D.C.Code § 28:4A–303.

The Restatement of Restitution provides the following definition of the discharge-for-value defense:

> A creditor of another or one having a lien on another's property who has received from a third person any benefit in discharge of the debt or lien, is under no duty to make restitution therefor, although the discharge was given by mistake of the transferor as to his interests or duties, if the transferee made no misrepresentation and did not have notice of the transferor's mistake.

Restatement (First) of Restitution § 14(1) (1937).

Thus, it is clear that the discharge-for-value defense allows a transferee to keep mistakenly transferred funds only when it has received no notice of the mistake and has made no misrepresentations. *In re Calumet*, 398 F.3d at 559. However, as the court pointed out in *In re Calumet*, few authorities have "specif[ied] the point in time by which notice of mistake must be received." *Id*. Previous cases addressing the discharge-for-value defense examined "*whether* the discharge-for-value rule applies in this setting, not *how* it applies." *Id*. (discussing *Gen. Elec. Capital Corp. v. Cent. Bank*, 49 F.3d 280 (7th Cir.1995) and *Banque Worms v. BankAmerica Int'l*, 77 N.Y.2d 362, 568 N.Y.S.2d 541, 570 N.E.2d 189 (1991)) (emphasis in original). For this reason, those cases do not offer substantial guidance in determining when notice must be received.

In re Calumet does provide a detailed analysis of this issue. . . . It rejected two possible interpretations of the notice rule: (1) that notice must occur before "a payment order ... is accepted by the beneficiary's bank" and (2) that notice must be actual, rather than constructive. 398 F.3d at 560.

Instead, the court reached two key conclusions. First, it reasoned that the "most desirable option" is to apply the discharge-for-value defense "unless the beneficiary receives notice of a mistake before the beneficiary of the transfer credits the debtor's account." *Id*. This approach is desirable because it is "consistent with one of the underlying principles of the discharge-for-value rule; namely, that the creditor has given value for the mistaken payment." *Id*. Second, it reasoned that "[a]ny sensible application of the discharge-for-value rule ... must account for constructive as well as actual notice of a mistake." *Id*.[10]

---

[10] This approach is consistent not only with the language in the Restatement but also with the official comment to § 4A–303(a). The official comment states that the discharge-for-value defense applies if a mistaken payment is received "in good faith in discharge of the debt." D.C.Code § 28:4A–303. It is clear that when a beneficiary receives actual or constructive notice that funds

In the present case, Winmar has provided no reason to reject the Sixth Circuit's conclusions. Accordingly, the discharge-for-value rule applies only if Winmar did not have actual or constructive notice before Winmar credited Al-Jazeera's account.

Here, QNB wired the second payment to the Citibank account on January 30, 2006, and the funds arrived in the account on the next day. On February 24, 2006, Al-Jazeera wrote a letter to Janson in which it stated that the $474,677 payment was a "mistake." . . . In Winmar's response on March 9, 2006, it acknowledged that it had been "unaware" prior to the receipt of this letter that "any wire had been accomplished on January 31st [2006]." *Id.* Winmar does not dispute that it did not become aware of the mistake until February 24, 2006, nor does it present any evidence that it credited Al-Jazeera's account prior to that date. In fact, it is clear that Winmar could not have credited Al-Jazeera's account prior to February 24, 2006 if it did not even know of the transfer until that date. Therefore Winmar's March 9, 2006 letter provides undisputed evidence that Winmar received actual notice of QNB's mistake before it credited Al–Jazeera's account.

Even if Winmar did not have actual notice that the payment was a mistake, it had constructive notice of the error. Less than two months after it received a payment of $474,677, it received a second payment of the exact same amount. That second payment substantially exceeded the $355,297 that Winmar had claimed it was owed in its January 23, 2006 certification. These two undisputed facts show that Winmar had constructive notice that the second payment had to have been a mistake. *See In re Calumet*, 398 F.3d at 560 ("[C]onstructive notice of a mistake may also occur simply as a result of the size of the transfer."). Winmar received this constructive notice at the moment the payment arrived in its account, which occurred prior to February 24, 2006. As discussed *supra*, Winmar could not have credited Al–Jazeera's account prior to February 24, 2006. Therefore, it had constructive notice prior to crediting Al-Jazeera's account. For these reasons, the discharge-for-value defense does not apply to QNB's mistaken payment to Winmar.

In *Credit Lyonnais[–New York v. Washington Strategic Consulting Group*, 886 F.Supp. 92, 93 (D.D.C.1995)], a case remarkably similar to the present one, the plaintiff bank received a request to confirm a previous payment made four days earlier of $171,821.30. Instead of responding to the confirmation request, the plaintiff bank mistakenly– as in this case–made a second wire transfer of the same amount to its affiliate. In that case, it took nearly six months for the plaintiff bank

---

were mistakenly transferred before he credits a debtor's account, he has not received the payment "in good faith in discharge of the debt."

to discover its mistake and demand return of the funds. Despite the substantial passage of time, Judge Robertson ruled for the plaintiff bank on the basis of "settled law: where one person receives money that in equity and good conscience belongs to another, action will lie for 'money had and received.' " *Credit Lyonnais*, 886 F.Supp. at 93 (citations omitted).

Accordingly, Winmar has not shown that it would be inequitable to require it to refund QNB's mistaken payment.12 See D.C.Code § 28:4A–303 (stating that in the case of a mistaken payment, a bank would "normally have a right to recover the overpayment" from the beneficiary); *In re Calumet*, 398 F.3d at 561 ("It is difficult to see what is unfair about requiring a bank to return money if it was notified of the mistaken payment before it gave value for the payment.") (internal quotation marks and citations omitted).

Questions and Problems 5.19. *Mistakes happen.* They come in many varieties. Consider how the following mistakes would be resolved under *Qatar Nat. Bank* or, more generally, under UCC § 4A-303.

> **a.** BayerCorp instructs Issuer Bank to transfer $100,000 dollars to Banco Merca for credit to SallerCo's account, and to debit its account at Issuer Bank for the amount of the transfer. Issuer Bank transfers $200,000 to Banco Merca for credit to SallerCo's account. (*See* UCC §§ 4A-303(a)(i), 4A-402(c).)
>
> **b.** BayerCorp instructs Issuer Bank to transfer $100,000 dollars to Banco Merca for credit to SallerCo's account, and to debit its account at Issuer Bank for the amount of the transfer. Issuer Bank transfers $10,000 to Banco Merca for credit to SallerCo's account. (*See* UCC §§ 4A-303(b), 4A-402(c).)
>
> **c.** BayerCorp instructs Issuer Bank to transfer $100,000 dollars to Banco Merca for credit to SallerCo's account, and to debit its account at Issuer Bank for the amount of the transfer. Later that day, Issuer Bank transfers $100,000 to Banco Merca for credit to SallerCo's account. On the following day, another payments clerk at Issuer Bank transfers $100,000 to Banco Merca for credit to SallerCo's account. (*See* UCC §§ 4A-303(a)(ii), 4A-402(c).)
>
> **d.** BayerCorp instructs Issuer Bank to transfer $100,000 dollars to Banco Merca for credit to SallerCo's account, and to debit its account at Issuer Bank for the amount of the transfer. Issuer Bank transfers $100,000 to Banco Merca for credit to SallerCo's account, but Banco Merca takes $5,000 in "processing fees" before crediting SallerCo's account with $95,000. (*See* UCC § 4A-303(b).)
>
> **e.** BayerCorp instructs Issuer Bank to transfer $100,000 dollars to Banco Merca for credit to SallerCo's account, and to debit its account at Issuer Bank for the amount of the transfer. Issuer Bank

transfers $100,000 to Banco Marcoa for credit to SellerCorp's account. (*See* UCC §§ 4A-303(c).)

f. What if BayerCorp failed to notice the mistake that Issuer Bank made in any of the preceding situations for four months? For a year? You may assume that the mistake would have been obvious from a review of the monthly bank statement. In answering this question, consider UCC § 4A-505. *See also Mendes Regatos v. N. Fork Bank*, 431 F.3d 394 (2nd Cir.2005) (applying § 4A-505); *National Bank of Commerce v. Shelton*, 27 So.3d 444, 451-452 (Miss. App. 2009) (raising issue to be resolved on remand).

5.20. There are in fact a varied group of provisions – *e.g.*, UCC § 4A-204 - 4A-205, 4A-303 - 4A-305 – that apply to various types of mistakes occurring in different contexts. How do these provisions compare with one another? Can more than one be applicable to the same transaction? The following case may over some helpful guidance in answering these questions.

NATIONAL BANK OF COMMERCE V. SHELTON
27 So.3d 444 (Miss. App. 2009)

BARNES, J., for the Court.

[National Bank of Commerce (NBC) mistakenly established of a recurring transfer from a customer's account to the account of another customer, when the originating customer had only requested a one-time transfer. The trial court granted the customer's motion for summary judgment, awarding him the full amount of the erroneous transfers but only 90 days of interest on the transfers occurring within 90 days of customer's notification to bank of the error. Both parties appealed.]

. . . Justin Shelton filed a negligence action against [NBC] as a result of electronic transfers of funds from Justin's account at NBC to the account of W.J. "Sonny" Shelton at NBC.[1] Applying Mississippi Code Annotated section 75–4A–204 (Rev.2002), the circuit court granted Justin's motion for summary judgment and awarded him $54,611.74 in damages, which included the amount of the transfers, ninety-days' interest on $2,242.50 (the amount received in transfers ninety days prior to notification) and attorney's fees. NBC appeals, arguing that the circuit judge: (1) applied the incorrect section of the UCC to the facts of this case; (2) failed to enforce the contractual obligations between Justin and NBC; and, alternatively, (3) failed to ap-

---

[1] Sonny has admitted his liability for any judgment awarded in favor of Justin. . . .

ply the statute of repose set forth in the UCC or the general three-year statute of limitations. Justin filed a cross-appeal claiming that the circuit judge erred by awarding Justin interest on the $2,242.50 for only ninety days rather than from the date he notified the bank of the erroneous transfers until the date of refund.

We affirm the trial court's finding of liability on the part of NBC, albeit on different grounds; however, we reverse and remand on the issue of the interest awarded to Justin and whether the liability of NBC must be reduced by application of the three-year statute of limitations or the UCC's one-year statute of repose.

SUMMARY OF FACTS AND PROCEDURAL HISTORY

On October 2, 1995, Justin opened a checking account with First Federal Bank of Savings—now NBC—in Columbus, Mississippi. In October 1999, Justin International, a company owned by Justin, issued two paychecks to Sonny. The bookkeeper for Justin International, Susan T. Noland, inadvertently deposited those checks into Justin's account instead of Sonny's account. Both accounts were held by NBC. When Noland realized the error, she contacted the bank and requested that the funds be transferred from Justin's account to Sonny's account. NBC completed the transfer as requested.

However, a computer error by the bank caused the transfer to recur each month. As a result, $747.50 was transferred from Justin's account to Sonny's account each month. Justin failed to notice the error until April 2005—over five years later. Justin notified the bank, and the transfer for April 2005 was credited back to Justin's account. The mistake resulted in a total transfer of $49,335 from Justin's account to Sonny's account.

Justin filed a complaint alleging negligence, gross negligence, and a breach of fiduciary duty on the part of NBC as a result of the transfers. Both NBC and Justin filed motions for summary judgment. Following a hearing, the circuit court denied NBC's motion for summary judgment. NBC then filed a motion for reconsideration that was denied on August 21, 2007. . . .

I. Whether the trial court erred in applying section 75–4A–204.

. . . The circuit court found that the facts of this case required the application of Mississippi Code Annotated section 75–4A–204 (Rev.2002) concerning unauthorized payment orders. NBC argues that the circuit court erred because the facts of this case require the application of Mississippi Code Annotated section 75–4A–205 (Rev.2002) concerning erroneous payment orders. Justin responds that the matter is properly controlled by section 75–4A–204; thus, the circuit court did not err. [The court then quoted UCC §§ 4A-204(a)-(b), 4A-205(a)-(c).]

NBC argues that section 75–4A–204 does not apply as Justin was unable to prove that NBC accepted a payment order from him that was not authorized. We agree with NBC, as Justin did issue the one authorized payment order. However, we do not accept NBC's claim that the subsequent monthly transfers were erroneously-transmitted duplicates under section 75–4A–205. While the official comments to the UCC were not adopted by our Legislature, "[s]till we look to official comments about uniform laws, when those laws have been adopted all but verbatim by the [L]egislature, as the most informed source explaining provisions of the original enactment." *Holifield v. BancorpSouth, Inc.*, 891 So.2d 241, 248(¶ 28) (Miss.Ct.App.2004). Having found no variation between Mississippi's version of Article 4A and the model version, we find the official comments of the UCC instructive. The official comments confirm that the error in this case is not the type of transmission error covered by section 75–4A–205:

> This section concerns error in the content or in the transmission of payment order. It deals with three kinds of error. *Case 1.* The order identifies a beneficiary not intended by the sender.... *Case 2.* The error in the amount of the order.... *Case 3.* A payment order is sent to the receiving bank, and then, by mistake, the same payment order is *sent to the receiving bank again.* In Case No. 3, the receiving bank may have no way of knowing whether the second order is a duplicate of the first or is another order.

U.C.C. § 4A–205 cmt. 1 (2002) (emphasis added). The transmission at issue in section 75–4A–205 is, thus, a duplicate transmission of a payment order from the sender to the receiving bank, not a duplication of that order by the receiving bank. Neither Justin, nor anyone acting on his behalf, ever "transmitted" a duplicate payment order to NBC so as to bring the case within the provisions of section 75–4A–205. Therefore, neither 75–4A–204, nor section 75–4A–205, are applicable to the facts in this case.

We find, upon our de novo review of the record and of Article 4A of the UCC, that the reason the facts of this case do not fit neatly within either of these sections is the transfers were, in fact, erroneously-executed payment orders, governed by Mississippi Code Annotated section 75–4A–303 (Rev.2002). [The court quoted from UCC § 4A-303(a)(ii).]

In this case, the receiving bank, NBC, executed the only payment order issued by Justin by transferring $747.50 from Justin's account into Sonny's account at the oral request of Justin's agent, Noland.

Thereafter, NBC's computer system, due to "an entry error" improperly duplicated that payment every month for over five years. The requirements of Mississippi Code Annotated section 75–4A–402(c) (Rev.2002) were satisfied as the funds transfer was completed; therefore, under section 75–4A–303, NBC is entitled to recover from Justin, the sender, the amount of his order–that is, one payment of $747.50. The official comment to UCC section 4A–303 confirms that: "If erroneous execution causes the wrong amount to be paid the sender is not obliged to pay the receiving bank an amount in excess of the amount of the sender's order." U.C.C. § 4A–303(1) cmt. 1 (2002). By way of example, the comment continues:

> Subsection (a) also applies to duplicate payment orders. Assume Originator's Bank properly executes Originator's $1,000,000 payment order *and then by mistake issues a second $1,000,000 payment order in execution of the Originator's order.* If Beneficiary's Bank accepts both orders issued by the Originator's Bank, Beneficiary's Bank is entitled to receive $2,000,000 from Originator's Bank but *Originator's Bank is entitled to receive only $1,000,000 from Originator.* The remedy of Originator's Bank is the same as that of a receiving bank that executes by issuing an order in an amount greater than the sender's order. It may recover the overpayment from Beneficiary to the extent allowed by the law governing mistake and restitution and in a proper case as stated in Comment 2 may have subrogation rights if it is not entitled to recover from Beneficiary.

Id. at cmt. 3 (emphasis added).

Justin's failure to discover NBC's error prevents his recovering interest on the majority of the transfers; it does not make him liable to NBC for the bank's duplicate payments to Sonny. [The court quoted UCC § 4A-304.]

This outcome makes sense when one recalls that it was NBC, not Justin, that erroneously duplicated the payment. The computer "entry error" occurred at NBC. In drafting Article 4A of the UCC, "a critical consideration was that the various parties to funds transfers need to be able to predict risk with certainly, to insure against risk, to adjust operational and security procedures, and to price funds transfer services appropriately." U.C.C. § 4A–102 cmt. (2002). Competing interests of the banks that provide funds-transfer services, the commercial and financial organizations that use those services, and the public interest were thoroughly considered. "The rules that emerged represent a careful and delicate balancing of those interests and are intended to be the exclusive means of determining the rights, duties and liabilities of the affected parties in any situation covered by particular provisions of the Article." *Id.* Therefore, we find that the facts of this case are covered by Mississippi Code Annotated sections 75–4A–303 and 75–4A–304. NBC erroneously executed Justin's payment order and may recover from him only the amount of his order. Justin, having failed in his duty to exercise ordinary care to determine that the order was erroneously executed, is precluded from recovering most of the interest on his refund; he is not, however, liable to NBC for failing to detect the bank's error.

The result of the judgment is the same as if Mississippi Code Annotated section 75–4A–204 had applied as found by the trial judge: Justin is entitled to a refund of the amount erroneously debited from his account; but he is granted interest only on funds transfers made within ninety days of his notifying NBC of its error. This Court, therefore, affirms the trial court's finding of liability on the part of NBC, albeit on different grounds.

However, we must reverse and remand on the issue of computation of the interest by the trial judge. Justin, in his cross-appeal, asserts that he was entitled to interest on $2,242.50 of the $49,335 from the date of NBC's receipt of his notification of the unauthorized transfers (January 2005) *until the date of refund*. We agree. Although the trial court correctly noted that interest could only be applied to the funds received ninety days from the notification of the error—$2,242.50, the trial judge incorrectly computed the interest to be $44.23, which is only ninety-days' worth of interest on the $2,242.50. Section 75–4A–204 states that the bank "shall pay interest on the refundable amount calculated from the date the bank received payment to the *date of the refund*." Miss.Code Ann. § 75–4A–204(a) (emphasis added). Although we find that section 75–4A–204 is not applicable in this case, the computation of interest is the same for 75–4A–304. That section provides that the bank is not obligated to pay interest "on any amount refundable to the sender under Section 75–4A–402(d) for the period before the bank learns of the execution error." Miss.Code Ann. § 75–4A–304. It does not state that only ninety-days' interest is allowed. Rather, it is implicit that the interest will accrue until the date of refund. Therefore, we find Justin's argument on cross-appeal meritorious and reverse and remand for computation of the interest by the trial court consistent with this opinion. . . .

Index

References are to Pages
